View of St. Peter's Chapel and place of Execution.

NOTICES

OF THE

𝕳istoric 𝕻ersons

BURIED IN THE

CHAPEL OF ST. PETER AD VINCULA,

IN THE

TOWER OF LONDON.

WITH AN ACCOUNT OF THE DISCOVERY OF THE SUPPOSED
REMAINS OF QUEEN ANNE BOLEYN.

By DOYNE C. BELL, F.S.A.

"In truth there is no sadder spot on earth than this little cemetery."—MACAULAY.

WITH ILLUSTRATIONS.

LONDON:
JOHN MURRAY, ALBEMARLE STREET.
1877.

The right of Translation is reserved.

LONDON:
PRINTED BY WILLIAM CLOWES AND SONS,
STAMFORD STREET AND CHARING CROSS.

TO

HER MOST GRACIOUS MAJESTY

QUEEN VICTORIA,

THIS VOLUME IS BY SPECIAL PERMISSION

𝔇𝔢𝔡𝔦𝔠𝔞𝔱𝔢𝔡

BY

HER MAJESTY'S MOST DEVOTED AND
DUTIFUL SERVANT,

DOYNE C. BELL.

PREFACE.

Some years ago I was occupied during my leisure hours in collecting various memoranda respecting the death and burial of the sovereigns of England and their issue, and whilst engaged upon this task I visited several places of their interment.

At Westminster Abbey and at Windsor due care and attention had been bestowed upon the Royal resting places, but when I came to the chapel of St. Peter in the Tower, I regretted to find that the graves of the two unhappy Queens in the chancel remained unmarked by any memorial stone, and the condition of the whole chapel was also such as could not fail to awaken feelings of a painful nature. The wish which I then entertained that this interesting building might ere long be restored, and that some record might be placed there of the historic personages who had been interred within its walls, has now been fulfilled, and few persons will be disposed to cavil at the conscientious and careful manner in which the works of restoration have been carried out.

A deep debt of gratitude is undoubtedly due to the late Lord De Ros for the active interest with which (whilst holding the office of Deputy Lieutenant) he so zealously advocated the claims of the Tower to public consideration; and it should also be recorded that it is in great measure due to the present Constable, Sir Charles Yorke, supported by the energy of the Office of Her Majesty's Works, that we are indebted for this last work, the restoration of the chapel of St. Peter.

I must take this opportunity of tendering my sincere acknowledgments to Colonel Milman, the Resident Governor of the Tower, for the facilities which he has kindly afforded me for consulting the records which are in his custody, and which have been so admirably arranged and catalogued under the direction of the late Lord De Ros.

D. C. B.

Plan of the Tower, 1877.

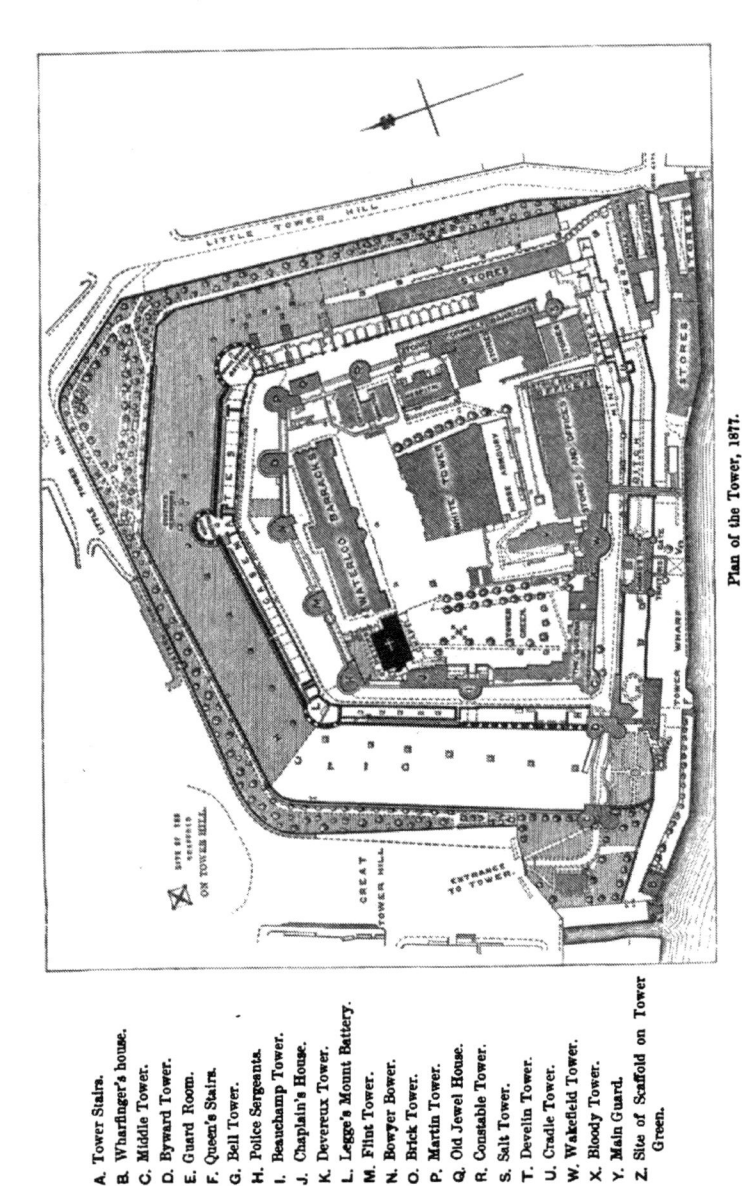

A. Tower Stairs.
B. Wharfinger's house.
C. Middle Tower.
D. Byward Tower.
E. Guard Room.
F. Queen's Stairs.
G. Bell Tower.
H. Police Sergeants.
I. Beauchamp Tower.
J. Chaplain's House.
K. Devereux Tower.
L. Legge's Mount Battery.
M. Flint Tower.
N. Bowyer Bower.
O. Brick Tower.
P. Martin Tower.
Q. Old Jewel House.
R. Constable Tower.
S. Salt Tower.
T. Develin Tower.
U. Cradle Tower.
W. Wakefield Tower.
X. Bloody Tower.
Y. Main Guard.
Z. Site of Scaffold on Tower Green.

CONTENTS.

CHAPTER I.
THE HISTORY OF THE CHAPEL .. ..   PAGE 1

CHAPTER II.
THE RESTORATIONS IN 1876-7 10

CHAPTER III.
THE OPERATIONS OF 9TH AND 11TH NOVEMBER, 1876; AND OF 13TH APRIL, 1877 19

CHAPTER IV.
THE MONUMENTS 32

CHAPTER V.
THE BURIAL REGISTER 42

CHAPTER VI.
THE BURIALS IN THE CHAPEL 50

BIOGRAPHICAL NOTICES.

	PAGE
GERALD FITZGERALD, EARL OF KILDARE	59
JOHN FISHER, BISHOP OF ROCHESTER	60
SIR THOMAS MORE	76
GEORGE BOLEYN, VISCOUNT ROCHFORD	91
QUEEN ANNE BOLEYN	94
THOMAS CROMWELL, EARL OF ESSEX	109
MARGARET PLANTAGENET, COUNTESS OF SALISBURY	116
QUEEN KATHARINE HOWARD	122
JANE, VISCOUNTESS ROCHFORD	122
THOMAS, LORD SEYMOUR OF SUDELEY	127
EDWARD SEYMOUR, DUKE OF SOMERSET	134
SIR RALPH VANE	149
SIR THOMAS ARUNDEL	149
JOHN DUDLEY, DUKE OF NORTHUMBERLAND	153
LADY JANE GREY	164
LORD GUILDFORD DUDLEY	164
HENRY GREY, DUKE OF SUFFOLK	177
THOMAS HOWARD, DUKE OF NORFOLK	185
SIR JOHN PERROTT	200
PHILIP, EARL OF ARUNDEL	205
ROBERT DEVEREUX, EARL OF ESSEX	217
SIR THOMAS OVERBURY	231
THOMAS, LORD GREY OF WILTON	240
SIR JOHN ELIOT	250
WILLIAM, VISCOUNT STAFFORD	255
ARTHUR CAPEL, EARL OF ESSEX	263
JAMES, DUKE OF MONMOUTH	268

CONTENTS.

	PAGE
GEORGE, LORD JEFFREYS	278
JOHN ROETTIER	285
EDWARD, LORD GRIFFIN	291
WILLIAM, MARQUIS OF TULLIBARDINE	296
WILLIAM, EARL OF KILMARNOCK	301
ARTHUR, LORD BALMERINO	301
SIMON, LORD FRASER OF LOVAT	313

APPENDIX.

PEDIGREE OF THE HOUSE OF NORFOLK AND ARUNDEL	325
NOTE ON THE "BAGA DE SECRETIS"	326

INDEX 329

LIST OF ILLUSTRATIONS.

	PAGE
View of St. Peter's Chapel and place of Execution .. .. *Frontispiece*.	
Plan of the Tower in 1877	x
Interior of the Chapel in 1820	8
View of the Chancel before the restorations in 1876..	12
View of the Chapel as restored in 1877	13
Suggested Plan of Interments in the Chancel	52
View of the Bell Tower	63
Plan of the Prison Room in the Bell Tower	66
Traitors' Gate, from the River	96
Traitors' Gate and St. Thomas's Tower	97
Chapel of St. John in the White Tower	160
View of the Lieutenant's Lodgings and Gentleman-Gaoler's House ..	165
Jane. Lady Jane Grey's name inscribed in the Beauchamp Tower ..	177
Plan of the Tower in 1597	187
View of the Bloody Tower	194
View of the Beauchamp Tower before the restorations in 1852	207
Inscription of Philip, Earl of Arundel..	208
Prisoner's Room in the Beauchamp Tower	210
Passage and Cell in the Beauchamp Tower	214
Processional Axe	306
Execution of the Earl of Kilmarnock and Lord Balmerino, on Tower Hill .. .. } *To face*	308
Coffin-plates of the Earl of Kilmarnock and Lords Balmerino and Lovat	312
Gravestone of the three Scotch Lords..	312
Axe, Block, and Executioner's Mask	324

ST. PETER'S CHAPEL

IN THE

TOWER OF LONDON.

S.T PETER AD VINCULA.

CHAPTER I.

THE HISTORY OF THE CHAPEL.

WITH the exception of the Abbey Church of St. Peter's at Westminster, there is no ecclesiastical edifice in the United Kingdom, in which (so far as it has been used as a place of sepulture) is centred so much historical interest as the chapel of St. Peter ad Vincula in the Tower of London. Within its walls have been received the mortal remains of many, whose names, though not recorded on the stones of its pavement, must yet ever live in the pages of English history.

The chapel of St. John, in the White Tower, is a building of earlier date doubtless as to its foundation, and the original Norman structure still remains; but St. Peter's (though not the present building) can also lay claim to a nearly equal antiquity, and was founded not long after the chapel of St. John; in all probability by Henry I. It is at any rate known to have been in existence in the reign of King John.

In Henry III.'s reign the King issued a warrant dated Windsor, 10th December, 1241, directing the chancel of St. Mary, and the Royal Stalls in the chancel of St. Peter, to be repaired, ornamented, and painted, for the use of himself and his Queen: and the "little Mary, with her tabernacle, and the figures of St. Peter, St. Nicholas, and St. Katherine, to be newly coloured, all with the best colours; the beam beyond the altar of St. Peter, and the little cross with its images, to be refreshed with good colours: that two fair tables be made with the histories of St. Nicholas and St. Katherine before their altars in the said church; also two fair cherubim with cheerful and pleasant countenances[1] to be placed on either side of the great crucifix; and a marble font with columns to be provided."[2]

Again, ten years later, bells for the church are ordered by the King,[3] and in 1272, at his decease, mass is ordered to be said there for the repose of his soul, and his son Edward I. directs the payment of fifty shillings per annum to be paid to the priest as a recompense for such services.[4]

Some slight remains of this earlier building may be detected in the crypt, and perhaps in some parts of the walls, but the present church owes its origin to King Edward I., who, towards the end of his reign in 1305-6, issued orders for its erection, and in a warrant dated Fotheringay, the 11th July, he authorises "Ralph de Sandwich, Constable of our Tower of London," to be re-imbursed for the various outlays incurred by him "in the construction of our new chapel within the Tower."[5]

The chapel then erected, and which still remains, is situated in the inner ward of the Tower, at the north-west angle of the open space, which is now called the Parade, and on which was formerly erected the scaffold for the execution of those who "suffered on the Green within the Tower."

It consists of a nave and chancel, and one aisle on the north side of the nave; between the nave and the aisle is a row of columns which belong to the so-called "decorated" period of architecture. It is sixty-six feet in length, fifty-four feet in width, and the height from the pavement to the roof is twenty-five feet.

The dedication of the chapel to "St. Peter ad Vincula"

---

[1] Cum hyllari vultu et jocoso: et praeterea unum fontem marmoreum cum columpnis marmoreis bene et decenter incisis.

[2] Rot. lib., 25 Hen. III. m. 20.
[3] Rot. claus., 35 Hen. III. m. 16.
[4] Rot. lib., 1 Ed. I. m. 1.
[5] Rot. claus., 34 Ed. I. m. 8.

(St. Peter in chains or bonds) is peculiar, and at once points to its use as the place of worship for the prisoners within the fortress, in contradistinction to the chapel of St. John, which was rather for the accommodation of the Sovereign and court when residing in the Tower. With the exception of the church of S. Pietro in Vincoli at Rome, where the chains of the saint are annually exhibited to the faithful on the 1st August, I am not aware of any similar dedication.

Various grants for the maintenance of service in the church have been made from time to time. Henry III. and Edward I. granted to the chaplains who performed service, the yearly sum of fifty shillings, which was an allowance similar in amount to that received by all the royal chaplains.[1] In 1354 Edward III. proposed to convert the chapel into a sort of collegiate church, with a dean and three canons, but this does not appear to have been effected, as he subsequently granted "certain rents, at a certain custom of Stabotes or Stalbotes (a kind of fisher-boats)," for the maintenance of a rector and three chaplains, and later he added two more chaplains, in order that the sacraments and divine services might be better administered to his officers and servants residing in the Tower:[2] for their remuneration, he granted also certain allowances or tithes, to be paid for some tenements in London, and at Tower Hill and Petty Wales;[3] fifty-eight shillings per annum from the Hospital of St. Katherine; ten marks per annum to be paid by the Constable of the Tower, and twenty shillings per annum of his good will; thirteen shillings per annum from the Master of the Mint, and of every artificer and stipendiary a certain tithe out of their wages and stipends."[4]

[1] Rot. lib., Hen. III.
[2] Tanner's 'Notitia Monastica,' p. 321.
[3] "Some are of opinion that these great stone buildings, the ruins whereof do yet remain, were sometime the lodging appointed for the Princes of Wales, when they repaired to this city, and that therefore the street (Thames Street) in that part is called Petty Wales, which name remaineth there most commonly until this day, even as where kings of Scotland were used to be lodged betwixt Charing Cross and Whitehall, it is likewise called Scotland (Yard), and where the earls of Briton were lodged without Aldersgate, the street is called Britain Street (Little Britain)."—Stow.
[4] Maitland's 'Hist. of London,' vol. i. p. 148; Bayley, 'Hist. of the Tower,' p. 127.

This grant was confirmed in subsequent reigns, and Henry V., in addition, grants to John Salmonby, rector of the chapel in the Tower, sixty shillings rent, and the appurtenances in Candlewick Street, for and towards his subsistence.[1]

Such then were the emoluments of the clergy at that period, but the duties of the rector do not seem always to have been limited to the services of his church, for Stow records that "in the year 1419 Friar Randolph was sent to the Tower, and was there slain by the parson of St. Peter's in the Tower."

"From the accounts of the various grants," says Maitland, "it has been collected that the bounds of this rectory, are, all the compass of the Tower, and it hath some territories without, as Little Tower Hill, which was therefore called the King's soil of Little Tower Hill, adjoining to which was a place called 'the King's waste of Rosemary Lane' or 'Hog Lane;' but these boundaries, as well as the precinct of the Tower, which contains all the soil and liberty between Barking Church and Crutched Friars, St. Mary Gracious and St. Katherine's, have been an old controversy[2] between the magistrates of the city, and the officer of the Tower."[3]

Edward IV., in lieu of the rector and chaplains, instituted a dean and three canons, whom he incorporated by the name of the "Dean and Canons of the Royal Free Chapel of the King's household within the Tower of London;" but the King dying before this grant was completed, his intentions were rendered ineffectual.

Very extensive alterations in the structure were made in the reign of Henry VIII., who in 1532 ordered a general survey to be made, and a report to be drawn up of the condition of the Tower. The chapel had then suffered much

---

[1] Rot. lib., 8 Hen. V. m. 5.
[2] This controversy continued till late years: in 1730 a dispute arose between the inhabitants of the Tower liberty without and those within the Tower, whether the church was parochial or not: the case was then tried in the King's Bench, and decided in the negative.—Northouck, 'Hist. of London,' p. 525.
[3] Maitland, vol. i. p. 149.

from fire,[1] as well as from general decay, and the repairs and restorations which were then carried out by the King's order brought the church into the architectural condition in which we now see it. The present windows, except that over the west entrance door, the arches, and the timber roof, are all of that period. The removal of the plastering on the east wall of the aisle has recently disclosed a small piscina, of the same date as the window tracery; and close by it is a hagioscope or squint: there were two altars in the church, the chief altar being dedicated to St. Peter, and the other to St. Mary, and this hagioscope was to enable the officiating priest at St. Mary's altar to observe the high altar: the view through it is now blocked by the Blount monument in the chancel.

The interesting series of historical interments in the chapel, of which we have any definite records, commences in this reign. Edward VI. subjected the chapel to the Episcopal authority of the Bishop of London, and Queen Mary confirmed the jurisdiction of this prelate by the following order, dated 12 Oct. 1555:—"Item, it is alsoe orderede for advauncement of devyne service and religion that the curate nowe servinge within the saide Towere, and his souccessores for ever, shall take instruction of the bysshope of London and his souccessores for the time being, by the name of the parsone of the Towere; and that the saide parsone and his successores, and all inhabittauncyes within the saide Towere, shall perpetually be reputed and takyne to belonge to the speciall jurysdyctyon of the bysshope of London and his successores."

In the same ordinance is the following passage respecting the appointment of the "parsone of the Tower":—"And whereas there is a churche within the Tower, and therein divine sarvis daylie usede, and yet neither parsone nor vicare of the same, and so apperinge but donative at the Kinge and Queene's Majesties' pleasure, whereby no parsone

---

[1] Stow expressly mentions that the "chapel in the Tower" had been burnt in 1512, and during the recent restorations in 1876 several indications of fire have been observed on the walls.

abide to have cure sowle, which is to be remedid, and therefore their Majesties' pleasure is, the same to be established into perfecyon, as to their Grace's counsell, and the ordinary shall be thought convenient."

This jurisdiction of the Bishop ended upon the establishment of the Protestant succession in the following reign, and the chapel then became, as it still remains, a "Benefice donative; where the Bishop can neither visit nor deprive."[2] There is no account of any particular occurrences connected with the architectural arrangements, or with the services in the chapel during the reign of Queen Elizabeth; but the doctrine of one of the preachers in the chapel appears to have been called in question, as amongst the State papers is a "Declaration dated 4th June, 1587, of the substance of the doctrine preached in the sermon by Mr. Mathewe, minister of St. Michael's, Cornhill, before Sir Owyn Hopton, Lieutenant of the Tower, and the prisoners with the rest of the audience then present on Whit Sunday, wherein he accused the Presciscians of disturbing the Church against the Queen and the Bishop."[3]

In the time of James I. a dispute arose about the solemnization of marriages and christenings[4] in this chapel, and Mr. Hayes, the then curate, was put in confinement by the High Commission for performing those ordinances: but Sir William Waade, the Lieutenant of the Tower, demanded and obtained his release.[5] The question was nevertheless still agitated, and in 1620, Mr. Hubbock the rector, and his son

---

[1] Britton and Brayley, 'Tower of London,' p. 308; Newcourt's 'Repertorium,' vol. i. p. 530.

[2] "The statutes and records being shewed to the Archbishops Whitgift and Bancroft, they said they would not meddle with us."—Tower Records.

[3] State Papers, Dom. Eliz. 1587, p. 415.

[4] The fragments of the font, which ppear to have been broken up designedly, were found in 1876 hidden within the monument of Sir Richard Cholmondeley. It is hoped that they will furnish sufficient data for a satisfactory restoration or copy of the old font, which, from the character of the fragments, appears to be of the time of Edward III.: they are of stone, and therefore not parts of the marble font given by Henry III. Allen, in his 'History of London,' vol. ii. p. 512, says there was no font in this church, and that he had seen a slop basin used for the rite of baptism.

[5] There are several memoranda on this subject, and on other matters concerning the rights and privileges of the Tower which were drawn up by Sir William Waade, now preserved in the Tower records.

the curate, were excommunicated by the Archbishop of Canterbury, and the excommunication was published on the following Sunday, in All Hallows, Barking, and in St. Katherine's Churches; the right to celebrate marriages and christenings was however soon afterwards fully established, and has since been enjoyed without interruption.[1]

In Charles I.'s reign differences of opinion appear to have arisen between Sir W. Balfour, the Lieutenant of the Tower, and the chaplain of St. Peter's, and the former appears to have had recourse to somewhat strong measures. On 25th May, 1641, Archibald Mackellar, who had been appointed by the King to St. Peter's, petitions His Majesty that "Sir William Balfour will not allow him to perform his duties, but continued to molest him; that he had agreed to exchange his living with Dr. Shipsen, upon which he was thrust out of his cure before the exchange was completed, and for trying to obtain some redress he was imprisoned by the Lieutenant in the Tower."[2]

During the subsequent reigns the chapel appears to have undergone the various changes to which the majority of our ecclesiastical buildings have been subjected. A cumbersome reredos with heavy cornice, and pews placed in various positions, were added; and in some such "family pew" Pepys doubtless sat on the occasion of his visit.

"February 28th, 1663-4. Lord's day. The Lieutenant of the Tower, Sir J. Robinson,[3] would needs have me by coach home with him; where the officers of his regiment dined with him. I did go and dine with him, his ordinary table being very good, and his lady a very high carriaged, but comely-big woman:[4] I was mightily pleased with her. After dinner to chapel in the Tower with the Lieutenant, with the keys carried before us, and the warders and gentleman porter going before us; and I sat with the Lieutenant in his pew in great state. None it seems of the prisoners in the Tower that are there now, though they may, will come to prayers there."[5]

The gallery was added in the reign of George II. for the accommodation of the troops in the garrison: and thus

[1] Bayley, p. 128; Tower Records.
[2] MSS. Records: House of Lords.
[3] Constable from 1660 till 1678.
[4] Anne, daughter of Sir George Whitmore, of Barnes, in Surrey.
[5] Pepys' Diary, vol. ii. p. 101.

in the present century these various additions had reduced the building to a condition more resembling that of a neglected and insignificant parish church, than of the Royal Chapel of the old metropolitan fortress.

Macaulay has thus recorded his impressions after visiting it :—" I cannot refrain from expressing my disgust at the barbarous stupidity which has transformed this interesting little church into the likeness of a meeting house in a

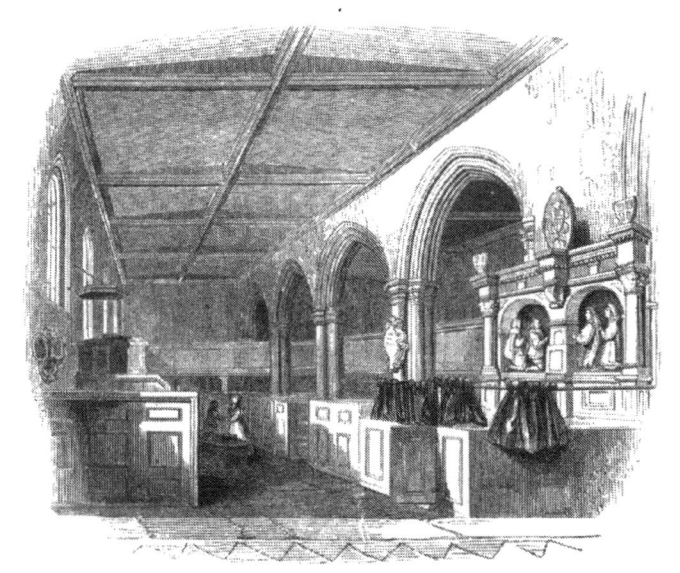

Interior of the Chapel in 1820. From Bayley's 'History of the Tower.'

manufacturing town." In truth there is no sadder spot on earth than this little cemetery. Death is there associated, not, as in Westminster and St. Paul's, with genius and virtue, with public veneration and with imperishable renown; not, as in our humblest churches and churchyards, with everything that is most endearing in social and domestic charities : but with what ever is darkest in human nature and in human destiny; with the savage triumph of implacable enemies, with the inconstancy, the ingratitude, the cowardice of friends, with all the miseries of fallen greatness and of blighted fame.

"Thither have been carried through successive ages, by the rude hands of gaolers, without one mourner following, the bleeding relics of men, who had been the captains of armies, the leaders of parties, the oracles of senates, and the ornaments of courts." [1]

[1] Macaulay's 'Hist. of England,' vol. i. pp. 628-9.

CHAPTER II.

THE RESTORATIONS IN 1876-7.

ENCUMBERED as it was by high pews and unsightly galleries, the pavement broken and uneven, the walls and columns disfigured with whitewash and unimportant tablets, the sight of the interior of the chapel may well have awakened Lord Macaulay's eloquent protest, and for some years it had been desired to improve this state of things, and to restore the chapel to a decent and sightly condition.

In 1862, the insignificant porch on the south side, by which the building had been entered since the time of Queen Elizabeth, was removed, and the original old doorway at the west end, which had been bricked up and concealed by plaster, was reopened, and the fragments of the window above, being found there, they were restored to their original position. The lath and plaster covering was at the same time removed from the ceiling, and the old chesnut beams of Henry VIII.'s roof were disclosed to view.[1]

At length the necessity for a thorough restoration and repair became imperative for sanitary reasons, and in the early part of the year 1876 the Constable, Sir Charles Yorke, took the necessary steps for submitting the proposed plan for the decision of Her Majesty the Queen. It was then decided that the chapel should be, as far as possible, architecturally restored to its original condition, and also suitably arranged as a place of worship for the use of the residents and garrison of the Tower.

---

[1] It is impossible to speak too highly of the active interest which the late Lord De Ros showed whilst holding the office of Deputy Lieutenant of the Tower: amongst the numerous instances of his zeal for everything relating to the Tower, may be mentioned the admirable care with which the records and documents are arranged.

View of the Chancel before the restoration in 1876.

View of the Chapel as restored in 1877.

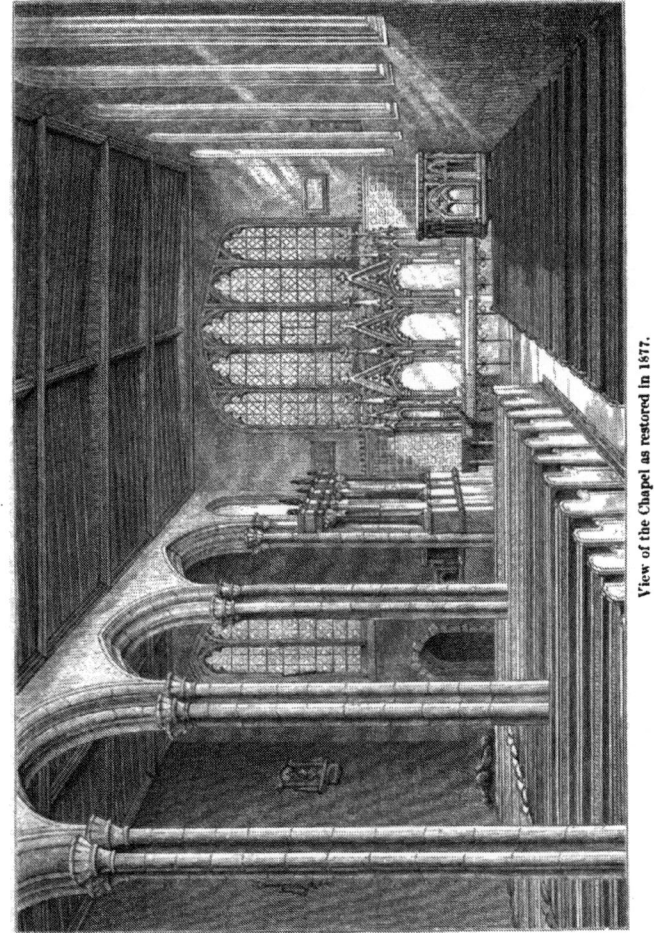

The question then came under the consideration of the First Commissioner of Her Majesty's Works, when Mr. John Taylor of that Department prepared comprehensive plans for its restoration: these were submitted to Mr. Salvin, the architect under whose superintendence all the other works of restoration throughout the Tower have been carried out, and the operations were commenced in the month of August, 1876.

When the designs for the repair and restoration of the chapel came under consideration, the necessity for relaying the pavement, which had sunk and become uneven in many parts, became very evident; and upon the removal of the pews, it was at once seen that nothing could be done until a level and safe foundation was prepared, upon which the new pavement could be placed; it was moreover intended that a heating apparatus should be fitted in the church.

On removing the stones of the pavement it was found (as reference to the burial register too abundantly proved) that the resting places of those who had been buried within the walls of the chapel during the troublous times of the sixteenth and seventeenth centuries, had been repeatedly and it was feared almost universally desecrated.

When the Tower ceased to be a residence of the sovereign or a state prison, the chapel of St. Peter appears to have gradually come to be regarded too much in the light of a mere ordinary parish church, in which the interment not only of those who had lived in the Tower, but even of residents in the neighbourhood, was freely permitted.

It is true that the bodies of those who had perished on the scaffold, or died as prisoners within the walls of the Tower, were buried (no doubt intentionally) "in great obscurity;"[1] but even if some memorial stone had recorded their burial place, it is doubtful whether that would have protected their remains, for in the instance of the three Scotch lords (Lovat, Balmerino, and Kilmarnock) although their grave was specially marked by a stone, which is still preserved,[2] it was found that their bones had been much

[1] Northouck, p. 768.
[2] See p. 312. This stone still remains in its original position in the pavement near the west door.

disturbed, so much so indeed as to be beyond all possible means of identification. It is even feared that in some instances coffins had been designedly broken up and their contents scattered in order to make room for some fresh occupant of the ground.

Many of the more recent interments were barely two feet below the surface, and in no instances were any graves found lower than five or six feet; a continual sinking of many parts of the surface was certain to occur, and moreover, for sanitary reasons, it was most imperative that the ground should be cleared and readjusted to a proper level. It was therefore considered advisable to take immediate steps for removing all the remains into the crypt, only retaining in position some of the brick vaults which were found in different parts and which appeared to be in perfectly sound condition.[1]

The Constable of the Tower submitted this proposal for the approval of the Queen, and Her Majesty, while expressing her great regret at learning that so little respect should have apparently been shown to the remains of the dead, gave her sanction to the plan, with the express condition that the greatest care and reverence should be exercised in this removal, and that a careful record should be kept of every sign of possible identification which might come to light.

These conditions have been scrupulously observed, and the operations have been carried out by the Office of Works, and under the immediate personal supervision of Major General Maitland, the Lieutenant, and of Colonel Milman, the resident governor of the Tower.

All the human remains which were found beneath the floor of the chapel were carefully collected and enclosed in boxes, with suitable inscriptions; and all the coffins which were found intact were at once removed to the crypt.[2]

The works had progressed so far, when in October, 1876,

---

[1] These have now been covered with a firm bed of concrete.

[2] The crypt is on the north side of the chapel, and it is not unlikely that it was beneath the old chapel. It was originally entered from the chapel, and a door leading towards it, which had been bricked up, was recently found in the north wall.

it became necessary to consider the arrangements for the restoration of the chancel; and it was pointed out that as the Queens Anne Boleyn and Katharine Howard, and the Dukes of Somerset, Northumberland, and Monmouth, were undoubtedly known to have been buried there, it would be very desirable (although other interments certainly had been permitted) to allow this portion of the chapel to remain undisturbed; and at a meeting which took place in the chapel, at which Major General Maitland, the Hon. S. Ponsonby Fane, Colonel Milman, Colonel the Hon. G. Wrottesley,[1] and Mr. Doyne C. Bell, were present, it was resolved that this pavement should remain intact, and that the new pavement should be laid over it.

A subsequent examination by the Surveyor of the Office of Works showed however that this was practically impossible, as in two places the pavement had sunk, and showed signs of considerable hollowness beneath it. It was therefore decided that the pavement must be removed in order that this sinking might be rectified, but that as little disturbance of the ground as possible should take place.

The documents contained in the following chapter will show how this decision was carried into effect.

The restorations progressed steadily during the winter and spring of 1876-7, and the works which were carried out may be thus briefly enumerated. The old plastering and whitewash were removed from the walls and columns, and as has been already mentioned, a doorway in the north wall and the piscina and hagioscope on the east wall of the aisle were discovered. The galleries, the wooden pulpit and the high pews, with which the chapel had been disfigured, were all removed: a carved stone reredos and pulpit were erected; and a reading desk, and open benches of oak were substituted for the pews. The inconvenient wooden structure (also a modern barbarism) near the west entrance door, which had served as a vestry, was pulled down, and a new vestry, giving easy access to the chancel, was built outside the eastern end of the aisle. Lastly, a suitable and hand-

[1] As representative of the family of Sir John Burgoyne.

some pavement has been laid down in the chancel; this pavement is formed of green and red marble, with octagon panels of white marble, in which are inserted the armorial bearings of those historic persons who were interred in the chancel; their names being inscribed on the border of yellow Siena marble which surrounds each panel.[1]

The chapel was completed and re-opened for divine service in June, 1877.

[1] The restorations have all been carried out under the superintendence of Mr. John Taylor of Her Majesty's Office of Works; Mr. Salvin having been consulted upon the drawings. Mr. McCleish acted as Clerk of the Works.

CHAPTER III.

THE OPERATIONS OF 9TH AND 11TH NOVEMBER, 1876;
AND OF 13TH APRIL, 1877.

ST. PETER AD VINCULA,
9th November, 1876.

PRESENT:

The Right Hon. GERARD J. NOEL,
  First Commissioner of Her Majesty's Works.
Mr. A. B. MITFORD,
  Secretary to the Commissioners of Her Majesty's Works.
Colonel G. BRYAN MILMAN, C.B.,
  Resident Governor of the Tower.
The Hon. SPENCER PONSONBY FANE, C.B.,
  Comptroller in the Lord Chamberlain's Department.
Dr. FREDERIC J. MOUAT, F.R.C.S.,
  Local Government Inspector.
Mr. DOYNE C. BELL,
  Secretary to Her Majesty's Privy Purse.

AT a meeting held in the chapel of St. Peter ad Vincula in the Tower on Thursday, 9th November, at half-past twelve o'clock, Mr. Mitford produced a plan which had been prepared by the Clerk of the Works; this plan showed the present condition of the pavement of the chancel, and recorded the memorial stones with their inscriptions. He also explained that it was intended to repair the chancel with tiles or symmetrical paving, so as to bring it into harmony with the restorations which were being carried out in the rest of the chapel. It had been at first decided that this pavement should not be moved, and that the tiles, or new pavement, should be fixed upon it: one reason for this decision was, that the chancel had been less disturbed for recent interments than the other parts of the chapel, and it was therefore hoped that the remains of some of those, who were known to have been interred on this spot in the sixteenth century, might still be remaining *in situ*.

Mr. Bell then showed a plan which he had prepared, showing the relative positions in which it was believed that these persons had originally been buried. This plan had been prepared after consulting various historical authorities.

Mr. Mitford explained that a recent examination of the pavement showed however that it would not be safe, or of good construction, to place any new pavement upon the present stones, as two portions, which he pointed out, had considerably sunk and bore every evidence of being hollow underneath, so that further sinking would in all probability shortly take place; the small brick grave in which Sir John Burgoyne had been buried in 1870 was indeed the only spot in the chancel which could be thoroughly relied upon.

Upon this evidence, it was decided that the pavement should be raised, in order to remedy any further sinking; that the greatest caution should be used in removing every spadeful of earth; that the earth should be carefully examined with a sieve; that whatever remains were found should be re-interred on the same spot; and that these operations should be carried out under the supervision of some, or all, of the persons who were then present.

The pavement was then lifted on the spot which was marked on the plan as the place of Queen Anne Boleyn's interment, and the earth removed to a depth of two feet; it had certainly not been disturbed for upwards of a hundred years.

At this depth the bones of a female were found, not lying in the original order, but which had evidently for some reason or other been heaped together into a smaller space: all these bones were examined by Dr. Mouat, who at once pronounced them to be those of a female of between twenty-five and thirty years of age, of a delicate frame of body, and who had been of slender and perfect proportions; the forehead and lower jaw were small and especially well formed. The vertebræ were particularly small, especially one joint (the atlas), which was that next to the skull, and they bore witness to the Queen's "lyttel neck."[1] He thought that these female bones had lain in the earth for upwards of three hundred years, and they were certainly all those of one person. No other female bones were found on this spot.

Not much doubt existed in the minds of those present that these were the remains of Anne Boleyn, who is recorded to have been buried in front of the altar by the side of her brother George Rochford, and these being the first burials in the chancel, the graves were in all probability dug to the right or dexter side of the altar, the so-called "place of honour." Rochford was buried on the 17th May, and the grave into which, at noon on the 19th May, the old elm-chest containing the remains of his sister Anne was cast, was dug by the side of him. Stow says "he lieth with the rest."

Some male bones belonging to a man of considerable stature, and of about fifty years of age, were found close to those of the Queen, but they were lying separate, and no intermixture had taken place; these were few in number, and appeared also to have been collected and placed together for some special reason.

It was evident that when the ground had been disturbed, probably about one hundred years ago, the re-arrangement of these remains had been effected with considerable care; and that much respect had undoubtedly been shown to them.

When the grave for Sir J. Burgoyne was prepared, some bones corresponding to the male bones now found, were discovered lying loosely in the earth; these had been all placed together more towards the east wall, near the spot where the Duke of Monmouth's remains lie; it is supposed that the bones now found had fallen out of position when

[1] See p. 104.

Hannah Beresford was interred, and they were therefore not seen when Sir J. Burgoyne was buried in 1870.

These large male bones are doubtless those of the Protector Somerset; he and John Dudley, Duke of Northumberland, were buried between the two Queens, Anne Boleyn and Katharine Howard, and in front of the altar. The Duke of Somerset being buried in 1551, and Northumberland two years later.

The bones of George Rochford may have been removed at the same period, or else they lie more towards the north wall; but it was not thought desirable or necessary to examine that ground, especially as it might have affected the stability of the Blount monument.

The removal of another two feet of earth disclosed the cause of the sinking of the pavement, and also explained in some measure the reason why, and furnished the probable date when the remains of Queen Anne Boleyn had been gathered together. The lead coffin of Hannah Beresford, August 1750, aged fifty-four years, was reached, and this had decayed and collapsed, leaving the ground above it loose and hollow to such an extent that the workman was able to pass his arm freely up the cavity.

All the remains which had been discovered were carefully sorted and immediately locked up in a box, to remain in the custody of Colonel Milman, the Resident Governor of the Tower, until suitable receptacles could be made and the ground prepared for their re-interment.

At a quarter past three o'clock the operations were suspended.

(Signed)

G. J. NOEL.	S. PONSONBY FANE.
A. B. MITFORD.	F. J. MOUAT.
G. B. MILMAN.	DOYNE C. BELL.

11th *November*, 1876.

PRESENT:

The Right Hon. GERARD J. NOEL,
First Commissioner of Her Majesty's Works.
Mr. A. B. MITFORD,
Secretary to the Commissioners of Her Majesty's Works.
Lieut.-Colonel G. BRYAN MILMAN, C.B.,
Resident Governor of the Tower.
Dr. FREDERIC J. MOUAT, F.R.C.S.,
Local Government Inspector.
Mr. DOYNE C. BELL,
Secretary to Her Majesty's Privy Purse.

A meeting was again held in the chapel of St. Peter in the Tower, on Saturday the 11th November, at half-past eleven o'clock.

Mr. Mitford had pointed out on the 9th November that the pavement had sunk very considerably on the south as well as on the north side of the chancel, and it had therefore been decided to lift the stones of that portion; this had been done when we arrived, but the earth had not been removed at any part.

Mr. Bell indicated on his plan the spot where John Dudley, Duke of Northumberland, and Queen Katharine Howard are recorded to have been interred, and he also expressed an opinion that Margaret of Clarence, Countess of Salisbury, had been buried near Katharine Howard, as she was beheaded soon after that Queen, and it is said she "rested with the attainted group" in the chancel.

Lady Rochford was beheaded on the same day as Katharine Howard, and might very possibly have been buried by her side.[1]

It was recommended that the ground nearest to Sir John Burgoyne's grave should be first examined; this was the

---

[1] Bayley says she was, but does not give his authority for this statement.

spot where the Duke of Northumberland is recorded to have been buried. About two feet below the surface, and precisely in the position which had been expected, were found the male bones of a person of about fifty years of age: a large skull was found with them, and it is specially recorded that the Duke's head was not exposed on London Bridge or elsewhere, but buried with his body.[1]

There appeared no reason to doubt that these were the remains of John Dudley, Duke of Northumberland; they had been much shaken during the formation of Sir J. Burgoyne's grave, but most of the skeleton was collected.

Close by, somewhat in a south-east direction, and nearer to the wall of the chancel, gathered together in two distinct groups, were found the bones of two females; these were examined and carefully sorted, they appeared to belong to a person of about thirty to forty years of age, and to another who must have been considerably advanced in years. It is worthy of note that these latter remains were a little to the south-east of the younger female.

These groups had been much disturbed, and many bones are missing: the younger female had been of rather delicate proportions, the elder had been tall, and certainly of above average height.

These remains are believed to be those of Lady Rochford and Margaret of Clarence, Countess of Salisbury: and, as was subsequently discovered, they had been removed somewhat to the east of their original resting places, in order to make room for two unknown persons, who had been buried close to the step of the chancel, probably about one hundred years ago.

No remains which could be identified as those of Queen Katharine Howard were found; it should, however, be borne in mind that lime has been most extensively used in these interments, and as Katharine Howard was only twenty years old when she was beheaded (at which age the bones have not become hard and consolidated), it is very possible that even when Judge Jeffreys was interred in the chancel, her

[1] See p. 163.

remains had already become dust. It was at first supposed, as she had been buried on this spot, that her remains had been discovered, when the group of female bones were found lying near the Duke of Northumberland; but a closer examination showed that the age and size of the bones (Katharine Howard is said to have been very small in stature) would not support that supposition, and these are now believed to be the remains of Lady Rochford.

A large male skeleton was found beneath the stone which formerly bore the name of Sir Allan Apsley, Lieutenant of the Tower, who was buried in 1630.

Close against the east wall, and lying partly on the concrete foundation of that wall, were discovered the leg bones of a tall man: they were not lying in the usual position, east and west, but north and south.

James, Duke of Monmouth, was buried "under the communion table," and there can be no doubt of this identification of his remains.[1]

At a depth of six inches lower than the grave of the Duke of Monmouth was found a large male skeleton, lying north-east and south-east, the skull, face downwards, being towards the altar and close to the legs of the Duke of Monmouth. This body was at first supposed to be that of Judge Jeffreys, who it is recorded was buried "by the Duke of Monmouth." But it was afterwards ascertained that although interred here in 1689, his body was removed to the church of St. Mary, Aldermanbury, in 1692.[2] These remains have not yet been identified. It was evident that this interment had much deranged that of Sir A. Apsley, and might also have caused some removal of the remains, believed to be those of Margaret of Clarence, Countess of Salisbury.

A broken tobacco pipe of the 17th century and a fragment of silk were found between this body, and the supposed remains of Lady Rochford and the Countess of Salisbury.

The cause of the sinking of the pavement on this side of the chancel was now discovered, as close beyond the remains of Sir A. Apsley, the earth suddenly collapsed, and it was

---

[1] The earth was only partially removed, so that only the leg bones were seen. [2] See pp. 48, 485.

then ascertained that this was occasioned by the interment of Colonel Maclean, in 1816; either his coffin had much collapsed, or else the earth had been too loosely filled in after his burial.

It was decided to make no further examination of the ground, and the excavation was therefore at once filled up.

All the remains that had been taken out were examined seriatim by Dr. Mouat, and were carefully sorted and placed apart. These several parcels were duly labelled and fastened up, and then conveyed in boxes to the "Queen's House," where they will remain locked up in the custody of Colonel Milman, until the leaden coffers are ready to receive them, when they will be re-interred in the same positions in which they were found.

(Signed)
G. J. NOEL.   F. J. MOUAT.
A. B. MITFORD.   DOYNE C. BELL.
G. B. MILMAN.

[MEMORANDUM BY DR. MOUAT.]

QUEEN ANNE BOLEYN.

The bones found in the place where Queen Anne Boleyn is said to have been buried are certainly those of a female in the prime of life, all perfectly consolidated and symmetrical, and belong to the same person.

The bones of the head indicate a well-formed round skull, with an intellectual forehead, straight orbital ridge, large eyes, oval face, and rather square full chin. The remains of the vertebræ, and the bones of the lower limbs, indicate a well-formed woman of middle height, with a short and slender neck. The ribs show depth and roundness of chest. The hand and feet bones indicate delicate and well-shaped hands and feet, with tapering fingers and a narrow foot.

They are all consistent with the published descriptions of the Queen, and the bones of the skull might well belong to the person portrayed in the painting by Holbein, in the collection of the Earl of Warwick.

The Duke of Northumberland.

The bones supposed to be those of the Duke of Northumberland are of a tall powerful man, above fifty years of age, and they have been very long in the ground, quite three centuries I should say.

Countess of Salisbury.

The bones found are few in number, but are all of the same person, a tall aged female.

The absence in the vicinity of this grave of any of the bones of Queen Katharine Howard, is quite consistent with the fact of her youth. The bones at the age at which she was executed are softer in texture, and a great portion of them are more cartilaginous than when growth is completed, and the framework of the body consolidated; so that they would disintegrate and disappear much more rapidly than had she been fully formed, and the whole process of ossification been completed. The large admixture of lime with earth which was found in the grave would accelerate this process; there is nothing therefore inconsistent with the fact of her having been buried there, in the absence of any portion of her remains after a lapse of more than three centuries.

The portions of the skeleton of the second female found, were those of a woman probably of forty years of age, of larger frame than Katharine Howard. They may possibly therefore have been those of Lady Rochford, who was executed at the same time.

Queen Anne Boleyn.

Frontal bone: tolerably complete, showing a forehead moderate in height, and of fair breadth; orbits large; superciliary ridge straight.

A large portion of the occipital bone; in excellent preservation.

Two portions of both upper maxillary bones.

Several portions of the parietal bones; in good condition.

Fragments of both temporal bones; much eroded in external plate.

Small portions of the ethnoid and sphenoid bones.

Lower jaw: two thirds perfect; the other third, on the left side, was broken off and not found: eight teeth remaining in jaw; four more teeth found loose (they had just fallen out), all in excellent preservation; one molar tooth of left side was slightly decayed.

The form of the head appears to have been round, and the face of an oval shape; the forehead straight and ample, and denoting considerable intelligence.

The lower part of the face, judging from the form of the jaw, must have been moderately full, with a somewhat square chin.

Vertebræ—the atlas; very small, much eroded. Three dorsal vertebræ; probably the first and third. Three lumbar vertebræ, very perfect; the other vertebræ are much eroded. Judging from these vertebræ, her height might have been about 5 feet, or 5 feet 3 inches, not more.

Four ribs, tolerably perfect; the rest fragmentary, in fifty-two pieces.

Collar-bone and clavicle; the left side perfect; a small portion of the right clavicle only remaining.

Two fragments of the head of the scapula left side.

Judging from the curvature of the ribs, she must have had a deep and well-formed chest.

Eight fragments of the pelvis, very much eroded, and the characters almost obliterated.

Portions of both legs: the left thigh bone, in tolerably good preservation, though broken off above, is singularly delicate and well formed; several portions of the tibiæ and fibulæ of both legs.

Patella (knee-cap) of left leg very perfect.

Her limbs evidently bore a due proportion to the rest of her body.

Portions of the humerus, and radius of the right side; the radius remarkably slender.

Scaphoid bone of the right foot, and eleven bones of feet; all tarsal and metatarsal bones.

Eleven finger bones; phalanges. The middle metacarpal bone of the right hand, and last bone of the little finger of left hand very perfect. These bones showed a slender and delicate formation of the hands.[1]

Fifty-two other fragments, very much eroded, and not susceptible of exact identification.

---

[1] "There was founde indeede upon the side of her naile upon one of her fingers some little shew of a naile which yet was so smale, by the report of those that have seen here, as the woork maister seemed to leave it an occasion of greater grace to the hand, which with the tip of one of her other fingers might be, and was usually by her hidden without any lest blemish to it."—Wyatt's 'Life,' p. 4.

It was at first thought that this malformation could be traced on one of the finger bones, but a more careful examination dissipated that impression.

THE DUKE OF NORTHUMBERLAND.

These bones evidently belonged to a large man, about six feet in height; and aged about 50 years. They all belong to one person, and appear to have been in the ground at least 300 years.

MARGARET COUNTESS OF SALISBURY.

The bones believed to be those of Margaret Countess of Salisbury, are all those of a tall and aged female.

Skull: considerable portion of the frontal bone with the left orbit: petrous portion of the temporal bone; two small fragments of the side of the skull.

The upper portion of the sternum (breast-bone); tolerably perfect.

Six fragments of ribs.

The sacrum; tolerably complete.

Two portions of the pelvis.

Portions of the radius of both arms; in good preservation.

Portions of both clavicles.

One dorsal and three lumbar vertebræ.

Two fibulæ; nearly complete.

One finger bone.

A portion of the humerus.

Most of these bones in tolerable condition, but some eroded by lime.

It was not considered necessary to make any further detailed examination of the other remains.

FREDERIC J. MOUAT, M.D., F.R.C.S.,
Formerly Professor of Medicine and Medical Jurisprudence.

November 15, 1876.

13th *April*, 1877.

PRESENT:

General Sir CHARLES YORKE, G.C.B.,
Constable of the Tower.

Major-General C. L. MAITLAND, C.B.,
Lieutenant of the Tower.

Colonel G. BRYAN MILMAN, C.B.,
Resident Governor of the Tower.

Mr. A. B. MITFORD,
Secretary to the Commissioners of Her Majesty's Works.

The Hon. SPENCER PONSONBY FANE, C.B.,
Comptroller in the Lord Chamberlain's Department.

Rev. E. JORDAN ROGERS,
Chaplain of St. Peter's Chapel.

Mr. DOYNE C. BELL,
Secretary to Her Majesty's Privy Purse.

A meeting was held in the chapel of St. Peter in the Tower, on Friday, the 13th April, at twelve o'clock, when Colonel Milman produced seven cases, which contained the remains that had been exhumed from the chancel on the 9th and 11th November last.

These remains had been soldered up in thick leaden coffers, and then fastened down with copper screws in boxes made of oak plank, one inch in thickness. Each box bore a leaden escutcheon, on which was engraved the name of the person whose supposed remains were thus enclosed, together with the dates of death, and of the year (1877) of the re-interment.

The cases were then placed in the respective positions in the chancel in which the remains had been found, and the ground having been opened, they were all buried about four inches below the surface, the earth was then filled in, and concrete immediately spread over them.

The various positions of these interments are recorded upon a plan which will be copied on vellum, and deposited among the records belonging to the Tower.

    CHARLES YORKE, S. PONSONBY FANE.
    CHARLES L. MAITLAND. E. JORDAN ROGERS.
    G. B. MILMAN.   DOYNE C. BELL.
    A. B. MITFORD.

CHAPTER IV.

THE MONUMENTS.

SIR RICHARD CHOLMONDELEY, 1522.

THE oldest monument in the chapel is that of Sir Richard Cholmondeley, Lieutenant of the Tower in the reign of Henry VII., and of his wife Elizabeth.[1] Upon it are the recumbent life-size effigies, in alabaster, of Sir Richard and his wife. He is represented in plate armour, his head resting on a helmet, and his feet upon a lion: his hands are closed in prayer, and he wears a collar of SS round his neck. His wife lies on his left side, her head resting on a cushion: she wears a pointed head-dress. These effigies have originally been coloured and gilt. The tomb is ornamented with lozenges enclosing blank shields, which do not appear ever to have been carved: the base is adorned with foliage.

The inscription has been partly destroyed; the only remaining portion is—

"Hic Jacent corpora Richardi Cholmondeley, militis, et dñe Elizabethe consortis sue, qui ——————, quorum aiabus (animabus) Deus propietur. Amen."

This tomb was not improbably erected by Sir Richard Cholmondeley during his lifetime, as the date of his death is left blank in the carved inscription.

It originally stood in the centre of the nave in front of the chancel,[2] but many years ago was removed to the north-

---

[1] Maitland, vol. i. p. 149. Bayley, p. 123.

[2] It would be very desirable to restore it, and place it in its original position. For an engraving of this monument, see Bayley, p. 122.

west corner of the north aisle: it has now again been removed to the north-east end of the same aisle. When it was taken down in December, 1876, it was found to contain no human remains, but the fragments of the old stone font were discovered packed within it.

Sir Richard Cholmondeley was of an old Cheshire family. He served under the Earl of Surrey at the battle of Flodden Field, in 1513. He was afterwards knighted, and was made Lieutenant of the Tower. In 1518, when a riot arose between the Londoners and the Lombards and other merchant strangers, he discharged some artillery of the fortress against the city, with a view of intimidating the rioters. "Whilst this ruffling continued Syr Richard Cholmley, Knight, Lieutenant of the Towre, no great frende to the citie, in a frantyke fury losed certayn peces of ordinance, and shot into the citie, whiche did little harme, howbeit his good wyll apeered."[1] He died in 1544.

Sir Roger Cholmondeley, Lord Chief Justice of England, was a natural son of Sir Richard, who had no legitimate issue.

SIR RICHARD BLOUNT, 1564.   SIR MICHAEL BLOUNT, 15—.

On the north side of the chancel is a large and splendid monument, erected to the memory of Sir Richard Blount, Knight, and Sir Michael his son, both Lieutenants of the Tower. It is formed of alabaster and marble: it is in fact two monuments, the western portion having been erected by Sir Richard in 1564, the eastern portion added by Sir Michael Blount, thirty-two years later. They now form one uniform design, which is composed of three Corinthian columns, enclosing four arched recesses, within which are twelve effigies in alabaster. Sir Richard, who died in 1564, is represented on one side, in armour, with his two sons kneeling, and opposite are the figures of his wife and two daughters, also kneeling. The figures representing

[1] Hall's 'Chronicle.'

Sir Michael Blount and his family fill the other recesses. They are all dressed in the costume of the time. A tablet bears this inscription:—

"Hic jacet Richardus Blountus miles auratus qui Henrico octavo e quatuor atriensibus unus Edouardo sexto a privato cubiculo fuit: et in varia hujus imperii officia ab Elizetha regina selectus, Turri Londinensi ab eadem praefectus, ex hac dignitate in coelos a Deo susceptus est. Is uxorem duxit filiam Richardi Listeri militis itidem aurati primarii totius Angliae judicis, et ex ea filios habuit, Michaelem Blountum qui Mooram sibi in matrimonium sumpsit: et Richardum Blountum quem solum sine conjuge celibem reliquit: filias Elizabetham et Barbaram habuit, quarum alteram Nicholaio Seintihone, alteram Francisco Sherleio in conjugium dedit. Ex hac vita vir ille bonus discessit, annos natus quinquaginta nonos, undessimo die Augusti Anno Domini 1564. Et in hoc tumulo ex sumptu Elizabethae uxoris suae sepultus acquiescit. Tuum est O Deus omnium cadavera ad extremum vivificare et una tecum glorificare per sanctum Christum tuum. Amen."

Sir Michael Blount is represented in armour, attended by his three sons, his wife, and daughter, all in the attitude of prayer. On the tablet is this inscription:—

"Here lyeth buried Sir Michael Blount, Knight, sonne and heayre of Sir Richard Blount, Knight, whoe succeeded his father in y° office of Lieutenantcy of y° Tower of London xxv. yeares after y° death of his sayd father, and left issue by Mary his wife, sister and one of y° coheayres of Thomas Moore of Bissiter,[1] Richard, Thomas, and Charles, Catherine, and Frances. Richard maryed Cecily, youngest daughter of Sir Richard Baker, of Kent, Knight. Catherine, his eldest daughter, maryed to John Blount, alias Croke of Stydley, in y° countie of Oxon, Esquier, sonne and heayre apparant to John Blount, alias Croke of Chilton, in y° countie of Buckingham, Esquier, and hath issue John, Henry, and Charles; and Dame Mari, y° wife of y° sayd Sir Michael, died on Saterdaye, being y° 23rd daye of December in A° Domi. 1592,[2] and she lyeth here buried."

Below this monument is a tablet to the memory of Lyster Blount, an infant, with the following inscription:—

"Lyster Blount, January the 20, 1683.
"Underneath this place was interred y° body of Lister Blount, who diseased at 2 yeares 3 months of age, being lineally discended from

---

[1] Bicester, pronounced Bister. [2] See p. 47.

3 lieutenants of the Tower; viz. Sir Allen Apsley, who in this chapple gave Joyce his only daughter by his second wife, to y² father of this child Lyster Blount, y² third sonn of Sir Richard Blount, sonn and heire of Sir Michael Blount, sonn and heire of Sir Richard Blount, both Lieutenants of this Tower, as above declares.

"Here they all lye to expect y² coming of our sweet Saviour Jesu. Amen, Amen."

SIR ALLAN APSLEY, 1630.

Against the wall, on the south side of the chancel, is an oval tablet of black marble to the memory of Sir Allan Apsley : it is enclosed in a stone frame, on which are carved his armorial bearings. The inscription is,

"M. S.

"Here lyeth interred the body of Sir Allan Apsley, K⁶, late Leiftenant of y² Tower,[1] w²ʰ place he executed for y² space of 14 years. He was victualler of his Maʸ Navye Royall of Engl: and Ireland 21 yeares. He maried two wives; y² first was Ann, daughter and heire of Sir Peter Carew, K⁶, by whome he had issue Peter Apsley, Esq. sonne and heire; Joice, maried to Lister Blount, 2nd sonne of S⁶ Richᵈ Blount, of Maple Durham, K⁶; and Carew, who died at nurse. His second wife was Lucy, daughter of Sir John S⁶ John, of Lidyard, K⁶, by whome he had issue Allan, and John that died younge; William, James, Lucy,[2] Barbara now livinge, Elizabeth, Mary, Ann and Edward, whoe lye buried in the Tower; and havinge lived 61 yeares he departed this mortall life in the Leiftenant's Lodginges in the Tower on Monday the 24ᵗʰ of May, 1630."

Sir Allan Apsley held a small appointment at Queen Elizabeth's court, but having lost his money at play, he joined the expedition of Lord Essex to Cadiz, where he served as a victualler in the navy: he was afterwards employed in Ireland, and knighted by James I. He was appointed victualler to the navy, and Lieutenant of the

---

[1] "March 1616-17. Sir Allen Apsley, the 3 of this month, was sworn Lieutenant of the Tower in the room of Sir George Moore, who was wearye of thatt troublesome and dangerous office."— 'Letters of Lord Carew,' Camden Soc. p. 91.

[2] Wife of Colonel John Hutchinson.

Tower. He died, " after he had three years before languished of a consumption, that succeeded a fever, which he got in the unfortunate voyage to the Isle of Rhee." He was buried in the chancel, where a brass plate formerly marked the spot of his interment.[1]

It was Sir Allan Apsley's descendant, "Henry Bathurst, Baron Apsley, Earl Bathurst, and Lord Chancellor," who built Apsley House in Piccadilly.

GEORGE PAYLER, ESQ., LADY MARIA CAREY HIS WIFE.

On the south wall of the chancel is a singular mural monument, consisting of two life-size marble busts of George Payler, Master Surveyor of the Ordnance, and his wife Lady Maria Carey: between them is an oval frame, within which is the recumbent effigy of a child, in alabaster: around the frame is inscribed—

"Here is buried Robert Payler, sonne of George Payler and the Lady Maria Carey. Dyed the 8 December, aged 41 weeks 2 dayes."

Beneath this is another oval frame, also containing two recumbent figures of children in alabaster which is supported by two standing figures of children. Below, on a black marble tablet, is inscribed—

"Neere unto this place sleepeth the bodies of Samuell and Maria Payler, the second sonne and eldest daughter of George Payler, Esq., Mr. Surveyor of th' Ordinance, and of the Lady Maria Carey, his wife, daughter and heire to Sir Robert and the Lady Margrett Jackson, and late wife to Sir Pelham Carey. Maria departed this life the 25th of July, 1646, and Samuel the 8th day of February, 1649. 'The Lord gave, and the Lord hath taken away: blessed be the name of the Lord.' Job i. 21."

[1] Memoirs of Col. Hutchinson, p. 12. Bayley, p. 124.

TALBOT EDWARDS, 1674.

On the south wall of the nave is the gravestone of Talbot Edwards, who was Keeper of the Regalia when Colonel Blood made his desperate attempt, on 9th May, 1673, to seize the crown, &c.[1] It bears this inscription :—

"Here lieth yᵉ body of Talbot Edwards, gentᵃ late Keeper of his Maᵗⁱᵉ Regalia, who dyed yᵉ 30 of September, 1674, aged 80 yeares and 9 moneths."[2]

This stone was found in 1852 in one of the old houses in front of the Beauchamp Tower, where it had been used as an ordinary paving stone. Lord De Ros caused it to be removed into the chapel and placed on the south wall, where we now see it. Its original position was at the west end of the chapel.

VALENTINE PYNE, 1677.

On the north wall there is a monument with this inscription, done in gold letters on black marble :—

"Erected in memory of Capt. Valentine Pyne, late master gunner of England; second son of George Pyne, of Currimullet, in the county of Somerset, gent., who following the footsteps of his father, in loyalty and obedience to his Sovereign, trailed a pike, under the command of his said father, in the late expedition at Calais, in the year 1625; and in the year 1627, in the expedition of the Isle of Rhee. After that he betook himself to His Majesty's fleet, where he served at sea until the late unhappy rebellion, and during that rebellion, in His Majesty's service, by land: after whose death he voluntarily followed the command of Prince Rupert for the space of fifteen years, both in his expedition at sea, and in the wars of Germany, till his now Majesty's happy restoration; since which time he commanded some of His Majesty's ships in the first war against the Dutch; and in recompence of his faithful service, His Majesty was graciously pleased to elect him Master Gunner of England. In which capacity he departed this life (which he led single) the last day of April, Anno Dom. 1677, in the twenty-eight year of His Majesty's reign.

[1] See Pennant's 'London;' Heath's 'Chronicle,' p. 580; and Bayley, p. 196, &c.
[2] See p. 48.

> "Vndaunted hero, whose aspiring mind,
> As being not willing here to be confin'd,
> Like birds in cage, in narrow trunk of clay,
> Entertain'd Death, and with it soar'd away.
> Now he is gone, why should I not relate,
> To future age, his valour, fame, and fate?
> Iust, loyal, prudent, faithful; such was he,
> Nature's accomplish'd, World's epitome.
> Proud he was not; and tho' by riches try'd,
> Yet virtue was his safe, his surest guide.
> Nor can devouring Time his rapid jaws
> Ere eat away those actions he made laws."

Beneath this black marble tablet is the representation of a ship, and on either side is a cannon carved in white marble.

Sir Jonas More, 1679.

This tablet was formerly affixed to one of the columns at the upper end of the nave, it is now placed against the north wall.

Sir Jonas More was Surveyor-General of the Ordnance in the time of Charles II. "He was a good mathematician, and a good fellowe. He dyed at Godalming, and was buried Sept. 2, 1769, at the Tower chapel, with sixtie pieces of ordinance equal to the number of his years. He was tall and very fat, thin skin, faire cleare grey eie."[1]

The inscription is—

"M. S.

"Jonae Mori Equitis Aurati in agro Lancastriensi apud Vicum Whitelee nati viij Die Februarii anno a partu virginis MDC.XVII. Qui, ob egregiam erga principem suum fidelitatem, summam in rebus mathematicis scientiam, et singularem in negotiis peragendis solertiam et industriam a Rege Carolo Secundo ad officium supervisoris generalis rei tormentariae bellicae evocatus est. Quo munere dum digne fungitur, ingenuas etiam disciplinas, artesque mecanicas, non magis ad animi sui oblectamentum, quam publica patriae commoda, studiosissime excoluit. Et inprimis astronomiae et nauticae artis fautorum beneticentissimum se praebuit; easque promovendi causa speculam Grenovicensem (jubente rege) exstrui coluit, instrumentis idoneis

---

[1] Aubrey's 'Lives.'

locupletavit, editisque mathematicis operibus utilissimis orbi inclarit. Vixit annos lxii. Devixit xxvij Augusti A° Christi MD.C.LXXIX.[1]

"Filium unicum de uxore charissima susceptum post se reliquit, qui eundem quem pater tenuerat et locum ut honoris gradum adeptus, prae propera morte extinctus, hic una sepultus est. Maria filia, e duabus natu major, ejusque maritus Gulielmus Hanway, generos: patri optimo, et fratri monumentum hoc.

"LL.MM.PP."

WILLIAM BRIDGES, 1714.

Against the north wall, and at the north-east angle of the church, is a monument of white marble with his bust, erected for William Bridges, Esq., on which is this inscription:

"To the memory of William Bridges, Esq., late inhabitant of this place, and surveyor general of y⁰ ordnance; in that and other considerable offices through which he pass'd at different times, a diligent and faithfull servant to the Crown and to his country and parliament.

"Assiduous in publick business, and in his private life possessing an happy equality of temper, adorned with exemplary sobriety and virtue.

"He died Oct. 20, 1714, and was buried at the east end of this chappel.

"Elizabeth Bridges his only surviving sister and executrix, as a grateful memorial of the best of friends and brothers, caused this monument to be erected. MDCCXXI."

JOHN GORE, 1794.

Against the west wall of the aisle is an oval tablet of white marble to the memory of

"John Gore, Esq., 16 years Deputy Lieutenant of the Tower, died 5 March, 1794, in the 70th year of his age.[2]

"Bellamira, his wife, died 17 June, 1791, aged 52 years.

"Eliza Maria, their 2nd daughter, died 19 May, 1788, in her 20th year.

"Their remains are deposited near the place, where this monument is erected by their youngest daughter, Bellamira Frances Gore, in dutifull and affectionate remembrance, 1794."

[1] See p. 48.
[2] In the burial register is "John Gore, Esq., Deputy-Governor of the Tower, buried 14th March, 1794."

HENRY FREDERICK GRIFFITHS, 1821.

This tablet is on the south wall.

" Near this place are deposited the remains of Henry Frederick Griffiths, Esq., late Ensign and Lieutenant in the Coldstream Regiment of Guards, who departed this life on the 19th Jan. 1821, whilst on duty in the Tower with the first Battalion, aged 29 years. At the memorable battle of Waterloo he was attached to the second battalion, and was severely wounded. On the 25th January he was buried in the church with military honours."

COLONEL JOHN GURWOOD, 1845.

A marble tablet to the memory of Colonel Gurwood, who is buried in the crypt, is affixed to the south wall of the nave:—

"To the memory of Colonel John Gurwood, C.B : K.T.S : Deputy Lieutenant of the Tower of London, whose remains are deposited in a vault in this chapel.

" Having served with distinction, and been repeatedly wounded in the glorious fields of the Peninsula, France, and Waterloo, he was honoured with the task of compiling the dispatches and other records of his illustrious commander, the Duke of Wellington.

"Kind as he was brave, he died on the 27th of December, 1845, aged 57. Deeply deplored by his family, and deservedly lamented by a wide circle of friends. He led the forlorn hope at C : Rodrigo, and received the sword of the Commander Gen : Barrie from the commander-in-chief on the field of battle."

JOHN HENRY ELRINGTON, 1857.

Three tablets at the west end of the chapel are inscribed—

" John Henry Elrington, died 6 June 1830, aged 16 years."

" James Loftus Elrington, died 13 Oct. 1851."

" In memory of John Henry Elrington (father of the above John Henry Elrington and James Loftus Elrington), 41 years Major of the Tower of London, who died 30 March 1857, in his 86th year."

A stone in the centre of the pavement in the nave, engraved I. H. E. 1821, marks the position of the vault in which the Elrington family are buried.

Sir John Fox Burgoyne, 1871.

Against the east wall of the chancel is a brass tablet, with the following inscription :—

"Near this spot lie the remains of Field-Marshal Sir John Fox Burgoyne, Bart., Knight Grand Cross of the Order of the Bath, Grand Officer of the Legion of Honour, Knight of the first class of the Order of Medjidie, Commander of the Tower and Sword of Portugal, Doctor of Civil Law, Fellow of the Royal Society, Colonel Commandant of Royal Engineers, Constable of the Tower of London, Lieutenant and Custos Rotulorum of the Tower Hamlets. Born 24 July, 1782. Died 7th October, 1871. This tablet was put up by his brother officers.

"'He being dead, yet speaketh.'"

Sir J. Burgoyne's armorial bearings are above, and around the border of the tablet are engraved the insignia of the orders which had been conferred on him.

Lord De Ros, 1874.

On the east wall of the chancel is a brass tablet, bearing this inscription :—

"To the memory of William Lennox Lascelles, XXII Baron de Ros. P. C. Colonel of the 4th Hussars, General in the Army, and Deputy Lieutenant of the Tower of London. Born vii. Sept. 1795. Died vi. Jan. 1874. Buried at Old Court Chapel, Strangford, Ireland.

"'They may rest from their labours, and their works do follow them.'—Rev. ch. xiv. v. 13."

Lord De Ros was Deputy Lieutenant of the Tower from Feb. 1852 until his death in Jan. 1874, when the office was abolished.

CHAPTER V.

THE BURIAL REGISTER.

The Register of the Christenings, Marriages, and Burials, which have taken place in St. Peter's, is contained in a tall narrow book, which measures eighteen inches and three quarters in height, by seven inches wide; it appears to have been rebound about the year 1780.

The entries of christenings commence in 1587, those of marriages in 1586, and those of burials in 1550.

A memorandum, written on the first leaf, states that: "This book was brought into a perfecte forme out of the old square bookes and loose papers, and other bookes from sundrie ministers gotten and procured, and entered in this booke and these callendars, for the rapid finding out the parties enquired for, by Thomas Michell."

This memorandum is not dated, but it was probably written about the year 1587, as at that date a line is drawn across the page of the register, with this remark, "These were taken out of the old book."

Unfortunately, not only previous to 1587, but in some subsequent years, the entries, especially in the list of burials, are but few in number, and until the middle of the seventeenth century the registers appear to have been very irregularly kept.

The register of the burials alone contains any names of historic interest. "Buried in the chappell" is the form of entry, but in some instances only the letter C is placed against the names. Many interments took place in the churchyard outside; for instance, Norris, Brereton, Weston, and Smeaton, were buried there in 1536.

There was also another burial-ground attached to the chapel, which was situated on the counterscarp beyond the moat at the east end of the Tower.

The following are some of the more interesting entries in the Burial Register.

1551.

"Sir Raff. A. Vane,[1] in the chappell."

"Sir Thomas Arundell,[2] in the chappell."

1554.

"Sir Roger Cholmley's Father, in the chappell."

Sir Roger Cholmondeley was Chief Baron of the Exchequer from 1546 till 1552, and Lord Chief Justice of the King's Bench from 1552 till 1553.[3] Having witnessed Edward VI.'s will, in which it was attempted to exclude Mary from the throne, and having shown an inclination to support Queen Jane, he was, upon the accession of Mary, committed to the Tower,[4] where he remained for six weeks, when he was liberated after paying a large fine.[5]

He was then restored to the Queen's favour, and made a Privy Councillor; and was on several occasions appointed to examine certain prisoners in the Tower, with the permission "to put them to such tortures as might be thought most convenient."[6]

He was the illegitimate son of Sir Richard Cholmondeley, whose tomb (with its recumbent effigy in alabaster) formerly stood in the centre of the church.

The above entry cannot, however, refer to Sir Richard, as he died in March 1522, but it may possibly have reference to Sir Roger Cholmondeley's father-in-law. Sir Roger died in 1565, and his wife Christine died in 1558.[7]

[1] See p. 153.
[2] See p. 153.
[3] King Edward enters in his diary, "The Chief Baron of the Exchequer, upon the surrender made by justice Leciter (Lyster), made Chief Justice 14 March, 1552."
[4] On 26th July, 1553 "at 5 of the clocke at nyght."—Machyn's 'Diary,' p. 38.
[5] On the 6th September.—Machyn's 'Diary,' p. 43.
[6] Foss's 'Judges,' vol. ii. pp. 293–6.
[7] "The vii Day of December was bered my Lade Chamley, the wyff of Ser Roger Chamley, Knyght and late Lord Cheyffe barne (baron), in the parryche of Saint Marten's at Ludgate: and ther was iiij branshe tapers, garnyshed with iiij dosen pensels, and the howse (hearse) hangyd with blake and armes, and ther was a harold of armes: and ij whyt branchys, and xxiiij torchys, and mony morners: and the morow masse and a sermon, and after a gret dener (dinner), and she had iiij baners of saintes."—Machyn's 'Diary,' p. 181.

1556.

" MR. LEWKNOR, buried in the chappell."

The following extracts from Machyn's 'Diary' will explain who Mr. Lewknor was:—

" The xv day of June (1556) was raynyd at Geldhall (arraigned at Guildhall) Master Lecknolle, grome porter unto King Edward and Quen Mare, the iii yere of Quen Mare and cast to suffer deth."[1]

" The vii day of September was bered within the Towre of London, the wyche was the evyn of the Natevetie of oure Lade, one master Lecknolle, sume tym grome porter unto Quen Mare, the wyche was kast to suffer deth for the consperacy agaynst the Kynge and the Quen."[2]

BETWEEN 1565 AND 1578.[3]

" MR. ARTHUR POOLE'S BROTHER, buried in the chapel."

" ARTHUR POOLE, buried in the chapel."

Arthur and Edmund Poole or Pole were the sons of Sir Geoffrey Pole, and grandsons of Margaret of Clarence, Countess of Salisbury; Cardinal Pole was therefore their uncle.

In 1562 they entered into a conspiracy, the objects of which were to depose Queen Elizabeth, to set Mary Queen of Scots on the throne, and to re-establish the Roman Catholic forms of worship; it was also alleged that one of them designed to marry the Queen of Scots.

They were tried for high treason at Westminster Hall, on the 26 Feb. 1562-3, and sentenced to be executed as traitors at Tyburn.[4]

Queen Elizabeth spared the lives of the two brothers, and imprisoned them for life in the Tower.

Their names are carved several times on the walls of the Beauchamp Tower; viz.: on the left side of the loophole in the third recess is—

" I : H : S . DIO . SEMIN : IN : LACHRIMIS : IN EXALTATIONE : METE : Æ. 21 . E : POOLE : 1562.' (He who sows in tears shall reap in joy. E. Poole, aged 21, 1562.)

On the right of the third recess is the name " EDMONDE : POOLE : ."
On the left of the loophole near the door of the principal chamber is an almost obliterated inscription, but the words " EDMONDE : POOLE * * SPERO . Æ. 27. E. P: A° 1568:" can be read. On

---

[1] Machyn's 'Diary,' p. 108.
[2] Ibid., p. 114.
[3] The entries under this heading are not specially dated, having been copied from the other record books.
[4] Their trial is in the Baga de Secretis : pouch xl., marked " The trial and conviction of Arthur Poole or Pole, pretending to the title of Duke of Clarence: Edmund Poole, and others." For " Baga de Secretis," see Appendix, p. 326.

the right of the next recess is the following inscription: "DEO : SERVIRE : PENITENTIAM : INIRE : FATO : OBEDIRE : REGNARE : EST. A : POOLE : 1564 . I.H.S:" (To serve God, endure penance, and obey fate, is to reign). Again, near to it is another sentence: "I . H . S . A : PASSAGE : PERILLUS : MAKETHE : A : PORT : PLEASANT : A° 1568. ARTHUR : POOLE : Æ : SUE : 37 : A. P."

Lastly, on the wall of the staircase leading to the chamber above, the name E : POOLE : occurs again.[1]

1587.

"NATHANIELL PARTRIDGE, buried y° xiii[th] of February."

He held the office of gentleman gaoler, and Lady Jane Grey lived in his house.[2]

A document in the Tower records states his emoluments from fees to be estimated at £10 per an. in 1574.

"MR. WILLIAM FOXLEY, buried 4 May. He slept fourteen daies and fifteen nights, and lived after forty-one years. Potmaker in the Mint."

"In the year 1546, the 27th of April, being Tuesday in Easter week, William Foxley, potmaker for the Mint in the Tower of London, fell asleep, and so continued sleeping, and could not be wakened with pricking, cramping, or otherwise burning whatsoever, till the first day of term, which was 14 days and 15 nights. The cause of this sleeping could not be known, though the same were diligently searched after by the King's physicians and other learned men : yea the King himself examined the said William Foxley, who was in all points found at his wakening to be as if he had slept but one night; and he lived more than 40 years after in the said Tower, to wit, until the year of Christ 1587, and then deceased on Wednesday in Easter week."[3]

1591.

"SIR THOMAS WILLIAMS, prisoner, buried y° xx[th] of August."

Sir Thomas Williams had held office in Ireland when Sir John Perrott was Lord Lieutenant, and he was committed to the Tower with Sir J. Perrott on being implicated in his proceedings.

[1] "Geffrye Poole, 1562," is also carved on the wall; this may be the name of their younger brother, or of their father. Both had previously been committed to the Tower.
[2] See p. 167. [3] Stow.

John Stanhope writes to the Earl of Shrewsbury, from Greenwich 10th March, 1590, saying, " Sir John Perrott and Sir Thomas Williams were this day committed to the Tower."[1]

In the state papers also we find two documents referring to him.

1. Dated 4th May, 1590. Notes delivered by Sir John Perrott for examination of Sir Thomas Williams and others, touching their knowledge of the priest Dennis Rougham.

2. A petition dated 15 December, 1590, addressed by Sir Thomas Williams to the Council, in which he vindicates his proceedings in obtaining the place of Muster Master by appointment from Sir John Perrott. Relation of the several conversations he had with Her Majesty on the subject. He also gives details of his long imprisonment in Ireland, when Sir J. Perrott would not interfere for his release, and concludes his letter by complaining of his present very close imprisonment.[2]

In a list of the " names of suche prisoners as have been receved in the Tower by Sir Michael Blount, Knighte, sithence the time that he hathe had the charge thereof," there occurs this entry, " Sir John Perrott, Knighte, and Sir Thomas Williams, Knighte, were committed close prisoners in the Tower by warrant, dated the viii[th] daie of Marche, 1590, signed by the late Lord Chancellor, the Lo: threr, Lo: Admirall, Lo: Chamberlaine, and Lo: Buckhurst. The saide Sir Thomas Williams died in the Tower the xx[th] of August, 1591, and the saide Sir John Perrott remaineth still close prisoner."[3]

" SIR THOMAS FITZHERBERT, buried y[e] xii[th] of October."

Sir Thomas Fitzherbert was a member of the Roman Catholic family of the Fitzherberts of Derbyshire; and already in July 1582 we find that his books were seized and examined; in November 1585 he writes to Walsingham, giving " particulars of his poor estate," and expresses his hope for the Queen's gracious consideration.

In March 1586, the names of Sir T. Fitzherbert and John Gage appear upon a list of recusants in the State Paper Office, under date of October 1586, marked " Interrogatories to be ministered to Sir Tho' Fitzherbert and others his people," on the following subjects. " His connection with the rebellion in the North, harbouring and receiving priests and Jesuits; sheltering Anthony Babington in the late conspiracy: Mass said in his house at Norbury by Father Parsons the Jesuit."[4]

Richard Topcliffe, writing to Lord Shrewsbury on 8 December, 1590, alludes to " the most dangerous and loathesome treasons that had been

---

[1] Lodge, vol. ii. p. 138.
[2] State papers, Dom. Eliz. 1590-1, p. 703.
[3] Bayley, p. lxxxiv.
[4] State papers, Dom. Eliz. 1586, p. 365.

moulded and tempered in the three houses of the family of Fitzherberts." [1]

His name also appears on Sir Michael Blount's list: "Sir Thomas Fitzherbert, Knighte, and John Gage, gen': were committed close prisoners in the Tower by warrant, bearinge date the xth daie of Januarie, 1590-1, signed by the late Lo: Chancellor : Lo: threr: Lo: Admiral : Lo: Chamberlaine, Lo: Cobham : Lo: Buckhurst: Sir Francis Knowles: Sir Thomas Heneage: and Mr. J^{no} Wolley.

The saide Thomas Fitzherbert died in the Tower the seconde daie of October, 1591, and the saide John Gage [2] remaineth still close prisoner.

On 1 December, 1591, a commission is issued to Henry Cavendish and six others, and to the escheater of Derbyshire to enquire after the death of Sir Thomas Fitzherbert. [3]

1592.

"SIR JOHN PRATT, condemned of high treason ; buried vth Oct. in the chappell." [4]

"SIR MICHAEL BLOUNT'S LADY, the Lady Mary; buried the xxvii Dec^r" [5]

1595.

"LORD ARUNDALL, buried ye xxi of Oct: in the chappell." [6]

1600.

"ROBERT DEVEREUX, Earle of Essex, was beheaded in the Tower, and was buried in the chappell the xvth of February." [7]

1613.

"SIR THOMAS OVERBURY, prisoner, poysoned; buried the xv of Sept." [8]

1614.

"LORD GRAY, a prisoner; buried xvith of July." [9]

---

[1] Lodge, vol. ii. p. 430.
[2] See inscription in Broad Arrow Tower, J. GAGE, 1591.
[3] State papers, Dom. Eliz. 1590-1.
[4] Sir John Perrott. See p. 205.
[5] See p. 34.
[6] See p. 216.
[7] See p. 231.
[8] See p. 238.
[9] Lord Grey of Wilton. See p. 249.

1630.

"Sir Allyn Apsley, Knight, Lieutenant of the Tower of London, was buried in the chappell of the Tower aforesaid, upon Monday, being the 24th day of May."[1]

1674.

"Mr. Edwards, ye Crown Keeper, buryed October ye 2nd."

The Keeper of the Regalia.

1679.

"Sir Jonas Moore, Surveyor of ye Ordnance; Sept : 2."[2]

1680.

"William Lord Viscount Stafford, beheaded; buried 29 Dec."[3]

1683.

"Arthur, Earl of Essex, cutt his own throat within the Tower; July 13th."[4]

1685.

"James, Duke of Monmouth, beheaded on Tower Hill, ye 15th, and buryed ye 16th July."[5]

1689.

"George, Lord Jefferies,[6] buried 20 April." (*Added in another handwriting*) "and removed 2 Nov : 93."

1703.

"John Rotier, 17 June, in the chappell."[7]

[1] See p. 36. [2] See p. 38. [3] See p. 263.
[4] See p. 268. [5] See p. 278. [6] See p. 284.
[7] See p. 290.

1710.

"EDWIN[1] GRIFFIN, LORD GRIFFIN, prisoner, buried on 15th Nov."[2]

1719.

"TALBOT EDWARDS, Keeper of ye Jewell Office, April 30th."

1746.

"WILLIAM MURRAY, ESQ., alias MARQUIS OF TULLIBARDINE, prisoner in ye Tower; on 11th July."[3]

"WILLIAM, EARL OF KILMARNOCK, and ARTHUR, LORD BALMERINO, beheaded on Tower Hill; on 18th August."[4]

1747.

"SIMON, LORD LOVAT, beheaded on Tower Hill; on 17th April."[5]

1758.

"JOHN TUDOR, an ancient Briton, who had been a warder in the Tower upwards of sixty years, aged 107 years; was buried September 21st."

---

[1] The name should be Edward.
[2] See p. 296.
[3] See p. 300.
[4] See p. 312.
[5] See p. 323.

CHAPTER VI.

THE BURIALS IN THE CHAPEL.

On a memorial tablet near the entrance door will be found the following

LIST OF REMARKABLE PERSONS BURIED IN THIS CHAPEL.

1. Gerald Fitzgerald, Earl of Kildare	1534
2. John Fisher, Bishop of Rochester	1535
3. Sir Thomas More	1535
4. George Boleyn, Viscount Rochford	1536
5. Queen Anne Boleyn	1536
6. Thomas Cromwell, Earl of Essex	1540
7. Margaret of Clarence, Countess of Salisbury	1541
8. Queen Katharine Howard	1542
9. Jane, Viscountess Rochford	1542
10. Thomas, Lord Seymour of Sudeley	1549
11. Edward Seymour, Duke of Somerset	1551
12. Sir Ralph Vane	1552
13. Sir Thomas Arundell	1552
14. John Dudley, Duke of Northumberland	1553
15. Lord Guildford Dudley	1554
16. Lady Jane Grey	1554
17. Henry Grey, Duke of Suffolk	1554
18. Thomas Howard, Duke of Norfolk	1572
19. Sir John Perrott	1592
20. Philip, Earl of Arundel	1595 [1]
21. Robert Devereux, Earl of Essex	1601
22. Sir Thomas Overbury	1613
23. Thomas, Lord Grey of Wilton	1614
24. Sir John Eliot	1632
25. William, Viscount Stafford	1680
26. Arthur, Earl of Essex	1683
27. James, Duke of Monmouth	1685

[1] Removed to Arundel in 1624.

28. George, Lord Jeffreys [1]	1689
29. John Rotier	1703
30. Edward, Lord Griffin	1710
31. William, Marquis of Tullibardine	1746
32. William, Earl of Kilmarnock	1746
33. Arthur, Lord Balmerino	1746
34. Simon, Lord Fraser of Lovat	1747

This list includes only those persons who were buried in the chapel. The names of other prisoners of distinction may occur to the reader, and it may therefore be as well to mention that—

Henry Earl of Surrey, beheaded 19th Jan. 1546-7, was buried in the churchyard of All Hallows, Barking, but removed to Framlingham in 1614.

Lady Arabella Stuart, who died in the Tower, was buried on 27th Sept. 1615, in the Stuart vault in Westminster Abbey.

Sir Walter Raleigh, beheaded in New Palace Yard on 29th Oct. 1618, was buried in the chancel of St. Margaret's, Westminster.

Wentworth, Earl of Strafford, beheaded on Tower Hill, 12th May, 1641, was buried at Wentworth Woodhouse, in Yorkshire.

Archbishop Laud, beheaded 10th Jan. 1644-5, was buried in the churchyard of All Hallows, Barking, but afterwards removed to St. John's College, Oxford.

The diagram on the following page is given as a suggestive plan, to show how the interments in the chancel may have been arranged up to the date of the Duke of Monmouth's burial, in 1685, and it has been based on the following authorities:—

"Here lieth, before the high altar in St. Peter's church, two Dukes between two Queens, to wit, the Duke of Somerset (3) and the Duke of Northumberland (4), between Queen Anne (2) and Queen Katharine (5), all four beheaded." (Stow.)

"Between the two Queens, before the high altar, lie

[1] Removed in 1692 to St. Mary's Aldermanbury.

52 ST. PETER AD VINCULA. CHAP. VI.

SUGGESTED PLAN OF INTERMENTS IN THE CHANCEL.

SOUTH.

		7 COUNTESS OF SALISBURY. 1541.		14 SIR T. OVERBURY. 1613.
		6 LADY ROCHFORD. 1542.		13. EARL OF ESSEX. 1601.
		5 QUEEN KATHARINE HOWARD. 1542.		12 EARL OF ARUNDEL. 1595.
ALTAR. 15 DUKE OF MONMOUTH. 1685.		4 DUKE OF NORTH- -UMBER- -LAND. 1553.		11 DUKE OF NORFOLK. 1572.
	3 DUKE OF SOMERSET. 1551.		10 *Duke of Suffolk.* 1554.	
	2 QUEEN ANNE BOLEYN. 1536.		9 *Lady Jane Grey.* 1554.	
	1 LORD ROCHFORD. 1536.		8 *Lord Guildford Dudley.* 1554.	

EAST.

SIR R. BLOUNT. MARY BLOUNT, 1592. SIR R. BLOUNT, 1664. LYSTER BLOUNT, 1633.

NORTH.

HAGIOSCOPE.

CHAP. VI.   THE BURIALS IN THE CHAPEL.   53

buried two Dukes, the Duke of Somerset, Edward Seymour, and the Duke of Northumberland, John Dudley." (Weever.)

"The Duke of Somerset was buried on the north side of the choir of St. Peter's." (Machyn's Diary.)

Lord Rochford (1) was beheaded on the 17th of May, two days before his sister, and it is very probable that on the 19th of May the spot for her interment was selected by his side.

Lady Rochford (6) was beheaded at the same time as Queen Katharine Howard, and they were probably buried in the same grave; Bayley says, "Lady Rochford accompanied her mistress in execution and in sepulture."

Bayley also states that the Countess of Salisbury (7) "lies with the attainted group" in the chancel.

Lord Guildford Dudley (8), his wife Lady Jane Grey (9), and her father, the Duke of Suffolk (10), were all executed in February 1554. There is no record of their burial in any particular part of the chapel, but as they were persons of high birth and distinction, the chancel would naturally have been chosen, and commencing on the "dexter," or north side, they would have been interred as marked on this plan.

There is particular mention that the Earl of Arundel (12) was buried in the chancel, in the same grave with his father.[1] It is also recorded that in 1601 the Earl of Essex (13) was laid by them in the chancel.[2]

Sir Gervas Elwys, the Lieutenant of the Tower, writes that he buried Sir Thomas Overbury (14) "in the quire of the chapel."[3]

Lastly, "under the communion table was interred James Duke of Monmouth, the handsome, profligate, and ungrateful son of King Charles 2nd."[4]

In any building, even in Westminster Abbey, it would be difficult to point to a spot where can be seen so closely grouped together more remarkable names than those which are inscribed on the memorial tablets in this chancel pavement. Names which must awaken many singular personal

[1] See p. 216.   [2] See p. 231.   [3] See p. 239.   [4] See p. 278.

as well as historical associations, and which cannot fail to bring to mind, not only stirring episodes in the lives of those who are there recorded, but also to recall many critical scenes and events in the history of our country in which they have been the chief actors.

In the centre, the two great Dukes, who had been engaged in life-long rivalry and strife for political and personal power in the realm, lie here side by side, having ended their days in the same prison, and on the same scaffold. Next to Somerset, the unfortunate Queen, who was supplanted by his sister in the affections of her husband and sovereign.

Katharine Howard, another consort of that same sovereign, and first cousin to the former Queen, was laid in the earth next to Northumberland, and by her side also, Lady Rochford, her accomplice in guilt, who had already assisted a husband and a sister-in-law to the scaffold.

The first group is completed by the venerable Margaret of Clarence, Countess of Salisbury, the last of a race, which had given more than one famous king to England, and who, at the age of seventy years, fell a victim for dynastic as well as political reasons, to the stern policy of the second Tudor sovereign.

Turning to the lower group,[1] we find in the centre the name of that Duke of Norfolk, who ambitiously aspired, from motives of religious and state policy, to the hand of Mary Stuart. By his side lay his son, a victim doomed on account of his political influence and stubborn theological opinions, to a lingering and life-long imprisonment. Next to him, that Earl of Essex, who so ill requited the especial favour which his sovereign had incessantly bestowed upon him.

On the other side, the names of Suffolk, his daughter and her husband, recall the abortive ending of all those ambitious schemes of Dudley, Duke of Northumberland, whose grave is but a few feet distant.

The names of Overbury, whose death exemplified the

---

[1] The original interments on this spot have been too much disturbed to admit of any satisfactory identification of the remains.

THE BURIALS IN THE CHAPEL.

profligacy of the court of the first Stuart Sovereign, and of Monmouth, who, basing his claims on his Stuart blood, had more than once intrigued to obtain the succession to the throne of England, complete the group.

When the list of names for the memorial tablet at the west end of the church had been drawn up, it appeared that it would be desirable to collect the references to those historical authorities, that had warranted the formation of this list, especially when, upon examination of the register, the notices of burial were found to be so deficient during the earlier years. It was, however, ultimately considered that a short biographical account of each of these persons, strung together in a consecutive narrative, and comprising all the available details of their imprisonment, and subsequent death, would more fully meet the requirements of the case, and at any rate prove more interesting than disjointed references, or a bare quotation of facts and dates.

The plan which has been adopted is, to give accounts of the arrest and committal to the Tower of those persons who are named on this list, any incidents of their imprisonment, and a short notice of their trial; and lastly, an account of their death and burial; this information being gathered, as far as possible, from the works and in the words of contemporary writers, or other authors of trustworthy authority.

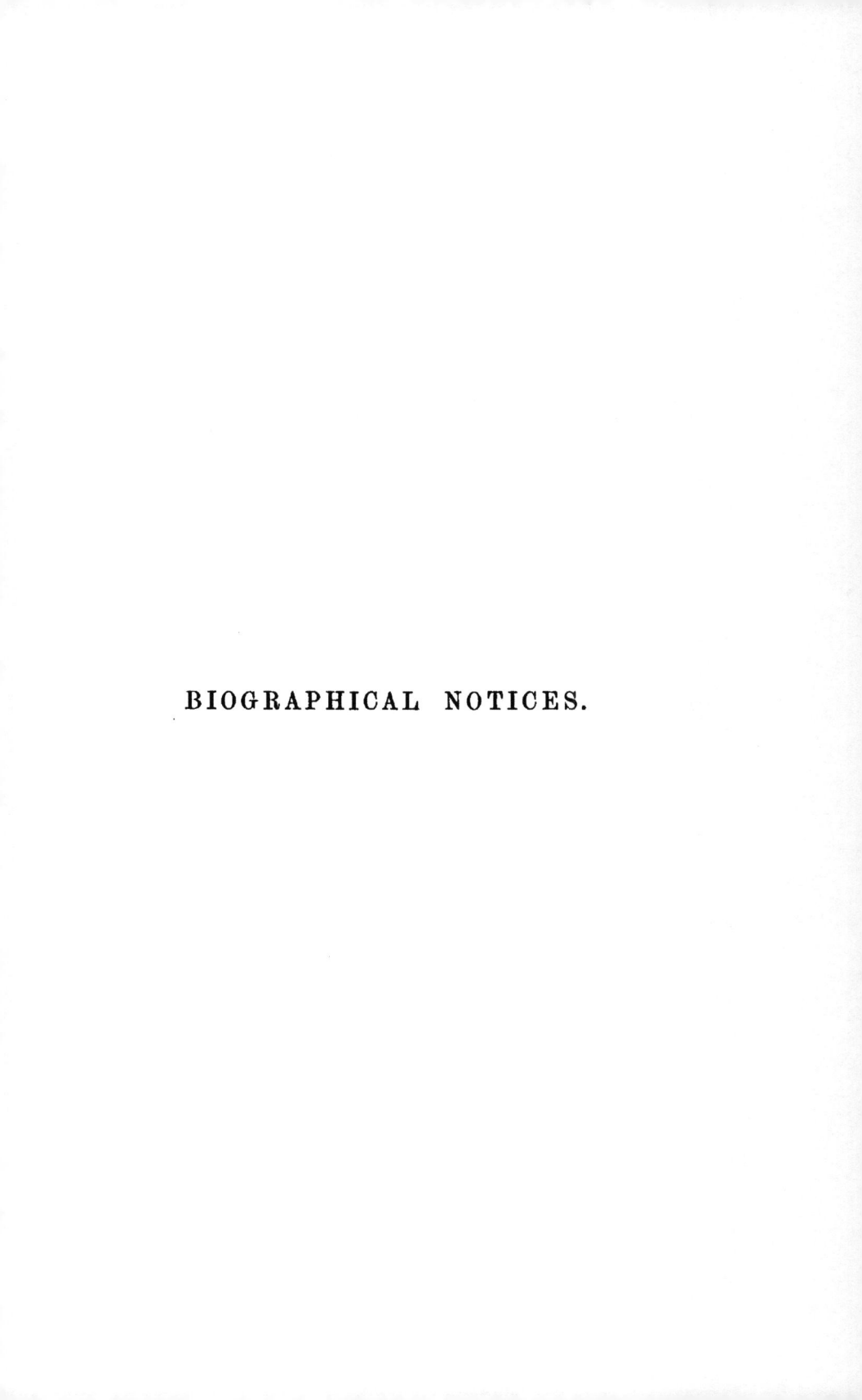

BIOGRAPHICAL NOTICES.

BIOGRAPHICAL NOTICES.

GERALD FITZGERALD, EARL OF KILDARE.
Died in the Tower, 12th December, 1534.

GERALD FITZGERALD, ninth Earl of Kildare, was Lord Deputy of Ireland for a considerable period, during the reign of Henry VIII. Already on two occasions he had been summoned to England at Wolsey's instigation, and committed to the Tower upon charges of maladministration, when in 1534 he was for a third time ordered to appear before the King, and answer for his alleged offences. On his arrival he was sent as a prisoner to the Tower, and whilst there, awaiting the inquiry into his conduct as Lord Deputy, he received the intelligence of the insurrection which had been organised in Ireland by his five brothers[1] and his son "silken Thomas."[2] It is said that this news so overwhelmed him with grief that he died of a broken heart.[3]

His son with his accomplices were afterwards taken prisoners, brought to London, committed to the Tower, and shortly afterwards executed as traitors at Tyburn.

The Earl of Kildare died on the 12th December, 1534, and was buried in St. Peter's.

"In the year 1580, when a grave was being dug to bury

---

[1] For a graphic account of this insurrection, see Froude, 'Hist. of England,' vol. ii. p. 275 et seq.

[3] "In this tyme dyed the Erle of Kyldare, a prisoner in the Tower."— Grafton. See also Wrottesley's Chron. (Camden Soc.), p. 25.

[2] In the Beauchamp Tower, near the entrance to the cells, his name is thus roughly cut:

AS : YT : IS : TAKY
THOMAS : FITZGera—

Ralph Hopton,[1] son of Sir Owen Hopton, Lieutenant of the Tower, a chest was found in the earth with this inscription: "Here lieth the corpes of the L: Gerald Fitzgerald, Earle of Kyldare, who deceased the 12th of December in the year of our Lord MCCCCCXXXIIII. On whose sole Jesu have mercey."[2]

He was said to have been one of the fairest men living when he succeeded to the title in 1513. Holinshed describes him as "a wise, deep, and far-reaching man; in war' valiant and without rashness; and politic without treachery: such a suppressor of rebels in his government, as they durst not bear armour to the annoyance of any subject. His great hospitality is to this day rather of each man commended than of any followed. He was so religiously addicted unto the serving of God, as what time soever he travelled to any part of the country, such as were of his chapel should be sure to follow him. He was also so well affected to his wife as he would not at any time buy a suit of apparel for himself, but he would suit her with the same stuff: which gentleness she recompensed with equal kindness; for after that he deceased in the Tower, she did not only ever after live a chaste and honourable widow, but also nightly, before she went to bed, she would resort to his picture, and there, with a solemn congé, she would bid her lord good night."[3]

Lady Elizabeth Fitzgerald, Surrey's "fair Geraldine," was the daughter of this Earl of Kildare.[4]

John Fisher, Bishop of Rochester.

Born 1456. Beheaded on Tower Hill, 23rd June, 1535.

Bishop Fisher had been called upon to attend during the session of Parliament in 1533-4, as Thomas Cromwell, the Secretary of State, was desirous that he should take the

[1] There are no entries in the burial register for this year.
[2] Collins's Peerage, vol. vi. p. 165.
[3] Holinshed.
[4] Walpole's 'Noble Authors,' Collins's Peerage.

new oath of the succession to the Crown:[1] but the bishop had excused himself more than once on account of ill-health, and had replied to the pressure which Cromwell evidently put upon him, by the following letter :—

"Master Cromwel, after my right humble comendation, I beseiche you to have some pytye of me, considryng the case and condition that I ame in: and I dowt not but yf ye myght see in what plyte that I ame ye woulde have some pytye uppon me, for in good faythe now almoste this six weekys I have hadde a grevous cowighe (cough), with a fever in the bigynnynge thereof, as dyvers others heare in this countre hathe hadde, and dyvers have dyed thereof. And now the mattyer is fallen downe in to my leggis and feit, with suche swellinge and aiche that I maye nother ryde nor goo, for the which I beseiche you eftsonys[2] to have some pytye uppon me, and to spare me for a season, to the ende the swellinge and aiche of my leggis and feit maye swaige (assuage) and abait (abate), and then by the grace of our Lorde I shall with all speide obeye your commaundement. Thus far ye weall, at Rochestre the xxviij daye of January.

"By your fathefull Beadman, "Jo: Roffs."[3]

At last he was peremptorily summoned to appear on the 13th April, 1534, before the Commissioners who had been appointed, in accordance with the terms of the Act of Parliament (25 Hen. VIII. cap. 22), to administer the oath of succession to all the clergy.[4]

Before setting out he made his will, and took leave of all his friends, and "passing through the city of Rochester, there were a great multitude of people gathered together to take their leave of him, both citizens and countrymen, to whom he gave his blessing, riding by them all the while bareheaded. When he came to the top of Shooter's Hill, there he alighted to rest himself, and ordered such victuals to be brought before him as he had caused to be provided

---

[1] For the act and the oath, see Burnet, 'History of the Reformation,' bk. ii. vol. i. p. 296, and Strype's 'Eccles. Hist.' vol. i. p. 268: "The object being that the issue of Queen Katharine should be cut off from succeeding to the Crown, and that of Queen Anne Boleyn should have the right of succession vested in them."

[2] "Eftsonys," eftsoons, in a short time; shortly.

[3] MSS. Cotton. Vespasian, F. xiij fol. 154 b.

[4] The Commissioners were the Lord Chancellor (Sir Thomas Audley), the archbishop (Cranmer), and the Dukes of Norfolk and Suffolk, Mr. Secretary Cromwell, and the Abbot of Westminster.

for that purpose, saying, he would now make use of his time and dine in the open aire while he might; after he had dined he cheerfully took his horse againe, and came to Lambeth that night."[1]

On the following day at Lambeth he met his old friend Sir Thomas More, who had also been sent thither on the same account. "Sir Thomas glad to see the Bishop thus saluted him: 'Well met, my Lord, I hope we shall meet in heaven.' To which the Bishop replied: 'This should be the way, Sir Thomas, for it is a very straight one.'"[2]

The interrogatories of the Commissioners failed to obtain any admission from Bishop Fisher: he declined to take the oath, upon which, "he having desired some time to consider of it, the Commissioners allowed him five days to go to his house till then."[3] During this time, several of his friends visited him, in order to take leave of him, for they felt sure he would be committed to prison. "Among these were Mr. Seton and Mr. Bransby, who came in the name of the Masters and Fellows of the two colleges of Christ's and St. John's (Cambridge), to which the Bishop had shown himself so much a friend." They asked him to confirm and seal the statutes which had been drawn out; but he desired first to look through them. "Alas," said they, "we fear your Lordship's time is now too short to read them before you go to prison." The Bishop said, "It was no matter, he would then read them in prison:" and on their answering, that he would hardly be allowed to do it there, his Lordship replied: 'Then God's will be done, for I shall hardly be drawn to put my seal to that which I have not well considered.'"[4] He afterwards signed them when in the Tower.[5]

On the 17th April he was again summoned before the

---

[1] Lewis, 'Life of Fisher,' vol. ii. p 134.
[2] Lewis, vol. ii. p. 135.
[3] Lewis, vol. ii. p. 137.
[4] Lewis, vol. ii. p. 138.
[5] In the archives of St. John's College, Cambridge, is preserved an indenture, dated 22nd Feb. 1525, between John Fisher, Bishop of Rochester, of the first part, Christ's College, Cambridge, of the second part, and St. John's College, Cambridge, of the third part, as to the institution of an obit for him on the 3rd February in each year.

JOHN FISHER, BISHOP OF ROCHESTER. 63

Commissioners, to whom he decisively replied, "If you will needs have me answer directly, my answer is, that, forasmuch as my own conscience cannot be satisfied, I absolutely refuse the oath."

Archbishop Cranmer then wrote to Cromwell on the same day on behalf of both Fisher and Sir Thomas More. His

View of the Bell Tower.

letter is dated "From my manor at Croydon, the 17th day of April," he having returned there after the examinations at Lambeth.[1]

However, on Tuesday the 21st April, Fisher was committed to the Tower, and lodged in the Bell Tower.[2]

---

[1] Original letter is in Cotton. MSS. Cleopatra, E. vi. p. 181. See also Weever, p. 279, and Lewis, vol. ii. p. 181.

[2] This tower is situated at the south-west angle of the inner ward, and is still surmounted by the wooden bell turret, in which formerly hung the bell for regulating all the movements of the officials and the prisoners. The walls are from 9 to 13

Rowland Lee, Bishop of Lichfield and Coventry,[1] was the next day sent to him, to endeavour to persuade him to take the oath, but without success.

Bishop Lee thus writes to Cromwell:—

"Pleaseth you to be advertised that I have been with my Lord of Rochester, who is as you left him, that is to say, ready to make his oath for the succession, and to swear never to meddle more in disputation of the validity of the matrimony or invalidity with the lady Dowager (Queen Katharine) but that utterly to refuse. But as for the case of the prohibition Levitical, his conscience is so knit, that he cannot send it off from him whatsoever betide him. And yet he will & doth formally profess his allegiance to our sovereign lord the King, during his life. Truly the man is nigh going, and doubtless cannot continue, unless the King and his council be merciful to him; for the body cannot bear the clothes on his back, as knoweth God, Who preserve you. In haste, scribbled by your own most bounden,

"Roland, Cov: et Litch: electus et confirmatus."[2]

Parliament met in November, when an Act (26 Hen. VIII. c. 22) was passed attainting Fisher of treason, and his bishopric was declared to be vacant from 2nd January; his household goods were seized, and also his library, which he had intended to give to the College of St. John's at Cambridge.

It was on the 22nd December, 1534, that he addressed the

---

feet thick. It formed part of the "Lieutenant's Lodgings," and is now attached to the house of the resident governor. Queen Anne Boleyn, and in all probability, Queen Elizabeth when princess, were lodged in this tower: the apartment above is spacious and airy; it was perhaps the best prison in the Tower, and was used for prisoners of distinction, and as the only mode of ingress or egress was through the lieutenant's house, he was enabled to guard them very vigilantly. In a room, adjoining to this tower, and forming part of the "lodging," was imprisoned Margaret, Countess of Lennox, and the following inscription is over the chimney-piece: "Upon the twenty daie of June in the yere our Lord a thousande five hundred three score and five, was the right honorable Countes of Lennox grace commettede prisoner to thys lodgynge for the marreage of her sonne my Lord Henry Darnle and the Queene of Scotland. Here is their names that do wayte upon her noble grace in thys place: M. Eliz[th] Hussey, M. Jane Baily, M. Eliz[th] Chamberlain, M. Robert Partington, Edward Cuffin. Anno Domini, 1566."

See transactions of London and Middlesex Archæological Society for an account of the Bell Tower.

[1] Rowland Lee, Bishop of Lichfield, from 1534 till 1543.

[2] Cotton. MSS. Cleopatra, E. vi. p. 165; Strype, Cranmer, vol. i. p. 338, Appendix, No. x.

following letter to Cromwell, describing his miserable condition in prison:—[1]

"After my most humbyl commendations, whereas ye be content that I shold wryte unto the King's Hyghnesse, in gude faithe I dread mee that I kan not be soo circumspect in my wryteing but that sume worde shal escape me wherwith his grace shal be moved to sum further displeasure againste me, wherof I wold be veray sorry. For ass I wyll answer byfore God, I wold not in any manner of poynte offend his grace, my dutey saved unto God, whom I muste in every thyng prefer. And for this consideration I am full loth and full of fear to wryte unto his hyghnesse in this matter. Nevertheless, sythen I conceyve that itt is your mynde that I shal soo doo I wyll endevor me to the best that I kan. But first here I must beseeche you, gode Master Secretary, to call to your rememberance that att my last beyng befor yow, and the other Commyssionars, for taking of the othe concernyng the King's most noble succession, I was content to be sworne unto that parcell concerning the succession. And there I did rehcars this reason, which I sade moved mee, I dowted nott but the prynce of eny realme with the assent of his nobles and commons myght appoynte for his succession royal such an order ass was seen unto his wysdom most accordyng; and for this reason I sade, that I was content to be sworne unto that part of the othe ass concernyng the succession. This is veray trowth as God help my sowl att my most neede. All be itt I refused to swear to sum other parcels[2] by cause that my conscience wold not serve me so to doe.

"Furthermoor I byseche yow to be gode, master, unto me in my necessite; for I have neither shirt nor sute, nor yett other clothes, that ar necessary for me to wear, but that bee ragged and rent to shamefully. Notwithstanding I might easily suffer that, if thei wold keep my body warm. Butt my dyett allso, God knoweth how slendar it is at meny tymes, and noo in myn age my sthomak may nott awaye but with a few kynd of meats, which if I want, I decaye forthwith, & fall in to coafes & diseases of my bodye, & kan not keep myself in health. And ass our Lord knoweth, I have nothyng laft un to me for to provide any better, but ass my brother of his own purs layeth out for me to his great hynderance. Wherefoor gode master secretarye eftsones I byseche you to have sum pittee uppon me, and latt me have such thyngs ass ar necessary for me in myn age, & specially for my health. And allso that it may pleas yow by yo hygh wysdom, to move the Kyng's Highness to take me unto his gracious favor agane & to

---

[1] Bishop Fisher was also confined in the White Tower: in one of the dungeons below is an inscription, almost obliterated, in which his name can be read: it was probably cut by one of his servants.

[2] The validity of the marriage of Queen Katharine, &c., in the preamble of the Act.

F

restore me unto my liberty, owt of this cold and paynefull emprysonment; whearby ye shall bynd me to be your pore beadsman for ever unto Allmighty God, who ever have you in his proteccion & custoody. Other twayne thyngs I mustt allso desyer uppon yow: thatt oon is, that itt may pleas yow that I may take some preest with in the Towr, by the assyngment of master levetenant, to hear my confession againste this hooly tyme: the other is, that I may borow sum bowks to styr my devotion mor' effectuelly thes hooly dayes for the comfort of my sowl. This I byseche yow to grant me of your charitie. And thus our Lord send you a mery Christenmass and a comforthable to your harts desyer. At the Towr, the xxii day of December.[1]   "Yo pore Beadsman,
                      "Jo. Roffs."[2]

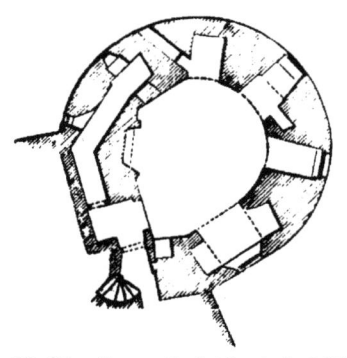

Plan of the Prison Room on the first floor in the Bell Tower.

This severe treatment of Fisher, writes Burnet, "was understood at Rome, and Pope Clement by an officious kindness to him, or rather to spite King Henry, declared him a

[1] Cotton. MSS. Cleopatra, E. vi. f. 172; Lewis, vol. ii. pp. 330-3; Fuller's 'Church History,' bk. v. p. 203; Bayley, pp. 135-6; Strype's 'Cranmer,' vol. i. p. 337, App. No. ix.

[2] In the Cottonian MSS. is preserved this memorandum:

"The Charges of certayne persons in the towre; in it appeare the following items:

"The Bysshope of Rochester for xiiijth monthys after xx s. le weke. } Lvj.li.

"Sir Thomas More for iijth monthis unpayd after x s. le weke, and his servainct v. s. le weke. } ix.li.

Cotton. Titus, B. i. fol. 155.

Twenty shillings a week ought to have supplied the Bishop with more necessaries than he appears to have enjoyed, but doubtless Mr. Lieutenant had his profit upon the sum charged. After all, Fisher was better treated than More, who was allowed five shillings less, & had a servant to share the pittance with him.

cardinal, and sent him a red hat. When the King heard of this, he sent to examine him about it; but he protested he had used no endeavour to procure it, and valued it so little that, if the hat were lying at his feet, he would not take it up. It never came nearer him than Picardy, yet did this precipitate his ruin." [1]

Fisher had managed to carry on a secret correspondence with his friend Sir Thomas More, who was also a prisoner in the Tower, through George Gold, the lieutenant's man, and Wilson, his own servant; but one of his letters was intercepted,[2] and an enquiry was then ordered to be held upon this matter, and on the 2nd June, the King desired a commission to be issued and an indictment for high treason to be drawn up, and, on the 12th June, the Commissioners visited him in the Tower, when "thirty-one interrogatories were ministered unto John Fissher, Doctour of Divinitie, late Busshop of Rochester, on the 12 daye of June, in the 27 yere of the reign of King Henrie the eight, within the Towre of London, in the presence of Sir Edmund Walsingham, Knight, Lieutenant of the Tower, by the right worshipfull Mr. Thomas Bedyll, Mr. Doctour Aldridge, Mr. Richard Layton, and Mr. Richard Curwen, being of the King's Counsaill, in the presence of Harrie Felstede and John Wolley, witnesses, and me John ap Rice, notary publick; with the aunsweres of the said Mr. Doctour Fissher to the same." [3] The result was that Fisher's liberty was further restricted, and he was henceforth debarred the use of pen, ink, and paper.[4]

On the 1st May, 1535, some of the Council [5] were sent to reason with him, but he declared that he must act as his own conscience dictated to him, and, he added, "I think I am able to give your Lordships reasons that perhaps may seem

---

[1] Burnet, bk. iii. vol. i. p. 707.
[2] George Gold then came and told him "that Mr. More was in a peck of troubles."—Lewis's 'Life,' vol. ii. p. 163.
[3] Cotton. MSS. Cleopatra, ed. vi. p. 169; and 'Archæologia,' vol. xxv. p. 95.
[4] Lewis, vol. ii. p. 160. He had already written "A godly treatise declaring the benefits, fruits, and commodities of prayer: a spiritual consolation to his sister Elizabeth, at such time as he was prisoner in the Tower of London." Published London, 1577. 16mo.
[5] The Lord Chancellor (Audley), the Duke of Suffolk, the Earl of Wiltshire, and Mr. Secretary Cromwell.

sufficient why my conscience stands affected as it doth, and could be well content that you heard them, could I declare my mind with safety and without offence to His Majesty and his laws. After which not a word more was said for that time, but the Lords calling for the Lieutenant re-delivered the Bishop into his custody, giving him a strict charge that no further conference or message should pass betwixt the Bishop and Sir Thomas More, or any one else."[1]

When the result of this visit was reported to the King he "swore that they were all fools, and asked them if there were not more ways to the wood than one? they should make him take the oath, or he would see better reasons why they could not than any they had yet given him; wishing them to see his face no more until it were done."[2]

Richard Rich,[3] the King's Solicitor-General, was next sent to him, but still Fisher stood firm.

Some time previous to this examination he had been taken ill, "and the King sent his own physician to recover him, but being now in a better state of health he was, on Thursday the 17th of June, brought from the Tower to the Court of King's Bench at Westminster, and, because he was not able to walk all the way on foot, he rode part of it on horseback, in a black cloth gown, and the rest of the way he was carried by water. But the tide not serving to go through bridge, he was carried to the Old Swan, the very next stairs on the other side of it, to take water there. As soon as he was come into Westminster Hall he was there presented at the barre in the Court of King's Bench before the Commissioners, who were all there sat ready in their places against his coming. Being thus brought before them, he was commanded by the name and title of John Fisher, late of Rochester, clerk, otherwise called John Fisher, late Bishop of Rochester, to hold up his hand, which he did with a most chearful countenance and uncommon firmness and constancy. Then was read to him his indictment. When it was all read

---

[1] Lewis, vol. ii. pp. 166-7.
[2] Lewis, vol. ii. p. 168.
[3] Richard Rich, then Solicitor-General, appointed Lord Chancellor by Edward VI. in 1547. Died in 1568, and was buried at Felsted.

he was asked whether he was guilty of this treason or no? whereunto he pleaded, Not guilty. Then was a jury of twelve men, being freeholders of Middlesex, called and sworn to try this issue."[1]

The jury being thus sworn the trial proceeded, Rich, the Solicitor-General, being the only witness produced.[2] The verdict of "Guilty of High Treason" was found by them, and the Lord Chancellor then asked the Bishop what he had to say in arrest of judgment. Fisher replied, "Truly, my Lord, if that which I have already said be not sufficient I have no more to say; but only to desire Almighty God to forgive them who have thus condemned me, for I think they know not what they have done." The Chancellor then pronounced the sentence on those convicted of treason in the usual terms.[3]

The Lieutenant of the Tower, standing ready with his men to receive and carry back his prisoner, Fisher was, after a short speech to the judges, conveyed back to the Tower in the same manner as he was brought from thence to his trial, partly by water and partly on horseback. When he was come to the Tower gate, he turned back to the guard of halberdeers which had conducted him thus forward and backward, and spake to them as follows: "My masters, I thank you all for the great labour and pains which ye have taken with me to-day; I am not able to give you anything in recompense, because I have nothing left, and therefore I pray you accept in good part my hearty thanks."[4] And this he spoke with so good a courage, so amiable a countenance, and with so fresh and lively a colour in his face, as he seemed rather to have come from some great feast or banquet than

---

[1] Lewis, vol. ii. pp. 180-1, where the names of the jurymen are given.

[2] Fisher objected that two witnesses were necessary in a case of treason: the chancellor answered this objection, saying that this was a case in which the King was personally concerned, so the rules for two witnesses did not apply.

[3] The trial is preserved in the Baga de Secretis, Pouch vii. See Appendix, p. 327. "On 23rd Aug. 1535, Cromwell writes to Sir John Wallop, the King's ambassador at the court of France, directing him in what manner to justify the King's actions in the matter of the divorce, and the execution of Sir Thomas More and the Bishop of Rochester."—MSS. belonging to Marquis of Bath, and Harleian MSS. 288, pp. 39-46.

[4] Lewis, vol. ii. pp. 188-9.

from his trial and condemnation, showing by all his carriage and outward behaviour nothing else but joy and satisfaction.[1]

He had not been in the Tower above three days when the writ for his execution was sent to the Lieutenant, and on 21st June "those whose service and attendance was to be used were ordered all to be in readiness against the next morning; and because when the writ was brought it was very late at night, when the Bishop was supposed to be asleep, the Lieutenant was loath to disturb him and hinder his rest for that time; and therefore in the morning (22nd June) early, before five of the clock, he went to the chamber in the Bell Tower, where, finding him fast asleep in his bed, he waked him, telling him that he was come to him on a message from the King. After some preamble, used to prevent the Bishop's being surprised by the fatal message, and putting him in mind that he was now an old man, and could not by reason of his great age live long according to the course of nature, he at last told him that he was come to signifie unto him that it was the King's pleasure he should suffer death that forenoon. 'Well,' said the Bishop, 'if this be your errand you bring me no great news, for I have sometime looked for this message. I most humbly thank His Majesty that it pleaseth him to rid me from all this worldly businesse, and I thank you also for your tidings. But pray, Mr. Lieutenant,' added he, 'when is mine houre that I must go hence?' 'Your hour,' said the Lieutenant, 'must be nine of the clock.' 'And what hour is it now?' said he. 'It is now about five,' said the Lieutenant.

---

[1] "The bishop being thus returned to the place of his confinement did not continue there above three or four days. But before the time came that was appointed for his execution, a false report was, it seems, raised of his being to be executed such a day; upon which his cook, who used to dress his victuals, and carry them daily to him, dressed no dinner at all that day. When therefore the cook came next unto him, the bishop asked him why he brought him not his dinner as he used to do. 'Sir,' said the cook, 'it was commonly reported that you was to die that day, and therfore I thought it to no purpose to dresse anything for you.' 'Well,' said the bishop, merrily, to him again, 'for all that rumour thou seest me yet alive, and therfore, whatsoever newes thou shalt heare on me hereafter, let me no more go without my dinner, but get it ready for me as thou usedst to do: and if thou seest me dead when thou comest, then eat it thyself; but I promise thee if I am alive, by God's grace, to eat never a bit the lesse.'"—Lewis, vol. ii. p. 192.

'Well then,' said he, 'let me by your patience sleep an hour or two, for I have slept very little this night; and yet to tell you the truth, not for any fear of death, I thank God, but by reason of my great weaknesse and infirmity.' 'The King's further pleasure is,' said the Lieutenant, ' that you should use as little speech as may be upon the scaffold, especially as to anything concerning His Majesty, whereby the people should have any cause to think otherwise than well of him and his proceedings.' 'For that,' said the Bishop, 'you shall see me order myself so, by God's grace, as that neither the King nor any one else shall have occasion to dislike what I say.' With which answer the Lieutenant left him, and so he fell asleep again very soundly for two hours. When he awaked, he called to his man to help him up. But first of all, he ordered him to take away the hair shirt, which he used by way of mortification to wear next to him, and to convey it privily away, and instead thereof to lay him out a clean white shirt and all the best apparel he had as cleanly brushed as might be. As he was adressing himself, his man, perceiving in him a greater curiosity and more care for the neat and cleanly wearing of his clothes than ever he was wont to have before, asked him the reason of this sudden alteration, telling him that his lordship knew well enough that he must put off all again within two hours and lose it. 'What of that,' said the Bishop, 'dost thou not mark that this is our wedding-day, and it becomes me therefore to be more nicely drest than ordinary for the solemnity of the occasion?' About nine of the clock the Lieutenant came again to his prisoner, and, finding him almost ready, said to him that he was now come for him. 'I will wait upon you straight,' said the Bishop, 'as fast as this thin body of mine will give me leave.' Then said he to his man, 'Reach me my furred tippet to put about my neck.' 'O, my lord,' said the Lieutenant, 'what need you be so careful for your health for this little time, which you know is not much above an hour?' 'I think the same,' said the Bishop; 'but yet in the meanwhile I will keep myself as well as I can till the very time of my execution. For I tell you truly tho' I have, I thank our Lord, a very good desire and a willing mind to die at this present, and so trust that of His infinite goodness He will continue it; yet will I not willingly incommode my health in the meantime one minute of an hour, but will still continue the same as long as I can by such reasonable ways and means as Almighty God hath provided for me.' With that, taking a little book in his hand, which was a Latin New Testament that lay by him, he made a crosse on his forehead, and went out of his chamber with the Lieutenant, being so weak that he was scarce able to go downstairs. Wherfore at the stairs foot he was taken up in a chair between two of the Lieutenant's men, and carried to the Tower gate, with a limited number of weapons about him, there to be delivered to the sheriffs of London and Middlesex in order to his execution. When they were come thither they made a halt, till such time as one was sent to know in what readiness the sheriffs were to receive him. During this stop the Bishop rose up out of his chair, and stood leaning against the wall with his eyes lifted up to heaven. In this posture he opened the New Testament in his hand and said, 'O Lord, this is the last time that I shall ever open this book, let some comfortable place now chance to me whereby I, thy poor servant, may glorifie Thee in this my last hour.' With that, looking into the book, the first words he espied there were these: 'And this is the life eternal, that they might know Thee the only true God, and Jesus Christ whom Thou hast sent. I have glorified Thee on the earth: I have finished the work which Thou gavest me to do. And now, O Father, glorifie Thou me with Thine own self.' Words most suitable to the Bishop's case and present circumstances. Having therefore read them, he shut the book and said, 'Here is learning enough for me to my life's end.'

"The sheriffs' men being now ready to receive him, the Bishop was again taken up in his chair and carried to the scaffold, which stood on that part of Tower Hill which is called East Smithfield, beyond the postern, he praying to himself all the way, and meditating on the words of the

Gospel which he had lately read. When he was come to the foot of the steps by which he was to go up to the scaffold, they who carried him offered to help him up. But he said, 'Nay, masters, seeing I am come so far, let me alone, and you shall see me shift for myself well enough.'

"As he was going up the stairs, the south-east sun shone full in his face: on which he said to himself, holding up his hands, 'Accedite ad eum et illuminamini, et facies vestræ non confundentur.' ('Come ye unto him and be ye enlightened, and your faces shall not be confounded.') By the time the Bishop was upon the scaffold it was about ten of the clock, where the executioner being ready to do his office, kneeled down to him, as the custom is, and asked him forgivenesse. 'I forgive thee,' said the Bishop, 'with all my heart, and I trust thou shalt see me overcome this storm with courage.'

"Then was his gown and tippet taken from him, so that he stood stript to his doublet and hose, in the sight of all the people who were there gathered together in great numbers to see this execution. In his address the Bishop spake to them to the following effect. He told them he was come thither to die for the faith of Christ's Holy Catholic Church, and that hitherto he thanked God he had not been afraid of so doing: that he desired the assistance of their prayers, that he might at the very point of death, and the instant of the stroke, which was about to be given to him, continue stedfast, without wavering, in any one point of the Catholic faith, and free from any fear. He concluded with his prayers for the King and the realme, that it might please God to hold his hand over it, and to send the King good counsel. This short speech was spoken by him with so cheerful a countenance, so much life and gravitie, that he seemed not only free from fear but glad to die. Besides, he uttered his words so distinctly, and with so loud and clear a voice, as perfectly surprised those who heard him; since he was so much wasted as to look death itself in humane shape. And no doubt but it must be very affecting to see one of the Bishop's great age and character, who was as it were dying, already brought thither to be put to death by the public executioner. After the Bishop had thus ended what he had to say, he kneeled down on both his knees and repeated certain prayers, among which was the hymn, 'Te Deum laudamus,' and the 31st Psalm, 'In te Domine speravi.' When he had made an end of praying, the executioner came, and bound a handkerchief about his eyes: after which the Bishop, lifting up his hands and heart unto heaven, said a few short prayers, and then laid down his head on the block, where the executioner standing ready with a sharp and heavy axe cut asunder his slender neck at one blow, which bled so abundantly that it was wondred so much blood should issue out of so slender and lean a body."[1]

According to Cardinal Pole, "the lifeless body was treated with every description of contumely, and by direction of the King was exposed entirely naked at the place of execution, as a sight for the rabble to gaze at." He adds that so great was the popular dread of Henry, that no one approached the body except those who came for the sake of treating it with indignity, and the persons who stripped it of its clothes.[2]

Dr. Hall's account is that "the executioner stripping the body of his shirt and all his clothes, departed thence, leaving the headless carcase naked upon the scaffold, where it remained after that sort for the most part of that day, saving that one, for pity and humanity sake, cast a little straw over it; and about eight of the clock in the evening commandment came from the King's Commissioners, to such as

---

[1] Lewis, vol. ii. pp. 194–8. "Thus," says Burnet, "died John Fisher, Bishop of Rochester, in the 80th year of his age. He was a learned and devout man, much addicted to the superstitions in which he had been bred up, and that led him to great severities against all that opposed them. He had been for many years confessor to the King's grandmother, the Countess of Richmond; and it was believed that he persuaded her to those noble designs for the advancement of learning, of founding two colleges in Cambridge, St. John's and Christ's College, and divinity professors in both universities. And in acknowledgment of this, he was chosen Chancellor of the University of Cambridge. Henry VII. gave him the Bishopric of Rochester, which he, following the rule of the primitive church, would never change for a better: he used to say, his church was his wife, he would never part with her, because she was poor."—Burnet, bk. iii. vol. i. p. 708.

[2] "Mortui corpus nudum prorsus in loco supplicii ad spectaculum populo relinqui mandaverat." Poli Apol. ad Cæsar. 96; Lingard, vol. v. p. 21; 'Archæologia,' vol. xxv. p. 86. Ellis's 'Orig. Letters,' 2nd series, vol. ii. p. 58.

watched about the dead body (for it was still watched with many halberds and weapons), that they should cause it to be buried. Whereupon two of the watches took it upon a halberd between them, and so carried it to a churchyard by, called All Hallows Barkin, where, on the north side of the churchyard, hard by the wall, they digged a grave with their halberds."[1]

The head of the aged prelate was placed on London Bridge. Dodd in his 'Church History' says, " that after an exposure of fourteen days on London Bridge, the head was taken down and thrown into the Thames, in consequence of a report that rays of light were observed to shine around it."[2] Hall merely says that " the face was observed to become fresher and more comely day by day, and that such was the concourse of people who assembled to look at it, that almost neither cart nor horse could pass."[3]

"Here, in the chapel of St. Peter," writes Weever, " lie interred the headless remains of John Fisher, doctor of divinity, sometime Bishop of Rochester, brought up a scholar in Cambridge, master of our college (I mean Queen's College, in Cambridge), and chancellor of that university. He was made Cardinal St. Vitalis, the one and twentieth of May, which honor was to him 'parum vitalis,' for the cardinal's hat and his head never met together,[4] he being beheaded on Tower Hill, the twenty-second of June following, anno dom. 1535. His body was first buried in Barking churchyard,[5] and afterwards upon occasion as followeth, removed to this place."[6]

" In 1773 the remains of a tomb which he caused to be

[1] Hall's 'Life,' p. 210.
[2] Dodd, vol. i. p. 161.
[3] Hall, p. 212.
[4] The cardinal's hatt was already upon the way coming towards the Bishop of Rochester, not only as a worthy rewarde of his merite, butt also for a buckler under the which the Pope thought to handle his cruell sworde: his Highnes, I say, fearyng the example of his predecessour Kynge John, or ever they had arryved, shaved the bishop's crowne by the shoulders, to see afterward where the pope would bestow his cardinal's hatt. — William Thomas's Defence of Henry VIII.
[5] " In the churchyarde of Barkyne by the northe dore."—'Grey Friars' Chron.' p. 38.
[6] Weever's 'Funeral Monuments.' "Sir Thomas More, some tyme Chaunsler of Inglond, was beheddyd at Towrehyll, then was tane up the byshoppe agayne, and both of them burryd within the Tower." — 'Grey Friars' Chron.,' p. 38.

prepared for himself in St. John's Chapel, Cambridge, were discovered, and it is believed that Torregiano had furnished the design for it. A small chapel at the east end of the college chapel had been arranged for it, and above was the motto, 'Faciam vos fieri Piscatores hominum.' At the 'stalls endes was graven by ye joyner, a Fisher, and an eere of wheat' (Harl. MSS. 7047, p. 16). The remains of this tomb being exposed to the weather, in 1774 were entirely spoiled."[1]

Sir Thomas More.

Born, 1480. Beheaded on Tower Hill, 6th July, 1535.

Sir Thomas More, like Bishop Fisher, was summoned to Lambeth to take the oath of succession, and on the same day as Fisher: so on Monday the 13th April (1534) "he left his house at Chelsea with heavy forebodings," and (writes William Roper his son-in-law), "whereas he evermore used before his departure from his wife and children, whom he tenderlie loved, to have them bringe him to his boate, and theare to kisse them and bid them all farewell, then would he suffer none of them forth the gate to follow him, but pulled the wickett after him, and shutt them all from him, and with a heavie heart, as his countenance it appeered, with me and our foure servants theare tooke boate towards Lambethe."[2]

On his arrival at Lambeth Palace the form of the oath was shown him, "which when he had read unto himself, he answered, that he neither would find fault with the oath, nor with the authors of it, nor would blame the conscience of any man that had taken it; but for himself he could not take it without endangering his soul of eternal damnation: which he having said, the Lord Chancellor replied that all there were heartily sorry he should make such an answer; and they showed him a catalogue of nobility and others who

[1] Lewis, vol. i. Introd. xx.   [2] Roper's 'Life,' p. 70.

had taken it, &c. He was then commanded to walk in the garden awhile: others were called in, who took the oath; and all took it except Bishop Fisher and Dr. Wilson, Vicar of Croydon."[1] Again the oath was shown to him, and the list of those who had just subscribed to it; More's decision was immovable, and after that he was given into the custody of the Abbot of Westminster[2] for four days, during which time the King consulted with his council "what order weare meet to be taken with Sir Thomas More." And albeit in the beginning they weare resolved that with an oathe, not to be acknowe,[3] whether he had to the supremacie been sworne, or what he thought thereof, he should be discharged: yet did Queen Anne by her importunate clamour soe sore exasperate the Kinge against him,[4] that contrary to his former resolution he caused the saide oathe of the supremacie[5] to be ministered unto him. Who albeit he made a discreet quallified answere, nevertheless was forthwith committed to the Tower."[6]

This was on Friday the 17th of April: when Sir Richard Southwell,[7] who conveyed him to the Tower, advised him to send home his chain of gold that he wore about his neck " to his wife, or to some child or friend of his. 'Nay, sir,' quoth he, 'that I will not: for if I were taken in the field with mine enemies, as I am a knight, I would they should fare somewhat the better for me.'"[8]

He was conveyed by the river from Westminster to the Tower, and at his landing the Lieutenant was ready at the Tower gate to receive him, "where the porter demanded of him his upper garment. 'Mr. Porter,' quoth he, 'heere it is,' and tooke off his capp, and delivered it to him, saying, 'I am very sorry it is noe better for thee.' 'Noe, sir,' quoth

---

[1] Cresacre More's 'Life of Sir T. More,' pp. 233-4.
[2] William Benson, called "Boston," from his birthplace: he was the successor of Islip at Westminster, and the last of the abbots and the first dean: he died in 1549, and was buried in the abbey.
[3] Acknowledged.
[4] More had previously refused to be present at her coronation.
[5] This should be "succession," as the Act of Supremacy was not passed until 15th Jan. 1535. It is 26 Hen. VIII. c. 1.
[6] Roper's 'Life,' p. 71.
[7] Roper attributes this to Sir Richard Cromwell: Cresacre More writes "Sir Richard Wingfield."
[8] Harpsfield's 'Life.'

the porter, 'I must have your gowne.' And soe was he by Mr. Lieutenant conveyed to his lodginge."[1]

He was allowed to have one of his own servants with him, John A. Wood, who could neither write nor read, and who was sworn to report to the Lieutenant "anything that he might hear spoken or written against the King."

Not long after his arrival at the Tower, he wrote the following letter to his favourite daughter, Margaret Roper:—

"Myne owne good daughter: our Lorde be thanked, I am in good helthe and bodye, and in good quiet of minde; and of worldlye thinges, I no more desyer than I have. I besecho hym make you all mery in the hope of heaven. And such thynges as I somewhat longed to talke with you all, concerning the worlde to come, our Lorde put them into your myndes, as I truste be dothe, and better to, by hys holy spirite: who blesse and preserve you all.

"Written wyth a cole[2] by your tender loving father, who in hys pore prayers forgetteth none of you all, nor your babes nor your nurses, nor your good husbandes, nor your good husbandes shrewde wyves, nor your father's shrewde wyfe neither, nor our other frendes. And thus fare ye hartely well, for lacke of paper.[3]

"THOMAS MORE, Knighte."

When he had been in prison about a month, his daughter by her "earneste suite at lengthe got leave to goe unto him:" but there is another version of her special mode of obtaining access to her father. It is, "that longing to see him she wittiely invented this craft: she wrote a letter and sent it to her father, wherein she seemed to labour to persuade him to take the oath. She nothing doubted but that the letter would be intercepted: but this she did to winne thereby credit with Master Cromwell, and soe to git libertie to have free access to her father: which by this sleight she obtained. Others say it was seriouslie written, and soe her father tooke it, and thereon did write to her againe accordingly."[4]

After this visit occurred the conversation (so characteristic of More's humour) with the Lieutenant of the Tower:

---

[1] Roper's 'Life,' pp. 89, 90.
[2] Charcoal or a burnt stick.
[3] Roper's 'Life,' Appendix, p. 148.
[4] MS. Life at Lambeth Library, in Wordsworth's 'Eccles. Biography,' vol. ii. p. 145.

"who coming into his chamber to visit him rehearsed the benefites and friendships that he had many waies received of him, and howe muche bounde he was thearfore to entertain him, and to make him good cheere, which since the case standinge as it did, he could not, without the Kinge's indignacion; he trusted, he saide, he would accept his good will and suche poore cheere as he had.' 'Mr. Lieutenant,' quoth he again, 'I verilie believe, as you maie, soe are you my good frend indeed, and would, as you saie, with your best cheere entertaine me, for the which I most hartelie thanke you; and assure yourselfe, Mr. Lieutenant, I doe not mislike my cheere, but whensoever I soe doe, then thrust me out of your doores.'"[1]

He employed his time in the Tower by writing, and began a treatise on the Passion of Christ:[2] but when he came to expound the words, "and they laid hands upon him and held him," he was deprived of his books, ink, and papers, so that he could write no more.[3] "Which being done, he applied himself wholly to meditation, keeping his chamber windows shut and very dark: the occasion whereof Mr. Lieutenant asking him, he said, 'When all the wares are gone, the shop windows are to be shut up.'"

"Yet by stealth," adds Cresacre More, "he would gett little peeces of paper, in which he would write diverse letters with a coale; of which my father left me one, which was to his wife; which I accounte as a precious jewell, afterwards drawen over by my grandfather's sonne with inke."[4]

At the beginning of the next year (1535) he was again visited by his daughter, and also by his wife, who at her first coming, like a simple ignorant woman, bluntly advised him to "do as all the bishops and best learned in the King's realm had done," so that he might again be "abroad with his liberty: but her persuasions moved him but a little."[5]

---

[1] Roper's 'Life,' pp. 73–4. Fuller's 'Worthies,' vol. ii. p. 69.

[2] Whilst in prison he wrote his three books of comfort against tribulation: a treatise to receive the blessed sacrament, the treatise on the Passion above mentioned, and various devout instructions and prayers.

[3] Probably on account of the discovery of his clandestine correspondence with Bishop Fisher. See p. 67.

[4] C. More's 'Life,' pp. 253–4. Roper's 'Life,' p. 78.

[5] Ibid., pp. 249–50.

And now the Act of Supremacy having been passed, it was thought desirable to get Sir Thomas More's adhesion to that oath, as well as to the question of the succession; so the "Lord Chancellor, the Dukes of Norfolke and Suffolke, with Mr. Secretarie and certaine other of the privie councell came at two severall times, by all pollicyes possible, procuringe him either preciselie to confesse the supremacie or preciselie to deny it. Wherunto, as appeareth by his examinations they could never bring him."[1] It was to them that he said the Act of Supremacy was "like a two-edged sword, for if one answer one way it will confound his soule, and if the other way, it will confound his body;"[2] and this speech was subsequently used against him at his trial.

Richard Rich, the Solicitor-General,[3] Sir Richard Southwell, and "one Mr. Palmer, Mr. Secretary's man," were also sent to examine him, and to endeavour by "pretending to talk friendly" to obtain some admission from him which might serve as evidence against him.

He was arraigned on 7th May, but his trial was postponed till the 1st July, in the hope of strengthening the case for the Crown.[4]

At length, on Thursday the 1st July, he was summoned to appear before the Special Commission in the Court of King's Bench at Westminster Hall. He went thither on foot, through the streets of London, to Westminster, "leaning on his staff, because he had been much weakened by his imprisonment: yet his countenance cheerful and constant."

His judges were Audley (the Lord Chancellor), Sir John Fitzjames (the Lord Chief Justice), Sir John Baldwin,[5] Sir Richard Leicester,[6] Sir John Port, Sir John Spelman, and Sir Walter Luke,[7] and Sir Anthony Fitzherbert. He pleaded not guilty, when the Attorney-General proceeded to read the

---

[1] Roper's 'Life,' p. 79.
[2] Herbert's 'Henry VIII.' p. 393.
[3] Sir Richard Rich, afterwards Lord Chancellor, died in 1566.
[4] Campbell's 'Chancellors,' vol. ii. p. 59.
[5] Chief Justice of the Common Pleas.
[6] Or Lyster, Chief Baron of the Exchequer.
[7] Puisne judges of the King's Bench.

lengthy indictment, which stated that "he had behaved maliciously and traiterously against the crown and regall dignitie of his sacred majestie."[1] More then said: "When I think how long my accusation is, and what heinous matters are laid to my charge, I am stricken with fear, lest my memory and wit, both which are decayed, together with the health of my body, through an impediment contracted by my long imprisonment, so as I shall not be able to answer these things on a sudden, as I ought and otherwise could. After this there was brought him a chair, in which when he was sate,"[2] he addressed the Court in reply to the indictment. Rich, Sir Richard Southwell, and the Mr. Palmer, were the witnesses produced against him; to whose evidence Sir Thomas More ably replied: but "for all that ever he could do or say, the jury of twelve men[3] going together and staying scarce one quarter of an hour (for they knew what the King would have done in that case) returned with their verdict guilty."

The Chancellor then pronounced upon him the frightful sentence in cases of treason, and ordered that his head should be placed on London Bridge.[4]

After a short speech to the judges, he left the Court,[5] an axe being carried before him with the edge towards him, and he "departed to the Tower again, led by Sir William Kingston,[6] a tall, stronge, and comelie knight, and his

[1] For the indictment, see 'Archæologia,' vol. xxvii. pp. 361–374, printed from Arundel MSS. No. 152, p. 308, in British Museum.
[2] C. More's 'Life,' p. 257.
[3] The following are the names of the jury:—Sir Thomas Palmer, Sir Thomas Pierte, George Lovell, Thomas Burbage, Geoffrey Chamber, Edward Stockmore, William Browne, Jasper Leake, Thomas Billington, John Parnell, Richard Bellamy, George Stoakes.
[4] The sentence was changed into beheading, because he had borne the highest office in the realm, of which mercy of the King's word being brought to Sir Thomas, he merrily said, "God forbid the King should use any more such mercy to any of my friends, and God bless all my posterity from such pardons."—C. More's 'Life,' p. 271; Herbert in 'State Trials,' vol. i. p. 394.
[5] The proceedings of the trial are preserved in Baga de Secretis, Pouch vii. bundle 3. See also Campbell's 'Lives of Chancellors,' and Froude's 'Hist. of England,' vol. ii. pp. 376–380; MS. Life in Wordsworth's Eccles. Biographies,' vol. ii. pp. 151–169; C. More's 'Life,' p. 256 et seq.
[6] Sir William Kingston was captain of the Yeomen of the Guard from 1523 to 1536, and Constable of the Tower in 1535. The record of the trial in the 'Baga de Secretis' shows that Sir Edward Walsingham, the Lieutenant, attended him to and from Westminster.

verie dear friend. Who when he had brought him (by water) from Westminster to the ould Swan towards the Tower, theare with a heavie heart, the tears runninge downe his cheeks, bade him farewell."[1]

As Sir Thomas More passed out of the court at Westminster, "his only son,[2] my grandfather," says Cresacre More, "like a dutiful child, casteth himself at his father's feet, craving humbly his blessing, not without tears; whom he blessed and kissed most lovingly, whose love and obedience Sir Thomas afterwards in a letter praised."[3]

When he arrived at the Tower ward, "his daughter, my wife," writes Roper, "desirous to see her father, whome she thought she should never see in this world after, and alsoe to have his finall blessinge, gave attendance about the Tower wharfe, wheare she knewe he should passe before he could enter into the Tower. There tarrynge his comminge, as soon as she sawe him, after his blessinge, uppon her knees reverentlie received, she hastinge towards him, without consideracion or care of herselfe, pressinge in amongst the midst of the throng and companie of the garde, that with holbards and bills went round about him, hastelie ranne to him, and there openlie in sight of them, imbraced him, and tooke him aboute the neck and kissed him. Who well likinge her most naturall and deere daughterlie affection towards him, gave her his fatherlie blessinge and manie godlie wordes of comfort beside.[4] From whome after she was departed, she not satisfied with the former sight of him, and like one that had forgotten herselfe, beinge all ravished with the entire love of her father, havinge respect neither to herselfe, nor to the presse of people and multitude that weare theare about him, suddainlie turned back againe, ranne to him as before, tooke him aboute the necke, and

---

[1] Roper's 'Life,' p. 90; C. More's 'Life,' p. 274.

[2] John More, born 1510.

[3] C. More's 'Life,' p. 274. The following is the letter referred to: "Commend me, when you can, to my son John: his towardly carriage towards me pleased me very much. God bless him, and his good wife and their children, Thomas and Augustine, and all that they shall have."—C. More's 'Life,' p. 39.

[4] She was not able to say any word but "Oh, my father! oh, my father!" —C. More's 'Life,' p. 276.

divers times kissed him lovinglie,[1] and at last with a full and heavie heart, was faine to depart from him.[2] The beholdinge whereof was to manie that were present soe lamentable, that it made them for verie sorrow thereof to weape and mourne."[3]

On Monday, the 5th-July, "he sent," writes Roper," his shirt of haire, not willing to have it seene, to my wife, his deerlie beloved daughter, and a letter, written with a cole, which was the laste thinge that ever he wrote."[4]

"Oure Lorde blesse you good daughter, and youre good husbande, and youre lyttle boye, and all yours, and all my chyldren and all my godde chyldren, and all oure frendes.

"Recommende me when ye maye to my good daughter Cicely,[5] whom I beseeche oure Lorde to comfort. And I send her my blessyng and to all her children, and praye her to praye for me. I send her an handkercher, and God comfort my good sonne her husbande. My good daughter Daunce[6] hathe the picture in parchemente that you delivered me from my Lady Coniers, her name is on the backside. Shew her that I hartelye praye her, that you may send it in my name to her agayne for a token from me to praye for me. I lyke spesiall wel Dorothy Coly, I pray you to be good unto her, I would wytte whether thys be she that you wrote me of. If not yet I praye you bee good to the tother, as you maye in her affliction, and to my good daughter Joone Aleyn[7] too. Geve her I praye you some kynde answere for she sued hither to me this day to pray you be good to her. I comber you good Margaret much, but I would be sorry for it should

[1] "Whereat he spoke not a word, but carrying still his gravity, tears fell also from his eyes: few could refrain from weeping, no not the guard themselves."—C. More's 'Life,' p. 277. Roper's 'Life,' p. 91.

[2] "At last, with a heavy heart, she was severed from him, at which time Margaret Giggs embraced him and kissed him also; and mine aunt's maid, Dorothy Collie, did the like, of whom he said after, it was homely, but very lovingly done."—C. More's 'Life,' p. 277; for Margaret Giggs and Dorothy Collie, see pages 84, 87.

[3] ". . . The blushing maid
Who through the streets as through a desert stray'd,
And when her dear, dear father passed along,
Would not be held: but bursting through the throng
Halbert and axe, kissed him o'er and o'er,
Then turned and wept, then sought him as before,
Believing she should see his face no more."—
ROGERS'S 'Human Life.'

[4] Roper's 'Life,' p. 161.
[5] Cecilia, his third daughter, married to Giles Heron.
[6] Elizabeth, his second daughter, married to John Dance.
[7] This was one of Margaret Roper's servants.

be any longer than to-morrow. For it is Saint Thomas even, and the Utas[1] of St. Peter; and therefore to-morrow long I to go to God: it were a day verye mete and convenient for me: I never liked your maner toward me better than when you kissed me late:[2] for I love when daughterly love and deere charitye hath no leysure to loke to worldlye curtesy.

"Farewell, my dere chylde, and pray for me, and I shall for you, and all youre frendes, that we maye merelye mete in heaven. I thanke you for youre gret cost. I sende now to my good daughter Clement[3] her algorisme stone, and I send her and my godsonne and all hers God's blessing and myne.

"I praye you at time convenient recommende me to my good sonne John More. I liked well his natural fashion.[4] Our Lorde blesse hym and his good wyfe[5] my loving daughter, to whom I praye him to be good, as he hathe greate cause: and that if the lande of myne come to his hande, he breake not my wyll concernynge hys sister Daunce.

"And oure Lord blesse Thomas and Austen[6] and all that they shal have."

"And soe uppon the next morowe, Tuesdaie (6th July), earlie in the morninge, there came to him Sir Thomas Pope, his singular good frende, on message from the Kinge and counsaile that he should the same daie before nine of the clock in the morning suffer deathe, and that therefore he should forthwith prepare himself thereto."[7]

"Mr. Pope," quoth Sir Thomas More, "for your good tidings I hartelie thanke you.

"I have been alwaies muche bounden to the Kinge's Highnes for the benefites and honours that he hath still from time to time most bountifullye heaped uppon me: and yet more bounden am I to his Grace for puttinge me into this place, wheare I have had convenient time and space to have remembrance of my end. And soe, God helpe me,

---

[1] Octaves.
[2] See *ante*, p. 82.
[3] Margaret, the wife of Clement, not his daughter, but who had been brought up from a child with his own daughters.
[4] His son having asked his blessing as he left Westminster after his trial. See *ante*, p. 82.
[5] John More married Annie Cresacre.
[6] John More's children. Cresacre More says, "Thomas, who was my father, and Augustine, who died unmarried." (C. More's 'Life,' p. 280; Roper's 'Life,' p. 162.)
[7] Sir Thomas Pope, b. 1508, d. 1559. He was then a privy councillor: he held many offices, and amongst others he was Master of the Jewel-house in the Tower. He founded Trinity College, Oxford.

most of all, Mr. Pope, am I bounden to his Highnes, that it pleaseth him so shortlie to ridd me from the miseries of this wretched world, and therefore will I not faile earnestlie to praie for his Grace bothe heere and allsoe in the worlde to come. The Kinge's pleasure is farther, quoth Mr. Pope, that at your execution you shall not use manie words. Mr. Pope, quoth he, you doe well to give me warninge of his Grace's pleasure, for otherwise at that time had I purposed somewhat to have spoken, but of noe matter whearwith his Grace or any should have had cause to be offended."[1]

More then asked that his daughter Margaret might be present at his burial. "The Kinge is content alreadie, quoth Mr. Pope, that your wife and children, and other your freends shall have libertie to be present thereat."

"Whearwithal Mr. Pope, takeinge his leave, could not refraine from weepinge.

"Quiet yourselfe, good Mr. Pope, said Sir Thomas, and be not discomforted: for I trust that we shall once in heaven see eache other full merrilie, wheare we shall be sure to live and love together in joyfull blisse eternalie."[2]

"Uppon whose departure Sir Thomas More, as one that had binne invited to some solemn feast, he changed himselfe into his best apparel, and put on his silk camlet gown, which his entire friend, Mr. Anthony Boudise, a noble citizen of the state of Lucca, gave him, which Mr. Lieutenant espieing advised him to put it off, sayeinge, that he that should have it was but a javell.[3] 'What, Mr. Lieutenant,' quoth he, 'shall I account him a javell, that shall doe me this daie soe singuler a benifit? Naie, I assure you, weare it cloath of gold, I should thinke it well bestowed on him, as Saint Cyprian did, who gave his executioner thirty pieces of gold.' But at length through the Lieutenant's importunate persuasion he altered his apparel, and put on his gown of frieze; yet after the example of the holie martyr, Saint

---

[1] Roper's 'Life,' p. 93.
[2] And further to put him from his melancholy, Sir Thomas More did take his urinal, and cast his water, saying merrily, "I see no danger but the man that owns this water may live longer, if it please the King."—C. More's 'Life,' p. 283.
[3] Javell, a worthless fellow.—Nares' 'Glossary.'

Cyprian, did he, of that little money that was left him, send an angell of gold to his executioner, as a token that he maliced him nothing, but rather loved him extremely.[1]

"So about nine of the clock, he was brought by the Lieutenant out of the Tower, clad in the old frieze gown, his beard being long, which fashion he had never before used,[2] his face pale and lean, carrying in his hand a red cross, and casting his eyes often towards heaven."[3]

"As he thus passed by a good woman's house, she came forth and offered him a cup of wine, which he refused, saying, 'Marrie, my good wife, I will not drinke nowe, my Maister had easell[4] and gall, and not wine given him to drinke.'

"There came another woman after him, crying unto him for certain books, which she had given into his custody when he was Lord Chancellor, to whom he said, 'Good woman, have patience but for one hour's space, and by that time the King's majesty will rid me of the care I have of thy papers, and all other matters whatsoever.'"[5]

The scaffold was "ill constructed, weak, and ready to fall," so he said merrilie to the Lieutenant, "I praie you, Mr. Lieutenant, see me safe up, and for my comminge downe, let me shift for myselfe." Then desired he all the people thereabout to praie for him, and to beare witness with him that he should now there suffer death in and for the faithe of the Holy Catholick Church.[6] He then knelt down and repeated the 'Miserere' (the 50th Psalm) to the end, with some prayers; after he had ended and risen, the executioner asked him for forgiveness: Sir Thomas kissed him, and said, "Plucke up thy spirits, man, and be not afraide to doe thine office. I am sorie my neck is verie short, therefore strike not awrie for savinge of thine honestie."[7]

The executioner offered to tie his eyes. "I will cover them myself," he said; and binding them in a cloth which

---

[1] Roper's 'Life,' p. 94. See also C. More's 'Life,' p. 281 et seq.
[2] All the portraits of Sir Thomas More represent him as close shaven.
[3] Roper's 'Life.' C. More's 'Life,' p. 284.
[4] Vinegar.
[5] C. More's 'Life,' pp. 284–5.
[6] Roper's 'Life,' p. 94.
[7] C. More's 'Life,' p. 286, &c.

he had brought with him,[1] he knelt and laid his head upon the block.

"The fatal stroke was about to fall, when he signed for a moment's delay while he moved aside his beard: 'Pity that should be cut,' he murmured, 'that has not committed treason,' with which strange words, the strangest perhaps ever uttered at such a time, the lips most famous in Europe for eloquence and wisdom closed for ever."[2]

His head was put upon London Bridge, where traitors' heads are set up upon poles:[3] his body was buried in the chapel of St. Peter, in the Tower, in the belfrey, or as some say, as one entereth into the vestry, near unto the body of the holy martyr Bishop Fisher.[4]

"That which happened about Sir Thomas' winding sheet, was reported as a miracle by my Aunt Roper, Mrs. Clement,[5] and Dorothy Collie, wife unto Mr. Harris. Thus it was: his daughter Margaret, having distributed all her money to the poor, for her father's soul, when she came to bury his body at the Tower, she had forgotten to bring a sheet: and there was not a penny of money left amongst them all." The servant Dorothy told Mrs. Roper, who said she might try to get it on credit: "I am not known in this neighbourhood," replied the servant. "At any rate," said Mrs. Roper, "go and do what you can." "She went to the next draper's shop, agreed about the price, and pretending to look for some money in her purse, she found there the exact sum for which she had agreed with the draper, not one penny more or less, though she knew before, certainly, that she had not previously one cross (farthing) about her. This the same Dorothy affirmed constantly to Doctor Stapleton, when they both lived at Douay, in Flanders, in Queen Elizabeth's reign."[6]

---

[1] Probably a corpus christi cloth.—More's 'Life,' p. 287.

[2] Froude, vol. ii. p. 384. Hall's version is, "I pray you let me lay my beard over the block, least ye should cut it: thus with a mocke he ended his life."—Hall's 'Chronicle.'

[3] In a Latin account of his death, it is said "priusquam exponetur, acquâ ferventi decoctum est, quo plus habe-ret horroris!"

[4] C. More's 'Life,' p. 288.

[5] Stapleton says that he had seen the shirt stained with blood, which More had worn when executed, and that it was in the possession of Margaret Clement.

[6] C. More's 'Life,' pp. 288-9. See also Stapleton's 'Life,' cap. xx. p. 71.

Another story, which is characteristic of the period, is told, that one day Mrs. Roper was "passing under the bridge, and looking on her father's head, said 'that head has laid many a time in my lap, would to God it would fall into my lap as I pass under:' she had her wish, and it did fall into her lap, and is now preserved."

The true version is, however, to be found in Stapleton, who states that she obtained the head by bribing the executioner (corruptâ pecuniâ carnefice): he also records that she most carefully preserved it with aromatic substances, as long as she lived, but he appears not to have been aware of its ultimate destination, as he says that after Mrs. Roper's death it "remained with one of her relations."

She kept it in a leaden box, and it was buried with her in 1544, in the vault of the Roper family at St. Dunstan's Church, Canterbury. Gostling in his 'History of Canterbury' (1774), says, "in a vault under the family chancel of Roper is kept a skull, said to be that of the great Sir Thomas More: it is in a niche of the wall, secured by an iron grate. Some say that his favourite daughter, Mrs. Roper, who lies here, desired to be buried with it in her arms."

The Rev. J. Bowes Bruce, of Canterbury, records that in 1835 "wishing to ascertain whether Sir Thomas More's skull was really there, I went down into the vault, and found it still remaining in the place where it was seen many years ago, in a niche in the wall, in a leaden box, something of the shape of a beehive, open in the front, and with an iron grating before it."[1]

It was also seen, and a drawing made of it, in 1715; which drawing was exhibited by Mr. Pownall at the meeting of the Kent Archæological Society, on 11th April, 1866; and on the same day many members of the society, and visitors, went down into the vault, where the leaden box was exposed to view.

It has been asserted that Mrs. Roper removed her father's

---

[1] Campbell's 'Chancellors,' vol. ii. p. 68.

body to Chelsea Church, but I am inclined to consider that this was not the case.[1]

Her husband makes no mention of it in his life of Sir T. More. Stapleton, writing in 1588, and who was intimate with members of the family, as well as with Mrs. Roper's servant, expressly describes the burial of the body under Mrs. Roper's superintendence, in the chapel of St. Peter: and by the side of his friend Fisher, as he had in his latter days expressly wished, and whose body, as has been already stated, was removed from Barking churchyard to be reinterred by Sir Thomas More.

Weever in the following passage seems to have been the first to state that More's body was removed to Chelsea. "On the sixth day of July following the decollation of Bishop Fisher, Sir Thomas More, Lord Chancellor of England, was likewise beheaded on the Tower Hill, for the like denial of the King's supremacy: he was first buried in this chapel (St. Peter's), and the body of his dear friend Fisher was removed out of Barking churchyard, and buried with him in the same grave, for agreeing so unanimously in their opinions living, it was (belike) thought unfitting to part them being dead: but how long they lay together in this their house of rest, I certainly know not; yet this is certain, that Margaret, the wife of Master Roper, and daughter of the said Sir Thomas More, removed her father's corps not long after, to Chelsea: and whether she honored the Bishop by another remove to the place of her father's burial or not, I know not, yet she might by all probability."[2]

Anthony à Wood also states that More's body was removed to Chelsea Church, but he probably merely adopted Weever's statement, which I do not find confirmed in any other accounts: as far therefore as More is concerned, the monument, which he erected for himself in Chelsea Church, and in which he had deposited the body of his first wife, remains a mere cenotaph.

---

[1] If she had done so, she would probably have placed her father's head in that tomb with his body, and not have caused it to be taken to Canterbury.
[2] Weever's 'Funeral Monuments.'

The antiquary Lysons thus records his opinion: "A few years before his death, Sir Thomas More caused a vault to be made on the south side of the chancel of Chelsea Church, to which he removed the bones of his first wife, designing it for the place of his own interment. It has been a matter of dispute whether his body was deposited there or not: some authors[1] say that his daughter Margaret removed his corpse from the Tower, where it had been buried, to the vault at Chelsea. Neither C. More, the Chancellor's great grandson, who wrote his life, nor Roper mention this fact: and it has been thought unlikely, from the circumstance of Bishop Fisher's body having been removed to the Tower by Margaret Roper, that it might be interred, according to his request, near her father, who was there buried." [2]

Sir Thomas More's personal appearance is thus described: "He was of mean stature, well proportioned, his complexion tending to phlegmatic, his colour white and pale, his hair neither black nor yellow, but between both; his eyes grey, his countenance amiable and cheerful: his voice neither big nor shrill, but speaking plainly and distinctly, it was not very tunable, though he delighted much in music: his body reasonably healthful, only that towards his latter time, by using much to write, he complained much of the ache of his breast."[3]

"In his youth he drunk much water; his common drink was very small ale: and as for wine he did but sip of it, and that only for company's sake, or for pledging his friends. He loved salt meats, especially powdered beef, and usually he did eat of brown bread, which he rather used to punish his taste, than for any love he had unto it."[4] His contemporary, the chronicler Hall, writes: "I cannot tell whether

---

[1] Quoting Weever and Anthony à Wood.
[2] Lysons, vol. ii. p. 53. See also 'Remarks on More's Life,' by Rev. Dr. King, 1717.
[3] C. More's 'Life,' p. 294. His friend Erasmus says "dexter humerus paulo videtur eminentior lævo, præsertim cum incedit, id quod non accidit naturâ, sed assuetudine:" he also says, "his hands were a little clumsy and rustic, in comparison with the rest of his body:" and this may be the reason why Holbein represented him as sitting with his hands folded together, and partly covered with the sleeves of his gown.
[4] 'Life,' by J. Hoddesdon, p. 175.

I should call him a foolish wise man, or a wise foolish man, for undoubtedly he, beside his learning, had a great wit, but it was so mingled with taunting and mocking, that it seemed to them that best knew him, that hee thought nothing to be well spoken except he had uttered some mocke in the communication."

Hoddesdon concludes his Life of More with a "view of his wit and wisdom," which chapter he says, addressing the reader, "after this tragicall story, looks like a comedy, and may serve as wine and bisket at a funeral, to allay thy sadness."[1]

GEORGE BOLEYN, VISCOUNT ROCHFORD.

Born, ———. Beheaded on Tower Hill, 17th May, 1536.

Lord Rochford was arrested at Greenwich, on Tuesday the 2nd May, with Brereton, Weston, Norris, and Smeton, and was examined by the Duke of Norfolk and other members of the King's council, but it does not appear that he was immediately sent with the others to the Tower, as Sir William Kingston in one of his letters to Cromwell, written apparently on 2nd May, says that Queen Anne Boleyn on her arrival had asked him, "I pray you tell me where my Lord Rochford ys? and I told her I saw hym afore dyner in the Cort. O wher ys my swete brother? I sayd I left hym at York Place:[2] and so I dyd."[3]

In all probability he was lodged in the Tower on the evening of that day.

The next mention of him is found in another letter from Kingston, who reports to Cromwell that Rochford "desyred to know at what tyme he should come before the Kynge's counsell for, sayde he, I thynk I shal not cum forthe tyll I cum to my account, wepying very bitterlie."[4]

The grand juries of Middlesex and Kent returned true bills on 10th and 11th May.

---

[1] 'Life,' by J. Hoddesdon, p. 181.
[2] Afterwards Whitehall Palace.
[3] Cotton. MSS. Otho, c. x. f. 225.
[4] Ibid. c. x. f. 2096.

Norris, Weston, Brereton and Smeton, were tried at Westminster on Friday the 12th May, and on the 15th May, immediately after sentence had been passed on his sister, Queen Anne, Rochford was brought before the court sitting in the King's Hall in the White Tower.

"The Duke of Norfolk presided as High Steward, assisted by the Duke of Suffolk, the Marquis of Exeter, and twenty-four other peers.[1] The Lord Mayor of London and his brethren the aldermen, the wardens, and some persons of most every the twelve principall companies were, however, present."[2]

Rochford was found guilty, and condemned to be beheaded and quartered.[3] The latter part of his sentence was remitted, and he was to suffer death on Tower Hill with Norris, Brereton, Weston, and Smeton[4] on the 17th May.

Sir William Kingston had on the 16th May submitted some petition which had been addressed by Rochford to the King: the substance of it does not appear, he merely reports to Cromwell that it was answered, and adds—

"The sayd Lord meche desyreth to speke with you, weche touchet hys conscyens meche, as he sayth, wherin I pray you I may knowe your plesur, for bycause of my promyse made unto the sayd lorde to do the same."

The interview was probably not granted by Cromwell, and Rochford was ordered to prepare for his execution, as in the same letter Kingston says—

"I have told my Lorde of Rochford that he be in a redyness to-morrow to suffer execusyon, and so he accepse it very well, and will do his best to be redy. Notwithstanding he wold have reysayved hys ryghts,[5] weche hathe not bene used, and in especiall here. Sir, I shall desyre you that we here may know the Kyng's plesur here as

---

[1] The Earl of Wiltshire, father of Anne and Rochford, had been included in the special commission, and was present when Norris and the others were tried at Westminster, but he was absent during the trial of his children. The Earl of Northumberland was absent "on account of sudden illness."

[2] Holinshed.

[3] The trial is in the Baga de Secretis, Pouch xx. See Appendix, p. 327.

[4] It is uncertain whether Smeton was beheaded or hanged. In the 'Grey Friars' Chronicle' it is stated that he was beheaded. See also 'Excerpta Historica,' p. 263.

[5] Received the sacrament.

shortlie as may be, that we here may prepayre for the same what ys necessary, for the same we here have now may for to do execusyon."[1]

When brought with the others to the scaffold, he exhorted them to die courageously. He said to the bystanders that he came to die as the King had ordered: and in leaving them, would exhort every one not to trust to courts, states, or kings, but to rely on heaven alone. For his sins, he had deserved heavy punishment from heaven, but none from the King, whom he had never offended, and for whom he now prayed a long and happy life.[2]

The following account of his execution is believed to have been written by an eye-witness: "A scaffold was built up before the Tower of London, on a Wednesday, which was the 17th of May. And then they led out of the Tower, wherein they had been imprisoned, the Queen's brother, and the four accused gentlemen, all closely guarded, as they are wont to guard those guilty of such things."

"And my Lord of Reujafort (Rochford), for that was the name of the Queen's brother, said three times[3] with a loud voice, to the whole city there gathered together. 'O ye gentlemen and Christians, I was born under the law and I die under the law, forasmuch as it is the law which hath condemned me,' and then he proceeded to speak in this wise."[4]

The speech given by the writer is somewhat amplified, but it quite corresponds in substance with the version which is recorded in the 'Chronicle of Calais.' I prefer to give this latter version.

"The words of Ser Gorge Boleyne, brothar to qwene Anne, warden of the V portes, on the xvij of May, when he toke his deathe at the Towre Hill at London, he sayde thre tymes:

"Christen men, I am borne undar the lawe, and judged undar the lawe, and the lawe hathe condemned me. Mastars all, I am not come

[1] Harl. MSS. 283, fol. 134. Ellis's 'Orig. Letters,' 1st series, vol. ii. p. 62; also Singer in Cavendish's 'Wolsey,' p. 227.

[2] Meteren, p. 21; Turner's 'Hist. of Henry VIII.,' vol. ii. p. 447.

[3] The meaning is that he addressed the people from each of the three sides of the scaffold.

[4] 'Excerpta Historica,' p. 363. The translation of a Portuguese letter.

hether for to preche, but for to dye, for I have deserved for to dye yf I had xx lyves, more shamefully than can be devysed, for I am a wreched synnar, and I have synned shamefully, I have knowne no man so evell, and to reherse my synnes openly it were no pleaswre to you to here them, nor yet for me to reherse them, for God knowethe all; therefore, mastars all, I pray yow now take hede by me, and especially my lords and gentlemen of the cowrte, the which I have bene amonge, take hede by me, and beware of such a fall, and I pray to God the Fathar, the Sonne and the Holy Ghoste, thre persons and one God, that my deathe may be an example unto yow all, and beware trust not in the vanitie of the worlde and especially in the flateringe of the cowrte. And I cry God mercy, and aske all the worlde forgevenes as willingly as I would have forgevenes of God; and yf I have offendyd any man that is not here now, eythar in thowght, worde, or dede, and if ye here any suche, I pray yow hertely in my behalfe pray them to forgyve me for God's sake. And yet my mastars all, I have one thing for to say to yow: men do comon and saye that I have bene a settar forthe of the worde of God, and one that have favored the Ghospell of Christ; and bycawse I would not that God's word shuld be slaundered by me, I say unto yow all, that yf I had followed God's worde in dede as I dyd rede it and set it forthe to my power, I had not come to this. I dyd red the Ghospell of Christe but I did not follow it; if I had, I had bene a lyves man amonge yow; therefore I pray yow mastars all, for God's sake sticke to the trwthe and folowe it, for one good followere is worthe thre redars, as God knowethe."[1]

And then he knelt down upon his knees and his head was stricken off.

"His body with the head was buried in the chappel of the Tower; the other foure in the churchyarde there."[2]

Bayley in his 'History of the Tower,' states that Rochford was buried in front of the altar.

Queen Anne Boleyn.

Born 1501 (?) or 1507. Beheaded on the green within the Tower, 19th May, 1536.

"On May-day (1536) were a solemne Justes kept at Grenewyche, and sodainly from the Justes the King departed, having not above six persons with him, and came in the

---

[1] 'Chronicle of Calais,' Camden Soc. pp. 46-7.   [2] Holinshed; Stow.

evening from Grenewyche to his place at Westminster. Of this sodain departyng many men mused, but most chiefely the Quene, who the next day was apprehended and brought from Grenewyche to the Tower of London."[1]

Such is the record of the chronicler Holinshed; but some preliminary investigation into the Queen's conduct had already been held on the 24th April; and formal special commissions of oyer and terminer had been issued to the justices of Middlesex and Kent. On the 2nd May, she was examined by some of the Lords of the Council at Greenwich, and she afterwards complained to Sir William Kingston that she was "cruelly handled at Greenwich with the King's council, with the Duke of Norfolk, he said, 'Tut, tut, tut!' shaking his head three or four times."[2]

Queen Anne was brought by water from Greenwich to the Tower, on the same day, viz. Tuesday the 2nd May, at about five o'clock in the afternoon, by "Sir Thomas Audley, Lord Chancellor, Thomas Cromwell, Secretary, and Sir William Kingston, Constable of the Tower;" and when she "came to the Tower gate,[3] entering in she fell on her knees before the saide Lords, beseeching God to help her, as she was not guilty of that whereof she was accused, and then she desired the said Lords to beseech the King's grace to be good unto her, and so they left her there prisoner."[4]

---

[1] Holinshed.

[2] Kingston to Cromwell.—Cotton. MSS. Otho, c. x. f. 224; Ellis's 'Orig. Letters,' 1st series, vol. ii. p. 59; Cavendish's 'Wolsey,' vol. ii. p. 224.

[3] Her daughter Elizabeth, when sent to the Tower, also entered it by this water-gate (Traitors' Gate). "She refused to land, then sharply rejecting an offer of assistance, she sprung out upon the mud. 'Are all those harnessed (armed) men there for me?' she said to Sir John Gage, who was waiting with the Tower guard. 'No, madam,' Gage answered. 'Yes,' she said, 'I know it is so; it needed it not for me, being but a weak woman. I never thought to have come in here a prisoner:' She went on, turning to the soldiers: 'I pray you all, good fellows and friends, bear me witness, that I come in no traitor, but as true a woman to the Queen's majesty as any is now living, and thereon will I take my death." She threw herself down upon a wet stone. Lord Chandos begged her to come under a shelter out of the rain. 'Better sitting here than in a worse place,' she cried; 'I know not whither you will bring me.'"—Froude, vol. vi. pp. 209-10. Both mother and daughter are believed to have occupied the same rooms in the Lieutenant's lodgings whilst in the Tower. On a wall in the Martin Tower is seen the word "Boullen," the letter H, and a Tudor rose: this may have been cut by one of the gentlemen who were executed with Rochford.

[4] Holinshed.

"After those who had brought her to the Tower were departed, the said Constable went before her into her lodging, and then she said to him, 'Mr. Kyngston, shall I go into a dungeon?' He answered her, 'No, madam, you shall go into your lodging, that you lay in at your coronation;' upon which she said, 'It is too good for me,' and further said, 'Jesu, have mercy on me:' and then kneeled down, weeping a great pace, and in the same sorrow, fell into

Traitors' Gate, from the river.

a great laughing: and so she did several times afterwards."[1]

Archbishop Cranmer interceded on her behalf, and on the 3rd May wrote to the King, saying, "I think your Grace best knoweth, that next unto your Grace, I was most bound unto her of all creatures living, and my mind is clean amazed, for I never had better opinion in woman, than I

---

[1] Strype, vol. i. p. 431. See also Kingston to Cromwell, Cotton. MSS. Otho, c. x. f. 225, in Ellis's 'Orig. Letters,' 1st series, vol. ii. p. 53.

Traitors' Gate and St. Thomas's Tower.

had in her: which maketh me to think that she should not be culpable—I wish and pray that she may declare herself inculpable and innocent."[1]

It was on the 6th May that she wrote the well-known letter to King Henry.[2]

"SIR,—Your Grace's displeasure and my imprisonment are things so strange unto me as what to write or what to excuse I am altogether ignorant.

"Whereas you send unto me (willing me to confess a truth, and so to obtain your favour) by such an one whom you know to be mine antient professed enemy. I no sooner conceived this message by him than I rightly conceived your meaning: and if, as you say, confessing a truth indeed may procure my safety, I shall with all willingness and duty perform your command.

"But let not your Grace ever imagine that your poor wife will ever be brought to acknowledge a fault where not so much as a thought thereof proceeded. And to speak a truth, never prince had wife more loyal in all duty and in all true affection, than you have ever found in Anne Boleyn; with which name and place I could willingly have contented myself, if God and your Grace's pleasure had been so pleased. Neither did I at any time so far forget myself in my exaltation or received queenship, but that I always looked for such an alteration as now I find: for the ground of my preferment being on no surer foundation than your Grace's fancy, the least alteration, I knew, was fit and sufficient to draw that fancy to some other subject. You have chosen me from low estate to be your queen and companion, far beyond my desert or desire. If then you found me worthy of such honour, good your Grace, let not any light fancy or bad counsel of mine enemies, withdraw your princely favour from me; neither let that stain, that unworthy stain, of a disloyal heart towards your good Grace, ever cast so foul a blot on your most dutiful wife and the infant princess your daughter.

"Try me good King, but let me have a lawful trial; and let not my sworn enemies sit as my accusers and my judges; yea, let me receive an open trial, for my truth shall fear no open shame. Then shall you

---

[1] See Cotton. MSS. Otho, c. 10. Burnet, book iii. vol. i. p. 402.

[2] The authenticity of this letter has been called in question, but it is accepted as genuine by Mr. J. A. Froude and the late Sir H. Ellis, who remarks, "the original is not remaining now, but the copy was found among Cromwell's papers, with Sir William Kingston's letters, and is certainly in a handwriting of the time of Henry VIII. Queen Anne was too closely guarded to allow of any one concerting such a letter with her."—Ellis's 'Orig. Letters,' 1st series, vol. ii. p. 53. Turner's Henry VIII. vol. ii. p. 439. —It is endorsed "To the King from the Ladye in the Tower," in Cromwell's handwriting.

see either mine innocency cleared, your suspicions and conscience satisfied, the ignominy and slander of the world stopped, or my guilt lawfully declared; so that, whatsoever God or you may determine of me, your Grace may be freed from an open censure; and mine offence being so openly proved, your Grace is at liberty, both before God and man, not only to execute worthy punishment on me, as an unlawful wife, but to follow your affection already settled on that party for whose sake I am now as I am, whose name I could some good while since have pointed unto; your Grace not being ignorant of my suspicion therein.

" But if you have already determined of me; and that not only my death, but an infamous slander, must bring you the joying of your desired happiness; then I desire of God that He will pardon your great sin therein, and likewise my enemies, the instruments thereof; and that He will not call you to a straight account for your unprincely and cruel usage of me, at His general judgment seat, where both you and myself must shortly appear; and in whose judgment I doubt not, whatever the world may think of me, mine innocence shall be openly known and sufficiently cleared.

" My last and only request shall be, that myself may only bear the burden of your Grace's displeasure, and that it may not touch the innocent souls of those poor gentlemen, who, as I understand, are likewise in strait imprisonment for my sake. If ever I have found favour in your sight, if ever the name of Anne Boleyn hath been pleasing in your ears, then let me obtain this request; and I will so leave to trouble your Grace any further; with mine earnest prayers to the Trinity to have your Grace in His good keeping, and to direct you in all your actions. From my doleful prison in the Tower, this 6th of May.[1] Your most loyal and ever faithful wife,

"ANNE BOLEYN."

The Queen was strictly guarded by Sir W. Kingston during the days preceding her trial, and all her conversation was duly reported by letter to Cromwell.[2]

In a letter, written probably on Monday, the 8th May, Kingston says that he has charged

"The gentelwemen that atende apon the Quene that they shuld have now commynycascon with hyr unlese my wyf ware present:

---

[1] Cotton. MSS. Otho, c. 10, f. 228; Burnet, bk. iii.; Records, No. iv.; Herbert's 'Henry VII.,' p. 382. See also Ellis's 'Orig. Letters,' vol. ii. p. 53; Turner's 'Henry VIII.,' vol. ii. p. 439; Froude, vol. ii. pp. 465–7.

[2] These letters (Cottonian MSS. in British Museum) have unfortunately been much injured by fire in 1731.

my Lady Boleyn[1] and meystrys Cosyn lyes on the Quene's pallet, and I and my wyf at the dore withyowt. I have everythyng told me by mestrys Cosyn that shee thynks met for mee to knowe."[2]

All preliminary legal steps had been taken, and on the 15th May the trial of the Queen took place. The charges against her were adultery, and its consequent treason.

"There was a great scaffold made in the Kinge's Hall,[3] and there was made benches and seates for the Lordes. My Lorde of Norfolke[4] sittinge under the clothe of estate, representinge there the Kinge's person as Highe Steward of Englande[5] and uncle to the Quene; he holdinge a longe white staffe in his hande, and the Earle of Surrey, his sonne and heire, sittinge at his feete before him holdinge the golden staffe for the Earle Marshall of Englande, which sayde office the sayde Duke had in his handes; the Lord Audley, Lord Chancellour of England sittinge on his right hande, and the Duke of Suffolke[6] on his left hande, with other marquesses, earles, and lordes, everie one after their degrees."

"And first the Kinge's commission was redd and then the Constable (Sir William Kingston) and the Lieutenant (Sir

---

[1] Her aunt, wife of Sir Edward Boleyn, and Mrs. Cosyns, one of her ladies: both of them were disliked by Queen Anne. She said, "The Kyng wyst what he dyd when hee put two abowt me as my Lady Boleyn and Mestres Cosyn."—Kingston to Cromwell.

[2] Cotton. MSS. Otho, c. x. p. 225; Ellis's 'Orig. Letters,' 1st series, vol. ii. p. 55.

[3] On the second floor in the White tower adjoining the chapel of St. John.

[4] Thomas Howard, third Duke of Norfolk, created Earl Marshal in succession to Charles Brandon, Duke of Suffolk. He was uncle to both Anne Boleyn and Katharine Howard, and upon the attainder of the latter wrote to Henry VIII. saying "the abominable deeds done by two of my nieces against your Highness have brought me into the greatest perplexity that ever poor wretch was in," &c.—'State Papers, Domestic,' vol. i. p. 721. He was afterwards imprisoned in 1546, attainted by Act of Parliament, and the warrant for his execution was sent to the Lieutenant of the Tower: but his life was saved by the death of the King early on the following morning, the Royal executors being unwilling to carry out the sentence. He remained a prisoner until the accession of Queen Mary. He died in 1554, and was buried at Framlingham. For a table showing the genealogy of the Dukes of Norfolk, &c., see Appendix A. p. 325.

[5] For the commission appointing him High Steward, see Birch MSS. in British Museum, No. 4293; Turner's 'Hist. of Henry VIII.,' vol. ii. pp. 443-4.

[6] Charles Brandon, Duke of Suffolk, who married Mary Tudor (the French queen), daughter of Henry VII. and sister of Henry VIII. He died in 1545, and was buried at Windsor.

Edmund Walsingham), brought forthe the Queene to the barre, where was made a chaire for her to sitt downe in, and then her indictment was redd afore her, wherunto she made so wise and discreet answeres to all thinges layde against her, excusinge herselfe with her wordes so clearlie, as thoughe she had never bene faultie to the same.[1] And at length they putt her to the triall of the Peeres of the Realme, and then were twenty-six of the greatest peeres theere present, chosen to passe on her, the Duke of Suffolke being highest, and after they had communed together, the youngest lorde of the saide inquest was called first to give verdict, who sayde guiltie, and so everie lorde and earle after their degrees sayde guiltie to the last, and so condemned her. And then the Duke of Norfolke gave the sentence on her, sayinge: 'Because thou haste offended our Sovereigne the Kinge's Grace, in committinge treason against his person, and here attaynted of the same, the lawe of the realme is this; That thou shalt be brent here within the Tower of London, on the Greene, else to have thy head smitten off as the Kinge's pleasure shal be further knowen of the same.'"

The Duke of Norfolk was in tears as he pronounced this sentence. "I hearde saye that the water roune in his eyes: I blame hym not though it greved him."[2]

The Earl of Northumberland,[3] the Queen's former lover, had left the hall under the plea of illness.[4]

Until recently the impression prevailed that Queen Anne Boleyn had been tried in secret, and condemned almost unheard; it was surmised that all judicial documents relating to her trial had perished, and Sir Henry Ellis even

---

[1] "Having an excellent quick wit, and being a ready speaker, she did so answer all objections that her acquittal was expected."—Harl. MSS. No. 2194.

[2] Constantyne's 'Memorial' in 'Archæologia,' vol. xxiii. p. 66.

[3] Henry Percy, 6th Earl of Northumberland. He died at his house in Hackney, and was buried in the choir of Hackney Church, 30th June, 1537.

—Collins's 'Peerage,' vol. ii. p. 394.

[4] "He was taken with a sudden fit of sickness, and was forced to leave the court. This might have been casual; but since he was once in love with the Queen, and had designed to marry her, it is no wonder if so sad a change in her condition did raise an unusual disorder in him."—Burnet, vol. i. p. 728.

stated, "whether purposely destroyed by Henry VIII. or Queen Elizabeth is not known."[1]

The discovery, however, of the so-called "Baga de Secretis," or pouches containing the legal records of the Court of the King's Bench, has set this matter at rest, and these records, which are now in the State Paper Office, throw much light upon the whole question of the Queen's trial, which is to be found in Pouch ix.: "Sessio tent' apud Turrim, London, coram Thoma Duce Norff: hac vice Senescallo Anglie," &c.; the whole is inscribed on twenty-one membranes.[2] From these documents it is evident that, as has been recently most justly observed, the trial was conducted "with a scrupulousness without a parallel in the criminal records of the time,"[3] and that instead of the summary process of an attainder by Act of Parliament: the ordinary course of justice was followed, and special care was taken to preserve all the original records connected with the trial.[4]

After the trial the Queen was taken "back to warde agayne and two ladies wayted on her, which came in with her at the first, and wayted still on her, whose names were the Ladie Kingstone and the Ladie Boleyn, her aunte."[5]

On Wednesday, the 17th, she was taken to Lambeth to confess to Cranmer; and it is supposed that any statements which she made to him were induced by the prospect of saving her life.[6]

Sir William Kingston continued his reports to Cromwell, and writing on the 16th May, says, "Thys daye at dynar the Quene sayd that she should go to Anveres (Antwerp [7]) and ys in hope of lyf."[8]

[1] Ellis's 'Orig. Letters,' 1st series, vol. ii. p. 52, note.
[2] For 'Baga de Secretis,' see Appendix B. p. 326.
[3] Froude, vol. ii. pp. 479–491. Harl. MSS. No. 2194.
[4] One of these documents is the original panel of the Peers: it is dated Monday, 15th May. The names are pricked off in the margin, probably as they answered to their names when called over, and against each name is written the abbreviated word "Cul" in the handwriting of the Duke of Norfolk: and this in two columns, being evidently the answer "culpabilis" upon each arraignment. See Third Report of Deputy Keeper of Public Records, 1842.
[5] Wrottesley's 'Chronicle,' p. 38.
[6] Burnet, bk. iii. vol. i. p. 411.
[7] Bayley, p. 372, erroneously gives this as "Hanover." Harleian MSS. 283, f. 134.
[8] Ellis's 'Orig. Letters,' 1st series, vol. ii. p. 63.

At times she was cheerful, laughed heartily, and ate her meals with a good appetite. She said to Kingston, "If any man accuse me, I can say but nay, and they can bring no witness:"[1] she also said to him, "I think the King does this to prove me, and did laugh withal and was very mery," and then added, "I shall have justice, I have no doubt therein.[2]

"The day before she suffered, upon a strict search of her past life, she called to mind, that she had played the stepmother too severely to Lady Mary (Princess Mary) and had done her many injuries. Upon which, she made the Lieutenant of the Tower's lady sit down in the chair of state; which the other, after some ceremony, doing, she fell down on her knees, and with many tears charged the lady, as she would answer it to God, to go in her name, and do, as she had done, to the Lady Mary, and ask her forgiveness for the wrongs she had done her."[3]

The following interesting letter addressed to Cromwell has been much injured by fire in 1731, but it had been previously copied by Burnet: it is dated 18th May:—

"SYR,—Thys shal be to advertyse you I have resayved your lettre, wherin you wuld have strangerys conveyed yowt of the Towre, and so they be by the means of Richard Gressum and William Loke and Wythepoll, bot the number of strangerys is not xxx, and not mony of them armed: Hothe and the imbassidor of the Emperor had a servant there, and honestly put yowt. Syr, yf we have not an owre serten as it may be knowen in London, I thynke here wil be bot few, and I thynk a reasonable numbur ware best; for I suppose she wyll declare hyrself to be a good woman for all men bot for the Kyng at the owre of hyr dethe. For thys mornyng she sent for me that I myght be with hyr at soche time as she reysayved the gud lord[4] to the intent I shuld here hyr speak as towchyng hyr innosensy alway to be clere and in the writyng of thys she sent for me, and at my commyng she sayd, 'Mr. Kyngston, I hear say that I shal not dye affore none, and I am very sory therfore; for I thowth to be dede by thys time, and past my payne.' I told hyr it shuld be now payne it was so sottel; and then she sayd, I have hard say the execut' was very gud, and I have a lyttel neck, and put her hand abowt it lawyng hartely.

"I have sen many men and also wemen executed, and that they

---

[1] Lingard, vol. v. p. 33.
[2] Cotton. MSS. Otho, c. x. fol. 224; Cavendish's 'Wolsey,' vol. ii. p. 224.
[3] Burnet, bk. iii. vol. i. p. 410.
[4] The sacrament.

have been in grete sorrow; and to my knowlidge thys lady hasse meche joy and plesur in dethe. Syr, her almoner ys continewaly with hyr and hasse bene syns ij of the clocke, after mydnighte. This is the effect of hony thyng that ys here at thys tyme, and thus fare you well.

"Yours,

"To Mas^{tr} Secretory.   WILL^M KYNGSTON."[1]

Queen Anne Boleyn was brought to the scaffold a little before noon on the 19th May, where "a great company came to look on the last scene of this fatal tragedy : the chief of whom were the Dukes of Suffolk and Richmond,[2] the Lord Chancellor and Secretary Cromwell, with the Lord Mayor, the Sheriffs, and Aldermen, of London.[3]

An account of the Queen's execution, which bears every appearance of being that of an eye-witness, is contained in a letter from a Portuguese gentleman to a friend in Lisbon, which is preserved in the Library of the Monastery of Alcobaca, in Portugal.[4]

"From London, the 10th day of June, 1536.

* * * * * *

"On the next Friday, which was the 19th of the same month, the Queen was beheaded according to the manner and custom of Paris, that is to say, with a sword, which thing had not before been seen in this land of England. And a scaffold, having four or five steps, was then and there set up. And the unhappy Queen, assisted by the Captain of the Tower, came forth, together with the four ladies who accompanied her; and she was wholly habited in a robe of black damask, made in such guise that the cape, which was white, did fall on the outer side thereof. And then she besought the Captain of the Tower that he would in no wise hasten the minute of her death, until she should have spoken that which she had in mind to say; which he consented to, she said as followeth:

"Good friends, I am not come here to excuse or to justify myself, forasmuch as I know full well that aught that I could say in my defence doth not appertain unto you, and that I could draw no hope of life from the same. But I come here only to die, and thus to yield myself humbly to the will of the King my Lord. And if in my life I did ever offend the King's grace, surely with my death, I do now atone

---

[1] Cotton. MSS. Otho, c. x. f. 223; Ellis's 'Orig. Letters,' 1st series, pp. 64, 65.

[2] Henry Fitzroy, natural son of Henry VIII., to whom precedence had been granted in 1525 above all Dukes excepting those of the Blood Royal; he died in 1536.

[3] Burnet, bk. iii. vol. i. p. 412.

[4] A translation by Viscount Strangford is given in Sir H. Nicolas's 'Excerpta Historica,' pp. 260–5.

for the same. And I blame not my judges, nor any other manner of person, nor anything save the cruel law of the land by which I die. But be this, and my faults as they may, I beseech you all, good friends, to pray for the life of the King my Sovereign Lord and yours, who is one of the best princes on the face of the earth, and who hath always treated me so well that better could not be: wherefore I submit to death with a good will, humbly asking pardon of all the world."

This speech agrees in the main with that which is recorded in Hall and Stow's chronicles. The following is Hall's version:

"Good christen people, I am come hether to dye, for accordyng to the lawe and by the lawe I am judged to dye, and therefore I wyll speake nothyng against it. I am come hether to accuse no man, nor to speake anything of that whereof I am accused and condempned to dye, but I pray God save the King and send him long to reigne over you, for a gentler nor a more mercyfull prince was there never, and to me he was ever a good, a gentle and soveraigne lorde. And if any persone will meddle in my cause, I require them to judge the best. And thus I take my leve of the worlde, and of you all, and I heartley desyre you all to pray for me."[1]

"Then with her own hands she took her coifs from her head[2] and delivered them to one of her ladies, and then putting on a little cap of linen to cover her hair withal she said, "Alas, poor head, in a very brief space thou wilt roll in the dust on the scaffold. And ye, my damsels, who, whilst I lived, ever showed yourselves so diligent in my service, and who are now to be present at my last hour and mortal agony, as in good fortune ye were faithful to me, so even at this my miserable death yet do not forsake me.[3] And as I cannot reward you for your true service to me, I pray you take comfort for my loss; howbeit, forget me not; and, in your prayers to the Lord Jesu, forget not to pray for my

[1] Hall's 'Chronicle.' The following is the version of the speech in Constantyne's 'Memoirs': "Good people, I do not intend to reason my death, but I remit me to Christ wholly, in whom I trust, desiring you all to pray for the King's majesty that he may long reign over you; for he is a very noble prince and full gently hath handled me."

[2] "Then with the aid of her maids, she undressed her neck with great courage."—Meteren, 'Hist. des Pays Bas;' Burnet, bk. iii. pt. iii. vol. v. p. 231.

[3] It is said she died with resolution, and so sedately as herself to cover her feet with her garments.—Turner's 'Hist. of Henry VIII.,' vol. ii. p. 455.

soul." And being minded to say no more, she knelt down upon both knees, and one of her ladies covered her eyes with a bandage, and then they withdrew themselves some little space and knelt down over against the scaffold, bewailing bitterly and shedding many tears.

And thus, and without more to say or do, was her head stricken off; she making no confession of her fault, and only saying, "O Lord God, have pity on my soul!" and one of her ladies then took up the head and the others the body, and covering them with a sheet did put them into a chest which there stood ready, and carried them to the church which is within the Tower, where, they say, she lieth buried with the others."[1]

"Her head," says Burnet, "was cut off by the hangman of Calais, who was brought over as being more expert at beheading than any other in England: her eyes and lips were observed to move after her head was cut off, as Spelman writes, and her body was thrown into a common chest of elm tree, that was made to put arrows in."[2] Stow says, "Suddenly the hangman of Calais smote off her head at one stroke with a sword; her body with the head was buried in the quire of the chapel in the Tower."[3]

---

[1] 'Excerpta Historica,' pp. 260-265; Turner's 'Henry VIII.' vol. ii. p. 463-4.
[2] Burnet, bk. iii. vol. i. p. 412.
[3] Stow; Weever. A romantic and fanciful story is printed in Disraeli's 'Curiosities of Literature,' which is taken from Houssaie's 'Memoirs,' vol. i. p. 435. Disraeli says, "it may have been preserved by tradition in France."

"Anne Boleyn, being on the scaffold, would not consent to have her eyes covered with a bandage, saying she had no fear of death. All that the divine who assisted at her execution* could obtain from her was, that she would shut her eyes. But as she was opening them at every moment, the executioner could not bear their tender and mild glances; fearful of missing his aim, he was obliged to invent an expedient to behead the queen.

"He drew off his shoes, and approached her silently; while he was at her left hand, another person advanced at her right, who made a great noise in walking, so that this circumstance drawing the attention of Anne, she turned her face from the executioner, who was enabled by this artifice to strike the fatal blow without being disarmed by that spirit of affecting resignation which shone in the eyes of the lovely Anne Boleyn."— Disraeli's 'Curiosities of Literature,' vol. ii. p. 297.

Miss Strickland makes reference in her 'History of the Queens of England' to a Norfolk tradition, viz., that the remains of Anne Boleyn were "secretly removed from the Tower church under cover of darkness, and privately conveyed to Salle church, the ancient burial-place of the Boleyns. A plain black marble slab without any inscription is still shown in Salle church as a monumental memorial of this queen."

Another tradition, also mentioned by

* No divine attended her on the scaffold.

108   ST. PETER AD VINCULA.

The closing scene is graphically described by a recent historian: "A little before noon on the 19th of May, Anne Boleyn, Queen of England, was led down to the green, where the young grass and the first daisies of summer were freshly bursting in the sunshine. A single cannon stood loaded on the battlements, the motionless cannoneer was ready, with smoking linstock at his side; and, when the crawling hand upon the dial of the great tower clock touched the mid-day hour, that cannon would tell to London that all was over. The yeomen of the guard were there, and a crowd of citizens; the Lord Mayor too, and the deputies of the guilds, and the sheriffs, and the aldermen; they were come to see a spectacle which England had never seen before—a head which had worn the crown falling under the sword of the executioner."[1]

In February, 1866, a communication was by command of Queen Victoria addressed to the First Commissioner of Works, stating Her Majesty's wish that the spot where Queen Anne Boleyn and others had been executed should be protected by a railing, and that an inscription on a brass plate which records that event should be renewed.

On a stone within the railing are the following words, "Site of the ancient scaffold: on this spot Queen Anne Boleyn was beheaded on the 19th May, 1536."

Miss Strickland, is that, "a nameless black marble slab in the church of Hornden on the hill in Essex," is believed to cover Anne Boleyn's remains. —'Queens of England,' vol. iv. p. 293.

These traditions are not supported by any definite evidence, and are not even alluded to by the historians of the counties of Norfolk and Essex: they may be therefore considered as baseless, as the tradition that Charles I. was buried in the dead of night on Naseby field; that the body of Lady Jane Grey was removed to the chapel at Bradgate; that it was not James Duke of Monmouth, who was executed in 1685, and similar other popular beliefs.

[1] Froude, vol. ii. pp. 497-8.

Thomas Cromwell, Earl of Essex.

Born, —— Beheaded on Tower Hill, 28th July, 1540.

"Cromwell, surnamed the Great, whom Wolsey first raised from the forge to eminent good fortunes,[1] lies here interred. He followed the same steps to the same stage upon the said Tower Hill, and acted there the same part which his two friends, More and Fisher, had done before him, and that within five years after."[2]

Such is the statement of the antiquary Weever, and the story of Cromwell's life is one of the most remarkable episodes in the history of that period of startling change and stirring excitement in which he lived.

The circumstances of his arrest and committal to the Tower are thus related: "The King's wrath was kindled against all those that were preferrers of this match,[3] whereof the Lord Cromwell was the chiefe, for the which, and for dealing somewhat too far in some matters beyond the King's good liking, were the occasions of his hastie death."[4]

On the morning of the 10th June, Cromwell attended as usual in his place at the House of Lords, but at three in the afternoon of the same day "being in the Counsaill chamber he was sodainly apprehended and committed to the Tower of London, the whiche many lamented, but more rejoysed, and specially suche as either had been religious men or favoured religious persones, for they banqueted and triumphed together that night, many wisshying that that daie had been seven yere before; and some fearynge least he should escape, although he were imprisoned, could not be mery. Others who knewe nothing but truth by hym bothe lamented hym, and hartely praied for hym. But this is true that of certain of the clergie he was detestably hated, and specially of suche as had borne swynge and by his meanes was put from it, for indede he was a man that in all his doynges seemed not to

---

[1] "He was borne in Putney, a village in Surrey, by the Thames side, about four miles west from London, and was sonne to a blacksmith, in his later days a brewer."—Stow.

[2] Weever, p. 282.

[3] The King's marriage with Anne of Cleves.

[4] Stow.

favor any kynde of Popery, nor could not abide the snoffyng pride of some prelates, which, whatever els was the cause of his death, did shorten his life and procured the ende that he was brought unto; whiche was that the xix daie of the said monethe he was attaynted by Parliament and never came to his answere, which lawe many reported he was the causer of the making thereof;[1] but the truthe thereof I knowe not. The articles for which he died apperith in the record where his attaynder is written, which are too long to bee here rehersed, but to conclude was there attainted of heresy and high treason."[2]

His friend Cranmer endeavoured to intercede on his behalf, and wrote thus to the King:

"I heard yesterday at your Grace's council that the Earl of Essex is a traitor, yet who cannot bee sorrowful and amazed that he should bee a traitor against your Majesty; he whose surety was only by your Majesty; he who loved loved your Majesty (as I ever thought) no lesse than God; he who studied alwaies to set forward whatsoever was your Majesties will and pleasure. He that cared for no man's displeasure to serve your Majesty; he that was such a servant in my judgment, in wisdom, diligence, faithfulnesse, and experience, as no prince in this realm ever had. He that was so vigilant to preserve your Majesty from all treasons, that few could be so secretly conceived but he detected the same in the beginning? If the noble Princes of memory, King John, Henry the second, and Richard the second, had had such a counsellor about them, I suppose they should never have been so traiterously abandoned and overthrown as those good Prince's were." After which, he saies again: "I loved him as my friend, for so I took him to be, but I chiefly loved him for the love which I thought I saw him bear towards your Grace, singularly above all other, but now, if he be a traitor, I am sorry that ever I loved him, or trusted him, and I am very glad that his treason is discovered in time; but yet againe I am very sorrowfull; for who shall your Grace trust hereafter, if you might not trust him? Alas! I bewaile and lament your Grace's chance herein, I wot not whom your Grace may trust. But I pray God continually night and day to send suche a counsellor in his place whom your Grace may trust, and who for all his qualities can and will serve your Grace like to him, and that will have so much sollicitude and care to preserve your Grace from all danger, as I ever thought he had."

[1] See p. 119.   [2] Hall's 'Chronicle.'

"All of which," says Lord Herbert, "as being a character of Cromwell in Cranmer's opinion, I have faithfully copied out of the originall."[1]

Fox remarks of his conduct and demeanour whilst a prisoner in the Tower, "Who so long as he went with full sayle of fortune, how modderately and how temperately hee did ever beare himselfe in his estate, before hath beene declared; so now the sayd Lord Cromwell, alwayes one man, by the contrarie winde of adversitie being overblowen, received the same with no less constancie and patience of a christian hart."

"Being in the Tower a prisoner, how quietly he bore it, how valiantly he behaved himselfe, how gravely and discretly he aunswered and entertained the Commissioners sent unto him, it is worthie of noting. Whatsoever articles and interrogatories they propounded, they could put nothing unto him, either concerning matters ecclesiasticall or temporall, wherein he was not more ripened and more furnished in everie condition than they themselves. Amongst the rest of those Commissioners which came unto him, one there was whome the Lord Cromwell desired to carry from him a letter to the King, which then he refused, saying that he would carry no letter to the King from a traytor; then the Lord Cromwell desired him at least to do from him a message to the King. So that the other was contented and granted, so that it were not against his allegeance. Then the Lord Cromwell, taking witnesse of the other lords what he had promised, 'You shall commend me (sayd he) to the King and tell him, by that he hath so well tryed and thoroughly proved you as I have done, he shall finde you as false a man as ever came about him.'"

The bill of attainder was brought into the House of Lords on the 17th June, it accused him of heresy and high treason, and stated that, though "raised by the King from a base degree to great dignities and high trusts, yet he was now by a great number of witnesses, persons of honor, found to be the most corrupt traitor and deceiver of the King and

[1] Herbert's 'Life of Henry VIII.' p. 457.

Crown that had been known during the whole reign."[1] It was read for a second and third time on the 19th June, and without any opportunity of receiving any reply from Cromwell, or of hearing any witnesses on his behalf, it was received from the House of Commons with certain amendments and passed on the 29th June, after which he was condemned to death.[2]

On the 30th June he wrote imploringly to the King, and concluded his letter with these words :

"I, a most woeful prisoner, ready to take the death when it shall please God and your Majesty; and yet the frail flesh inciteth me continually to call to your Grace for mercy and grace for mine offences.

"And thus Christ save, preserve and keep you.

"Written at the Tower, this Wednesday the last of June, with the heavy heart and trembling hand of your Highness' most heavy and most miserable prisoner and poor slave,

"THOMAS CROMWELL.

"Most gracious Prince, I cry for mercy, mercy, mercy!"[3]

"Beside this, he wrote also a letter from the Tower to the King, whereof when none durst take the carriage upon him, Sir Ralfe Sadler[4] (whome he also had preferred to the King before, being ever trustie and faithful unto him) went to the King to understand his pleasure, whether he would permit him to bring the letter or not; which, when the King had granted, the sayd Mr. Sadler as he was required presented the letter unto the King, when he commanded thrice to bee read unto him, insomuch as the King seemed to be moved therewith." This refers to a letter written on the 3rd July, when he again addressed the King at considerable length,

---

[1] Burnet, bk. iii. No. xvi. Records.
[2] The peers are said to have voted unanimously, and Cranmer was present when the bill was read a third time; but there is nothing to show that he was present at the division.
[3] Burnet, bk. iii.; Records, pt. xvii.
[4] Sir Ralph Sadler was born in 1507, brought up by Cromwell, and was his clerk when solicitor to Wolsey; was introduced to Henry VIII.'s court by Cromwell, appointed one of the King's Secretaries and a Privy Councillor: Queen Elizabeth appointed him Chancellor of the Duchy of Lancaster, and in 1571 he was (with Lord Burleigh and Sir Walter Mildmay) one of the Commissioners for inquiring into the conduct of the Duke of Norfolk: he died in 1587.

and replied to the charges of treason that had been brought against him, and says:

"As to your commonwealth, I have, after my wytt, power and knowledge, travayled therein, having had no respect to persons, your Majestie only except and my duty to the same."

He repeatedly asks for pardon, and declares he never

"thought treason to your Highness, your realme, or posteritie,"

and he concludes thus,

"wrytin with the quaking hand and most sorowfull harte of your most sorowful subject and most humble servaunt and prisoner: this Satyrday, at your Tower of London.   "THOMAS CROMWELL."[1]

Whatever inclination for mercy these letters may have awakened in King Henry was probably overruled by the influence of Gardiner and the Duke of Norfolk, and the 28th July was fixed for Cromwell's execution.

On that morning "first calling for his breakfast, and therewith eating the same, and after that passing out of his prison, downe the hill within the Tower, and meeting there by the way the Lord Hungerford, going likewise to his execution, and perceiving him to be all heavy and doleful, with chearful countenance and comfortable words, asking him why he was so heavy, hee willed to pluck up his heart and to be of good comfort; for, sayd he, there is no cause for you to feare; if you repent and be heartilie sorie for that you have done there is for you mercie enough of the Lord, who for Christe's sake will forgive you, and therefore be not dismaid; and though the breakfast which we are going to be sharpe, yet, trusting in the mercie of the Lord, we shall have a joyfull dinner. And so went they together to the place of execution and took their death patientlie."[2] The following was his speech to the people, which he is said to have spoken on the scaffold.

[1] Cotton. MSS. Titus, E. 1, f. 267; Burnet, bk. iii. pt. iii.; Records, p. 218; Bayley, App. xliii.; and Ellis's 'Orig. Letters,' 2nd series, vol. ii. p. 162, give the entire letter.
[2] Fox's Acts, p. 1095.

"THE WORDES OF THE LORDE CROMWELL, SPOKEN AT HIS DEATH.

" I am come hether to dye, and not to purge myself, as maie happen, some thynke that I will, for if I should so do, I wer a very wretche and miser: I am by the lawe condempned to die, and thanke my Lord God that hath appoynted me this deathe, for myne offence: For sithence the tyme that I have had yeres of discrecion, I have lived a synner, and offended my Lorde God, for the whiche I aske hym hartely forgeveness.

" And it is not unknowne to many of you that I have been a traveler in this worlde, and beyng but of base degree, was called to high estate, and sithence the tyme I came thereunto, I have offended my prince, for the whiche I aske hym hartely forgeveness, and beseche you all to praie to God with me, that he will forgeve me. O father forgeve me, O sonne forgeve me, O holy Ghost forgeve me: O thre persons in one God forgeve me.

" And now I praie you that be here, to beare me record I die in the Catholicke faithe, not doubtyng in any article of my faith, no, nor doubtyng in any sacrament of the churche. Many hath sclaundered me, and reported that I have been a bearer of suche as hath mainteigned evill opinions, whiche is untrue, but I confesse that like as God by his holy spirite doth instruct us in the truth, so the devill is redy to seduce us, and I have been seduced: but beare me witnes that I dye in the Catholicke faithe of the holy churche.[1] And I hartely desire you to praie for the Kinge's grace, that he maie long live with you in healthe and prosperitie. And after him that his sonne Prince Edward, that goodly ympe, maie long reigne over you. And once again I desire you to praie for me, that so long as life remaigneth in this fleshe, I waver nothyng in my faithe."[2]

This speech was printed and circulated and was considered as authentic by Hall, the chronicler; from his pages it has been transferred into English history, but Cardinal Pole, who had first believed it to be genuine, warned a correspondent, " on the authority of persons whose account could be relied upon, that the words which he really spoke were very different."[3]

---

[1] Burnet says, "he died a Lutheran. The words 'Catholic faith,' used by him in his speech seemed to make it doubtful: but that was then used in England in its true sense, in opposition to the novelties of the see of Rome; so his profession of the Catholic faith was strangely perverted, when some from thence concluded that he died in the communion of the Church of Rome." —Burnet, bk. iii. vol. i. p. 570.

[2] Hall's 'Chronicle'; Fox; Stow, &c.

[3] Froude, vol. iii. p. 521.

It is not possible to determine what words he really did use, but the following from the Harleian MSS. is apparently genuine, and may be the record of an eye-witness. It is certainly more touching than the foregoing set speech,[1] "printed by authority and to be circulated through Europe."

"And then kneeled he adowne and saide his prayeres, in the which prayeres were contayned thys worde: 'O Lord, grant me that when these eyes lose their use, that the eyes of my soule may see Thee;' and also, 'O Lord and father, when thys mouth shall lose his use that my heart may say "O Pater, in manus tuas commendo spiritum meum;"' and after thys prayer he stoode uppe agayne, and said, 'Pray for the Prince, and for all the lordes of the councelle, and for the clergye, and for the commonaltye, and nowe I pray you all ageyne that ye wille pray for me.' And then he turned hym abowte and sayde, 'Farewelle, Wyatt,[2] and gentylle Wyatt, pray for me.'"[3]

"And after that, he committed his soule into the handes of God, and so paciently suffered the stroke of the axe by a ragged and boocherly miser,[4] which very ungoodly performed the office."[5]

His body was brought back into the Tower, and buried in St. Peter's.

His character has been thus given:—"Great scholar he was none, the Latin Testament gotten by heart being his masterpiece; nor studied lawyer, never admitted to the Inns of Court; nor experienced soldier, though necessity cast him upon it; nor courtier, till bred up in Cardinal Wolsey's court: yet that of the lawyer in him so helped the scholar, that of the soldier the lawyer, that of the courtier the soldier, and that of the traveller all the rest: being no stranger to Germany, well acquainted with France, most familliar with Italy; that the result of all together made him for endowments eminent, not to say admirable. His apprehension was quick and clear; his judgment methodical and solid; his memory quick and rational; his tongue fluent and

---

[1] It was published by Redman, "cum privilegio ad imprimendum solum."
[2] Sir Thomas Wyatt, the elder, b. 1503, d. 1541.
[3] Harleian MSS. No. 3362.
[4] Miser—a miserable or wretched fellow.
[5] Stow; Hall: Fox, 'Acts and Monuments.'

pertinent; his presence stately and obliging; his heart large and noble; his temper patient and cautious; his way industrious and indefatigable; his correspondence well laid and constant; his converse insinuating and close. None more dexterous to find out by his setting-dogs and decoy ducks, none more reserved to keep a secret. He was equal, saith my author, to the French politicians when under his master, he ever over-reached them when alone; doing more in one month with his subtle head than the other in twelve months with his stately train." [1]

MARGARET PLANTAGENET, COUNTESS OF SALISBURY.

Born, 1470. Beheaded within the Tower, 27th May, 1541.

Margaret Plantagenet, Countess of Salisbury, and widow of Sir Richard Pole, was the daughter of George, Duke of Clarence, and niece of King Edward IV.: she had been appointed by Katharine of Arragon to be governess to the Princess Mary, and her name appears in the household lists in that capacity from 1525 to 1533.[2]

"But," says Sandford, "proving as great an eye sore to King Henry VIII. as her brother[3] had been to King Henry VII., she was condemned in Parliament (31 Hen. 8) for high treason, and committed to the Tower."[4]

Cardinal Pole was her son, and she was accused of being concerned in the treasonable plots of the Cardinal and his brothers, and in the "Pilgrimage of Grace." It was also alleged that she had opposed the suppression of the monasteries, and had designed to marry her son, Reginald Pole, to the Princess Mary. In November, 1538, Lord Southampton [5] and the Bishop of Ely [6] were sent by Cromwell to her resi-

---

[1] Lloyd's 'State Worthies,' p. 58.
[2] See Madden's 'Expenses of Princess Mary.'
[3] Edward, Earl of Warwick, beheaded on Tower Hill, 28th Nov. 1499.
[4] Sandford, p. 441.
[5] William FitzWilliam, created Earl of Southampton in 1537, Admiral of England. He died in 1543.
[6] Thomas Goodrich, Bishop of Ely from 1534 to 1554.

dence, at Warblington,[1] near Havant, to examine her, and to obtain evidence against her. They reported to Cromwell in the following letters.

"Please it your good Lordshippe to bee advertised that as by our oodre lettres wee signified to the same wee wold, so yesturday the xiij[th] of this Novembre, wee travayled with the Ladie of Sarisbury al day both before and aftre none, til almost night. Albeit, for all that wee could doo, thoughe wee usely her diversely, she wold uttre and confesse little or nothing more than the first day she did, but stil stood and persisted in the deniall of all togidres. And this day between viij and ix in the morning, having received your Lordshippe's lettres dated from Westminster the said xiij[th] wee furthwith upon recete of the same, eftsones repayred unto the said Lady. And first afore wee came to hir sight, calling hir men servaunts afore us, according to the continew of your said lettres, wee apprehended Standishe: and that doone went in hand with hir.

"And althoughe wee than entreatid her in both sorts, some tyme with doulx and myld wordes, now roughly and asperly, by traytring her and her sonnes to the ix[th] degree, yet woll she nothing uttre, but making herself clere, and as unspotted, utterly denieth all that is object unto hir: and that with most stif and ernest wordes: sayeng that if ever it bee found and proved in her that she is culpable in any of those things that she hath denied, that she is content to be blasund in the rest of all the articles layd against her. Surely, if it like your Lordshippe, wee suppose that there hatbe not been seen or heard of a woman so ernest in her   *   *   , so manlique in contenance, and so precise as well in gesture as in wordes.
    *   *   *   *   *[2]

"Nowe that wee have seized her goodes and given her notice that the Kinge's pleasure is she shall go, she seemeth thereat to be somewhat appaled.
       *   *   *   *   *

"Thus the holy Trinitee preserve your Lordshippe. From the manor of Warblington, the xiiij[th] of Novembre, late in the night.
  "Your Lordshippes assured
              "W. SOUTHAMPTON.
              "THOMAS ELIEN."[3]

On the 16th November they again write:

"Wee have now removed the Lady of Sarisbury, & this last night arrived with the same at Cowdrey.[4] And where in the same our

---

[1] Some slight ruins of the castle are still remaining.
[2] Much of this letter has perished.
[3] Cotton. MSS. Caligula, D. xi.
Ellis's 'Original Letters,' 2nd series, vol. ii. pp. 111–13.
[4] Cowdray, near Midhurst, then the residence of Lord Southampton.

118   ST. PETER AD VINCULA.

Lettres wee touched our opinions, that beeing removed, she would perhappes uttre something more than alreadie she had doone: so this shall bee to advertise you that syns our arrivall here, travayleng sondry tymes and aftre sondry sortes with her, somwhat elles of newe have wee goten of her wich wee deeme materiall. And likwise laboreng with Standishe have pycked owt of him more than in the beginning wee could.   *   *   *   *   *

"Wee assure your Lordshippe wee have dealid with suche a one, as men have not dealed withal to fore us: we may call her rather a strong and constant man, than a woman.
     *   *   *   *   *   *

"In Standishe's chambre were found lettres, wherein were enclosed certayne bulles graunted by a bushoppe of Rome."[1]   *   *   *

Robert Warner writes to Lord Fitzwalter:

"21 Nov.

"My Lady Marques of Exceter ys in the Tower, and my Lady of Salysbery ys in holde; but where I cannot tell: but ther ys lyke to be a fowle worke among them."[2]

After remaining a few days at Cowdray, she was brought to the Tower.

The immediate grounds of her arrest were the opposition which her son, Cardinal Pole, had offered to some measures of the King, but nothing could be urged against her, and she behaved with so much firmness, in the conscious integrity of innocence, as to disconcert her persecutors. An attempt was therefore made to attaint her without trial or confession, and at length her name, with others, was introduced into a bill of attainder,[3] found against several persons who had been condemned by the lower courts, though none of them had confessed any crime, or had been heard in their own defence.

"Some," says Burnet, "were to be attainted who had been accused of holding correspondence with Cardinal Pole, who was then trafficking with foreign princes, and projecting a league among them against the King. Some were to be attainted in absence: others they had no mind to bring to

[1] Cotton. MSS. Caligula, D. xi.; Ellis's 'Orig. Letters,' 2nd series, vol. ii. pp. 112–15.
[2] Cotton. MSS. Tib. b. i. f. 140. Ellis's 'Orig. Letters,' 1st series, vol. ii. p. 96.
[3] "The eight and twentieth daie of Aprill (1539) began a parliament at Westminster, in the which, Margaret, Countess of Salisbury, and Gertrude, wife to the Marques of Excestre, were attainted of high treason."—Hall.

make their answer, but yet designed to attaint them. Such were the Marchioness of Exeter and the Countess of Sarum, mother to Cardinal Pool, whom, by a gross mistake, Speed fancies to have been condemned without arraignment or trial, as Cromwell had been by Parliament: for she was now condemned, a year before him. About the justice of doing this there was some debate; and to clear it, Cromwell sent for the judges, and asked their opinions whether a man might be attainted in parliament without being brought to make his answer? They said it was a dangerous question: that the parliament ought to be an example to all inferior courts: and that when any person was charged with a crime, he, by the common rule of justice and equity, should be heard to plead for himself. But the parliament being the supreme court of the nation, what way soever they proceeded, it must be good in law; and it could never be questioned, whether the party was brought to answer or not: and thus a very ill precedent was made, by which the most innocent person in the world might be ruined. And this, as has often been observed in the like cases, fell very soon heavily on the author of the counsel."[1]

Amongst some of the accusations against her were, " that bulls from the Pope were found in her house: that she kept up correspondence with her son, and that she forbade her tenants to have the New Testament in English, or any other books that had been published by the King's authority."[2]

She was examined more than once whilst in prison, and Burnet records that though nearly seventy years of age, she showed by the answers which she made, that she had a vigorous and masculine mind.

Cromwell writes to Henry VIII. on 19th April, 1539. "The Marquise hath been examined, and in effect, albeit she pretendeth ignorance and no knowledge of the person that shuld reporte the tale, yet nevertheles she confesseth in substance the moch like wordes to have ben told her."[3]

---

[1] Burnet, bk. iii. vol. i. p. 530. Ellis's 'Orig. Letters,' 2nd series, vol. i. p. 138.
[2] Ibid., bk. iii. vol. i. p. 721.
[3] Cotton. MSS. Titus, B. i. f. 265.

Towards the close of the session of parliament in 1540, Henry sent in a general pardon for many political prisoners, but in particular "exempted the Countess of Sarum, with many others then in prison." He probably kept her in the Tower as a hostage, "designing to oblige her son, Cardinal Pole, and her friends, to a better behaviour," but upon a fresh provocation by a new rebellion in the north,[1] she was beheaded, and in her the name and line of Plantagenet determined.[2]

The Marchioness of Exeter had previously died a natural death in the Tower.

"Shortly after," writes Lord Herbert, "followed the Countesse of Salisbury's execution (27 May, 1541). The old lady being brought to the scaffold (set up in the Tower), was commanded to lay her head on the block: but she (as a person of great quality assured mee) refused, saying, so should traitors do, and I am none: neither did it serve that the executioner told her it was the fashion; so turning her gray head every way, shee bid him if hee would have her hedd, to get it as hee could: so that he was constrained to fetch it off slovenly."[3]

Lingard, quoting from a letter of Cardinal Pole,[4] states that her last words were, "Blessed are they who suffer persecution for righteousness sake."[5]

She was buried in the church at St. Peter, and Bayley, referring to the interments in the chancel, says, "here rests amid the attainted group, the mangled corse of the venerable and innocent Margaret, Countess of Salisbury."[6] During her imprisonment, we find that Thomas Phillips, one of the jailers in the Tower, writes probably to some member of the Privy Council—

"The Lady Salisbury maketh great moan, for that she wanteth necessary apparel, both for to change, and also

---

[1] In 1541 five priests and ten secular persons, some of them being gentlemen of quality, were raising a new rebellion in Yorkshire, which was suppressed in time, and the promoters of it being apprehended, were attainted and executed: but this occasioned the death of the Countess of Sarum.

[2] Burnet, bk. iii. vol. i. p. 722.

[3] Herbert's 'Henry VIII. (1649),' p. 468.

[4] 'Epist. Reg. Pole,' vol. iii. p. 76.

[5] Lingard, vol. v. p. 62.

[6] Bayley, vol. i. p. 120.

to keep her warm. Her gentlewoman, Mistress Constance, hath no manner of change, and that that she hath is sore worn. Another gentlewoman she hath, that is master comptroller's maid, and hath been with her one whole year and more, and very sorry she is that she hath not to recompense them at the least their wages."[1]

The result of this letter is shown in the following memorandum of the Privy Council.

On 1st March, 1541, a "letter was sent to Stutt, the Queene's tailor, to provide and make meet for the late Countess of Sarum, being prisoner in the Tower, the parcels of apparel and other necessaries ensuing: Inprimis, a night gown furred, a kirtle of worsted, and petticoat furred. Item, another gown of the fashion of night gown of saye,[2] lined with satin of eyprus, and faced with satin. Item, a bonnet with frontlet. Item, four pair of hose. Item, four pair of shoes and one pair of slippers."[3]

The payments for these articles appear in a 'Book of Household Payments' for 1541.

Item "paid to Johne Stutt, the Queene's tailor, by the Kinge's warrente, dated xii Aprilis A° xxxij for certain apparaile by him bought and made for Margret Pole, late Countesse of Salisbury, xj*li*. xvj*s*. iiij*d*. Also item, paid to Sir Edward Walsingham,[4] Lieutenant of the Tower, for the board wages of a woman for attending on the late Countess of Salisbury in the Tower, the space of eighty-three weeks at 18*d*. the week, 6*l*. 4*s*. 6*d*. Charges for provisions for one year and a half, 60*s*.; other necessaries, 66*s*. 8*d*. Total, 12*l*. 11*s*. 2*d*."[5]

She was Lady of the manor of Christchurch, in Hampshire, and had erected in that church on the north side of the altar the elegant chapel, still called the Salisbury chapel, for her own burial-place. In the central boss of the fan tracery of the roof is a representation, much mutilated, of

---

[1] Miscellaneous Exchequer Documents, 1st series, No. 1752.
[2] A kind of cloth.
[3] 'Acts of Privy Council,' vol. vii. p. 147.
[4] Sir Ed. Walsingham was lieutenant for twenty-two years.
[5] Account book of Henry VIII. Arundel MSS. 97, fol. 185, and Green's Letters, vol. iii. p. 94.

the Trinity, with the figure of the Countess in front, kneeling at the feet of God the Father. The armorial bearings of the Countess were on the eastern boss, and below can still be read her motto "Spes mea in deo est." The commissioners for the suppression of monasteries reported, "in thys churche we founde a chaple and monument curioslie made of Cane stone, paryd (prepared) by the late mother of Regnold Pole for herre buryall, whiche we have causyd to be defacyd, and all the arms and badgis clerly to be deleted:" and in this condition does the chapel remain at the present time.

During the repairs in 1834, two receptacles for coffins were discovered below the floor of this chapel, which were probably intended for the countess, and her son the cardinal, but seemed never to have been used.[1]

Queen Katharine Howard,

Born, 1520.   Beheaded within the Tower, 13th February, 1542,

and

Jane, Viscountess Rochford,

Born, ——.   Beheaded within the Tower, 13th February, 1542.

King Henry VIII. left Hampton Court for Oatlands upon receiving the first intimations of the immoral conduct of which Queen Katharine Howard was accused; and the Archbishop of Canterbury (Cranmer) and the Lord Chancellor (Audley) and the Duke of Norfolk were appointed to have an interview with the Queen, so as to endeavour to obtain from her either some refutation or confession of her guilt.

The result of two interviews was communicated by Cranmer in a letter addressed to the King, which he received "with

---

[1] Ferrey's 'Christ Church,' p. 40.

such inward sorrow that it was the most woful thing to see it. His heart was so pierced with pensiveness, that it was long before he could speak and utter his sorrows to us; but finally, with plenty of tears, which was strange to his courage, he gave vent to his feelings."[1]

Katharine Howard was placed under arrest, and the council ordered, on Friday, 11th November, that on the Monday next coming she should remove from Hampton Court to Sion House;[2] this she accordingly did, and Lady Rochford accompanied her.[3]

Specific instructions for her accommodation were given, and the following is the order of the Privy Council addressed to "Archbishop Cranmer, Mr. Controllour, and others:"—

Westminster, 11th Nov., 1541.

First, the King's pleasure is, that the Queen, with convenient diligence, remove to the house of Syon, there to remain till the matter be further ordered, in the state of a Queen, furnished moderately, as her life and conditions hath deserved; that is to say, with the furniture of three chambers, hanged with mean stuff without any cloth of estate; of which three, one shall serve for Mr. Baynton and the others to dine in, and the other two to serve for her use; and with a mean number of servants, according to a book which wee send unto you herewith; the proportion whereof to be augmented or diminished the King's Hignes reserveth to your discretions, who, His Majesty thinketh, will not excede a necessary furniture. The King's Highness pleasure is, that the Queen have, at her election, four gentlewomen and two chamberers; foreseeing alwayes that my Lady Baynton bee one, whose husband, the King's pleasure is, should attend uppon the Queen, to have the rule and government of the whole house; and with him the Almoner (Nicholas Heath, Bishop of

---

[1] Herbert's 'Life of Henry VIII.' p. 473; Turner's 'History,' vol. ii. p. 511.

[2] Sion was granted to the Protector Somerset, and then to John Dudley, Duke of Northumberland: Queen Mary re-established it as a monastery. In 1604 King James gave it to Henry Percy, Earl of Northumberland.

[3] Jane, Viscountess Rochford, was the daughter of Henry Parker, son of Lord Morley and Monteagle, who died in his father's lifetime.—Dugdale's 'Baronage,' vol. ii. p. 307.

Rochester) to be also associate. Besides which three personages by name, that is to say, Mr. Baynton, his wife, and the almoner, the King's Highnes appointeth none specially to remaine with her; and the number of the rest, before specified, besides those that bee at her choice, to be appointed by your discretions, such only to remain at Hampton Court, to abide the Queen's removing, as after the order before specified shall bee attendant at Syon: doing you, Mr. Controullour, to understand that Mr. Weldon,[1] Master of the Household, hath been here spoken unto, which he also doth, to make provision of wine, beer, and other necessaries at Syon for that purpose.[2]

The Queen and Lady Rochford remained thus as state prisoners at Syon until the 10th February, but on the 16th January, 1541-2, Parliament was opened, and on the 21st a bill of attainder against them was read for the first time. On Saturday, the 28th January, both Houses resolved "to desire of the King certaine petitions: First, that he would not vexe himself with the Queene's offence, and that she and the Lady Rochford might be attainted by Parliament:

"Secondly, and because protractyng of tyme, which the more should be to his unquietnesse, that he would under his great seale give his royall assent, without tarrying the ende of the Parliament.

"The which peticions the King graunted, saying that he thanked the Commons that they tooke his sorrow to be theirs."[3]

The Privy Council held another meeting to consider the question on the following day, Sunday the 29th, and on the 30th the Lord Chancellor moved the House of Lords to consider "the case the King was in by the Queen's ill-carriage," and proposed that some of the peers should be sent to examine the Queen.[4] "Whereupon the Archbishop of

---

[1] Sir Anthony Weldon, his great grandson, was Clerk of the Board of Green Cloth. For an account of the Weldon family, see Nichols' 'Progresses of James I.' vol. iii. p. 299.

[2] See Aungier's 'History of Syon,' p. 536; 'State Papers,' vol. i. part ii. p. 691.

[3] Grafton.

[4] See Froude's 'History of England,' vol. iv. p. 135.

Canterbury, the Duke of Suffolk, the Earl of Southampton, and the Bishop of Westminster,[1] were sent to her. How much she confessed to them is not very clear, neither by the Journal[2] nor the Act of Parliament,[3] which only says that she confessed without mentioning the particulars. Upon this, the processes of those that had been formerly attainted being also brought as an evidence, the Act passed in both Houses."[4]

The bill was hastened through the two houses, and brought to the Lords by the Chancellor ready signed by the King and with the great seal appended to it. "Whilst the officer proceeded to summon the attendance of the Commons, the Duke of Suffolk with some others reported that they had waited on the Queen, who acknowledged her offences against God, the King, and the nation; and expressed a hope that her faults might not be visited on her brother's family; she had also begged as a last favour that she might divide a part of her clothes among her maids: by this time the Commons had arrived, and the royal assent was then given in due form."[5]

Lady Rochford was sent to the Tower on the 9th February, and on the 10th, "the Queene was had by water from Syon to the Tower of London, the Duke of Suffolke, the Lord Privie Seale, and the Lord Great Chamberlaine, havinge the conveyance of her."[6]

"On Saterday, being the xi day of February, the King had sent his assent to the bill, then all the lordes were in their robes and the Common house called up, and there the acte redde, and his assent declared, and so, on the thirteene

---

[1] Thomas Thirlby, the first and only Bishop of Westminster, who held that office from 1540 till 1550. He died at Lambeth, 26 Aug., 1576, and was buried there. In 1783, when making a grave for Archbishop Cornwallis, his body was discovered in very tolerable preservation: a cap was on his head, and a hat of peculiar shape was under his arm.

[2] Lords' 'Journals,' vol. i. p. 176.

[3] 33 Henry VIII. c. 21.

[4] Burnet, bk. iii. vol. i. pp. 625-6. The trial, the mass of evidence collected, and the indictments against Derham, Culpepper, Lady Rochford, &c., now preserved in the Baga de Secretis, Pouch xiii. bundle 1, at the State Paper Office, were not accessible to Burnet: these records are contained on 58 membranes. See Appendix, p. 327.

[5] Lingard, vol. v. p. 77.

[6] Wrottesley's 'Chronicle,' p. 133.

daie, these two ladies were beheaded on the greene within the Tower with an axe, and confessed their offences and died repentant."[1]

The execution took place on Monday, the 13th February, on a scaffold which was erected on the green in front of the chapel, and on the same spot on which Queen Anne Boleyn had suffered.

The following letter, written by an eye-witness, furnishes the only record which we have of the last moments of the Queen and Lady Rochford.

OTWELL JOHNSON *to his brother*, JOHN JOHNSON, *a merchant of the staple at Calais.*

"At London the 15th day in February, 1541.[2]

"From Calleis I have harde nothing as yet of your sute to my Lord Gray; and for news from hens, know ye, that even, according to my writing on Sonday last, I se the Quene and the Lady Rotcheford suffer within the Tower the day following, whos sowles (I doubt not) be with God, for thay made the moost godly and christyan's end, that ever was hard tell of (I thinke) sins the world's creation: uttering thayer lively faeth in the blode of Christe onely, and with goodly words and stedfast countenances thay desyred all christen people to take regard unto thayer worthy and just punishment with death for thayer offences, and agenst God, hainously from thayer youth upward, in breaking all his commandements, and also agenst the King's royall majesty very daungeriously: wherfor thay being just condempned (as thay sayed) by the lawes of the realme and parlement, to dye, required the people (I say) to take example at them, for amendement of thayer ungodly lyves, and gladdly to obey the King in all things, for whos preservation thay did hartely pray: and willed all people so to do: commending thayer sowles to God and ernestly calling for mercy upon him: whom I besieche to geve us grace, with suche faeth hope and charitie at our departing owt of this miserable world to come to the fruytion of his Godhed in joy everlasting. Amen.

"Your loving brother,
"OTWELL JOHNSON."

"With my harty commendacions unto Mr. Cave and Mistress Cave, not forgetting my syster your wiff; I pray you lett them be made partakers of thies last newes, for surely the thing is well worth the knowledge."[3]

[1] Hall's 'Chronicle.'
[2] *I. e.* 1541-2.
[3] Ellis's 'Orig. Letters,' 1st series, vol. ii. p. 128.

"The xiij day February was the Qwene Kateryne and Lady Rocheford beheddyd within the Tower & there burryd."[1]

Weever, recounting the interments in St. Peter's, says, "Within the choir of this chaple lieth buried near the relics of the said Anne Bollein, the body of Katharine, the fifth wife of King Henry VIII., who having continued his wife but the space of one year, six months, and four days, was attainted by Parliament and beheaded here in the Tower upon the 13th of February, 1541."[2]

It has been always believed that Lady Rochford was buried by the Queen, and Bayley states, that "she accompanied her mistress in execution and in sepulture."

THOMAS SEYMOUR, LORD SEYMOUR OF SUDELEY.

Born, ——. Beheaded on Tower Hill, 20th March, 1548-9.

Thomas, Lord Sudeley, Admiral of England, and brother to Queen Jane Seymour and the Protector Somerset, was a man of restless ambition. He had married Katharine Parr, widow of King Henry VIII., and after her death (of which it was said, perhaps unjustly, that "he had holpen her to her end") he had designed to marry the Princess Elizabeth.[3] He intrigued against his brother, the Lord Protector, and had made for himself many enemies.

At length in January, 1548-9, his seal of office as Admiral was demanded from him, and his brother having summoned him to come to his house, the Admiral declined in the following letter:—

"Your servant was with me even now to come to speke with your grace: this shal be to desyr you to holde me excused tyll tomorow at the parlement chamber, or at Westminster in the afternoon, so that the consell may be prysent: and thus I wyche your grace as well as I wold to myself, altho' ye shold do me wrong.

"From my howse this fryday night, vi[th] Jan. your grace's lovyng brother. "T. SEYMOUR."[4]

[1] 'Grey Friars' Chronicle,' p. 45.
[2] Weever, p. 286.
[3] For her reply to his offer, see Green's 'Letters of Illustrious Ladies,' vol. ii. p. 191.
[4] State Papers, Dom. Ed. VI. vol. vi. No. 1.

A warrant was then, on the 17th January, issued for his arrest,[1] upon which he declared "by God's precious soul, whosoever lays hands on me to fetch me to prison, I shal thrust my dagger in him."[2] He was nevertheless seized and conveyed on the 19th to the Tower, "there to remain tyll such furder ordre be taken with him as the case afterward uppon more ample consultacion shall require for the most surety of the Kinge's majestie and the realme."

He was there examined by members of the Privy Council, with regard to the numerous charges alleged against him;[3] and on the 22nd February a report upon the subject was made to the Privy Council. It is called "articles of high treason and other misdemeanours against the King's majesty and his crown, objected to Sir Thomas Seymour, K^t, Lord Seymour of Sudley, and high admiral of England."[4]

It consists of thirty-three articles, and, together with "the Lord Admiral's answer to three of the former articles," has been printed by Burnet.[5]

On the 23rd the whole Council, except the Archbishop of Canterbury and Sir John Baker, Speaker of the House of Commons, went again to the Tower to examine him. His only reply was, he would consider the articles if they were left with him.

On the 24th the Council resolved that they should lay the matter before the King; and the following is the entry in the Council Book:—"This day the xxiiij of February, the Lord Chauncellor, and the rest of the Lords, and others of the counsell making report to the Lord Protector of their proceedings the day before in the Tower with the Lord Admirall, upon consultation herein taken, it was thought convenient that the said Lord Chauncellor and the rest of the counsell should at after dinner make reaport to the King's

---

[1] For warrant, see 'Life of Sir Thomas Seymour,' by Sir J. Maclean, p. 73.
[2] State Papers, Dom. Ed. VI. vol. vi. This threat probably had reference to John Dudley, Earl of Warwick, afterwards created Duke of Northumberland.
[3] The examinations of the principal witnesses are preserved in the Cecil MSS. at Hatfield. See also State Papers, Domestic, Ed. VI.
[4] Privy Council Book, p. 236.
[5] Burnet, 'History of Reformation,' book i. part ii. No. 31, Records.

majestie, both of such heynous and trayterous attempts and doeings as the lord admirall had done and entended, and also of his obstinate refusall to answer to the same or to excuse himself, if, peradventure, there might be any hope for him either to be proved giltless or to receive pardon: and it was further apointed that the said lord chauncellor should demand and know the King's majestie's mynd, whether he would be content that for his majestie's surety, and for avoyding of further inconvenience towards his royall person and crown, his highness wold be content that his majestie's lawes should procede upon him according to th' order of justice and th' accustome of the realme in like cases: and specially forsomuch as thies things have chanced to be revealed in the time of his majestie's high court of parliament, that the parliament should have the determinacion and ordre thereof.

"According as it was determined in the counsell, so, immediately after the King's majesty had dined it was put in execucion. The lord chauncellor declared forth the heynous facts and treasons of th' admirall and his obstinate refusall, and made the demande and request aforesaid. Every one of the lordes and the rest of the counsell in order briefly declared their mindes and sentences to that effect. Lastly, the lord protector declaring how sorrowful a case this was unto him, said, that he did yet rather regard his bounden dewtie to the King's majestie and the crown of England than his own son and brother, and did wey more his allegiance than his bloode: and therefore he could not resist nor wolde not be against the lordes request, but as his majestie wolde he wolde most obediently be content, and if himselfe should committ suche offences against his highnes, he could not think himself worthy lief, and so muche the more as he was of all men most bounde to his majestie and therefore he could not refuse justice.

"Upon all this the King's majestie answered theis wordes, 'We do perceive that there is great things which be objected and layd to myn lord admirall myn uncle; and they tend to treason: and we perceive that you require but justice to

K

be done. We think it reasonable, and we will well that you procede according to your request.'

" With theis words, coming so sudenly from his grace's mouth of his own motion, as the lordes might well perceive, the said lordes and the rest of the counsell were merveilously rejoyced and gave his Highnes most hearty praise and thanks."[1]

It was, however, decided that before the bill of attainder was brought into parliament some members of both houses should go to the Tower and hear what replies could be obtained from the Admiral.

The Lord Chancellor, the Earls of Shrewsbury, Warwick, and Southampton, Sir John Baker (the Speaker), Sir Thomas Cheney,[2] and Sir Anthony Denny, then visited him.

He was still obstinate; and on the 25th of February the bill of attainder was introduced into the House of Lords: on the 26th and 27th it was read a second and a third time. On the 2nd of March it was brought into the House of Commons, where it met with much opposition; for it was argued that the Admiral should be allowed to plead for himself. However, on the 3rd it was read a second time, and also for the third time on the 4th; on the 5th March it received the royal assent.

The next proceedings are thus recorded in the Privy Council register:—"This day the xth of Marche, the lord Protector and the rest of the counsell meting in the King's majestie's palace at Westminster to consult and deliberate of the affaires of the realme, emongs other thinges, it was thought good that for so much as both the lordes of the upper howse, and also the Knightes, citizens, and burgesses of the lower howse of parliament had passed and assented unto the bill of the attainder of the lord admirall, that the same should be signified and declared to the King's Majestie, with further openynge of his heynous offences, conspiracies, and treasons; how that the said treasons were so heynous

---

[1] Council Book. 'Literary Remains of Edward VI.,' vol. i. pp. cxx-i. Howell's State Trials, vol. i. p. 492.

[2] Treasurer of the Household: made Privy Councillor in March, 1551-2.

and fearfull, and so daungerous, tending both to the extreme peryll of his most royall person, and to the subversion of the state of the realme, that of necessitie it behovid not to pass them over, but seriously to consider them; especially now after by bothe the howses of his highness' court of parliament it had been so adjudged. Therefore they should require his highness that they might proceed further for the suretie of his person according to justice. And forasmuch as they did perceive that the case was so heavy and lamentable to the lorde protector, his majestie's uncle, yf his highness were so pleased and so comanded them, altho' the thing itself (but onely that for his majestie's suretie it could not be omitted) were also to them sorrowfull, yet they wold further procede to justice herein as apperteigned, without troubling or molesting, in this hevy case either his highness or the lord protector.

"According as it was in the counsell determined, so after dyner the lord chauncellor and the rest of the counsell repayred to the King's majestie, to whom the said matters and requests were declared in the name of the counsell by the mouth of the lord chauncellor, the lorde protector being also there present.

"To which his highness answered, that he had well perceived their proceedings herein, and gave them his hartie thankes for their paines and travaile, and the great care his highness perceived that they had for his suretie, willing and commanding them that they should proceed as they required, without further molestation of his highness or the lord protector; and at th' end said, 'And I pray you my lordes so do.' With the which answer they toke their leave and departed."[1]

It is believed that the Protector now desired to have an interview with his brother, and endeavoured to intercede for him, but this was prevented. In a letter written by Princess Elizabeth to Queen Mary before going to the Tower, she says, "In late days I hearde my Lorde of Somerset say, that if his brother had bine sufferd to speke

[1] 'Literary Remains of King Edward VI.,' vol. i. p. 122. Burnet, book i. part ii. vol. iii. p. 206.

to him, he had never sufferd; but the perswasions wer made to him so gret, that he was brogth in beleefe that he could not live safely if the admirall lived; and that made him give his consent to his dethe."[1]

Goodriche, Bishop of Ely, was desired on the 15th March to communicate the sentence of death to the admiral and to "instruct him in the things as might apperteigne to the welthe of his sowle, and to the patient taking of his worthie execution."

On the 17th March the Bishop, " repairing again to the court, made report to Mr. Comptroller and Secretary Smith, of the lord admiral's request. The which were that he required Mr. Latimer[2] to come to him: that the day of his execution to be deferred: certain of his servants to be with him: his infant daughter to be with my Lady Duchess of Suffolk to be brought up: and such like. Touching which requests, the said lords and the rest of the council declared their minds to Mr. Secretary Smith;[3] willing him to write their answer, in a letter to the Lieutenant of the Tower, who would show in all these requests their resolute answer to the said admiral; the which was done accordingly."

The following warrant was then issued for his execution.

"This daye, the 17th of March, the lorde chancellor, and the rest of the King's counsell, meeting in his highness's palace of Westminster, heard the report of the bishop of Elye, who by the said lordes, and others of the counsell, was sent to instruct and comfort the lord admirall; after the hearing whereof, consulting and deliberating with themselves of the tyme most convenient for the execucion of the lord admirall now attainted and condempned by the parliament, they did condescend and agree, that the said lorde admirall should be executed on the Wednesday next following, betwixt the howers of nine and twelve in the forenoon the same day, upon the Tower Hill. His bodye and hedd to

---

[1] Ellis's 'Original Letters,' 2nd series, vol. ii. p. 256.

[2] Hugh Latimer, who had resigned his bishopric of Worcester in 1539.

[3] Sir Thomas Smith, Secretary of State, in the reigns of Edward VI. and Queen Elizabeth, born 1512. died 1577.

be buryed within the Tower. The King's writte (as in such cases as heretofore hath been accustomed) being first directed and sent forth for that purpose and effect. Whereupon calling to the counsell-chamber the bishop of Elye, they willed him to declare this their determinacion to the saide lord admirall; and to instruct and teach him, the best he could, to the quiete and patient suffering of justice, and to prepare himself to Almighty God.

E. SOMERSET.[1]

T. CANTUARIEN:	WILLIAM PAGET.
R. RICH, Chancel:	ANTHONY WYNGFIELD.
W. ST. JOHN.	WILLIAM PETRE.
J. RUSSEL.	A. DENNY.
J. WARWYCK.	EDWARD NORTH.
F. SHREWESBURY.	R. SADLEYR.

THOMAS SOUTHAMPTON."[2]

In the King's Diary is entered, "The Lord Sudley, admiral of England, was condemned to death, and died in March ensuing."

His execution was fixed for the 20th of March.

Burnet says, "What his behaviour was on the scaffold I do not find;" and there does not appear to be any record of any speech made by him to the people, but Strype tells us, that when ready to lay his head on the block he bid his servant "speed the thing that he wot of."

"These words were overheard, and the servant taken into examination, who confessed that they were the two letters which his master had written in the Tower to the Lady Mary and Lady Elizabeth, which he had been enjoined to take an opportunity of delivering; they had been written with great ingenuity; he had made his ink so craftily and with such workmanship as the like has not been seen. He

---

[1] It is thus evident that Somerset signed the warrant for his brother's execution; but when the bill of attainder was under discussion in Parliament, he had "for natural pity's sake asked leave to withdraw."

[2] Council Book, f. 247. Burnet, book i., part ii.; Records, No. 32.

made his pen of the aglet of a point that he plucked from his hose."[1]

"These two papers (which were but of a small quantity), were sewed between the sole of a velvet shoe of his. By this means these letters came to light, and fell into the hands of the Protector and council. The contents of them tended to this end, that the two sisters should conspire against the Protector, enforcing many matters against him to make these ladies jealous of him, as though he had, it may be, practised to estrange the King their brother from them, or to deprive them of the right of their succession. Both these papers Latimer himself saw, and reported publicly in his fourth sermon before the King, though in the last edition of his sermons the passage be left out."[2]

"As touching the kind of his death, whether he be saved or no, I refer that to God. In the twinkling of an eye He may save a man and turn his heart. What He did I cannot tell; and when a man hath two strokes with an axe, who can tell but between two strokes he doth repent? It is hard to judge; but this I will say, if they will ask me what I think of his death, that he died very dangerously, irksomely and horribly. He was a wicked man, and the realm is well rid of him."[3]

The chronicler Grafton remarks, in recording his death, "It was then commonly talked, that the fall of one brother would be the overthrow of the other, as soone after it came to passe."

EDWARD SEYMOUR, DUKE OF SOMERSET (THE LORD PROTECTOR).

Born ——. Beheaded on Tower Hill, 22nd January, 1551-2.

Edward Seymour, Duke of Somerset, and brother to Lord Seymour of Sudeley, was the life-long rival of John Dudley, Earl of Warwick and Duke of Northumberland; he was twice committed to the Tower, and "in 1549, the Earle of Warwick, espying opportunity drew about eighteen of the

[1] Strype, vol. ii. part ii. p. 198.
[2] Ibid.
[3] Latimer's 'Sermons;' see reprint by Parker Society in 1844.

Privy Council to knit with him against the Lord Protector. These did he so winde up to his purpose that they withdrew from the Court, fell into secret consultations, and walked in the citie with many servants weaponed and in new liveries."[1]

The incidents of his first arrest are described in the pages of Stow,[2] who was living in London at the time. "On the 8th of October (1549) after a common Councell in the Guild hall at London,[3] whither all the Lords of the Councell came (after first taking possession of the Tower), when the Lord Chancellor,[4] and others declared divers abuses of the Lord Protector, desiring the citizens to be ayding and assisting with them, for the preserving of the King's Majestie's person, which they greatly feared, being in his adversaries hands.

"The Lords dined with Master Yorke, one of the Sheriffes, and in the afternoon proclamation of the accusations was made in divers places of the citie with trumpets, heraults and Kings at armes, wherein was contained divers articles touching the evill government of the Lord Protector."[5]

Stow then gives a copy of this proclamation, which was signed by Lord Rich, the Chancellor, the Earl of Warwick, Lord Great Chamberlain, and many other peers and influential persons.

The Lords had already addressed a similar statement to the King, to which Somerset had replied from Windsor on the 8th October, 1549.[6]

On the 10th October, "by a common counsell at the Guildhall, was granted five hundred men of the citie, one hundred to be horsemen, to be ready on the next morrow; and this day, the Lords dined with Master Turke, one of the Sheriffes of London."

[1] Hayward's 'Edward VI.' p. 85–6.
[2] Born, 1525; died, 1605.
[3] Sir John Hayward says the first meeting was held at the Earl of Warwick's lodging at Ely House, in Holborn, and that the meeting at Guildhall was in the afternoon of the same day.
[4] Richard Lord Rich, Chancellor from October, 1547, till December, 1551.

For the Lord Chancellor's speech see Hayward's 'Edward VI.' pp. 86–91.
[5] Stow.
[6] Both these documents, which are in the British Museum (Cotton. MSS. Titus, B. 2, and Caligula, B. 7), will be found in Burnet, book i. pt. ii., Record., 41 and 42.

"Sir Philip Hoby was sent by them with letters to the King, beseeching his highness to give credit to that which he should declare in their names: and the King gave him libertie to speak, and most gentlie heard all that he had to saie, and trulie he did so wiselie declare his message, and so gravelie told his tale in the name of the Lords, yea therewithal so vehementlie and greevous so against the Protector, who was also there present by the King, that in the end, the Lord Protector was commanded from the King's presence."[1]

"The 11th of October, the Lords sitting at the Lord Great master's, Sir Anthony Wingfield, Captain of the Guard, was sent with a letter to the King at Windsor,[2] and severed the Lord Protector from his person, and caused the guard to watch him till the Lord's coming. Then on the morrow (12th October) the Lord Chancellor with the rest of the councell rode to Windsor to the King, and that night, the Lord Protector was put in ward into Beauchamps Tower in the castle of Windsor.

"On the 14th in the afternoon the Duke of Somerset was brought from Windsor, riding betwixt the Earles of Southampton[3] and of Huntingdon,[4] through Oldborne, in at Newgate to the Tower of London,[5] accompanied with divers Lords and gentlemen and with 300 horse: the Lord Mayor, Sir Ralph Warren, Sir John Gresham, Master recorder, Sir William Locke, and both the Sheriffes and other Knights sitting on their horses against Sopers Lane, and all the officers with halbards, and from Oldborne bridge to the Tower certain aldermen or their deputies on horseback in every streete, with a number of householders standing with bills as he passed.[6]

---

[1] Grafton's 'Chronicle.' For the letters, see Ellis, 1st series, vol. ii. pp. 169–171. Cotton. MSS. Caligula, B. vii. ff. 407-8, 10–12.

[2] This letter is to be found in the Privy Council Records, and is also given in Burnet, book i. pt. ii., Records, No. 43.

[3] Thomas Wriottesley, Earl of Southampton, formerly Lord Chancellor, died 31st July, 1550.

[4] Francis, second Earl of Huntingdon, died June 1561.

[5] "The Lordes came to Windsore toke him, and brought him through Holborn to the Tower."—' Edward VI.'s Diary.'

[6] Stow. Hayward's 'Edward VI.' pp. 96, 7.

"Shortly after, when the Duke had breathed a small time in the Tower, in December, the Lordes of the Council resorted to the Tower, and there charged the Duke with certain articles, twenty-nine in number."[1]

The result of this interview was that on the 2nd Jan. 1550-1 a bill was brought into parliament embodying the accusations mentioned in the proclamation,[1] and to it was appended a confession, signed by the Protector's own hand, who stated that he had made it on his knees before the King and Council, and had signed it on the 12th December.[2] This submission was, however, not considered sufficient, and another in most abject terms was signed by him on the 2nd February, 1550-1.[3]

On the 6th February the Duke was released from the Tower, and King Edward in his Diary records that "that night he supped at Sir John Yorke's, one of the sheriffes of London, where the Lords assembled to welcome him." He was so far pardoned and restored to the King's favour that he reappeared at the King's court on the 31st March, as in the King's diary we find under that date, "My Lord Somerset was delivered of his bondes, and cam to court." Again on the 27th April "it was agreed by the whole counsaill that the Kinge's majestie shulde be moved for the restitucion of the Duke of Somersett unto all his goods, his debts, and his leases yet ungiven,"[4] and the King enters in his journal under the same date "It was grauntid that my lord of Somerset shuld have al his movebal goodes and lesses, except thos that be alredie given."

On the 11th May the Council "determined to be sutors for the duke to the King, that he might be again admitted of the privie chamber," and the King on the 14th records that the Duke was again thus received.

Although friendship was so far restored between the Duke and the Earl of Warwick, that a marriage was made between

---

[1] *Vide* Hayward and Stow, who give these documents in full detail.
[2] See Burnet, book i. pt. ii. Records, No. 46.
[3] Burnet, book i. pt. ii. vol. iii. p. 292. Sir J. Hayward says it was thus signed: "written with my owne hand 23 December anno 3° Edw: Regis." Both these "submissions" are printed by Stow.
[4] *I.e.* not given away to other persons.

Lord Lisle, Warwick's eldest son, and Lady Anne Seymour, the Duke's daughter, on 3rd June, 1550, yet the old feud soon broke out again, and Warwick, who had in the meantime been created Duke of Northumberland, gave intelligence of a conspiracy, in which Somerset and others [1] were concerned.

On the 16th October, 1551, "being Fryday, the Duke was again apprehended, and committed to the Tower on a charge of high treason." [2]

The King records, under date 16th October, "This morning none was at Westminster of the conspiratours. The first was the duke, who came later than he was wont, of himself. After diner he was apprehendid."

Somerset had previously gone to Secretary Cecil, and said "he suspected there was an ill design against him; to which the Secretary answered, 'If he were not in fault, he might trust to his innocency; but if he were, he had nothing to say but to lament him.'" [3]

Thus, for a second time, was the Lord Protector a prisoner in the Tower.

Among the Cottonian MSS. at the British Museum is a paper endorsed in Cecil's hand, "Wryting of the Duke of Somerset in the Tower of London." It is a paper of questions (fifteen in number) which he put to the Duke when in the Tower. [4]

In the meantime preparations were made for the trial of the Duke.

Accordingly, on the 16th November the Council addressed letters severally to the sheriffs of Middlesex, Surrey, and Kent, to "gyve ordre that good and substantiall full juries of Knights and esquires of the best sorte within those counties may be returned agaynst Saturday next, uppon suche precepts as shal be directed unto them from the

---

[1] Sir Thomas Arundel, Sir Ralph Vane, &c., see p. 149.
[2] Grafton.
[3] Burnet, book i. part ii. vol. iii. p. 368.
[4] It has been printed by Sir H. Ellis in his collection of original letters "in order that it may be preserved, as it is so decayed, torn, and discoloured." With this paper is also preserved a list of the necessaries of "dress and other accommodation" which the Duke and Duchess prayed to have sent them whilst in prison in the Tower. These papers are interesting, but too long to quote here.—Ellis's 'Orig. Letters,' 2nd series, vol. ii. pp. 214–15.

Commissioners, that shal be appointed by the King's majestie for that purpose."[1]

On the 21st the indictment against the Duke was presented at Guildhall, and a true bill found by the jury of Middlesex;[2] and on the 22nd the Council sent a "lettre to the mayor of London to cause the watches within the citie to be doubled, and that twyse in the weeke, betweene this and Christmas, there be made thorowght the citie privie searche."

These precautions were adopted in consequence of the popularity of the Duke; and as the time of the trial approached, it is evident that Northumberland apprehended some demonstrations in the Duke's favour, for the Lord Mayor is again desired " to cause the citie to be well looked to and garded all day tomorrow and the next night."

The Council then addressed a letter to Mr. Hoby, the Lieutenant of the Tower (Sir Arthur Darcy), and the Knight Marshal (Sir Ralph Hopton), "signifying the ordre taken for the Duke of Somerset's conduction to Westminster tomorrow in the morning;" and every householder was ordered that he "should see to his family and keepe his house, having in a readinesse a man in harnesse in every house; but not to goe abroad till they should be called, if need were, and further that on the night following there should be kept a good and substantiall watch of householders in every ward, which was done."[3]

On the 23rd November the King had entered in his diary: "The Lord Treasaurour[4] apointed high stuard for the arraignment of the Duke of Somerset." The trial was to take place at Westminster, and accordingly on the 2nd December was the "sayde Duke brought out of the Tower of London, with the axe of the Tower borne before him, with a great number of billes, gleves, holbardes, and polaxes attending upon him; and was had from the Tower by water, and having shot London Bridge at five of the clock in the morning,[3] so came unto Westminster Hall, where was made in the

[1] Privy Council Register.
[2] See Howell's 'State Trials,' vol. i. p. 518.
[3] Stow.
[4] William Paulet, created Marquess of Winchester in Oct. 1555, was Lord High Treasurer until 1558, died 1572.

middle of the hall a new scaffold, where all the Lordes of the King's Counsaill sate as his judges, and there was he arreigned and charged with many articles both of treason and felony. And when, after much milde speeche, he had aunswered not guiltie, he in all humble manner put himselfe to be tryed by his peeres, who, after long consultations among themselves, gave their verdict that he was not guiltie of the treason, but of the felony."[1]

The following is the account of the trial which King Edward has recorded in his diary:—

"The duke of Somerset cam to his triall at Westmyster halle. The lord treasaurour sat as high stuard of England under the cloth of estate, on a benche betwene tow postes, 3 degrees high: al the lordes, to the number of 26, videlicet:—

Dukes
Southfolke
Northumberland

Marquesse
Northampton

Erlis
Derby.	Bath
Bedford.	Sussex
Huntingdon.	Worcetour
Rutland.	Pembroke

Viscount
Hereford

Barons
Bargeiney.	Stafford
Audley.	Wentworth
Wharton.	Darcy
Euers.	Sturton
Latimer.	Windsore
Bourough.	Crumwell
Souch.	Cobham
Bray.	

---

[1] Grafton. The proceedings of the trial are preserved in the Baga de Secretis, Pouch xix.

"This (these) sate a degree under, and hard the matter debated. First after the inditements rede, 5 in number, the lerned counceill laid to my lord Somerset Paulmers confession. To which he answerid that he never minded to rayse the North, and declared al ill he could devise of Paulmer, but he was aferd for brutes (bruits), and that moved him to send to Sir William Harbert. Replied it was again that the wors Paulmer was the more he served his purpose. For the banket, first he sware it was untrue, and required more witnessis; when Cran(e)'s confession was rede, he wold have had him come face to face. For London, he ment nothing for hurte of any lorde, but for his owne defence. For the gend'armery it were but a made (mad) matter for him to enterprise, with his 100 against 900. For having men in his chambre at Grenwich, confessid by Partrege, it seemid he ment no harme, bicause when he could have done harme he did it not. My lord Straunges confession, he sware it was untrue, and the lord Straung toke his othe it was true. Nidegat's, Hammon's, and Alexander Scymour's confessions he denied, bicause they were his men.

"The lawers rehersid how to raise men at his house for an ille intent, az to kill the duke of Northumberland, was treason by an Act 3ᵉ anno of my raigne against unlaufull assemblis: for to devise the death of the lords was felony; to mind resisting his attachment was felony; to raise London was treason, to assault the Lordis was felony. He answerid he did not entend to raise London, and that sware the witness (who) were not their. His assembling of men was but for his owne defence. He did not determine to kill the duke of Northumberland, the marquese, etc., but spake of it and determined after the contrary; and yet seamid to confess he went about there death. The lordis went togither. The duke of Northumberland wold not agree that any searching of his death shuld bee treason. So the lordis acquited him of high treason and condemned him of treason feloniouse, and so he was adjudged to be hangid. He gave thanks to the lordis for there open trial and cried mercy of the duke of Northumberland, the marquis of Northampton, and th' erle of Penbroke[1] for his ill meaning against them, and made suet for his 'life' (*inserted above the line*), wife and children, servauntes and dettes, and so departed without the ax of the Toure. The peple knowing not the matter, shouted harf a douzen times so loud that from the halle dore it was hard at Charing Crosse plainely, and rumours went that he was quitte of all."[2]

King Edward gives another description of the trial in a letter addressed to Barnaby Fitzpatrick, dated from Westminster the 20th December, 1551.[3]

[1] William Herbert, created Earl of Pembroke in 1551; married Ann, daughter of Katharine Parr; died in 1569.
[2] 'Journal of King Edward VI.'
[3] See 'Literary Remains of Edward VI.,' p. 375.

The chronicler Grafton has also left us his version of the result of the trial:—" The people there present, which was a great number, heeryng the Lordes say not guiltie, which was to the treason, thinkyng most certainlie that hee was clerely acquitted, and chiefly, for that immediately upon the pronouncing of those wordes, he that carryed the axe of the Tower, departed with the axe; they made an outcrie and joy, as the lyke hath not bene heard, which was an evident declaration of their good willes borne towardes him.[1]

"But nevertheless he was condemned to the death, whereof shortlye after he tasted. The felony that he was condemned of, was upon the statute made the last yere agaynst rebelles and unlawfull assemblyes, wherein among other thinges is one braunch that whosoever shall procure the death of any counsellor, that every such attempt or procurement shall be felonye,[2] and by force of that statute the Duke of Somerset being accompanyed with certaine others, was charged that he purposed and attempted the death of the Duke of Northumberland. After the Duke was thus condemned, he was agayne returned to the Tower,[3] through London, where were bothe exclamations, the one cried for joye that he was acquitted, the other cried out that he was condemned. But howsoever they cried, he was conveyed to the Tower, where he remained until the xxij daye of January next following."[4]

Burnet says that all possible care was taken to divert the King's mind during the period that his uncle was under sentence of death, and we find in his journal many accounts of festivities held at court during the month of January. Yet, writes Burnet, "he was not much concerned in his uncle's preservation."

The question of the Duke's execution was, however,

---

[1] "They made such a shriek, casting up of caps, &c., that their cry was heard in the Long acre beyond Charing Crosse, which made the Lordes astonied."—Stow.

[2] "A law enacted, 3 Hen. VII., which made the very intent, nay imagination of killing a Privy Counsellor, punishable by death."—Godwyn's Annals, p. 247.

[3] "About 5 o'clock at night, at the Crane in the Vintry, and so was led through Candlewick Street to the Tower."—Stow. It was then dark, and doubtless a less concourse of people was then expected. He had been brought from the Tower in the darkness of the early morning for the same reason.

[4] Grafton.

brought specially under the King's notice, and in the British Museum is a paper in his writing, and endorsed by Cecil, " matters for the council, 18 Jan. 1551-2," in which is; " No. 3. The matter for the Duke of Somerset and his confederates to be considered as aperteineth to ourself and quietnes of our realme, that by there punishment and execution, according to the lawes, example may be shewed to others."[1]

Cecil has also marked this paper, " remembrances that was written and delyvered by the Kynges Matie to his Privie Counsell at Grenewiche in his Privie Chamber, the mondaye, being the 19th of January 1551. They were written with his Maties owne hand, and receved of his Maties owne handes by the Marquis of Wynchester, being then Lord Tresurer, being present the following," and then all the names are given, Cecil's object being thus to record the names of those [1] who were witness to this solemn step on the part of the King.

The " letters of warrantie, signed with our hand," directed the Chancellor to issue writs to the Lieutenant of the Tower, and to the sheriffs for the Duke's execution: and this is to be found in Rymer's ' Fœdera,' xv. p. 295, being reprinted from the close roll, 6 Ed. VI. p. 7, m. 16.

Friday, the 22nd of January, was fixed for the execution of the Duke. On that morning he was brought out of the Tower, and " according to the manner delivered to the sheriffs of London, and so with a great company of the guard, and others with weapons, he was brought to the scaffold where he should suffer."[2] And though, " according to a precept directed from the council to the mayor, the constables of every ward in London 'strictlie charged everie houshold of the same citie not to depart anie of them out of their houses, before ten of the clocke of that daie : meaning thereby to restraine the great number of people that otherwise were like to have been at the said execution; notwithstanding by seven of the clocke, the Tower hill was covered

[1] Cotton. MSS. Vespasian, F. xiii. p. 171. See also ' Literary Remains of Edward VI.' (Roxburghe Club), p. 490.
[2] Grafton; Holinshed.

with a great multitude, repairing from all parts of the citie, as well as out of the suburbs.'"[1]

Machyn, who was an eyewitness, writes, "the xxii of January, soon after eight of the clocke in the morning, the Duke of Somerset was beheaded on Tower Hill. There was as gret compeny as have beene syne: the Kinge's gard behynge there with ther halbards,[2] and a 1000 men with halbards of the privilege of the Tower, Ratcliffe, Lymhouse, Whytechappell, Saint Katheryn, and Stretford, Bow, Hogston, and Shoordyche, and ther were two shereffs ther present seying the execusyon of my Lord."[3] Then the Duke on the scaffold, "nothing changing voyce nor countenance, but in a manner with the same gesture that he partely used at home, kneling downe upon both his knees, and lifting up his handes, erected himselfe unto God. And after that he had ended a few shorte prayers, standing up agayne, and turning himselfe towards the East syde of the skaffolde, he uttered to the people these wordes."[4]

The following version of the speech, which is from the Cottonian MSS., corresponds in substance with that recorded by Grafton and Stow: I prefer to give it here, as being more terse, and as sounding more nearly like what was probably uttered. It was evidently written by some one who was present.

"Masters and good fellows, I am come hither for to die: but a true and faithful man as any was unto the king's majesty, and to his realme: but I am condemned by a law whereunto I am subject, and as we all are: and therefore to show obedience I am content to die: wherewith I am well content, being a thing most heartily welcome unto me: for the which I do thank God, taking it for a singular benefit and as great a benefit as ever might come to me any otherwise. For as I am a man, I have deserved at God's hand many deaths: and it hath pleased his goodness, whereas he might have taken me suddenly, that I should neither have known him nor myself, thus now to visit me and call me with this present death as you do see, when I have had time both to remember and knowledge him, and to know also myself: for which thing I do thank him most heartily. And, my friends, more

[1] Holinshed.
[2] The sergeants of the guards carried halberds until the reign of King George III.
[3] Machyn, p. 14.
[4] Grafton.

I have to say unto you as concerning religion. I have been always, being in authority, a furtherer of it to the glory of God, to the uttermost of my power, whereof I am nothing sorry, but rather have cause and do rejoyce most gladly that I have so done for the greatest benefit of God that ever I had, or any man might have in this world: beseeching you all to take it so, and to follow it on still, for if not there will follow and come a worse and great plague."

The MS. account then continues:

"Sodenly came a wondrous ffeare apon the peoplle after thos wordes of hym spoken, by a great sowend whych appered unto many abowe in the element, as yt had byne the sowend of gunpowder set on fyer in a close howes burstynge out, and by another sowend upon the growend as yt had byn the syght of a greate nomber of greate horses ronnynge on the people to overe roun them: so greate was the sowend of thys, that the peoplle fell dowen one apon the other, many wythe bylles, and others rone some thys waye some that waye, cryeng alowed 'Jesus save us! Jesus save us!' Many of the peopple cryeng 'thys waye thaye come, that waye thaye come, awaye, awaye.' And I loked when one or other shuld stryke me on the hedd, so was I stonned. The peopple beyng thus amassed, espyes Syr Anthony Browen[1] apone a lytell nage rydyng towards the scaffold, and there wythe burste out cryenge in a voyce, 'Pardon, pardon, pardon,' hurlyng up their cappes and clokes wythe these wordes, saying, 'God save the Kynge, God save the Kynge.'"[2]

Grafton says, "the truth of this hurlyburlye grewe hereof, as it was after well knowen. The manner and custome is that when such executions are done out of the Tower, the inhabitants of certayne hamlets round about London, as Hogsdon, Newyngton, Shordiche, and other, are commanded to give their attendaunce with weapons, upon the Lieutenant.

"And at this tyme, the Duke being upon the scaffolde by eyght of the clock in the morning, the people of one of the hamlets came late, and coming thorough the posterne gate and espying the Duke on the scaffolde, made haste and

[1] Sir Anthony Browne was then Sheriff of Surrey, he was created Viscount Montagu in 1554, and died 1592.

[2] See also Grafton's 'Chronicle,' and Hayward's 'Life of Edward VI.'

beganne to roune, and cryed to their felowes that were behind 'come away, come away.' The people sodainely beholding them to come running with weapons, and knewe not the cause, cried 'away, away,' by reason whereof the people ranne every way, not knowing whither or wherefore."[1]

The writer of the Cottonian MSS. account continues:—

"The good Duke all thys whyell stayed, and wythe hys cappe in hys hand wayted the people to come together, sayinge these wordes to ther wordes of pardon: 'there ys no suche thynge good people, there ys no suche thynge, yt ys the ordynans of God thus for to dye, where wythe we moste be content: and I praye you now lette us praye together for the Kynge's Majestic, to whose grace I have bynne allwayes a faythefull, trewe, and moste lovyng subject, desyros allwayes of his moste prosperos succes in all hys affayres; and ever glad of the furtherance and holpyng fortheward of the Common Welthe of thys Realme,' at whyche wordes the peoplie answered 'ye, ye, ye' and som sayd wythe a lowed voyce 'that is fowend now to trew.'

"To whose grace I beseeche God to send and grant to raynge moste prosperoslye to the pleasor of God.[2]

Grafton thus gives the close of his speech:

"And once agayne derely beloved in the Lord I require you that you will keepe yourselves quiet and still, least thorowe your tumult you might cause mee to have trouble, which in this case would nothing at all profite me, neyther be any pleasure unto yow. For albeit the spirite be wylling and readie, the fleshe is frayle and wavering, and through your quietnesse, I shall be much more the quieter: but if that you fall into tumult it will be great trouble and no gayne. Moreover I desire you to beare me witnesse that I die here in the fayth of Jesu Christ; desiring you to helpe me with your prayers, that I maye persevere constant in the same unto my life's ende."

"Then he turning himselfe about kneeled downe upon hys knees, unto whome Doctor Coxe,[3] which was there present to

---

[1] Grafton. "There was a sodain rumbelyng a lyttel a-for he ded, as yt had byn guns shuttyng, and grett horsys commyng, that many fell to the ground for fere: for thay that wher at the one syd thought no odur butt that one was kylling odur, that they fell down to the ground one apon anodur with ther holbards: sum fell into the dyche of the Towre, and odur plasys: and a hundred wer in the Towre dyche, and sum ran away for fere."—'Machyn's Diary,' p. 14.

[2] Cotton. MSS. in Ellis's 'Original Letters,' 2nd series, vol. ii. pp. 215–16.

[3] Richard Cox, appointed Dean of Westminster, 22nd Oct., 1549, but dispossessed and sent to the Tower 5th August, 1553, upon the accession of Queen Mary. In 1559 he was ap-

counsayle and advertise him, delivered a certaine scroll into his hande, wherein was conteyned a briefe confession unto God, which beyng read he stood up agayne on his feete, without any trouble of minde as it appeared, and first bade the Sherifes farewell, then the Lieutenant of the Tower and certayne other that were on the scaffolde, taking them all by the handes. Then he gave the executioner certayne money, which done, he put off his gowne, and kneling downe agayne in the strawe, untyed hys shirt strings, and then the executioner coming to him, turned downe his coller rounde about his necke, and all other things which did let and hinder him. Then he covering his face with his owne handkerchiefe, lifting up hys eyes unto heaven, where his onely hope remained, laid himselfe downe along, and then suffered the heavie stroke of the axe, which dissevered the head from his bodye, to the lamentable sight and griefe of thousands that heartily prayed God for him, and entirely loved him."[1]

Holinshed says: "He showed no manner of trouble or feare; neither did his countenance change, but that before his eyes were covered, there began to appear a red colour in the midst of his cheeks; and thus this most meeke and gentle duke lying along and looking for the stroke, because his doublet covered his neck he was commanded to put it off; then laying himself down again upon the block, and calling thrice upon the name of Jesus, saying 'Lord Jesu, save me;' as he was the third time repeating the same, even as the name of Jesu was in uttering, in a moment he was bereft both of head and life: and slept in the Lord Jesus, being taken awaie from all the dangers and evils of this life and resting now in the peace of God: in the preferment of whose truth and Gospell he alwaies showed himselfe an excellent instrument and member, and therefore hath re-

pointed Bishop of Ely by Queen Elizabeth: to him was addressed the celebrated letter:—

"Proud Prelate, you know what you were before I made you what you are; if you do not immediately comply with my request, by God, I will unfrock you. "ELIZABETH."

He died in 1581.

[1] Grafton. For a graphic account of the trial and execution, see Froude, vol. v. pp. 379–389.

ceived the reward of his labours. Thus, gentle reader, thou hast the true historye of this worthie and noble duke, and if anie man report it otherwise, let it be counted as a lie."[1]

"The people," writes Burnet, "were generally much affected by the execution: and many threw handkerchiefs into the Duke's blood, to preserve it in remembrance of him. One lady that met the Duke of Northumberland when he was led through the city in Queen Mary's reign, shaking one of these bloody handkerchiefs, said, 'Behold the blood of that worthy man, that good uncle of that excellent King, which was shed by thy malicious practice, it doth now begin apparently to revenge itself on thee.'"[2]

In King Edward's Diary we read the following cold and laconical entry of his uncle's death:—

"22 Jan. (1551-2). The Duke of Somerset had his head cut off upon Towre hill between eight and nine a cloke in the morning."

Machyn records: "And shortely ys body was putt into a coffin and carryed into the Towre and ther bered in the chyrche on the north syd of the qwyre of St. Peters: the wyche I beseeche God have mercy on ys sowlle. Amen."[3]

There is every reason to believe that the Duke of Somerset's bones remained in their original position until the burial of Sir John Burgoyne in 1871, when they were collected and removed somewhat nearer to the east wall of the chancel. A few that were apparently overlooked at that time were found in November, 1876, and these were enclosed in a leaden casket, and redeposited with the other remains in April, 1877.

[1] Holinshed; Hayward's 'Edward VI.,' pp. 138-140.
[2] Burnet, book i. part ii. vol. iii. pp. 383-4.
[3] Machyn's 'Diary,' p. 14. See also Collins's 'Peerage,' vol. i. pp. 160-1.

Sir Ralph Vane,
Born ———. Hanged on Tower Hill 26th Feb. 1551-2,
and
Sir Thomas Arundel,
Born ———. Beheaded on Tower Hill, 26th Feb. 1551-2.

Sir Ralph Vane was a gallant soldier; he had been knighted at the siege of Boulogne in 1544, and was afterwards made a banneret at Musselburgh, where he served as "Lieutenant of all the men at armes and demi-launces."

Hayward describes him as "a man of fierce spirit, both sodaine and bold, of no evill disposition, saving that he thought scantnesse of estate too great an evill." He had, however, become the enemy of the powerful John Dudley, Earl of Warwick, having quarrelled with him respecting some rights of pasturage, and he was, upon some unknown charge, arrested and committed to the Tower on the 27th March, 1551. He was released on the 5th October in the same year, but an opportunity soon after occurred of involving him in the alleged conspiracy of the Duke of Somerset, and King Edward records in his journal the evidence which was specially brought against him:—
"11th October: the Duke of Northumberland declared that Sir R. Vane had 2000 men in readiness."

Orders were therefore given for his arrest, and "being twice sent for, he fled, but upon pursuit was found in his servant's stable at Lambeth, covered with straw."[1]

He was then committed to the Tower, and the following entry appears in the King's journal:—"16th Oct. This morning none was at Westminster of the conspirators; Arundel and Vane were kept in chambers here[2] apart."

Sir Thomas Arundel was the son of Sir John Arundel, of Lanberne, in the county of Cornwall. He had been one of Wolsey's gentlemen of the privy chamber, was made a Knight

---

[1] Hayward's 'Edward VI.,' p. 131. "He was found by Jhon Piers in a stable of his man's at Lambeth under the straw."—Edward VI.'s Diary.

[2] The King was then living in the Tower.

of the Bath at Anne Boleyn's coronation, was present at Prince Edward's christening in 1537, and had been appointed Receiver-General of the duchy of Cornwall in 1549.

He was first sent to the Tower in January 1549-50, when it is supposed he was implicated in the rebellion of Humphrey Arundel, Governor of St. Michael's Mount, who was hanged at Tyburn in January, 1549-50. In King Edward's journal we read:—"1549. Sir Thomas Arundel and Sir Jhon (his elder brother) committed to the Tower for conspiracies in the west partes."[1]

He was released on the 4th October, 1551, but re-committed to the Tower on the 16th of the same month, as he, like Vane, was accused of being concerned in the Duke of Somerset's conspiracy.[2] King Edward's journal states the alleged treason:—"11 Oct. 1551. Sir Thomas Arrondel had ashuerid my Lord that the Towre was sauf." On the 16th October he was sent to the Tower, and the King writes:— "16 Oct. Arrondel was taken."

It was not until after the execution of the Protector Somerset that Sir R. Vane and Sir Thomas Arundel were brought to trial; because, as Sir J. Hayward says, "it was not thought fit that such a person should be executed alone, who could hardly be thought to offend alone."[3]

Vane was first brought before the Council, and was charged with conspiring with the Duke of Somerset; but he stood upon his innocence: "his bold answeres termed rude and ruffian-like, falling into ears oft to take offence, either only caused or much furthered his condemnation. For besides his natural fierceness, influenced by his present disgrace, he was the more free by reason of his great services in the field. He said: 'the time hath been when I was of

---

[1] The entry in the Council book is:

"xxx Jan. 1549–50.

"Sir Thomas Arundel, Knight, committed to the Tower by the order of the board."

[2] Bishop Ponet, in his 'Treatise on Politic Power,' says, in reference to his arrest in 1549, "he conspired with that ambitious and subtil Alcibiades, the Earl of Warwick, after Duke of Northumberland, to pull down the good Duke of Somerset, King Edward's uncle and protector:" if this be correct it is singular that he should have been afterwards re-arrested for conspiring with Somerset against Northumberland.

[3] Hayward's 'Edward VI.,' p. 142.

some esteeme : but now we are at peace, which reputeth the coward and courageous alike ;' and so with an obstinate resolution he made choice rather not to regard death than by any submission to intreat for life." [1]

He protested that he had never practised treason against the King or against the lives of any of the Lords of the Council ; and added that " his blood would make Northumberland's pillow uneasy to him." [2]

He was found guilty, and the terms of his conviction were—" for moving, stirring, and procureing of dyvers persons for the felonyous taking, imprisoning, and killing dyvers of our privey counsell against the form of our statutes and lawes of our realme."

The King then enters in his diary :—" 27 Jan. 1551-2. Sir Rafe Vane was condemned of felony in treason, aunswering like a ruffian."

Machyn writes :—" The xxvii day of Januerii was reynyd (arraigned) at Westminster Hall, Ser Raff. A. Vane, Knight, of tresun, and qwyt of hytt (acquitted of it) and cast of felonye, to be hanged." [3]

Sir Thomas Arundel was tried on the day after Vane, and Machyn records :—" The xxviij day of Januarii was reynyd Ser Thomas Arundell, Knyght, and so the qwest cold not fynd ym[4] till the tomorow after, and so he whent to the Towre agayne, and then the qwest wher shutt up tyll the morow withowt mett or drynke or candylle or fyre, and on the morow he cam agayne (from the Towre to Westminster Hall), and the qwest qwytt ym of tresun, and cast hym of felonye, to be hangyd." [5]

The following is the entry in the Royal diary :—" 29th Jan. 1551-2. Sir Thomas Arundel was likewise cast of felony in treason, after long controversie, for the matter was brought in trial bie seven of the cloke in the morning 28th

---

[1] Hayward's ' Edward VI.,' p. 142.
[2] Heylin's ' History of Reformation ' (1674), p. 117.
[3] Machyn's ' Diary,' p. 15.
[4] " And as the inquest could not find him."
[5] Machyn, p. 15. The records of these trials are preserved in the Baga de Secretis, Pouch xx. bundles 1 and 2. In them the name is written " Fane," and not " Vane."

day: at none the quest went together: they sate shut up together in a house, without meat or drinke, bicause they could not agree, all that day and all night: this 29th day in the morning they did cast him." [1]

On the 29th, therefore, the Council issued orders to the Lieutenant of the Tower,[2] "that Doctour Bill[3] may from tyme to tyme resort to Sir Rauff Fane[4] for his instruction to dye well: and that Doctour Parker[5] may resort from tyme to tyme to Sir Thomas Arundell for the lyke purpose."

Also on the 11th February, "Mr. Perne[6] was allowed to resort to Sir Thomas Arundell to instruct hym to dye well;" and on the 22nd of the same month the Lieutenant receives instructions to give notice to "Sir Thomas Arundell and Sir Rauf Vane that they should against Friday next prepare themselves to dye according to their condempnation."[7]

Some influence was used on behalf of Sir Thomas Arundel, as his sentence was changed from hanging to the less degrading death by beheading. Vane's sentence remained unaltered, perhaps because he had defiantly answered, "like a ruffian." Accordingly, on the 23rd February a letter is written to the King's solicitor, "to make a warrant for the beheading of Sir Thomas Arundel and Sir Michael Stanhope and to perform the processe of the hanging of Sir

---

[1] In the account of Sir A. Darcy for divers prisoners, &c., occur charges for diets for Sir Thomas Arundell and Sir R. Vane, at so much per week, for the King's servants waiting upon them: for "fewell and candell:" for the hire of barges to take them to Westminster, and again for "the same barge, the next day for Sir Thomas Arundell when he went for his judgment."—Harleian MSS. 284, f. 98.

[2] Sir Arthur Darcy, appointed Lieutenant on 31st October, 1551, in succession to Sir John Markham, who had been dismissed because he allowed too much liberty to the Duke of Somerset. See Edward VIth's Diary.

[3] Dr. William Bill, Master of St. John's, and, in 1551, of Trinity College, at Cambridge, afterwards Provost of Eton, Dean of Westminster, and Almoner to Queen Elizabeth. He died in 1561, and was buried in Westminster Abbey.

[4] The name is also found spelt Phane, in the proceedings of the Privy Council respecting the will of Henry VIII. He was of the same family as the Fanes, Earls of Westmoreland.—J. G. Nichols, 'Literary Remains of Edward VI.'

[5] Matthew Parker, born 1504, Chaplain to Edward VI., Dean of Lincoln, and afterwards Archbishop of Canterbury from 1559 till 1575. He was buried at Lambeth.

[6] Mr. Perne. Probably Mr. William Peryn, Prior of the Black friars. He was a celebrated preacher. Died 1558. See Machyn's 'Diary.'

[7] Extracts from Council Registers. Sir Michael Stanhope and Sir Miles Partridge were to suffer death at the same time.

Rauf Vane and Sir Miles Partridge, who are appointed to be executed on fryday next between ix and xi before noone." [1]

The warrant for their execution is dated 25 Feb.,[2] and on the next day, Friday the 26th, Arundel was beheaded and Vane was hung on Tower Hill.

"The xxvjth day of Februarie, the wyche was the morow after saynt Mathuwe day, was heddyd (beheaded) on the Towre hyll, Sir Thomas Arundell, and incontenent was hangyd the seylffsame tyme Sir Raff A. Vane, Knyght, after, ther bodys wher putt into dyvers nuw coffens to be bered, and heds, into the Towre in cases, and ther bered."[3]

It is recorded in the Register that they were buried "in the Chappell."[4]

JOHN DUDLEY, DUKE OF NORTHUMBERLAND.

Born 1502. Beheaded on Tower Hill, 22nd August, 1553.

Edward VI. died on Thursday evening the 6th July, 1553, and the Duke of Northumberland endeavoured to conceal the fact of the King's death from the public, so that he might with more facility mature his plans for placing his daughter-in-law, Lady Jane Grey, on the throne. On the 8th July, however, the King's demise became known, and on Sunday the 9th, Northumberland saluted Lady Jane Grey as Queen, when she entered the Tower in state.

On the 14th July by order of the council, Northumberland and his sons left London to take command of the troops that had been sent out to capture the Princess Mary, but the sailors of the fleet at Yarmouth declared in her favour,[5] and the soldiers also began to mutiny against Northumber-

---

[1] Council Register. A warrant is issued on the 24th February, directing the Exchequer " to delyver to the lieutenant of the Tower lvili. xiijs. iiijd., to be distributed unto Sir Thomas Arundel, Sir Michael Stanhopp, Sir Rauf Vane, and Sir Myles Partriche. This was evidently to defray the charges he had incurred during their imprisonment.—J.G Nichols, 'Literary Remains of Edward VI.,' p. 395.

[2] See Rymer's 'Foedera,' xv. 296.

[3] Machyn's 'Diary,' p. 15.

[4] See page 43.

[5] 'Chronicle of Queen Jane and Queen Mary,' p. 8.

land, upon which the Duke received orders to lay down his arms and return to London.

Queen Mary was proclaimed on the 19th July, and orders were then sent for the arrest of Northumberland, at Cambridge.

It is in the pages of Holinshed that we find the best account of his arrest. "The twentieth of Julie the Duke of Northumberland being come backe to Cambridge, heard that the proclamation of Queene Marie was come thither, whereof he being advertised, called for a trumpeter and an herald, but none could be found. Whereupon, he riding into the market place with the maior, and the Lord Marquess of Northampton,[1] made the proclamation himselfe, and threw up his cap in token of joy.[2] Within an houre after, he had letters from the councell (as he said), that he should forthwith dismisse his armie, and not come within ten miles of London; for if he did, they would fight with him; the rumor whereof was no sooner abroad, but everie man departed, and shortlie after, the Duke was arrested in the King's College by one Master Sleg, sergeaunt at arms.[3] At the last, letters were brought from the councell at London, that all men should go each his waie. Whereupon the Duke said to them that kept him: 'Ye do me wrong to withdraw my libertie, see you not the councell's letters without exception, that all men should go whither they would.' At which words they that kept him and the other noblemen, set them at libertie, and so continued they for that night: insomuch that the Earle of Warwicke[4] was readie in the morning to have rode awaie. But then came the Erle of Arundell[5] from the Queene, to the Duke, into his chamber, who went out to meet him.

[1] William Parr, Marquis of Northampton, and brother of Queen Katharine Parr, was attainted in 1554, restored to his honours in 1559, and died in 1571.

[2] Crying out, "God save Queen Mary."—Burnet, book ii. part ii. vol. iii. p. 479.

[3] Roger Slegg, afterwards an alderman of Cambridge. See Cooper's 'Annals of Cambridge;' also Stow.

[4] Northumberland's eldest son.

[5] Henry Fitzalan, last Earl of Arundel, Lord Chamberlain to Henry VIII., and Lord Steward to Queen Mary and Queen Elizabeth from 1553 till 1568. He made a proposal of marriage to Queen Elizabeth, which being refused, he resigned his offices and went abroad to travel. He died in 1580, and was buried at Arundel. His daughter and heir, Lady

"Now as soone as he saw the Earle of Arundell, he fell on his knees, and desired him to be good to him for the love of God: 'Consider,' said he, 'I have done nothing but by the consents of you, and all the whole councell.' 'My Lord' (quoth the Erle of Arundell), 'I am sent hither by the Queene's majestie, and in hir name I doo arrest you.' 'And I obeie it my Lord' (quoth he), 'I beseech you, my Lord of Arundell, use mercie towards me, knowing the case as it is.' 'My Lord' (quoth the Erle), 'you should have sought for mercie sooner, I must doo according to commandement.' Herewith he committed the charge of him and the others to the guard and gentlemen that stood by."[1]

On Friday the 25th July, Northumberland was brought to the Tower by the Earl of Arundel, "with a great number of light horsemen, bowes, and speares. They came into London at Bishopsgate, all the streetes as he passed by standing with men in harnesse, afore every man's doore, till he came to the Tower wharfe."[2]

He remained in the Tower until Monday the 18th of August, when he "and the others (the Earl of Huntingdon[3] was except) were brought into Westminster Hall, and there arraigned of high treason, before Thomas, Duke of Norfolk, High Steward of England.[4] And being brought to the barre he used great reverence to his judges, and protesting his fayth and allegeance to the Queene's majesty, whom he confessed to have grievously offended: he said that he meant not to speake anything in defence of his fact, but would first understand the opinion of the court in two pointes.

"First, whether a man doing any acte or thing by authoritie of the Prince's counsaile, and by warrant of the

---

Mary Fitzalan, married Thomas Howard. the fourth Duke of Norfolk, in 1554. In right of descent from their son (Philip, first Earl of Arundel of the Howards) the present Duke of Norfolk holds the earldom by possession of the manor and castle of Arundel.

[1] Holinshed.
[2] Stow. Machyn's 'Diary,' p. 37.
[3] Francis, Earl of Huntingdon, married Katharine, daughter of Margaret Plantagenet, Countess of Salisbury, died in 1560.
[4] Thomas Howard, third Duke. "The old Duke of Norfolk was made Lord High Steward: the Queen thinking it fit to put the first character of honour on him, who had suffered so much for being the head of the Popish party."— Burnet, book ii. part ii. vol. iii. p. 488.

great seale of England, and nothing doing without the same, may be charged with treason for doing anything by such warrant.

"Second, whether any such persons as were equally culpable in that crime, and those by whose letters and commandments he was directed in all his doings, might be his judges, or passe upon his trial as his peeres?[1]

"Whereunto was answered: as to the first, that the great seale (which he layd for his warrant) was not the seale of the lawfull Queene of the realme, nor passed by her authority, but the seale of an usurper, and therfore could be no warrant to him.

"And to the second, that if any were as depely to be touched in that case as himselfe, yet so long as no attainder were of recorde against them, they were neverthelesse persons able in law in passe upon any trial, and not to be chalenged therfore, but at the prince's pleasure.

"After which answere, the Duke using a few words declaring his earnest repentance in the case, and moving the Duke of Norfolk to be his meane to the Queene for mercy, without further answere confessed the inditement, which was that he 'by machinating and compassing to depose the Queen from her crown and dignity, did with arms and artillery, levy war against the Queen,' by whose example the other lords arreyned with him, did in the like manner, and thereupon had judgment.

"When judgment was given, the Duke sayd, I beseech you my Lords all to bee humble suters to the Queene's majestie, to graunt me iiij requestes, which are theis: firste, that I may have that deathe which noblemen have had in tymes past, and not the other: secondarylie, that her majestie will be gratyous to my childer, that may hereafter do hir grace gode service, concydering that they went by my commandement, who am their father, and not of their

---

[1] This was perhaps an allusion to the will of Edward VI., and the warrant under the great seal which was affixed to it; but especially to the commission under the great seal, which, as general of the army, he had obtained from Queen Jane and her council.

owne free willes: thirdely, that I may have appoynted to me some learned man, for the instruction and quieting of my concyence: and iiijth, that she will sende ij of the counsayle to comon with me, to whom I will declare suche matters as shal be expedyent for hir and the comonwelthes, and thus I beseche you all to pray for me." [1]

The Lord High Steward then pronounced upon him the usual sentence for traitors, broke his wand of office and dissolved the court. Northumberland was reconducted to his prison in the Tower.[2]

Stephen Gardiner, Bishop of Winchester, visited him on the next day; to whom Northumberland pleaded with much earnestness that his life might be spared: he declared he was a Catholic, and had always been a Catholic. Gardiner is believed to have spoken to the Queen on his behalf: but it was decided that he could receive no respite, and a priest named Watson was sent to prepare him for death.[3]

Yet he still clung to the hope of life, and on 20th August, the night before his appointed execution, he wrote the following abject letter to the Earl of Arundel.

"Honble lord, and in this my distress, my especiall refuge, most wofull was the newes I receyved this evenynge by Mr. lieutenant, that I must prepare myselfe agst to morrowe to receyve my deadly stroke. Alas my good lord, is my cryme so heynous as noe redemcion but my blood can washe awaye the spottes thereof? An old proverb there is, and it is most true, that a lyving dogge is better than a dead lyon. Oh! that it would please her good grace to give me life, yea, the life of a dogge, if I might but lyve and kiss her feet, and spend both life and all in her hon^{ble} services, as I have the best part already under her worthie brother, and most glorious father. Oh! that her mercy were such as she would consyder how little profit my dead and dismembered body can bringe her; but how great and glorious an honour it will be in all posterityes when the report shall be that soo gracious and mightie a queene had graunted life to soe miserable and penitent an object. Your hon^{ble} usage and promise to me since these my troubles

---

[1] 'Chron. of Queen Jane and Queen Mary,' p. 17.—Stow; Holinshed. The proceedings of the trial are to be found in Baga de Secretis, Pouch xxi.

[2] In the Beauchamp Tower: on the walls of the principal room are two inscriptions which have been attributed to him or his sons. See Bayley, pp. 146–162; 'Archæologia,' vol. xiii. pp. 69–70; Dick's Inscriptions.

[3] Froude, vol. vi. p. 67.

have made me bold to challenge this kindnes at your handes. Pardon me if I have done amiss therin, and spare not, I pray, your bended knees for me in this distresse. The God of heaven, it may be, will requite it one day, on you or yours; and, if my life be lengthened by your mediacion, and my good lord Chauncellor's (to whom I have also sent my blurred letters), I will ever owe it to be spent at your hon[ble] feet. Oh! my good lord, remember how sweet life is, and how bitter the contrary. Spare not your speech and paines; for God, I hope, hath not shut out all hopes of comfort from me in that gracious, princely, and woman-like hart; but that, as the doleful newes of death hath wounded to death both my soule and bodye, soe the comfortable newes of life shall be as a new resurrection to my wofull hart. But if no remedy can be found eyther by imprisonment, confiscation, banishment and the like, I can saye noe more, but God grant me pacyence to endure, and a hart to forgeve the whole world. Once your fellowe and lovinge companion, but now worthy of noe name but wretchedness and misery.

"J. D."[1]

The execution of the Duke, together with that of Gates and Palmer, was at first appointed to take place on Thursday the 21st August, and Henry Machyn, the merchant taylor and citizen of London, has recorded in his diary the preparations that were made.

"The xxi of August, was by viij of the cloke in the morning, on Towre hylle, abowte 1000 men and women for to have seen the execussyon of the Duke of Northumberland, for the skaffold was mad ready, and sand and straw was browth, and all the men that belonged to the Towre, as Hogston, Shordyche, Bow, Ratclyff, Lymhouse, Saint Kateryns, and the warders of the Towre, and the gard, and shyreyffs offesers, and evere man standing in order with ther holbardes, and lanes made, and the hangman was ther, and sodenly they wher commondyd to departe. And the sam tym after was sent for my lord mer and the aldermen and cheyffest of the craftes in London, and dyvers of the counsell, and ther was mas said afor the Duke and the rest of the presonars."[2]

This respite of twenty-four hours was doubtless obtained by Gardiner, in order to afford an opportunity of showing

[1] Harleian MSS. No. 787, f. 61; Tierney's 'Hist. of Arundel,' vol. i. p. 333; Bayley, p. 422.
[2] Machyn's 'Diary.' p. 42.

JOHN DUDLEY, DUKE OF NORTHUMBERLAND. 159

to the people the spectacle of the Duke and the other prisoners conforming to the celebration of the Catholic form of worship, by hearing mass, and confessing publicly in the chapel of St. John in the White Tower.

The following circumstantial account of the scene is in all probability from an eyewitness.

"On Mondaye the xxi[st] of August, it was appoynted the Duke with others should have suffered, and all the garde were at the Tower, but howsoever it chaunced he did not: but he desired to heare masse and to receave the sacrament, according to the olde accustumed manner. So about ix of the clocke, the alter in the chappell was arraied, and eche thing prepared for the purpose: then Mr. Gage[1] went and fetched the Duke: and Sir John à Bridges,[2] and Mr. John à Bridges dyd fetche the Marques of Northampton, Sir Androwe Dudley,[3] Sir Herry Gates, and Sir Thomas Palmer, to masse, which was sayde both with elevation over the hed, the paxe geving, blessinge, and crossinge on the crowne, breathinge, towrninge aboute, and all the other rytes and accydentes of olde tyme appertayning: and when the tyme came the prysoners shoulde receive the sacrament, the Duke tourned himselfe to the people and saide, first, theis wordes, or suche like:

"My masters, I lett you all to understande that I do most faithfullie belyve this is the right true waie, oute of the which true religion you and I have been seduced theis xvi yeres past, by the false and erronyous preching of the new prechers, the which is the onelie cause of the great plagges and vengeaunce which hath lighte apon the holye realme of Englande, and now likewise worthely falne apon me and others here presente for owr unfaythfulnesse. And I do believe the holye sacramente here most assuredlye to be owr Saviour and Redeemer Jesus Christe; and this I praye you all to testifye, and praye for me."

After which wordes he kneeled down and axed all men forgivenes, and likewise forgave all men. Emongest others standing by (were) the Duke of Somersetes sonnes. Then

---

[1] Sir John Gage, b. 1479, was Constable of the Tower, and Lord Chamberlain to Queen Mary. He died April 1556, and was buried at West Firle, in Sussex.

[2] Sir John Brydges, the Lieutenant of the Tower.

[3] Lord Ambrose Dudley.

160   ST. PETER AD VINCULA.

all the rest confessed the declaration aforesaide, and so receved the sacrament most humbly. Note, that a littell before masse was begonne, there was sent for into London for diverse of the best comoners and comon counsaill of the citye, to come and here the convertion of the Duke, amongst whom one Hartop, a goldsmith, and one Baskerfield, were there:[1] and the Lady Jane loking throughe

Chapel of St. John in the White Tower.

the windowe sawe the Duke and the rest going to the churche."[2]

[1] "Divers merchants to the number of 14 or 15 were by the counsell commanded to come to the Queen's chappell, and there tarry tyll masse was don: Mr. Thomas Locke was one, Mr. Clement Newse, and divers others in Cheapside."—Letter of William Dalby, 22 Aug. 1553, in Harleian MSS. No. 353.

[2] 'Chron. of Queen Jane and Queen Mary,' pp. 18–19. Northumberland was imprisoned in the Beauchamp Tower, and Lady Jane Grey looking out of a window in the master gaoler's house, would see him crossing the green to the chapel of St. John in the White Tower. It was doubtless by Gardiner's order that her attention was directed to the demonstration of Northumberland's adherence to the Catholic form of worship.

JOHN DUDLEY, DUKE OF NORTHUMBERLAND. 161

How far this conduct of Northumberland, in conforming thus openly to the Catholic worship, may have been stimulated by his hope of saving his life, it is impossible to say, but Foxe writes that hopes of pardon were held out to him, if he would recant and hear mass, and, relying on this assurance, he did what Gardiner required of him. Any such hopes were however defeated, and on the next day his execution took place.

"The two and twentieth of August Sir John Gage, Lieutenant of the Tower, had made redy the Indentures and delivered to the Sheriffs of London, these prisoners following, first, Sir John Gates was brought forth out of the Levetenants house, and set at the garden gate, then they went for the Duke of Northumberland, who within a littell while came fourthe. When the Duke and Sir John Gates met; 'Sir John' (sayd the Duke), 'God have mercie upon us, for this daie shall ende both our lives, and I praie you forgeve mee whatsoever I have offended, and I forgeve you with all my hearte, although you and your councell was a great occasion hereof:' 'Well my Lorde,' quoth Sir John Gates, 'I forgive you, as I would bee forgeven, and yet you and your auctoritie was the originall cause of all together, but the Lorde pardon you, I praie you forgeve me.' So either making obeisaunce to other, the Duke proceeded. The Duke of Somerset's sonnes stoode therby."[1]

Northumberland was attended on the scaffold by Heath,[2] Bishop of Worcester, and when he came upon the scaffold, "puttinge off his gowne of swane coloured damask," he leaned apon the raile towarde the Est, and addressed the people.[3]

---

[1] 'Chron. of Queen Jane and Queen Mary,' p. 21.—Stow. It is expressly recorded that the sons of the Duke of Somerset were present both on the 21st and 22nd, probably by Gardiner's direction, that they might be witnesses of the humiliation of their father's powerful rival.

[2] Nicholas Heath (had been previously Bishop of Rochester) was Bishop of Worcester from 1543 till 1554, when he was appointed Archbishop of York. He succeeded Gardiner as Chancellor in 1556. He was dispossessed of his archbishopric on the accession of Elizabeth, and retired to Chobham, in Surrey. He died in 1579, and was buried in Chobham Church.

[3] Among the acts of the council appears, "a letter to Sir Edmond Peckham for 41*l*. 14*s*. 4*d*. to the Lord Chamberlain, for soe much by him de-

His speech is to be found in the Harleian MSS., No. 284. It bears this heading, "The open confession off the Duke of Northumberlande, wch sufferid at Tower hyll 22 off August, 1553."

This version of Northumberland's speech bears evident indications of being prepared for public circulation, and may have been revised, if not in great measure written under Gardiner's inspection, I therefore prefer to give the speech which Stow has recorded in his chronicle, as it is simpler, and has a more genuine ring in it.

"Good people, all you that be heere present to see mee die, though my death bee odious, and horrible to the flesh, yet I pray you judge the best in God's workes, for hee doth all for the best, and as for mee, I am a wretched sinner, and have deserved to die, and most justly am condemned to die by law: and yet this act whereof I dye, was not altogether of me (as it is thought) but I was procured and induced thereunto by other: Howbeit, God forbid that I should name any man unto you, I will name no man unto you, and therefore I beseeche you looke not for it. I, for my part, forgive all men, and pray God also to forgive them. And if I have offended any of you here, I pray you, and all the world to forgive me; and mostly, chiefly, I desire forgiveness of the Queen's highnesse, whom I have most grievously offended.

"And I pray you all to witnesse with me, that I departe in perfect love and charitie with all the world, and that you will assist me with your prayers at this hour of death."

He concluded by making a confession of his belief.[1]

---

livered to the Duke of Northumberland, Sir John Gates, and Sir Thomas Palmer, to give almes at their execution."—Bayley, p. 423. Sir E. Peckham was then Treasurer of the Mint: he had been cofferer of the household to Henry VIII. and Edward VI.

[1] Stow.

Another record of the scene by an eyewitness may also be added:

"22 Aug. 1553.

"This present daye the duke of Northumberlande, sir John Gates, and master Palmere came to executione and suffered deathe. The duke's confessyon was in effecte but lytle, as I hard saye; he confessed himselfe worthie to dye, and that he was a greate helper in of this religion which is false, thearfore God had punished us with the lose of King Henry 8, and also with the lose of King Edward 6, then with rebellione, and after with the swetinge sickness, and yet we would not turne. Requiringe them all that weare presente to remember the ould learninge, thankinge God that he would vutsafe to call him nowe to be a Christyane, for this 16 yeares he had byne non. Theare weare a greate nomber turned with his wordes. He wished every man not to be covetous, for that was a greate parte of his distruction. He was asked further if he had anythinge

Stow then continues his narrative: "After the Duke had thus spoken hee kneled downe, saying to them that were about him, I beseech you all to beare mee witnesse that I die in the true Catholike faith, and then he sayd the Psalmes of 'Miserere,' and 'De Profundis,' his paternoster, and sixe of the first verses of the psalm 'In te Domine speravi,' ending with this verse: 'into thy handes O Lord, I commend my spirit,' and when hee had finished his prayers, the executioner[1] asked him forgivenesse, to whom hee sayd, 'I forgive thee with all my heart, and doe thy part without feare.'[2]

"And bowing toward the blocke, hee said, I have deserved a thousand deathes, hee layd his head upon the blocke, and so was beheaded.[3] Whose body, with the head, was buryed in the Tower, by the body of Edward, late Duke of Somerset: so that there lyeth before the high altar in St. Peter's Church, two Dukes betweene two Queenes, to wit, the Duke of Somerset, and the Duke of Northumberland between Queen Anne, and Queene Katherine, all foure beheaded."[4]

---

moare to saye, and he said nothinge but that he was worthie to dye, and so was more than he, but he cam to dye and not to accuse any mane. And thus bouldly he spak, tyll he layd his head on the block."—Letter of William Dalby, Harl. MSS. 353; 'Chron. of Queen Jane and Queen Mary,' p. 24. Bayley, Appendix, p. xlviii. Tytler, vol. ii. p. 230.

[1] Stephen Perlin, an ecclesiastic, in a description of England published in Paris in 1558, says that the "hangman was lame of a leg, for I was present at the execution, and wore a white apron like a butcher."—'Antiquarian Repertory,' vol. iv. p. 507.

[2] For the remarkable commentary by Lady Jane Grey upon the Duke's conduct and death, see page 167.

[3] He made the sign of the cross upon the sawdust, and kissed it, then laid down his head, and perished.—Froude's 'Hist. of England,' vol. vi. p. 72.

[4] Stow, "Theyr corpes, with the hedes, were buried in the chapell in the Tower: the Duke at the high altar, and the other two (Sir John Gates and Sir Thomas Palmer [for a graphic account of the scene at their execution see Froude, vol. vi. pp. 73–4]) at the nether end of the church.—'Chron. of Queen Jane and Queen Mary,' p. 24.

"Between the two Queenes before the high altar, lie buried two Dukes, to wit the Duke of Somerset, Edward Seymour, and the Duke of Northumberland, John Dudley."—Weever.

"His body with the head was buried in the Tower, by the body of Edward, late Duke of Somerset (mortal enemies while they lived, but now lying together as good friends), so as there lieth before the high altar in Saint Peter's church two Dukes between the two Queens; namely, the Duke of Somerset and the Duke of Northumberland between Queen Anne and Queen Katherine, all four beheaded."—Baker's 'Chronicle.'

LADY JANE GREY.

Born 1537. Executed on the Green within the Tower, 12th February, 1553-4.

LORD GUILDFORD DUDLEY.

Born ——. Executed on Tower Hill, 12th February, 1553-4.

Fuller, in his quaint style, remarks of Lady Jane Grey that "she had the birth of a princess, the learning of a clerk, the life of a saint, yet the death of a malefactor for her parent's offence, and she was longer a captive than a Queen in the Tower."

On Monday, the 10th July, 1553, she was brought down the Thames from Sion, which was then the residence of the Duke of Northumberland, and "in the afternoone about three of the clocke," she landed and entered the Tower of London as Queen. She was received "with a grett compeny of lords and nobulls, and ther was a shot of gunnes and chamburs as has nott bene sene oft, between four and five of the clocke." [1]

But on the 19th July, Queen Mary had not only been proclaimed but recognised as Queen throughout London, and measures had been taken to arrest the Duke of Northumberland. Queen Jane then desired to remove from the Tower; but "the Tower was a place not easy to leave save by one route too often travelled;" [2] and on the evening of that day Lady Throckmorton, the lady in attendance on Queen Jane, on entering the presence-chamber, observed that the canopy of state and all insignia of royalty had been removed. Queen Jane's short reign was over, and both she and her husband were now prisoners. They were separated, and confined in different parts of the Tower. Lord Guildford Dudley was lodged in the Beauchamp Tower, and Lady Jane Grey first in the Lieutenant's lodging, and afterwards in the gentleman gaoler's house which adjoins it. On the 21st August her father-in-law, the Duke of Northumberland,

---

[1] Machyn's 'Diary,' p. 35.   [2] Froude, vol. vi. p. 32.

View of the Lieutenant's Lodgings and Gentleman-Gaoler's House.

was taken from his prison in the Beauchamp Tower to the Chapel in the White Tower to hear mass and confess before his execution; when "Lady Jane looking throughe the windowe sawe the Duke and the rest going to the churche."[1]

The anonymous author of the diary, Harleian MSS. No. 194, has noted the following interesting incident: "On Tuisdaie, the 29th of Auguste, I dyned at Partrige's [2] House with my Lady Jane being ther present, she sitting at the bordes ende, Partrige, his wife, Jacob, my ladyes gentill-woman, and hir man. She comanding Partrige and me to put on our cappes, emongst our communycacion at the dyner, this was to be noted; after she had once or twice droncke to mee and bad mee hartellie wellcome, saithe she, 'The Quene's majesty is a mercyfull princess; I beseche God she may long contynue, and sende his bountefull grace apon hir.' After that we fell in discourse of mattiers of religion; and she axed what he was that preached at Polles (St. Paul's) on Sonday beefore, and so it was tolde hir to be one (*left blank in MS*.); 'I praie you,' quoth she, 'have they masse in London?' 'Yay, forsuthe,' quoth I, 'in some places.' 'It may so be,' quoth she, 'it is not so strange as the sodden convertyon of the late Duke; for who wolde have thought,' said she, 'he would have so done?' It was aunswered her, 'Perchance he thereby hoped to have had his pardon.' 'Pardon,' quoth she, 'wo withe him! he hathe brought me and our stocke in most myserable callamyty and mysery by his exceeding ambicion. But for the aunswering that he hoped for life by his tourning, thoughe other men be of that opynion, I utterly am not; for what man is ther lyving, I pray you, although he had been innocent, that wolde hope of life in that case; being in the felde ageinst the Quene in person as generall, and after his taking, so hated and evell spoken of by the Comons? and at his coming into pryson so

---

[1] See page 160, and 174 note.
[2] Nathaniel Partridge was the gentleman gaoler: his fees were estimated at 10*l*. per annum in an old book in the Tower records. He was buried on 13th Feb. 1587. See p. 45. His house was next to the Lieutenant's lodgings, and the room which was occupied by Lady Jane Grey is still pointed out. It is said that she inhabited the Brick Tower for a time.

wondered at, as the like was never harde by any man's tyme. Who was judge, that he shoulde hope for pardon, whose life was odyous to all men? But what will ye more? like as his life was wicked and full of dissimulacion, so was his ende therafter. I pray God, I, nor no frende of myne, dye so. Shoulde I, who am yonge and in my fewers (few years) forsake my faythe for the love of lyfe? Nay, God forbed! moche more he should not whose fatall course, althoughe he had lyved his just noumber of yeres, coulde not have long contynued. But life is swete, it appeered; so he might have lyved, you will saye, he dyd not care howe. Indede the reason is goode, for he that wolde have lyved in chaynes to have had his lyfe, by like wolde leave no other meane attempted. But God be mercyful to us, for he sayeth, 'Whoso denyeth him before men, he will not knowe him in his Father's kingdome.'

"With this and moche like talke the dyner passyd away: which ended, I thanked her ladyship that she would witsafe (vouchsafe) accept me in hir companye; and she thancked me likewise, and sayd I was wellcome.

"She thancked Partrige also for bringing me to dyner. 'Madam,' saide he, ' wee wer somewhat bolde, not knowing that your ladyship dyned belowe untyll we fonde your ladyship ther.' And so Partrige and I departed."[1]

In September, orders were sent by the Council to the Lieutenant of the Tower that the liberty of the walks within the garden of the Tower, was " at convenient times and at his discretion" to be granted to Lady Jane Grey and to Dr. Cranmer, " upon suggestion that divers be, and have been, evill at ease in their bodies for want of air."[2]

On the 14th September, the "libertie of the leades on Beacham's Tower" is granted to Lord Guildford Dudley and his brother, Lord Harry.[3]

Then came the pageant of Queen Mary's coronation on the

[1] 'Chron. of Queen Jane and Queen Mary,' pp. 25–6. Harleian MSS., No. 194. It originally belonged to Stow, the antiquary, and afterwards to Sir Simond D'Ewes.
[2] Bayley, p. 427.
[3] 'Chron. of Queen Jane and Queen Mary,' p. 27.

1st of October, and it was not until November that the trial of Lady Jane and her husband took place.

"On the xiii daie of November were ledd out of the Tower on foot, to be arraigned, to Yeldhall (Guildhall) with the axe before them, from theyr wardes, Thomas Cranmer, Archbushoppe of Canterbury. Next followed the Lorde Gilforde Dudley. Next followed the Lady Jane, and hir two gentyllwomen following hir. Next followed the Lorde Ambrose Dudley and the Lorde Harry Dudley.

"The Lady Jane was in a blacke gowne of clothe, tourned downe; the cappe lyned with fese velvett, and edget about with the same; in a French hoode, all black, with a black byllyment (habilment); a black velvet boke hanging before hir, and another boke in hir hande open." [1]

The trial was by special commission before the Lord Mayor (Thomas White), the Duke of Norfolk presiding as Lord High Steward, and other peers. The prisoners pleaded guilty, and confessed all their indictments; they were therefore attainted of high treason, "for assumption of the Royal authority by Lady Jane, for levying war against the Queen and conspiracy to set up another in her room." The sentence on Lady Jane Grey was that "she should be burned alive on Tower Hill or beheaded as the Queen pleases." These judgments were subsequently confirmed by Act of Parliament.[2] They were taken back on foot to the Tower; "from whence," says Grafton, referring to Lady Jane and her husband, "they never came but to the scaffold." On the 18th December orders are again given that Lady Jane should have "the libertie of the Tower, so that she might walk in the Quene's garden,[3] and on the hill," and Lord Guildford "had the libertie of the leds in the Bell Tower,"[4] and they were not without hope of life and liberty altogether if her father, the Duke of Suffolk, had not again joined in insurrection with Sir Thomas Wyatt: this rebellion was

---

[1] 'Chron. of Queen Jane and Queen Mary,' p. 32; Machyn, p. 48; Stow.
[2] Burnet, book ii. part ii. vol. iii. p. 515. The trial is in the Baga de Secretis, Pouch xxiii.
[3] See plan, p. 187.
[4] That is of walking to and fro on the leads extending from the Beauchamp to the Bell Tower: he was imprisoned in the Beauchamp Tower.

crushed on the 6th February (1553-4), and then "consultation was held what delinquents should be punished; when the first that was thought on was Lady Jane, in whom was verified 'the fathers have eaten sour grapes, and the children's teeth are set on edge;'[1] the innocent lady must suffer for her father's fault, for if her father, the Duke of Suffolk, had not this second time made shipwreck of his loyalty, his daughter had perhaps never tasted the salt waters of the Queen's displeasure; but now as a rock of offence she is the first that must be removed."[2]

Queen Mary was anxious to spare Lady Jane Grey's life, but after Wyatt's rebellion, "Renard in the closet, and Gardiner in the pulpit, alike told her that she must show no more mercy."[3]

We have no record of how her approaching execution was notified to Lady Jane Grey, or what she may have said on that occasion, but a few days before her death she wrote the following letter to her father, the Duke of Suffolk:—

"Father, although it hath pleased God to hasten my death by you, by whome my life should rather have beene lengthened, yet I can see patiently take it, that I yield God more hearty thanks for shortning my woful dayes, than if all the world had been given into my possession, with life lengthened at my owne will.

"And albeit I am very well assured of your impatient dolours, redoubled many wayes, both in bewayling your own woe, and especially as I am informed, my wofull estate: yet my deare father, if I may, without offence, rejoyce in my own mishaps, herein I may account myselfe blessed, that washing my hands with the innocence of my fact, my guiltless bloud may cry before the Lord, Mercy to the innocent! And yet though I must needs acknowledge, that beyng constrayned, and as you know well enough continually assayed, yet in taking upon me, I seemed to consent, and therein grieviously offended the Queene and her lawes, yet doe I assuredly trust that this my offence towards God is so much the lesse, in that being in so royall estate as I was, my enforced honour never mingled with mine innocent heart. And thus, good father, I have opened unto you the state wherein I presently stand, my death at hand, although to you perhaps it may seem wofull, yet to mee there is nothing that can bee more welcome than from this vale of misery to aspire to that heavenly

---

[1] Jeremiah, chap. xxi. ver. 29, and Ezekiel, chap. xviii. ver. 2.
[2] 'Baker's Chronicle,' p. 340.
[3] Froude, vol. vi. p. 181.

throne of all joy and pleasure, with Christ my Saviour; in whose stedfast faith (if it may be lawfull for the daughter so to write to her father) the Lord that hath hitherto strengthened you, soe continue to keepe you, that at the last we may meete in heaven with the Father, Sonn, and Holy Ghost. "I am,
"Your obedient daughter till death,
"JANE DUDLEY."[1]

Again she writes:

"*To the* DUKE OF SUFFOLK.

"The Lord comforte your Grace, and that in his worde, whearin all creatures onlye are to be comforted. And thoughe it hathe pleased God to take away ij of your children, yet thincke not, I most humblye beseach your Grace, that you have loste them, but truste that we, by leavinge this mortall life, have wunne an immortall life. And I for my parte, as I have honoured your grace in this life, wyll praye for you in another life. "Your Gracys humble daughter,
"JANE DUDDELEY."

Her unfortunate husband also wrote to his father-in-law:

"*To the* DUKE OF SUFFOLK.

"Your lovyng and obedyent son wischethe unto your Grace long lyffe in this world, with as muche joye and comforte as ever I wyshte to my selfe, and in the world to come joy everlasting.
"Your most humble son tel his death,
"G. DUDDELEY."[2]

The foregoing letters bear no date, but they were probably written just before the arrest of the Duke of Suffolk, which occurred on Saturday, the 10th February.

On the 8th February, Queen Mary, desirous if possible to convert Lady Jane to the Catholic faith, sent Feckenham[3] to commune with her. The theological dialogue which is recorded to have then taken place is too long for insertion here, but the reader will find it in the pages of Fox, in Sir

[1] Harleian MSS. 2194, f. 23. Nicolas's 'Memoir of Lady Jane Grey,' p. 47.
[2] Harleian MSS. 2342. 'Chron. of Queen Jane and Queen Mary,' p. 57.
[3] John Howman, called Feckenham, because he was born in Feckenham Forest, in Worcestershire, formerly a monk at Evesham, was appointed Dean of St. Paul's on 10th March, 1553-4, and Abbot of Westminster 21st Nov. 1556: he restored the shrine of Edward the Confessor to the condition in which we now see it: he was removed from Westminster in Jan. 1559-60 and sent to the Tower; he ultimately died at Wisbeach. He is described as "a short man of a round visage, fresh colour, affable, and pleasant."

H. Nicolas's 'Memoir of Lady Jane Grey,' and in Godwyn's 'Annals,' &c.

Feckenham is believed to have been touched by his interview with Lady Jane Grey, and to have endeavoured to intercede with Queen Mary on her behalf; a few days' respite was however the only result of his efforts.

Her execution was to take place on Monday, the 12th February, and the following "exhortation" was written by Lady Jane Grey to her sister Catherine on the previous evening, in the blank pages of a manuscript on vellum, now in the British Museum, containing an essay by Albertus Castellanus, 'De arte moriendi':—

"I have sent yō good suster Katherine a boke, wch, although it be not outwardly rimid with gold, yet inwardly it is most worth than peyous stones. It is the boke dere sust' of the laws of the Lord; it is his testament and last will, wch he bequeathed unto us wretches, wch shall lead yō to the path of eternall joye and yf yō with a good mīnde reade it, and with an earnest dissyre folow it, shall bring you to an imortale and everlasting lyfe. It wyll teach yō to lyve, and learne yō to dey: it shall wyne yō more then you sholde have gayned by the possessyon of y' wofull fathres lands, for as if God had p̄spered him, yō shold have inherited his lands, so if yō aply diligētly yo' boke, trying to directe yo' lyfe aft' it; yō shal be an inheritor of such riches as nither the covetous shall withdrawe from you, neither the thefe shal steale, neither yet ye mothe corrupte. Dessyre sist' to understand ye law of ye Lord yo' God. Lyve styll to dey y' yo by deth may purches eternell lyfe; or after yo' deth enjoye the lyfe purchessed yo by Christis death, and trust not yt y° tenderness of yo' age shall lengthen yo' life: for as sone, if God will, goith y° young as the old, and laboure alway to lerne to dey. Deney y° world, difey y° devell, and dispyse y° flesh. Delite yo' selfe onely in y° Lord. Be penitent for yo' syns, and yet despayre not. Be steady in faythe, yet p̄sume (presume) not and desyre with S. Pawle to be desolvid and to be with X' with whom even in death there is lyfe. Be lyke the good servant, and even at midnight be wakyng; least when death comyth and stealythe upon yō lyke a thefe in ye night, yo be with the evel servant found slepinge, and least for lacke of oyle ye be found lyk the first foulsh wence (foolish wench), and lyke him that had not on the wedding garment and then be cast out from the marriage. Risyst in ye, as I trust ye do, and seeing ye have y° name of a cristian, as neare as ye can folowe the stepes of your master Chrst, and take up yo' crosse; lay your syns on his backe and always embrace him; and as touchynge my deathe, rejoyce as I do, and adsist y' I shall be delyvred of y' corruption and put on incorruption, for I am assurede y' I shall for losyng of a mortall lyfe finde an immortal felisity. Pray God graunt yōu send yōu of his grace to lyve in his feare, and to dey in y° love (* *) of joy to you when the (* * * *) shall arrive, neither for love of lyfe nor feares of deathe.

"For if ye deney his truth to lengthen yur life, God will deney yō and shorten your dayes; and if you will cleave to him, he will plong (prolong) your dayes to your comfort and his glory, to wch glory, God beinge minde and yo herafter, when it shall please God to call yō.

"Farewell, good syst', put your onely trust in God, who onely must uphold you.   "Your loving syst',
                         "JANE DUDDLEY."[1]

The execution of Lady Jane Grey and her husband was to take place on Monday, the 12th February, and it had been originally intended that they should suffer together on Tower Hill, but the council, dreading the effect of their youth and innocence on the populace, changed the orders.

Lord Guildford Dudley was to be executed on Tower Hill, Lady Jane was to suffer on the green within the Tower.

Dudley, on the last morning, urgently requested to be allowed to see her; but although his wish was granted by Queen Mary, Lady Jane declined the interview, fearing the effect on her firmness; "the separation would be but for a moment, if the meeting would benefit either of their souls, she would see him with pleasure, but in her opinion it would only increase their trial, they would meet soon enough in the other world."[2]

Lord Guildford was first brought out for execution. "The Mondaie being the xii of Februarie at "about ten of the clocke ther went out of the Tower to the scaffolde on Tower Hill, the Lorde Guilforde Dudley, sone to the late Duke of Northumberland, husbande to the Lady Jane Grey, daughter to the Duke of Suffolke, who at his going out tooke by the hande Sir Anthony Browne, Maister John Throgmorton,

[1] Harleian MSS. No. 2370. A copy of this letter, but with some variations, &c., in modernised language, is given in Sir H. Nicolas's 'Lady Jane Grey,' p. 41, "from the end of a New Testament in Greek."

[2] Sir H. Nicolas's 'Lady Jane Grey,' p. lxxxvii.; Froude, vol. vi. p. 186.

and many other gentyllmen, praying them to praie for him; and without the bullwarke, Thomas Offeley,[1] the sheryve, receyved him and brought him to the scaffolde, where after a small declaration, having no gostlye father with him, he kneeled downe and said his praiers; then, holding upp his eyes and handes to God many tymes with teares, at last after he had desyred the people to pray for him, he laide himselfe along, and his hedd upon the block, which was at one stroke of the axe taken from him. Note, the lorde marques[2] stode upon the Devyl's Towre[3] and saw the executyon. His carcas throwne into a carre and his hed in a cloth, he was brought into the chappell within the Tower, wher the Lady Jane, whose lodging was in Master Partridge's house, dyd see his ded carcase taken out of the cart, as well as she dyd see hym before alyve going to deathe, a sight to hir no less than deathe."[4]

The chronicler then continues: "By this tyme was ther a scaffolde made upon the grene over agaynst the White Tower for the saide Lady Jane to die apon. Who with hir husband was appoynted to have ben put to deathe the Fryday before, but was staied tyll then, for what cause is not knowen,[5] unless yt were because hir father was not then come into the Tower. The saide Lady being nothing at all abashed, neither with feare of her own deathe, which then approached, neither with the sight of the ded carcase of hir husbande, when he was brought into the chappell, came fourthe, the Levetenaunt[6] leading hir, in the same gown wherein she was arrayned, hir countenance nothing abashed, neither her eyes anything moysted with teares, although her ij gentylwomen

---

[1] Sir Thomas Offley, merchant taylor and merchant of the Staple of Calais: sheriff of London in 1553, and Lord Mayor in 1557, when he was knighted. "He was the Zaccheus of London, not for his low stature, but his high charity, bequeathing the half of his estate unto the poor. He died in 1580, and was buried in St. Andrew Undershaft."—Fuller's 'Worthies.'

[2] The Marquis of Northampton.

[3] Devereux Tower, that which commanded the nearest view of the scaffold on Tower Hill. See plan at p. x.

[4] See Stow, and 'Chron. of Queen Jane and Queen Mary,' p. 55. Partridge's house was adjoining the Lieutenant's lodgings, from whence Lady Jane would see all that passed on the Tower green, and also look out towards the gate of the Tower and Tower Hill.

[5] The delay was in consequence of Feckenham's intercession with the Queen. See p. 172.

[6] Sir John Brydges, created Lord Chandos of Sudeley, in April 1554.

Mistress Elizabeth Tylney and Mistress Eleyn wonderfully wept, with a boke in her hande, wheron she praied all the way till she cam to the saide scaffolde, wheron when she was mounted, this noble young ladie, as she was indued with singular gifts both of learning and knowledge, so was she as patient and mild as any lambe at hir execution, a little before death uttered these wordes." [1]

Her speech is found in a rare tract, which is reprinted in the 'Archæologia.' [1]

"*The Ende of the* LADY JANE DUDLEY, *daughter to the* DUKE OF SUFFOLKE, *upon the scaffolde, at the houre of her death, being the* 12 *day of February.*

"Fyrst whan she mounted on the scaffolde, she sayd to the people standynge thereabout, good people, I com hether to die, and by a lawe I am condemned to the same. The facte, indede against the Queene's Highness was unlawful, and the consenting thereunto by me, but touching the procurement and desyre therof by me, or on my halfe, I doo wash my handes therof in innocencie before God and the face of you christian people this day, and therwith she wrong her hands, in which she had her booke. Then she sayd, I pray you all good christian people to beare me wytnes that I dye a true Christian woman, and that I looke to be saved by none other meane but only by the mercy of God, in the merites of the bloud of his onlye sonne Jesus Christe, and I confesse when I dyd know the word of God, I neglected the same, and loved myselfe and the world, and therefore this plague or punyshment is happely and worthely happened unto me for my sinnes. And yet I thanke God of his goodnes that he hath thus geven me a tyme and respet to repent. And now good people, while I am alyve I pray you to assyst me with your prayers." [1]

And then she knelying downe, she turned to Fecknam saying, Shall I say this psalm? and he said yea. Then she said the psalm of Miserere mei Deus in English in most devout maner to the ende. Then she stode up and gave her mayde, Mistres Tylney, her gloves and handkercher, and her boke to Maistre Thomas Brydges, the lyvetenantes brother. [2]

---

[1] 'Chron. of Queen Jane and Queen Mary,' pp. 55 and 56. Another speech is printed in Sir H. Nicolas's 'Lady Jane Grey,' p. 52.

[2] The book which she gave to Thomas Brydges for his brother, Sir John Brydges, Lieutenant of the Tower, is now in the British Museum. It is a manual of prayers, a small square vellum book, bound in modern times, and is No. 2342 in the Harleian MSS.; it is believed that Lady Jane Grey had borrowed it of Sir John Brydges, carried it with her to the scaffold, and then

Forthwith she untied her gowne. The hangman went to her to have helped her of therwith, then she desyred him to let her alone, turning towardes her two gentlewomen, who helped her of therwith, and also her frose paste[1] and neckercher, geving to her a fayre handkercher to knytte about her eyes.

Then the hangman kneled downe, and asked her forgevenes, whom she forgave most willingly. Then he willed her to stand upon the strawe, which doing she sawe the blocke. Then she sayd I pray you despatche me quickly. Then she kneled downe saying, "Will you take it of before I lay me downe?" And the hangman answered her, "No, madame." She tied the kercher about her eyes. Then feeling for the block, saide, "What shal I do, where is it?"[2] One of the standers by guyding her therunto, she layde her head downe upon the block, and stretched forth her body, and said, "Lord, into thy handes I commende my spirite," and so she ended.[3]

It is not recorded in what part of the church the bodies of Lady Jane and her husband were buried, but I have already, at page 53, stated the grounds for presuming that she and her husband were buried in the chancel. The recent examination of the chapel has failed to afford any means of identifying the spot.

The word JANE which is cut in the wall of the prisoners' room in the Beauchamp Tower may have been carved by

---

returned it, through the hands of his brother, with the following written in it:

"For as mutche as you have desyred so simple a woman to wrighte in so worthye a booke, good mayster Lieuftehante, therefore I shall as a frende desyre you, and as a christian require you, to call uppon God to encline your harte to his lawes, to quicken you in his wayes, and not to take the worde of trewethe utterlye oute of youre mouthe. Lyve styll to dye, that by deathe you may purchas eternall life, and remember howe the ende of Mathusael, whoe as we reade in the scriptures was the longeste liver that was of a manne, died at the laste; for as the precher sayethe, there is a tyme to be borne, and a tyme to dye: and the daye of deathe is better than the daye of oure birthe.

"Youres, as the Lord knowethe, as a frende.   "JANE DUDDELEY."

[1] Frontispiece, or frow's piece, a matronly head-dress.

[2] The popular representation of this scene by Paul Delaroche is not in accordance with the historical accounts.

[3] 'Archæologia,' vol. xii. pp. 406-8; 'Chron. of Queen Jane and Queen Mary,' p. 58. See also Holinshed.

Lord Guildford Dudley or one of his brothers who were there imprisoned, though Nichols in his 'History of Leicestershire,' vol. iii. p. 670, suggests that it was cut by John Dudley, Duke of Northumberland.

Henry Grey, Duke of Suffolk.

Born, ——. Beheaded on Tower Hill, 22nd February, 1553-4.

The Duke of Suffolk, father of Lady Jane Grey, was in command of the Tower, when his daughter was received there as Queen, in July, 1553, but on the 19th of the same month, after Queen Mary had been proclaimed in London, he received orders to deliver up possession of it. He submitted at once, and "himself came out of the Tower, having commanded his men to leave their weapons behind them, saying that he himself was but one man, and then himself proclaimed my Lady Mary Queen, on Tower hill, and so came into London, leaving the Lieutenant in the Tower."[1] As in the case of the Duke of Northumberland, his proclamation of Queen Mary as a last resource did not give sufficient cause for trusting his loyalty, and there being also reasons for suspecting that he was making some arrangements for joining Sir Thomas Wyatt in an insurrection, it was considered advisable to secure him, and on the 27th July he was committed as a prisoner to the Tower: however, on the 31st he was again liberated, upon his parole to return to prison should the Queen require it.

His movements and conduct soon again gave rise to much

---

[1] 'Chron. of Queen Jane and Queen Mary,' p. 12.

suspicion, and he was summoned to appear at court, when on the 25th January, 1553-4, the Duke "fled from his house." It is said that on the morning of the same day, "ther cam a messenger from the Quene that he shulde come to the court. 'Marye,' quoth he, 'I was comyng to her Grace; ye may see I am booted and spurred redy to ryde: and I will but breke my fast and go.' So he gave the messenger a rewarde, and caused hym to be made to drink, and so thence departed himself, no man knoweth whither."[1]

We next hear of him in a letter written by the Earl of Arundel to the Earl of Shrewsbury, dated 28th January, "The Duke of Suffolk is on Friday stolen from his house at Sheen,[2] and run away with his two brethren[3] into Leicestershire: for he was met at Stony Stratford. My Lord of Huntingdon is gone into those parts against him. He is proclaimed traitor."[4]

He then went to Leicester and on the 29th January, he and his brother appeared in the market-place there with a proclamation, the terms of which showed that he had joined in Wyatt's conspiracy: having thus endeavoured, unsuccessfully, to raise the neighbouring country in insurrection against Queen Mary, he then rode on to Coventry, and attempted to raise that town, but again without success, so now finding himself deserted by his followers, he began to think of his personal safety. He therefore fled to his own park of Astley, in Warwickshire, where he "put himself under the trust of one Underwood, a keeper, who concealed him for some days in a hollow tree, standing about two bow-shot south-westward from the church, but who being promised a reward betrayed him."[5]

His brother, Lord John Grey, was also captured, having been discovered hidden in some hay in the park.

On the 3rd February, it was announced in London that the Duke, and his two brothers "had been dyscomfeted

---

[1] 'Chron. of Queen Jane and Queen Mary,' p. 37.
[2] The Carthusian monastery of Sheen, near Richmond, had been granted to him after the attainder of the Duke of Somerset in 1552.
[3] Lord John and Lord Thomas Grey.
[4] Lodge's 'Illustrations of British History,' vol. i. p. 233.
[5] Dugdale's 'Warwickshire.'

by the Erle of Huntingdon,[1] and certayn of his horsemen taken, and that the Duke and his two brethren fledde in serving men's cottes;" and again, on "Satersday, being the 10th of February, the Erle of Huntingdon, and other gentyllmen to the nomber of 300 horse, brought into the Tower as prisoners, the Duke of Suffolke, and the Lord John Gray from Coventry, where he had remained three dayes after his taking, in the house and custody of Christofer Waren, alderman there."[2]

His brother, Lord Thomas Grey, got away for a time, but soon afterwards he was taken at Oswestry, by "Master Rycharde Myttoon of Shrosbery, being bailiffe."

Robert Swyft writes to the Earl of Shrewsbury, from London, 12th February, "The Lord Thomas was taken going towards Wales, and is coming up."[3]

On the 12th February his daughter, Lady Jane Grey, had been beheaded, and arrangements were then made for bringing him to trial.

"On Satersday the 17th daie of Februarie, the Duke of Suffolke was carried to Westminster, and there arrayned, being fetched from the Tower by the clerke of the cheke, and all the garde almoste: who at his going out went very stoutely and cheerfully enough, but at his coming here he landed at the water gate with a countenance very hevy and pensyfe, desyring all men to praye for him. (The

---

[1] Francis Hastings, second Earl of Huntingdon, succeeded his father as earl in 1551. He died at Ashby-de-la-Zouche 22nd June, 1560. His funeral is described in such detail in Machyn's 'Diary,' p. 239, that Machyn may have furnished it. For memoir and description of his monument see Nichol's 'Leicestershire,' vol. iii. pp. 580-583, and 619.

[2] 'Chron. of Queen Jane and Queen Mary,' pp. 53-4. Memoranda of the expenses incurred during his detention at Coventry, are to be found in the MS. records of the trading companies of that city.

[3] Lodge's 'Illustrations,' vol. i. p. 235. "He was apprehended, through his great mishappe, and folly of his man, that had forgot his cap-case with money behinde in his chamber one morning in his inne, and coming for it againe, uppon examination what he should be, it was mistrusted that his master should be some suche man as he was in deede, and so was stayde, taken, and brought up to London, where he suffered."— Holinshed. In the Privy Council Register is this entry, "21 Feb. Richard Mitton, Esquire, sheriff of Shropshire, brought this daye upp the Lord Thomas Graye, delivered unto him by indenture berynge date the xv day of Februarie by the Lord President and counsell of Wales, and comytted him to the Tower."

Lorde Courteney,[1] lying in the Bell Tower, sawe him both outwarde and inwarde)

"It is saide, the Earl of Arundell[2] sitting upon him in judgment, he shoulde saye that it was no treason for a pere of the realme, as he was, to raise his power, and make proclamacion onely to avoyde strangers out of the realme; and therapon he axed the sergeauntes standing by whether it was not soo or no, which they being abashed, they could not say it was treason by eny lawe. Then it was laidd to his chardge he mett with 200 men, the Quene's lieutenant in armes, being the Erle of Huntingdon, which was treason agaynst the Quene, forasmuch as the saide lieutenant represented hir own person. To the which he made answer that he knewe not the saide Erle to be no such lieutenant. 'But,' saith he, 'I met him indeede but with fyftye men or theraboutes, and wold not have shronken from him if I had had fewer.' And by theis wordes he confessed himself gilty of treason. Moreover, he partelie accused his brother, the Lorde Thomas, who he saide had perswaded him rather to flye into his country than to abyd, saying that 'it was to be feared he should be put agayn into the Tower; where being in his countrey, and amongst frendes and tenauntes, who durst fetch him?'"

"Further, towching the other artycles laide to his charge, he said, that he never knewe enything therof, saving that once he shold say at his table, over his supper, that he wolde undertake, for nede, onely with one hundred gentylmen, to sett the crowne upon Courtenay's hedd: and so he was condempned, and brought back to the Tower agayn."[3]

His execution followed shortly after his condemnation.

---

[1] Edward Courtenay, son of the Marquis of Exeter, who was proposed as a husband for Queen Mary. He had been released from the Tower on the 21st July, 1553, but in consequence of his rebellious conduct he was again sent to the Tower on the 12th Feb. 1553-4. In 1556 he was exiled, and died at Venice in September of that year.

[2] Henry Fitzalan, 10th Earl of Arundek. See p. 154.

[3] 'Chron. of Queen Jane and Queen Mary,' pp. 60-1.—Stow.

"The 17 day of February was the Duke of Suffolk rayned (arraigned) at Westmynster halle, and cast for tresun and cast to suffer deth."—Machyn's 'Diary,' p. 55. The trial is in Baga de Secretis, Pouch xxviii.

"Upon the Fridaie the three and twentith of Februarie, about nine of the clocke, the Duke of Suffolke was brought forth of the Tower unto the scaffold, on the Tower hyll. And in his coming thither, there accompanied him Doctor Weston,[1] as his ghostlie father, notwithstanding (as it would seeme), against the will of the said Duke. For when the Duke went up the scaffold, the said Weston, being on his left hand, pressed to go up with him. The Duke with his hand put him downe againe off the staires, and Weston taking hold of the Duke forced him downe likewise. And as they ascended the second time, the Duke againe put him downe. Then Weston said, it was the Queene's pleasure he should do so;[2] wherewith the Duke casting his hands abrode, ascended by the scaffold, and paused a prettie while after, and then said, 'Good people, this daie I am come hether to dye, being one whom the lawe hathe justlie condempned, and one who hathe no lesse deserved for my dysobedyence against the Quenes highnes, of whom I do moste humbly axe forgeveness, and I truste she dothe and will forgeve me.' Then Maister Weston, standing by, saide, 'my Lorde, hir grace hathe allredy forgeven and praieth for you.' With that, divers of the standers by said with meetly good and audible voice, 'such forgivenesse God send thee,' meaning Doctoure Weston.[2] Then saide the Duke, 'I beseche you all, goode people, to lett me be an example to you all for obedyence to the Quene and magestrates, for the contrarie thereof hath brought me to this end. And also I shall moste hartely desire you all to beare me witnes that I do dye a faythefull and true

[1] Dr. Hugh Weston, Dean of Westminster, and afterwards appointed Dean of Windsor, in 1556: in consequence of immoral conduct he was sent to the Tower, and remained there until the death of Queen Mary: he was then released, being in ill-health, and went to live in a friend's house in Fleet Street, where in a few days he died, and was buried in the church of the Savoy. He attended Sir Thomas Wyatt on the scaffold on 11th April, 1554. It is indicative of the state of alarm into which Wyatt's rebellion threw the metropolis, and also of the martial spirit of the time that "on Ashe Weddinsday that Wyatt was at Charinge Crosse, Doctor Weston did singe masse before the Queene in harnesse under his vestments. This Weston reported himself to Mr. Robards."—Harleian MSS. 419, f. 131.
[2] Holinshed; Fox.
[3] Fox.

christian, beleving to be saved by none other, but only by Allmightie God, thoroughe the passion of his son Jesus Christ: and nowe I praie you to praie with me.'

"Then he kneled downe, and Weston with him, and sayde the sallme of 'Miserere mihi Deus,' and 'In te, Domine, speravi:' the Duke one verse and Weston another. Which done, he arose and stode up, and dyd put off his gown and his doblet,[1] and delivered his cap and scarffe to the executioner, and therewith the executioner kneled downe, and asked the Duke's forgevenesse, and the Duke said, 'God forgive thee, and I doo: and when thou dost thine office, I praie thee doo it quicklie, and God have mercie to thee.'

"Then stood there a man and said, 'My Lord, how shall I doo for the monie that you doo owe mee?' and the Duke said, 'Alas, good fellow, I praie thee trouble mee not now, but go thy waie to my officers.' Then he knit a kercher about his face, and kneled downe and said, 'Our Father which art in heaven,' &c., unto the ende: and then he said 'Christ have mercie upon me,' helde up his handes to heaven, and laid downe his head on the blocke: the executioner toke the axe, and at the first chop stroke off his head,[2] and held it up to the people, according to the common custom of execution."[3]

Strype thus writes of him:

"To do right to this most noble prince, because he is so illy described, and passed over to posterity under such a wrong character, as I conceive, I shall here set down a truer and better." Sir John Hayward saith thus of him: "that he was a man for his harmless simplicity neither misliked nor much regarded." Bishop Burnet, "That for his weakness he would have died more pitied, if his practices had not brought his daughter to her end." But after that I leave this great peer to the opinion of the world,

---

[1] 'Chron. of Queen Jane and Queen Mary,' pp. 63–4.

[2] "The xxiij of February was heddyd the Duke of Suffolke, Dassett (Dorset) on the Towre hylle, betwyn ix and x of the cloke a-for-none."—Machyn, p. 57.

[3] Holinshed, p. 1101. Harleian MSS. No. 2194.

under the words of a good historian, that wrote before either of them. "Such was the end of this Duke of Suffolk: a man of high nobility by birth: and of nature to his friends gentle and courteous: more easy indeed to be led, than was thought expedient: of stomach stout and hard: hasty and soon kindled, but pacified strait again, and sorry, if in his heat ought had passed him otherwise than reason might seem to bear: upright and plain in his private dealings: no dissembler, nor well able to bear injuries: but yet forgiving and forgetting the same, if the party would seem but to acknowledge his fault, and to seek reconcilement: bountiful he was and very liberal: somewhat learned himself, and a great favourer of those that were learned. So that to many he shewed himself a very Maecenas. As free from covetousness, as void of pride and disdainful haughtiness of mind: more regarding plain meaning men, than claw-back flatterers. And this virtue he had, that he could patiently hear his faults told him by those whom he had in credit for their wisdom and faithful meaning towards him. He was an hearty friend unto the Gospel, and professed it to the last, although sometime he had not the hap to reforme himself therafter. Concerning this last offence for the which he died, it is to be supposed he rather toke in hand that unlawfull enterprice through others' persuasion than of his owne motion, for anye malicious ambition in himselfe." [1]

Although there is no record where the Duke of Suffolk was buried, I incline to the opinion that his body was interred in St. Peter's chapel, and I have therefore included a biographical notice of him in the present series. His daughter and her husband had been beheaded only a few days previously, and it may therefore be assumed with much probability that the Duke's remains were laid near them in the chapel.

His palace was in the Minories, being the old convent of St. Clare, which had been granted to him by King Edward VI., by a warrant dated, "Westminster 13 Jan. 1552," and

[1] Strype, vol. iii. pp. 1, 146-147. Holinshed, 'Chronicle of Queen Jane and Queen Mary, p. 127.

in the church of Holy Trinity,[1] which now stands on the site of the old convent chapel, there is preserved a head, which tradition asserts to be that of Henry Grey, Duke of Suffolk. It was no uncommon thing for some relative or faithful adherent to bribe the executioner on the scaffold and obtain possession of the head of the sufferer, so as to prevent its exposure on London Bridge or elsewhere.

If this should chance to be the head of the Duke of Suffolk, it is an argument in favour of the interment of his body in the Tower chapel, since if the body had not been removed into the fortress, it would doubtless have been buried with the head in the Duke's own chapel.

This head was found some years ago in a small vault on the south side of the altar. It had been preserved in a mass of oak sawdust, and is now completely dried up, or mummified; the tannin, which the oak sawdust contained, having reduced the flesh to the condition of leather.

It is not possible to determine for what length of time this head had remained buried; so powerful are the preservative qualities of tannin, that the cornea and the pupils of the eyes, which are wide open, are preserved in this desiccated condition.[2]

I had the advantage of examining this singular relic in company with Mr. A. B. Mitford, of the Office of Works, Mr. George Scharf, Keeper of the National Portrait Gallery, and Dr. F. J. Mouat; the latter has kindly furnished me with the following observations.

"The anatomical characters of the exposed bones show that the head belonged to a man past the prime of life. The narrow retreating forehead, flattened sides and roof of the skull, and disproportionate development of the occipital region, indicate moderate mental powers and strong animal faculties. The whole conformation, if there be any truth in

---

[1] The church was extensively repaired and almost rebuilt in 1708.

[2] On a door at Westminster Abbey, which was traditionally said to have been covered with the skins of some Danes, Sir Gilbert Scott has found remaining under the iron work some pieces of "white leather," which, upon being submitted to microscopic examination, were pronounced to be the "skin of a fair haired, ruddy complexioned man."—'Gleanings from Westminster Abbey,' G. G. Scott, pp. 48–50. Stanley's 'Westminster Abbey,' p. 430.

external cranial indications of mental and moral manifestations, tends to prove indecision of character, considerable self-esteem, and very moderate reasoning powers.

"That the head was removed by rapid decapitation during life admits of no doubt. A large gaping gash, which had not divided the subcutaneous structures, shows that the first stroke of the axe was misdirected, too near the occiput, and in a slanting direction.[1] The second blow, a little lower down, separated the head from the trunk below the fourth and fifth cervical vertebræ. The retraction of the skin, the violent convulsive action of the muscles, and the formation of a cup-like cavity with the body of the spinal bone at the base, prove that the severance was effected during life, and in cold weather.[2]

"The ears are small, well formed, and closely adhering to the head; the aperture being remarkably large, and the lobe clearly defined. The eyeballs must have been full, and a little prominent during life: all the hairs from the head, brows, lips and chin have fallen out: the cheek bones are somewhat high and the chin retreating."

Mr. George Scharf adds that "the arched form of the eyebrows and the aquiline shape of the nose, correspond with the portrait engraved in Lodge's series from a picture in the possession of the Marquis of Salisbury at Hatfield; a duplicate of which is in the National Portrait Gallery."

THOMAS HOWARD, DUKE OF NORFOLK.

Born 1536. Beheaded on Tower Hill, 2nd June, 1572.

Thomas Howard, fourth Duke of Norfolk, succeeded to the dukedom upon the death of his grandfather in 1554, his father, the Earl of Surrey, having been beheaded in 1547.[3]

---

[1] Holinshed, however, records that the Duke's head was severed by one blow of the axe. See p. 182.

[2] The Duke of Suffolk was beheaded on the 22nd Feb. 1554.

[3] See Appendix A. p. 325.

He owed his imprisonment and ultimate death on the scaffold to the intrigues of the Catholic party, who conspired to marry him to Mary Queen of Scots. The personal jealousy of the Earl of Leicester towards him may also have had some influence on his fate. He had been thrice married; first, to Mary, the daughter and heiress of Henry Fitzalan, the last Earl of Arundel, through which marriage the Arundel estates passed to the Howards, Dukes of Norfolk; secondly, to Margaret, daughter of Thomas Lord Audley, the Chancellor; thirdly, he married Margaret, daughter of Sir Francis Leybourne, and she died in the year 1567. In 1568 Camden relates: "It is whispered about this time that the Duke of Norfolk was to marry the Queen of Scots, and that a plot was laid to proclaim the Queen of Scots undoubted heir to the Crown, should Queen Elizabeth do otherwise than well."[1]

The Queen heard of the intrigue, and (being utterly averse to the marriage) when the Duke was dining with her at Farnham castle she advised him "to be careful on what pillow he laid his head." Soon after, when Elizabeth visited him at Titchfield, he "opened to her the whole business, and begged her pardon with all possible concern."[2]

"After this the Queen called the Duke to her into the gallery and roundly reprimanded him for attempting a match with the Queen of Scots without her cognizance, and commanded him, on his allegiance, to give over those pretensions. The Duke made her a very hearty and cheerful promise that he would; and, as if he had a very slight regard for the Queen of Scots, was not shy to affirm 'that his estate in England was worth little less than the whole kingdom of Scotland, and when in his bowling alley at Norwich he considered himself equal to a king of Scotland.'"[3]

As, however, he perceived that the Queen's manner towards him had much changed, and that Leicester "had laid aside the friend," he considered it prudent to withdraw for a time from Court. After a short residence at Kenninghall in Norfolk, he again returned, in order, as he said, to receive

[1] Camden.
[2] Collins's 'Peerage,' vol. i. p. 99.
[3] Camden; Collins's 'Peerage,' vol. i. p. 100; 'Howard Papers,' p. 155.

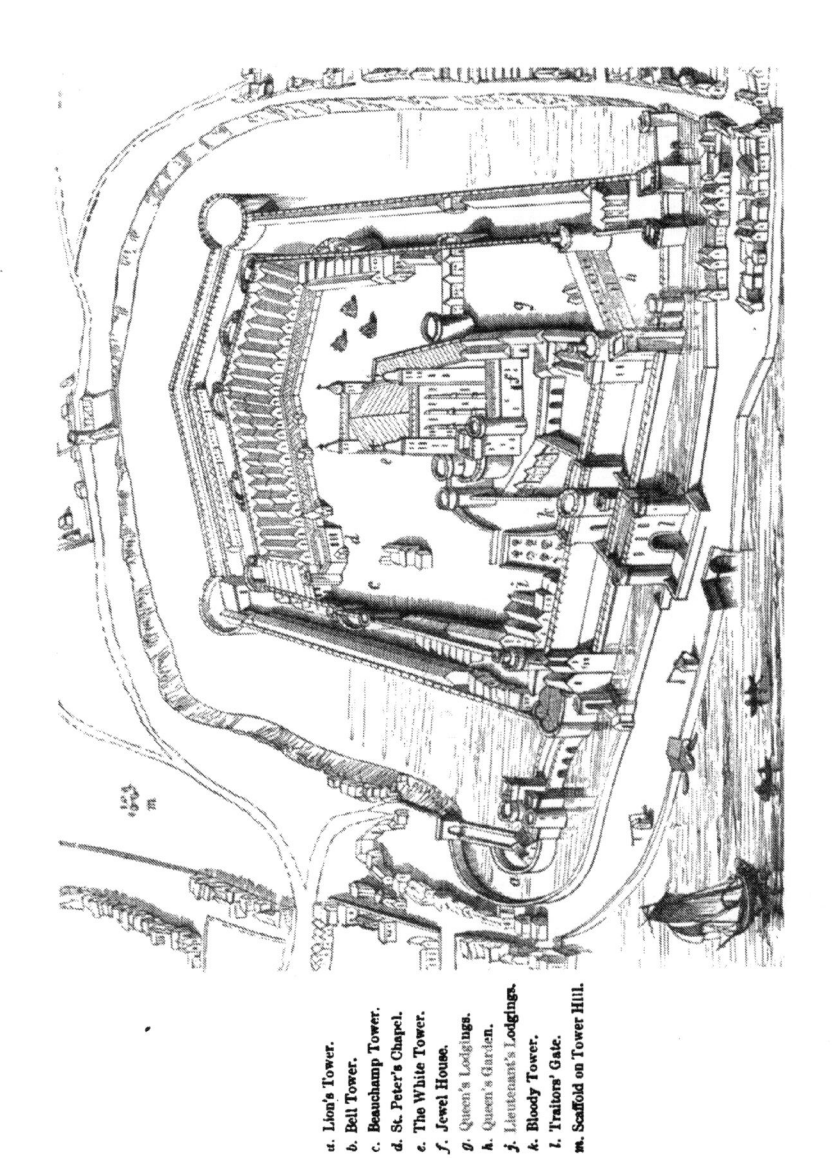

a. Lion's Tower.
b. Bell Tower.
c. Beauchamp Tower.
d. St. Peter's Chapel.
e. The White Tower.
f. Jewel House.
g. Queen's Lodgings.
h. Queen's Garden.
j. Lieutenant's Lodgings.
k. Bloody Tower.
l. Traitors' Gate.
m. Scaffold on Tower Hill.

the Queen's pardon. Upon his journey to Windsor, he was arrested at Uxbridge by Fitzgerald, a Lieutenant of the Band of Pensioners (some secret correspondence between himself and the Earl of Murray, Regent of Scotland, having been intercepted), and he was then placed in confinement at Burnham in Buckinghamshire. There he was examined by the Privy Council, and, after making some important confessions, he was committed to the Tower on the 11th October, 1569, upon a charge of high misdemeanour. Whilst he was in prison, a plot was organised "by several Norfolk gentlemen to set the Duke at liberty, by gathering a mob together at Harleston Fair on the 24th June (1570); but this plot was discovered and John Throgmorton and two others hanged."[1]

Shortly after the Duke declared "his mind was averse from thinking on, and his ears from hearing any mention of, the match with the Queen of Scots,"[2] and having entered into a bond not to concern himself further in the matter without Queen Elizabeth's knowledge,[3] he was removed from the Tower (where the plague was then raging) to his own residence, the Charter House[4] (then called Howard House) on the 4th August, 1570, and placed under the custody of Sir Henry Neville.[5] Yet there he was so slightly guarded that "at any time he could leap on horseback at his back door and ride away, and send word to the Queen that he was gone."[6]

In the following year, however, he was again engaged in treasonable intrigues. His correspondence with the Queen of Scots was discovered, in which she sent a long account of her plans, with several love-letters, to the Duke, written in cypher. Higford, the Duke's secretary, had been ordered

---

[1] Camden. Wright's 'Queen Elizabeth and her Times,' vol. i. p. 372.
[2] Stow.
[3] The following is the declaration which the Duke signed: "I do by this my writing, signed with mine own hand, and sealed with my seal, freely, voluntarily, and absolutely grant, promise, and bind myself, by the bond of my allegiance to your Majesty, as my Sovereign Lady, never to offend your Highness in the same, but do utterly renounce and revoke all that which on my part anywise hath passed, with a full intention never to deal in that cause of marriage of the Queen of Scots, nor in any other cause belonging to her, but as your Majesty shall command me."—Haynes' 'State Papers,' p. 598.
[4] It had been sold to him by Lord North in 1565 for 2500l.
[5] Collins's 'Peerage,' vol. i. p. 102.
[6] Cecil MSS. at Hatfield; Froude, vol. x. p. 288.

to burn these papers, but he hid them under the mats of the Duke's bed.[1] A bag containing money and letters to be remitted to Scotland by Mary Queen of Scots also came into possession of the Privy Council, and these being traced to Higford, he was sent to prison, where under the influence of the rack, he confessed the whole matter, and discovered where the letters were hid at Howard House. Several of his servants and agents were arrested and Sir Ralph Sadler was then ordered to watch the house closely; the Duke was brought before the Council, when, believing that the letters were burnt, he stiffly denied all that Higford and his servants had confessed: he was then committed to the Tower, on the 4th September (1571).[2]

On the 7th September he appeared again before the Lords of the Council, when they produced proofs of his treason, he then said, "I am betrayed and undone by my confidants, whom I knew not how to distrust: though diffidence is the very essence of wisdom," and, having been examined upon fifty articles, he confessed everything.

The Duke's popularity was very considerable, and with a view therefore of lessening that popularity, "the result of these examinations was reported to the Star Chamber, before the Peers and Lord Mayor and aldermen; and afterwards more publicly to all the citizens at Guildhall by Fleetwood, the Recorder."[3]

Lord Burghley writes to the Earl of Shrewsbury:[4]

"The Queen's majesty hath willed me to advertise you that she had found very dangerous attempts intended by the Queen of Scots, and

---

[1] Camden.

[2] "When the warrant for his committal was brought, the first peer in the land, the head of the proud house of Howard, and the aspirant for the hand of England's expectant Queen, fell upon his knees and cried for mercy like a poltroon. Mounted on a 'foot cloth nag,' between Sadler and Sir Thomas Smith, and attended only by their own servants, he was led through the streets to the Tower gates, amidst a crowd of women and idle boys and girls."—Froude, vol. x. p. 292.

[3] William Fleetwood, a natural son of Robert Fleetwood, of a Lancashire family, appointed Recorder in 1570, and Queen's Sergeant in 1592. He died on 28th Feb. 1594. Collins's 'Peerage,' vol. i. p. 103.

[4] George Talbot, 6th Earl of Shrewsbury, K.G., had the custody of Mary, Queen of Scots; presided at the Duke of Norfolk's trial; and after the Duke's execution, received the appointment of Earl Marshal of England. He died November 1540, and was buried at Sheffield.

the Duke of Norfolk to be privy thereof: who has made a very lamentable submission to her Majesty, with a request for her mercy; but I see her Majesty entered into a great indignation against him.

* * * * *

"Your Lordship may also let her (the Queen of Scots) know that her letters and discourses, in articles, being in cypher, to the Duke of Norfolk, are found, and he has confessed the same, and delivered the alphabet; so as she may not now find it strange that her Majesty uses her in this sort, but rather think it strange that it is no worse. Indeed, we have the Scottish Queen's writing, and the cyphers.[1]

"13 Sept. 1571.
"From Mark's Hall, in Essex.
"Your Lordship's at commandment,
"W. BURGHLEY."[2]

On Wednesday, the 16th January (1571-2), the Duke was brought to trial at Westminster Hall before twenty five of his peers, the Earl of Shrewsbury presiding as Lord High Steward.

The following account is written by Camden, who was present during the trial,[3] and it is an interesting record of the mode of conducting a trial of such importance in those days.

"The beginning of the new year presented the Londoners with a new and sorrowful spectacle in Westminster Hall. For a wooden scaffold was erected in the midst of the Hall, reaching from the gate to the upper end, where there was a tribunal built with seats on both sides, such a sight as they had not seen in full eighteen years. On the 16th of January was Thomas Howard, Duke of Norfolk, brought before the

---

[1] In the Cottonian MSS. Caligula 2, f. 53, are some of these cyphers, with the letters decyphered, which were addressed to the Duke of Norfolk by Queen Mary, together with a long paper of memoranda by Lord Burghley; it is endorsed by him: "Extract out of yᵉ letters and cyphers, &c., concerning yᵉ Scott: Queene & Duke of Norfolk." One letter from the Queen thus concludes: "I praie God protect you and kepe us bothe from deceitfull freindes. The last of Januarie, Your own faithfull to deathe, Queene of Scottes, my Norfolke." And another: "So I remayne yours till deathe, accordinge to my faithful and doutifull promess. I looke for good will and constancie againe, so I pray God, as I do daylie, to save you from all oure enemys. The xvi of this instant. Your owne." These papers were found under the tiles of the roof at the Charter House: they are now in the British Museum.

[2] Lodge's 'Illustrations of British History,' vol. i. pp. 526-7.

[3] Sir Thomas Gresham was foreman of the grand jury for Middlesex, who found a true bill against the Duke.

tribunal, between Sir Owen Hopton, Lieutenant of the Tower,[1] and Sir Peter Carew, Knights, the fatal axe being carry'd before him, with the edge turned from him. Upon the bench or tribunal sat George Talbot, Earl of Shrewsbury, constituted Lord High Steward of England for that day.

"After silence was proclaimed, the Commission was read, wherein the authority granted to the Lord Steward was contained. Then Garter King at Arms put a white rod into his hands, which the Lord Steward presently delivered to his gentleman usher, who standing by him held it upright all the time of the trial.

"Then were the earls and barons called over, and every one answered to his name. Silence being again proclaimed, the Lieutenant of the Tower was commanded to return his writ, and to bring the Duke to the bar. The Duke was presently brought. On the one side of him was the Lieutenant of the Tower, on the other Sir Peter Carew, and next him stood the axe-bearer, with the edge turned from the Duke. After silence was proclaimed again, the Clerk of the Crown spake to the Duke in these words : 'Thomas, Duke of Norfolk, late of Kenninghall, in the County of Norfolk, hold up thy hand.' When he had held up his hand, the clerk read, with a loud voice, the crimes he stood arraigned for."[2]

Camden then gives the details of the evidence, and speeches at the trial,[3] and continues :

"When it now grew late, the Lord Steward asked the Duke if he had anything more to say for himself. He answered, 'I confide in the equity of the laws.' The Lord Steward commanded the Lieutenant of the Tower to take the Duke from the bar; and, after silence proclaimed, turning to the peers he said, 'You have heard how Thomas, Duke of Norfolk, being charged with high treason and not confessing himself guilty, hath submitted his cause to God and you. It is for you therefore to consider with yourselves whether he

---

[1] See Sir Owen Hopton's 'Letter to Lord Burghley.' Ellis's 'Original Letters,' 3rd series, vol. iv. p. 67.
[2] Camden.
[3] See also Froude's 'Hist. of England,' vol. x. p. 322 et seq. for a graphic account of the trial; Collins's 'Peerage,' vol. i. pp. 103-5.

be to be held guilty, and to give in your verdict upon your conscience and honour.' And withal he ordered them to withdraw and advise together.

"After a short space they returned to their seats. Then the Lord Steward, beginning with the last, said, ' My Lord Delaware, is Thomas, Duke of Norfolk, guilty of that high treason charged against him or no?' He, rising up and laying his hand on his breast, answered, 'Guilty.' So answered the rest, being asked in their order.

"Then was the Duke brought again to the Bar, to whom the Lord Steward spake in this manner: 'Thomas, Duke of Norfolk, thou hast been arraigned upon divers crimes of high treason, and have submitted thyself to God and these peers, who have all found thee guilty.[1] Hast thou anything to say why sentence should not be passed upon thee?' The Duke answered, 'God's will be done, who will judge between me and my false accusers.'

"Silence being now kept, the edge of the axe was turned towards him; upon which Barham[2] required the Lord High Steward in the Queen's name to pass sentence; which he, with tears in his eyes, pronounced according to the usual form.

"When it was ended the Duke, with a presence of mind in a firm, but modest tone, said, 'Sentence is passed on me as a traitor; I have none to trust to but God and the Queen; I am excluded from your society, but hope shortly to enjoy the heavenly. I will fit myself to die; only one thing I crave, that the Queen would be kind to my children and servants, and take care that my debts be paid. God knows how true a heart I bear to Her Majesty, how true a heart to my country, whatever this day has been falsely objected to me. Farewell, my Lords.'" Camden concludes by saying that he heard these things himself, and penned them down exactly.[3]

---

[1] He was found guilty in the teeth of the statute of Edward VI., which enacts that no person shall be convicted of high treason but on the parole testimony of at least two witnesses, to be confronted with the accused.

[2] Nicholas Barham, the Queen's Serjeant, M.P. and Recorder of Maidstone. He died in 1577.

[3] Camden. The documents of the trial, with its lengthy indictment, is in Baga de Secretis, Pouch xlii.

The Earl of Shrewsbury broke his wand, and the court was dissolved: the Duke was then conveyed back to the Tower.[1]

He wrote a long address to "my loving children, Philip and Nan," after his return to the Tower; it is dated 20th January, 1571-2, and is to be found in the Harleian MSS., No. 787.[2]

View of the Bloody Tower, in which the Duke of Norfolk was confined.

On the 4th February he made a special statement in writing respecting his trial and conviction, this is also among the Harleian MSS., No. 787.[3]

On the 9th February Queen Elizabeth signed the warrant for the Duke's execution, which was ordered to take place on Monday the 11th. This fact was announced to him, and he wrote the following farewell letters on the day before.

[1] The Duke was imprisoned in the Bloody Tower. See letter of Sir Owen Hopton, 12 Jan. 1571, in Bayley, Appendix liii.

[2] See Wright's 'Queen Elizabeth and her Times,' vol. i. p. 402. Bayley, p. 475, &c.

[3] See also Bayley, lviii. to lxvii.

"*To* WILLIAM DYX.[1]

"Farewell good Dyx, your servys hathe bene so faythefull unto me as I ame sorye that I cane not make profe off my good wyll to recompense ytt. I trust my deathe schall not make no change in you towards myne, but that you wyll faythefullye perfourme the trust that I have reposyd in you. Forgett me, and remember me in myne. Forgett not wth planenes to cowncell and advyse Phylyp's and Nanne's unexperienced yeares: the rest off theyr brothers and systers well doyng restythe muche upon ther vertyous and consyderat dealyngs. God grant them his grace, whyche ys able to worke better in them than my naturall well meanyng harte cane wysh unto them. Amen. And so hopyng off your honestye and faythefullnes when I am deade, I bide you thys my last farewell, the 10 off febru. 1571-2.

"T. H."

"*To* GEORGE * * * *

"Good friend George, farewell. I have no other tokens to send my friends but my books, and I know how sorrowful you are, amongst the rest, for my hard hap, whereof I thank God, because I hope his merciful chastisement will prepare me for a better world. Look well throughout this book, and you shall find the name of Duke very unhappy. I pray God it may end with me, and that others may speed better hereafter. But, if I might have my wish, and were in as good a state as ever you knew me, yet I would wish for a lower degree.

"Be a friend, I pray you, to mine and do my hearty commendations to your wife, and to gentle Mr. Dennye. I die in the faith that you have ever known me to be of. Farewell good friend, 1571.

"Your dying as he was living,

"NORFOLK.[2]

"God bless my godson. Amen."

He also wrote to his son Philip a parting letter in a bible, and this also is to be found in the British Museum, Harleian MSS., No. 6991.

"*A copy of y^e* DEWKE OF NORFOLKE, *his writeinge in ye latter ende of ye boucke of Job. To his sunne* PHILIPP, EARLE OF SURREY *nowe of* ARUNDELL."

It concludes thus :

"11th of February, wythein fower (four) ouers myght be written with my hearte's bludde. Remember my lessons, and forgette me. Wrytten betweene 4 and 8 o'clocke."

[1] This letter is written in a copy of the New Testament, which the Duke sent as a parting gift to William Dyx, his steward. It is now in the possession of the Duke of Norfolk.

[2] Tierney's 'Hist. of Arundel,' p. 356.

"Your earthely wofull father, but joyefull, I moste humbly thanke the Lorde, that my tyme draweth so neere that my soule shall enjoy blysse, and leave this crowked lumpe of sinneful flesshe.
"Sumetyne NORFOLKE, now THOMAS HOWARD."

Beneath is written:

"Philipp Surreye and this boocke shoulde no waye be seperated, but be together allwayes; and I, Philipp Surreye, testyfy the same being written with my owen hande."

Norfolk was however respited, for on the Sunday the Queen sent order to delay the Duke's execution.

She had already consulted Burghley on the subject. "When she speaketh of the danger," he wrote, "she concludeth that justice should be done: when she speaketh of his nearness of blood, and his superiority in honour, she stayeth."

Elizabeth signed another warrant on the 27th February, and revoked it the next morning. On Thursday, the 10th April, she again signed a warrant and again revoked it in the following letter:

"MY LORD,—

"Methinkes that I am more beholdinge to the hindar part of my hed than wel dare trust the forwards side of the same, and therfore send to the Levetenant and the S, as you knowe best, the ordar to defar this execution till they here furdar. And that this may be done I doubte nothing, without curiositie of my further warrant, for that ther rasche determination upon a very unfit day was countermaunded by your considerat admonition. The causes that move me to this ar not now to be expressed lest an irrevocable dede be in mene while committed. If they wyl nides a Warrant, let this suffice, all written with myn owne hand.

"Your most lovinge Soveraine
"ELIZABETH R."

"Indorsed by Lord Burghley

"xi. April 1572. The Q. Ma*ty* with hir own hand, for staying of the Execution of the D. N.

"R*d* at 2 in the morning."[1]

Four months had elapsed, and at length, after some pressure from Burghley, and upon an address of a committee

[1] This letter is in Ashmolean MSS. at Oxford. See Ellis's 'Orig. Letters, 1st series, vol. ii. p. 263.

of both Houses of Parliament, the Queen signed the final warrant for his execution.

Camden gives an account of the Duke's death on Tower Hill.

"On the 2nd of June, at eight in the morning,[1] the Duke was brought to a scaffold erected upon Tower Hill, whereon he was no sooner mounted, and Alexander Nowell, Dean of St. Paul's,[2] who was there as his ghostly comforter, desiring the multitude that stood round to keep silence, 'but,' he said, '———'" the version of the speech in Camden appears to be merely an abbreviation of the following text of the Duke's speech and conduct on the scaffold, which is taken from the Harleian MSS. in the British Museum. It also supplies some additional particulars, not given by Camden, of the Duke's burial.

"The ende and confession of Thomas, Duke of Norff: beheaded at Towre Hill, the second day of June, 1572."

"It is not rare, good people, for a man to come here to die, althoughe thankes be to God, synce the begynninge of the quene's majestie's reigne, in this place hath not bene any.

"But synce it is my fortune to be fyrst, I pray God it may be the last; such have byn and is the mercifulnes of her ma^{tie} (whome God long preserve) as in this case of myne, yow knowe I have byn div'se tymes looked for ere this, in this place, but by her ma^{ys} clemencyes prolonged hetherto. It is not comon to se a man of my vocac'on to be a speaker, nevertheles I will be brief, and gladly shewe unto yow the state of my offences, as my conscyence doth burthen me; for I am founde by my peares worthy of deathe, whereof I do acquyte them, for I come not hether to justyfie my selfe, neyther yeat to charge my peares wth injustice, but rather submyttynge my selfe to this wch God hath prepared; and thus consideryngo the weaknes of my flesh and bloude, that at such tyme a man's senses wyll p'tely fayle, I do mynde to direct my speach into thre partes, desiringe yow to take it full and wholl, and not to tare it in peaces. For first, in dealing matt'e temporall toward the quene of Scottes, I dealte not as a good subjecte, for that I made not the quene's ma^{tie} privye thereunto, wch indeade I confesse I ought not to have done; and for thys offence I was commytted to this howse (poyntynge to the Tower), and upon my humble sub-

---

[1] "Between the hours of 7 and 8 of the clocke."—Stow.

[2] Alexander Nowell, Dean of St. Paul's for upwards of forty years; he died 13 Feb. 1601-2. See Milman's 'St. Paul's,' p. 306.

myssion deliv'ed thence, then makynge promysse to the quene's ma^{tie}, whom I pray God long to prosper, and prefer, never to deale in those matters agayne. But contrary to my promysse and submyssion to the quene's mat^{ies} clemencye towardes me, wch hath and doth greve me more than anythinge hath done, I dealt in that matter againe, partely for savinge my liffe and other causes wch I could alledge.' Here Mr Sheriffe Bramithe, standinge by the duke, desired him very courteously to make an ende as shorte as myght be, for tyme did spende. Then the duke did begyne againe, and said 'yt hath bene saide that I toke my othe and received the communion that I should not deale in those matters agayne, wch is untrue; and yeat the othe— (now M^r X'pofer, one of the officers, hearinge thies wordes, desired the duke to be shorte, for we are come hither to see you put to executi'on, and we must not delay, while thies speaches passe from yow, for in this we hassarde o^r lives). Then the duke said 'I do not excuse myself, but I come to discharge my conscience, and to acquyte my peares, and not to complaine of injustice, for I have deserved this, and more a greate deale, in that I have abused the quene's mercy toward me, for whome once agayne, with handes liftinge uppe, I pray God longe to p'serve and reigne over yow, and that my deathe may be an ende of all troubles. To augmente my faulte, it is said I had familiarite wth evill dealers; indeed I will confesse and tell yow that I nev' saw nor nev' had co'ference but with one Randolfe,[1] and yeat nev' agaynst the quene's ma^{tie}, God be my judge, although many lewd mocions and offers were made to me, for it is well knowne I had to do wth hym, by reason I was bounde to him in a recognysance for a greate some. And for the two l'res wch came from the pope, I confesse I did se them, the one ciphered and the other disciphered. I never consented unto them, neither was I consentynge to the last rebellion in the north, no'w^{th}standing I come not hither as unguylty. To the second parte I knowe I have byn thought not onelie to have byn a papyst, but to be a papyst, and a lover of papystri, and a mayntayner of them: God is my judge, before whom I stand, liftinge uppe myne eyes, that I was nev' papyst since I knewe what religion meant, but I did alwayes detest papistri and all the vayne or . . . . thereof, embrasinge ev' from the bottom of my harte, the trewe religion of Jesus Christ, trustinge through the assurance of my fayth in his bloude, that he is my onelie savio' and redemer; indeede I must confess that I had s'vants and freinds that were papists, but if thereby I have offended God's church or any protestant, I desire God and them to forgive me. Well, now to the third parte, wherein I have to shewe howe much I am bounden to the quenc's ma^{tie} for her ma^{ties} m'cifullnes

---

[1] Ridolfi or Ridolpho, a Florentine and agent of the Papal Court, lived long in London under the character of a merchant. His general commission was to sow sedition in England, and for this purpose he applied to the Queen of Scots, &c.—Lodge's 'Illustrations,' vol. i. p. 521.

toward me, in that her ma^tie hath promised to be good and gracius to my orphane children. I remember good father Latymer making a sermon in a more honourable place then this is, out of the pulpit, neyther do I compare myselfe unto him, sayd that God had often [taken] away the good and gracious prince for the synne and disobedience of his subjects, w^ch [I pray] God it be not in owr dayes, but that it will please God to contynue and increase her ma^ties yeares, yea, ev' unto the world's end, yf yt be his will and pleasure. Yow have a most gracious quene, as I must nedes confesse, and also a godly religion, therefore looke to yor living and conversac'ons; be godlye and answerable to the religion of Christe that yow professe, that God may prosper the prynce, overthrowe the pope, and mayntane yow in wealth and quietnes. Let not my person, good people, make my speech the worse, they that have facc'ons, I speake not p'ticularly but generally, let them beware and give ov' betymes, seeke not to p'vent God's doing lest God p'vent you."

"And thus the sheriffe hastinge him, he torned from the people to s^r Henry Lee,[1] the duke imbrasinge him, he said, 'I have, and alwayes have had, as trewe a harte to my prynce as any subject have had;' and so s^r Henry Lee stayinge him by the lefte arme, he kneled downe and asked the quene's majestie forgivenes, and risinge uppe agayne imbracinge m^r Deane of Paules often-tymes wth cherefull countynance, and afterwarde for the most p'te shakinge those that were upon the scaffolde by the handes, and desired them to pray for hym: amongst the rest, the executioner did on his knes desire forgivenes of his death, who did very courteously forgive hym, and put into his hands foure sovraignes of golde, and viii^s vi^d in silver. This done, the duke knelinge downe, and the deane of Paules wth hym, made his heartye prayers unto God, and readinge the one and fiftye psalme, saying ov' the last verse savinge one, wch doth say, 'and buylde uppe the walles of Jerusalem;' and he pawsed and said, 'the walles of Englande, good Lorde.' That psalme so finished, he began to read another, and at the vii^th verse of the psalme, he pawsed and said, 'I had almost forgotten, but not to late, I aske all the world forgiveness, and I likewise forgive all the worlde.'

[1] Sir Henry Lee, of Quarendon, Bucks, was Master of the Ordnance. He distinguished himself much at tilts and tournaments. He died in 1611.

That psalme, and those wordes finyshed, wth other prayers, he reade one prayer, counted in effect a petic'on unto God, that his faith nowe at the last howre should not fayle, and finishing the prayer, wth those wordes, in Latin and English, 'In manus tuas Domine commendo spiritum meum,' he rose uppe and pulled offe his velvet gowne, his blacke saten dublett, and his velvet night-cappe, and gave them to the executioner, and beinge in white fusthean waste, he said to m^r Deane, 'this is the white satten dublett I made to dye in, wch the preacher did speake of;' and kneeling downe at the blocke, he layd downe hymselfe, and did rise agayne, and did laye the strawe and other thing in such sorte, as he mighte in more convenyent manner yeld himselfe for the spediar execution; this done, his eyes and hands lifted upp, m^r Deane desired the people of sylence, and said, 'Nowe altogether with one voyce pray for hym, sayinge: Lord Jesus receyve thy soule, and after that, no more shouts nor noyce.' And so all people with one lowd voyce cryed, Lord Jesus receive thy soule. The duke yeldinge hymselfe to the blocke refused to have any handkercher before his eies, and so his heade, wth singular dexteritie of the executioner, was wth the appointed axe at one chop off, and shewed to all the people. Thus he finyshed his life, and afterward his corpes was put into the coffyn appertaininge to Barkynge Church, wth the head also, and the buryall clothe leade on hym, and so was caryed by fowre of the lyeftenants men and was buryed in the chappell in the Towre by m^r Dean of Paules."[1]

Sir John Perrott.

Born 1527. Died in the Tower, 29th Oct. 1592.

Sir John Perrott "was a goodly gentleman and of the sword: he was of a very vast estate, and came not to court for want; and to these advancements he had the endowments

[1] Harleian MSS. No. 834; Bayley, vol. ii. Appendix lxix.

of courage and height of spirit, had he alighted on the alloy and temper of discretion; the defect whereof with a native freedome and boldnesse of speech drew him on to a clouded setting, and layd him open to the spleene and advantage of his enemies, amongst whom Sir Christopher Hatton was professed.[1] He was yet a wise man and a brave courtier, but rough and participating more of active than sedentary motions, as being by his constellations destined for armes."[2]

Perrott had been sent as Lord Deputy to Ireland in 1583, but his haughty manner and the severity of his rule there, caused "strict enquiry to be made into his life and manners, his words and actions."[3] He was therefore recalled to England in 1588, but soon afterwards, in 1590, in consequence of some incautious and treasonable utterances, he was committed to the Tower, by warrant dated the " 8th daie of March, 1590, signed the Lo: Chancellor:[4] the lo: threr,[5] lo: admirall,[6] lo: chamberlaine,[7] and Lord Buckhurst."[8]

Thomas Kerry[9] writes to Lord Talbot:—

"London, xxiii Oct. 1590.

"Sir John Perrott is not yet clered, nor like to be: marry, I think no great matter will fall further but his great disgrace happely from the councell boorde, and some fyne in his apparell and countenance. He seemeth not to be any waie a prisoner."[10]

And, again, Francis Needham writes to the Earl of Shrewsbury:—

"London, xxiii. Nov. 1590.

"The pique and manner of proceeding with Sir John Perrot yieldeth matter to either side to work on, and hathe given to my Lorde

[1] He had offended Hatton often, and sneered at his dancing, saying, "He came to the Court by the Galliard."—Naunton.
[2] 'Naunton's 'Regalia,' pp. 85-6.
[3] Camden.
[4] Sir Christopher Hatton.
[5] Sir John Fortescue.
[6] Charles, Lord Howard of Effingham.
[7] Earl of Nottingham, Henry, Lord Hunsdon.
[8] Thomas Sackville, created Baron Buckhurst in 1567; appointed Lord High Treasurer in 1594, and created Earl of Dorset in 1604; died suddenly at the council table in 1608.
[9] Thomas Kerry, Clerk of the Privy Seal.
[10] 'Lodge's Illustrations of English History,' vol. ii. p. 417.

Treasurer some inwarde cause of dislike, for that Sir John was verie sodainly againe restrained, and his bookes and papers in my Lord Treasurer's house, and at his other house, serched and carried awaie by my Lord Chamberlaine and Lord Buckhurst, which was done without making his lordship previe thereto, but hath greatly appauled his Lordship, and disquieted him in his sleepe all that night."[1]

Perrott remained in the Tower "a close prisoner," and in a memorandum of Sir Michael Blount, it is recorded that "Thomas Vannor hathe the keepinge and lockinge upp of Sir John Perrott."

On 20th February, 1590-1, Sir John Perrott wrote to the Council, hoping they would consider his long imprisonment, protesting that he had never offended Her Majesty, and that he is innocent of the crimes that the unjust priest[2] accuses him of. He prays to be thoroughly charged and heard upon such points as their Lordships may think most material; he can then overthrow Sir Dennis Rougham's forgeries and inventions. He then requests permission to send to his house in the country for money. His poor servants want food and garments in their restraint.[3]

Again, on the 24th February, he writes to three persons (Thomas Lloyd, Roger Williams, and William Jones) at Bonall's Court; desires them to send him by six persons named, £1000 of certain moneys remaining in their hands, for payment of his debts and growing charges, to come from Tenby to Bristol by water; if sent by land, two more should come with it.[4]

6th March, of the same year, Sir John Perrott again addresses the Council, and renews his humble petition that "some good order may be taken to bring his troubles to an end. He is wronged by wicked practices, which cannot be made manifest till he is charged and heard."[5]

On the 21st March, 1591-2, Thomas Phillips writes to Thomas Barnes, that the Attorney and Solicitor General

---

[1] 'Lodge's Illust.' vol. ii. p. 428.
[2] Denis Rougham.
[3] State Papers, Dom. Eliz. 1591, p. 11.
[4] Ibid.
[5] State Papers, Dom. Eliz. 1591, p. 17.

are busily employed in considering the proofs against Sir J. Perrott.[1]

It was not until 1592 that his enemies succeeded in obtaining his impeachment, when he was, on the 27th April, brought to trial in Westminster Hall before Lord Hunsdon and other special commissioners. He was then accused of " having injured the Queene's Majestie with disgracefull speeches, so as to have said, that she was a base bastardly woman, fearefull and too curious: and she cared not for souldiers: that she hindred him from bringing the province of Ulster into good order: and that she would want his helpe shortly," &c.; also that he had treasonably intrigued with the King of Spain for an invasion of Ireland.

He admitted that he had used strong language, for which he was sorry, but said it did not " come from a bad meaning˙: that those words fell from him unadvisedly in his anger, when hindered in his good designs in Ireland, and were the result of the well-known heat of his temper; and that his heart was unstained by a disloyal thought." He " eagerly maintained his cause against Popham and the other pleading orators, even till eleven of the clocke at night: at last by his jury of twelve men he was pronounced guiltie of treason."[2] "Sentence," says Camden, "was not then pronounced, but deferred till another day, which was pronounced twenty daies after."[3] His alleged treasonable correspondence with Spain is believed to have been an entirely unjust accusation. It rested " chiefly on the evidence of a letter which was but a fiction of envy, and was soon after exploded by the priest's (Denis O. Rougham) own confession."[4]

The Queen, on hearing of his condemnation, swore " by her wonted oath" that the jury were all knaves.

On his return to the Tower after his trial, he said, with oaths[5] and with fury, to the Lieutenant, Sir Owen Hopton,

---

[1] State Papers, Dom. Eliz. 1591–2, p. 21.
[2] Camden.
[3] Camden. The documents of the trial, which are in the Baga de Secretis, Pouch li., show that he was tried on the 27th April, but not brought up for sentence until the 16th June.
[4] Naunton.
[5] Sir John Perrott was the first man of quality I find upon record to have sworn by " God's wounds."—Swift's ' Polite Conversation.'

"What! will the Queen suffer her brother[1] to be offered up as a sacrifice to the envy of my strutting adversaries?"

"Which being made known to the Queen, and the warrant for his execution tendered, and somewhat enforced, she refused to sign it, and swore he should not die, for he was an honest and faithful man."

He was respited, and remained in prison, but he died suddenly; it was said of a broken heart, at the end of September 1592. "His haughtiness of spirit," says Naunton, "accompanied him to the last, and still, without any diminution of courage therein, it burst the cords of his magnanimite."

Camden says he died "when, the Queen's anger being qualified, there was great hope of his life showed by her, who about those times was much used to commend the rescript of Theodosius, Honorius, and Arcadius: 'If any man speaks ill of the Prince, if it proceede out of the lightness of his minde, it is to be contemned; if out of madness, it is to be pitied; if out of any injury done to him before, it is to be pardoned.'

"Thus," he concludes, "did the unbridled untowardness of a roving tongue cause destruction to a worthy man, and one that deserved well of the Commonwealth: leaving an admonition to all posteritie, that reproachfull words against Princes finde a deepe impression in them, and commonly a very sharpe memorie."[2]

---

[1] He was supposed to have been a natural son of Henry VIII. by Mary, wife of Sir Thomas Perrott of Haroldstone in Pembrokeshire. "Compare his pictures, his qualities, gesture and voice with that of the King, which memory retains yet amongst us, they will plead strongly that he was a surreptitious child of the blood royal.

"He was of stature and size far beyond an ordinary man; seems never to have known what fear was, and distinguished himself by martial exercises."—Naunton.

"As he did exceed most men in stature, so did he in strength of body. His hair was auburn until it grew gray in his elder years. His countenance full of majestie, his eyes marvellous piercing, and carrying a commanding aspect. When in France in 1551, during a boar hunt, he had rescued a gentleman who was in danger, by giving the boar such a blow that it did well nigh part the head from the shoulders. The King (Henry II.) who stood in sight of this, came presently unto him and took him about the middle, and embracing him, called him Beaufoile, whereat he supposed the King came to try his strength, and taking the King also about the middle, lifted him high from the ground: with which the King was nothing displeased, but proffered him a good pension to serve him."—'History of Sir John Perrott.'

[2] Camden, pp. 68, 69.

The burial register records: "1592. Sir John P'ratt, condempned of high treason, buried vth Oct: in the Chappell." The place of his interment is not further indicated.

Philip, Earl of Arundel.

Born 28th June, 1557. Died a prisoner in the Tower, 19th October, 1595.

Philip, Earl of Arundel, was the only son of Thomas, fourth Duke of Norfolk; he was born on the 28th June, 1557, and baptized at Whitehall, Philip II. of Spain being his godfather.

The title of Duke of Norfolk had been forfeited by the attainder of his father in 1572, but he became Earl of Arundel as possessor of Arundel Castle through his mother, Lady Mary Fitzalan, only daughter of the Earl of Arundel. He was summoned to Parliament by that title in 1580.

He was shortly afterwards suspected of intriguing with the Catholic party on behalf of Mary Queen of Scots, and it is also believed that the Earl of Leicester was jealous of the attention which Queen Elizabeth seemed disposed to show him when at Court. In 1584, after the Queen had been entertained by him at Arundel House, he was informed that he must remain as a prisoner in his own house, and Lord Hunsdon was sent to examine him about his religious convictions,[1] "whereof the Queen began to have suspicions," and about his communications with Cardinal Allen and Mary Queen of Scots.

It was intimated to him that the Queen would restore his liberty if he would carry the sword of state and attend her to the services of the Reformed church in her chapel, but this he steadily refused to do.

He was on three occasions examined by the Privy Council, and one of the accusations brought against him was, that "if the Queen, at the opening of Parliament, attended a

---

[1] Fox, the ultra-Protestant and Martyrologist, had been his tutor, but he had now become a strict Roman Catholic.

sermon at Westminster, whilst the rest of the peers were alone in the chancel, he was 'loitering below in one of the aisles of the Abbey.'"[1]

No specific charges could be proved against him, and he was therefore in a few weeks set at liberty.

In order to free himself from further persecution, and being alarmed at the stringent laws which were directed against Jesuits and Roman Catholics, he determined to leave England for France, and he embarked at Littlehampton in a small vessel, with his two servants, William Bray and W. Burbace, late one evening about the middle of the month of April, 1585.

He had left a letter explanatory of his conduct with his sister, Lady Margaret Sackville, which was to be delivered to the Queen after his departure.[2]

He had, however, been already betrayed to Walsingham and the Council by one of his servants. As the night advanced, the captain hung out a light from the masthead. The signal was understood by those employed to watch for it, and shortly after the vessel was "boarded and stayed by one Kelloway, captain of a little man of war, who pretended himself to be a pirate."[3]

Arundel was seized and conveyed back to the shore. Here he was delivered into the custody of Sir George Carey, the son of Lord Hunsdon, who conveyed him to London. He was lodged one night on the way at Guildford, "where, seeing the master of the inn, who had sometime been his servant, weeping and sorrowing for his misfortune, he comforted them all, saying that he was not in custody of any crime or treason, but only for attempting to leave the kingdom."

On the 25th April, 1585, he was lodged in the Tower. Members of the Privy Council were twice sent by the Queen to the Tower to examine him, but he remained there until 17th May, 1586, when he was summoned before the Star

---

[1] He alludes to this accusation in the letter which he subsequently addressed to the Queen.

[2] For this letter, which is a lengthy document written in defence of his conduct, see Harleian MSS., No. 787. Stow, and MS. Life, pp. 31-51.

[3] MS. Life, p. 53.

Chamber.[1] The principal accusations were—attempting to leave the realm without permission from the Queen, and his being reconciled to the Church of Rome. After a rigid examination, to which he replied with much firmness, he was sentenced to pay a fine of 10,000*l.* to the Queen, and to be imprisoned during Her Majesty's pleasure; and "that

View of the Beauchamp Tower before the restorations in 1852.

imprisonment," says his biographer, "continued even till his dying day, ten years and more after the sentence given."[2]

He was probably first lodged in the Bell Tower, but at the

---

[1] Bryan Lassells writes on the 20th May to the Earl of Shrewsbury: "There were at his examination the Lord Chancellor, the Archbishop of Canterbury, the Lord Treasurer, the Lord Chamberlain, the Lord Cobham, the Lord Buckhurst, Sir Francis Knollys, Mr. Vice-Chamberlain, Mr. Secretary Walsingham, and the judges of every Bench, saving the Chief Justice of England, who was sick. Mr. Justice Periam gave the judgment, with his opinion, the first, whereto all the rest did consent."—Lodge's 'Illustrations,' vol. ii. p. 286.

[2] MS. Life, p. 65.

end of May, 1586, he was removed to the Beauchamp Tower,[1] and permitted to have the attendance of two of his servants, and to walk occasionally in the gallery within the Tower,[2] and in the garden (*i.e.* the Queen's Garden) with a keeper.[3]

Whilst imprisoned in the Beauchamp Tower he cut the inscription which is still to be seen in the window opening on the staircase leading from the first floor to the room above:

SICUT . PECCATI . CAUSA . VINCIRI . OPPROBRIUM . EST . ITA . E . CONTRA . PRO . CRISTO . CUSTODIAE . VINCULA . SUSTINERE . MAXIMA . GLORIA . EST.[4]

ARUNDELL,
28 OF MAY, 1587.

And also that which is visible above the fire-place in the prisoner's room.[5]

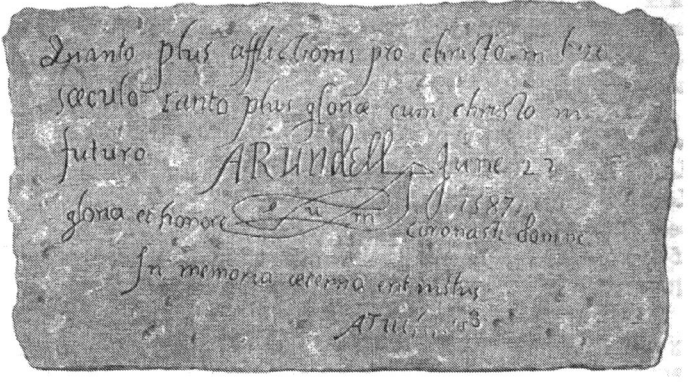

Inscription of Philip, Earl of Arundel.

[1] So called from having been the prison of Beauchamp, Earl of Warwick, in 1397.
[2] Probably in the Queen's Gallery; he had also the "liberty of the leads," a walk from the Beauchamp Tower to the Bell Tower.
[3] In the MS. Life an incident is related of his being annoyed by a man, whom he believed to be mad, continually bowing to him from the leads of the Salt Tower, whilst he was walking in the garden. (See plan, p. 187.)
[4] "It is a reproach to be bound in the cause of sin, but to sustain the bonds of prison for the cause of Christ is the greatest glory."
[5] "The more affliction we endure for Christ in this world, the more glory we shall obtain with Christ in the next."

Arundel, 22nd June, 1587.

"Thou hast crowned him with honour and glory, O Lord! In everlasting memory he will be just," &c.

For an account of the inscriptions see 'Archæologia,' vol. xiii. p. 70; Bayley, p. 139; and Dick's 'Inscriptions in the Beauchamp Tower.'

This latter sentence he "used often to show to his servants, as well to animate himself to suffer all his afflictions with patience and alacrity, as to incite them also to do the same." [1]

"At the beginning of the year 1588 he had found means (having much more liberty than ever he had either before or after) to meet his friends Sir Thomas Gerrard,[2] a knight of good worth in Lancashire, Mr. Shelly, a Sussex gentleman, and Mr. William Bennet, an old priest of Queen Mary's days, and to celebrate mass with them. This he did by mediation of the Lieutenant's daughter, who had thirty pound given her by the Earl's lady (as herself told me) for her endeavour in procuring it." [3]

This gave rise to a report that Arundel and his fellow-prisoners had prayed for the success of the Spanish armada, and it was said that he had "made prayer for four and twenty hours together for that end," and that Mr. Bennet had said "a mass of the Holy Ghost to the same effect."

The Earl was therefore again made a close prisoner, and was twice examined by some of the Council: first, by the Lord Chancellor (Sir Christopher Hatton), Sir William Cecil, Lord Treasurer, and Sir Thomas Heneage, "who had ever been a great enemy of his." [4] In addition to these members of the Council, Lord Hunsdon was specially sent by the Queen on the second occasion.

The examination of the Earl had reference to his religious opinions, and does not appear to have been always calmly carried on, as "one of the examiners said the Pope was an arrant knave, another called him a vile Italian priest, and the Lord Chamberlain, entering into passion, called the Earl 'beast and traitor,' and said rather than he should not be

---

[1] MS. Life, p. 111. A story is told that "whilst in time of his recreation he was engraving with his knife the sign of the holy cross in a stone of the wall of his chamber, he hurt his hand by the accidental slipping of the knife, a Protestant standing by, said, 'See how soon the Lord doth hinder this unlawful work!' 'Nay!' said the Earl, 'see rather how the devil hath applied himself to check so good an action.'"

[2] Sir Thomas Gerrard, created a baronet in 1611, when in consideration of his father's sufferings in the case of Mary, Queen of Scots, his fee of 1000*l.* was returned to him.

[3] MS. Life, p. 80.   [4] Ibid. p. 83.

hanged within four days, that he himself would hang him; repeating it once or twice." [1]

In the following year it was resolved to bring him to trial, and a commission was issued, appointing the Earl of Derby to be the Lord High Steward.[2]

Prisoner's Room in the Beauchamp Tower.

On the 14th April, 1589, he was brought from the Tower to the Court of King's Bench at Westminster Hall, and there arraigned before twenty-three peers, upon an indictment of high treason. "His tall and comely figure, which still bespoke the strength and elasticity of youth, contrasted strongly with his sunken eye and sallow countenance. He was dressed in a wrought velvet gown, furred with martens,

[1] MS. Life, p. 87.
[2] Henry, fourth Earl of Derby, K.G., was sent in 1584–5 to France to invest Henry III. with the Order of the Garter: was one of the Peers at the trial of Mary, Queen of Scots. Died 25th September, 1592, and was buried at Ormskirk.

laid about with gold lace, and buttoned with gold buttons; a black satin doublet, a pair of velvet hose, and a high black hat on his head. He made two obeisances to the state and to the nobles, and to the others present."[1]

When called upon to hold up his hand, he raised it very high, saying, "Here is as true a man's heart and hand as ever came into this hall. Behold a hand clear and a mind sincere."[2]

He was accused of conspiring with Cardinal Allen[3] to restore the Catholic faith in England, of having suggested that the Queen was unfit to govern, and of ordering masses to be said for the success of the Spanish Armada; that he intended to have withdrawn himself out of the realm to serve with the Duke of Parma against his native country, and that he had been privy to the measure of issuing the bull of Pope Pius V. for transferring the crown of England to King Philip of Spain. His friends Sir Thomas Gerard and Mr. Bennet were both brought as witnesses against him, but he denied their evidence "very stout and constantly."[4]

No charge of treason could be substantiated, except that he was reconciled to the Church of Rome, nevertheless he was found guilty of conspiring to dethrone the Queen.

His speeches during the trial evinced strong and polished talents. He repelled the partial and desultory attacks of Popham, the Attorney General,[5] by acute observations and prompt and ingenious argument, uttered occasionally with rhetorical elegance.

"The Attorney General," said he, "has managed the letters and confessions produced against me like the spider, who can suck venom out of the sweetest flowers, and find

---

[1] Tierney's 'Hist. of Arundel,' p. 389.
[2] Camden.
[3] William Allen, born in 1532, studied at Oxford; after the death of Queen Mary he retired to the Low Countries. At the time of the Spanish Armada he wrote an admonition exhorting the people of England to revolt in favour of the Spaniards. He was made a cardinal in 1587, and was afterwards appointed Archbishop of Mechlin. He died in 1594.
[4] MS. Life, p. 94.
[5] John Popham, appointed Solicitor-General in 1579 and Attorney-General in 1580. He was knighted by Queen Elizabeth in 1592, and appointed Chief Justice of the Common Pleas. In 1603 he was made Chief Justice of the Queen's Bench. He died in 1607.

materials for poison, where others would only obtain matter of a wholesome and harmless nature." [1]

The peers withdrew for an hour to consider their verdict, and on their return to the hall, each being questioned in succession, declared him guilty.

Arundel was then asked if he had anything further to say why sentence of death should not pass upon him, when he only used the same words which his father had done before him in the same place, "God's will be done." Sentence being pronounced, he desired leave to speak with his wife, that he might see his young son, who had been born since his imprisonment; that he might have the liberty to speak with his stewards, who had the accounts of his estate, and that his debts might be discharged. He likewise humbly desired the Queen would take his young son into her favour and patronage.

"Then the Lord Steward broke his staff, the badge of his office, and the Earl was carry'd back to the Tower, the fatal hatchet being carried the wrong way before him." [2]

"There were a great many that most heartily lamented the untimely fall of this young nobleman (for he was not above thirty-three years of age at the most), and as many on the other side were ready to cry up the Queen's wisdom and caution, who, by this example, had struck a kind of terror into the more powerful part of the Romish faction. The Queen, after all, gave him his life, and was well enough satisfied in having learned the power of so considerable a man, and one who was so great a bulwark of the Catholic cause." [3]

On the day after his condemnation he wrote the following letter to Lord Chancellor Hatton:—

"MY SPECIAL GOOD LORD,

"I am most hartily sorry that I was so prevented by my hasty departure from the bar, presently after the sentence pronounced upon me, as I wanted time to make humble suite for Her Majesty's favour.

---

[1] Tierney, vol. ii. p. 392.
[2] See Camden, whose account is interesting; also Tierney, vol. ii. pp. 388–397. The trial is in the Baga de Secretis, Pouch xlix.
[3] Camden.

And I am very glad that I have this opportunity of writing to your Lordship to make humble petition unto Her Majesty in my behalf for her gratious favour, together with my most harty grief for anything whereinsoever I have offended Her Highness in all the course of my life. As also to give your Lordship humble thanks for your honourable goodness always extended towards me, and to become a most earnest suiter for the continuance thereof to my wife and children.

"And as a dead man to this world, and in all good will whilst I live, your Lordship's most affectionate, I humbly take my leave, beseeching God to send you all honour and happiness in this world to his glory, and my poor soul a joyfull meeting with yours in heaven.

"The day after my condemnation, your Lordship's most humbly at commandement till my last.

"PHILIPP HOWARD."[1]

He also addressed a letter for Queen Elizabeth to the care of Hatton, but the chancellor declined to deliver it, by reason of his opinion that it would rather incense her against him.

In the following year, when Sir Owen Hopton was succeeded as Lieutenant of the Tower by Sir Michael Blount, the name of "Philipp, late Erle of Arundell," appears first on the list of the names of "all suche prisoners as Sir Owen Hopton, Knighte, delivered to the custodie of Michael Blount, Esquire, by indenture bearinge date the vith daie of Julie, 1590. A° Regni Reginæ Eliz: xxxii^{do};"[2] and with this memorandum added to it: "Phillipp, late Earle of Arundell, is a close prisoner, and hathe noe other libertie than he had in Sir Owen Hopton's tyme, which is to walke in the queen's gardeine twoe houres in the daie, with a servant of the lieutenant's to attende him, the gardeine doore beinge shutt at the tyme of his walkinge."

His life in prison was that of an ascetic, and his days were passed in a routine of praying and fasting. "His hour of rising in the morning was constantly at five of the clock, having to that end a Larum in his chamber, and was very carefull that it should be set overnight. Immediately as soon as he was risen out of bed, he fell down upon his bare

---

[1] MS. Life, pp. 96–7.
[2] Lansdowne MSS. Brit. Mus., No. 65; Bayley, lxxxii.

knees and breathed forth his devotions; with his kneeling in that manner, his knees were grown very hard and black."[1]

Blount appears to have treated him with much rigour. In a letter written in 1594 he complains that Blount's "injuries to me, both by himself and his trusty Roger, are intollerable, infinite, dayly multiplyd, and to those who

Passage and cell in the Beauchamp Tower.

know them not, incredible: and the most that you can imagine will be far inferior, I think, to the truth when you shall learn it."[2]

In a memorandum in Blount's writing is found this entry:—"Henrie Frewen hathe the keepinge and lockinge upp of the late Earle of Arundell, and twoe of the lieu-

[1] MS. Life, p. 109.   [2] Tierney, vol. ii. p. 399. MS. Life, p. 69.

tenant's servants with him, that is to saie, Robert Daubeney and Lawrence Whistler, which twoe doe attend him all the daie."[1]

He asked permission for his wife to visit him with his infant son, whom, having been born since his imprisonment, he had never seen, but this was refused, the reply being, "If he would once attend the protestant worship, his prayer should be granted, and he should be restored to his honours and estates, and to all the favours that the Queen could show him."

His sufferings were much increased by the attempt which was made to poison him. One of his discharged servants, Nicholas Raimberd, prompted by revenge, bribed the cook who prepared the meals of the prisoners, and in August, 1595, he "fell one day sitting at dinner so very ill immediately upon the eating of a roasted teal that he was forced to rise from the table."[2] But he still lingered on, till at length, in October, "his physitians comeing to visit him some few dayes before his departure, he desired them not to trouble themselves now any more, his case being beyond their skill, and he haveing then some business, meaning his devotions. Sir Michael Blount, who had been ever very hard and harsh unto him, took occasion to come and visit him, and kneeling down by his bedside, desired his Lordship to forgive him. 'Do you ask forgiveness, Mr Lieutenant?' said the Earl. 'Why then I forgive you in the same sort as I desire myself to be forgiven at the hands of God.' Then raising himself a little upon his pillow, he added, 'Mr Lieutenant, you have showed both me and my men hard measure. You must think when a prisoner comes hither to this Tower, he bringeth sorrow with him; then do not add affliction to affliction. Your commission is only to keep with safety, not to kill with severity. Farewell, Mr Lieutenant. For the time of my small abode, come to me whenever you please, you shall be heartely wellcome as my

---

[1] Bayley, Appendix lxxxvi.
[2] The cook is said to have come to him on his death-bed, and earnestly besought forgiveness for some offence, which, however, the Earl would not disclose.

friend:' the lieutenant then took his leave and went out of the chamber weeping." [1]

"About this time," writes Camden, "died Philip Howard, Earl of Arundel, in the Tower of London, having after his condemnation, in the year 1587, given himself up to his retired meditations, till by a religious kind of austerity he had reduced himself to a very languishing state."

Arundel died on Sunday, the 19th October, at about twelve o'clock noon. His body remained till the Tuesday following in the chamber where he died, and then, "being shrouded in a poor sheet, was put into a plain coffin, covered with a mean black cloth, and carried without any solemnity to the chappell in the Tower, and there buried in the chancel in the very selfsame grave where the Duke, his father, was." [2]

---

[1] MS. Life, pp. 116–19.
[2] MS. Life, p. 122. A curious account of the "words used at the Burial of Philip, late Earle of Arundel, on Oct. 22, 1595," is to be found in Lansdowne MSS., Brit. Mus., xciv. 49; see also Tierney, vol. ii. p. 409. The particular charges of the buriall of Phill Howard, late Earle of Arundell, in the church of the Tower of London.

Imprimis for a coffin	xs.
To the parson for breaking the ground in the chancel where the bodie was buried and for his attendance there	xls.
To the clerke for making the grave wth his attendance and for paving the same again	xiiis. iiiid.
For three yardes of black cloth to cover the coffyn	xxxs.
Sum	iiiil. xiiis. iiiid.

"Mr. Lieutenant desireth to knowe ye Lordshippes (Burleigh's) pleasure what shall be done with the said three yardes of black cloth that covered the coffyn.—(In another hand)—This yor Lo: hath appoynted to the minister of the church.—MSS. Lansd., lxxix. 74.

"Money remayning unpaid to Phil Howard, late Earle of Arundell, prison in the Tower, deceased, of her ma^{ties} pencōn assigned unto him by the R^t Honble the Lo: Treasur͡ of Englande. Imprimis, for the diett of the said late Earle not paied from Saterdaie, the xxviith of September, 1595, until Sondaie, the xixth of October followinge, in wch day the said late Earle died, being three weekes and one daie at viiil. the weeke=24l. Whereof due to the Lieutenant of the tower, for three weekes diett, xviiil., at the rate of vil. the weeke according to their agreem^t, and so resteth vil. wch the said late Earle hath given unto Thomas Rookwood, Gent., for his great paines, attending upon him by the space of three yeeres, as appeareth by a bill subscribed with the hand of the said late Earle. Also his pencoñ for his apparel, phisicke, and other his necessaries, for one quarter, ended in the feast of St. Michell the archangell 1595, after the rate of Cl. by the yeere, 25l. which is also given to the saide Thomas Rookewood, by the said late Earle, as appeareth by the said bill.

"Also for wages and liveries for three servants attendinge uppon the said late Earle for one-half yere, ended in the feast of St. Michell the archangell, 1595, 3l.
    Sum Total 54l."
Lansdowne MSS. Brit. Mus., lxxix. 74. Tierney, p. 398.

In the reign of James I. a licence for removal of the Earl's remains was obtained at the joint request of his widow and his son, and in the year 1624 they were removed from St. Peter's to West Horsley, in Surrey, the seat of the Countess of Arundel. Here they were placed in a small iron coffin or chest,[1] and then being transported to Arundel, they were deposited in the vault constructed for the family of the Howards.

When this vault was opened for the burial of Edward, Duke of Norfolk, in 1777, the coffin was seen, bearing on it the following inscription:—

"Philippi Comitis olim Arund: et Surr: ossa veneranda hoc loculo condita, impetratâ a Jacobo Rege veniâ, Annæ uxoris dilectissimæ diligenti curâ, Thomæ filii insigni pietate a Turri Londinensi in hunc locum translata sunt, anno 1624. Qui primo, ob fidei Cathol: professionem, sub Elizabethâ carceri mancipatus, deinde pœnâ pecuniariâ decem mille lib: mulctatus, tandem capitis iniquissimè condemnatus, post vitam in arctissimâ custodiâ in eadem Turri an: 10. mens: 6 sanctissimè translatum piissime XIX Octob: an: MDXCV. non absque veneni suspicione, in Domine obdormivit."[2]

He is described as "tall of stature, yet ever very straight; of a swarthy complexion, and long visaged, but of a comely countenance. His memory was excellent, his wit more than ordinary; he was naturally eloquent, and of a ready speech."[3]

ROBERT DEVEREUX, EARL OF ESSEX.

Born 10th Nov. 1567.   Beheaded on the green within the Tower, 25th Feb. 1600–1.

A certain halo of romance has always hovered over the career of Robert Devereux, second Earl of Essex, but of all

[1] This chest is nearly in the shape of a small coffin; but its widest part is in the middle, where it measures exactly 12 inches across; its length is 2 feet 6 inches.—Tierney, p. 630.

[2] Tierney, p. 630; Bayley, p. 146 MS. Life, p. 123.

[3] MS. Life, p. 126; Dodd's 'Church History,' vol. ii. p. 37.

the incidents of his eventful life few are more singular than his daring attempt to seize the person of Queen Elizabeth, and to compel her to dismiss from her court and councils those whom he regarded as his political and personal adversaries.

Sir Henry Wotton has thus written of him: "In their military services, the characters of the Earl's imployments were these: viz., his forwardest, was that of Portugal: the saddest, that of Rouen, where he lost his brave brother: his fortunatest piece I esteem the taking of Cadiz, and no less modest; for there he wrote with his own hands a censure of his omissions: his jealousest imployment was to the relief of Calais, besieged by the Cardinal Archduke; about which there passed then between the Queen and the French King much art: his voyage to the Azores was the best, for the discovery of the Spanish weakness, and otherwise almost a saving voyage: his blackest was that to Ireland, ordained to be the sepulchre of his father, and the gulph of his own fortunes."[1]

Already, in September 1599, his sudden return from the Irish expedition had brought him into disfavour with Elizabeth, and Sir John Harrington, who had been with Essex in Ireland, was witness of the Queen's anger against him. "When I came into her presence," he writes, "she chafed much, walked fastly to and fro, looked with discomposure in her visage, and, I remember, catched at my girdle, when I kneeled to her, and swore 'by God's son, I am no queen; that man is above me. Who gave him command to come here so soon? I did send him on other business.'"[2]

Essex was then committed to the custody of the Lord Keeper to be confined in York House.[3] He remained there

---

[1] Wotton's 'Reliquiæ; a Parallel,' &c., pp. 177-8.

[2] Harrington's 'Nugæ Antiquæ,' vol. i. p. 354. Harrington further adds: "She bid me go home. I did not stay to be bidden twice. If all the Irish rebels had been at my heels, I should not have made better speed."

[3] In the Strand; originally built in 1557, by Heath, Archbishop of York; it subsequently was the residence of the Duke of Buckingham. It was pulled down, and the site covered with streets, bearing the names and titles of the last possessor. George Court, Villiers Street, Duke Street, Of alley (now York Buildings) and Buckingham Street ('Handbook for London').

until the 19th March in the following year, when he was permitted to return to his own house, and after an inquiry, held by the Lords of the Council, into his conduct, he was released from confinement, but forbidden to come to Court.

He then endeavoured to reinstate himself in the Queen's favour, and wrote several letters to her;[1] but being unsuccessful he gave himself up to despair, and formed that daring plan which ultimately brought him to the scaffold. His friend Harrington remarked that "he shyftethe from sorowe and repentance to rage and rebellion so suddenlie, as well proveth him devoide of goode reason as righte minde. In my last discourse he uttered strange wordes borderinge on suche strange desygns, that made me hasten forthe and leave his presence."[2]

Meetings were held by the Earl and his disaffected friends at his own house, and also at Drury House.[3]

"The earle of Essex is now altogether at his howse near Temple barr, in no favour as yet with Her Majestie, but growing againe to wonted popularyty by beyng often visited by many of the nobility, as the Erles of Worcester, Southampton, Sussex, Rutland, Bedford, and others, with many captaines and cavaliers, and the whole pack of Puritanes, insomuch as now it is thought bothe the Queene and Mr. Secretary stand in some awe of hym, and would make hym surer if they durst."[4]

On Saturday, the 7th February, 1600–1, Essex received a

---

[1] In one of these letters he says, "that he humbly kisst the hand, and the rod of the Queene, which only corrected him and not overthrowed him; that he should never live a happy day, till he saw those blessed eyes of hers, which had been his stars, wherby he had sailed on happily, and kept his course on at a just measure. Now he had resolved to repent earnestly, and to say with Nebuchadnezzar, 'my habitation is amongst the wilde beasts of the field, that I may eat hay like an ox, and be watered with the dew of heaven, till such time as it shall please the Queene to restore my sense to me againe.' The Queen, says Camden, was so jocond at these words, that she said, 'I wish his deeds and words would jump together. He hath long tried my patience. Sure I am my father would not have borne with his perverseness. But I will not look back lest like Lot's wife, I am turned into a pillar of salt."

[2] Harrington's 'Nugæ Antiquæ,' vol. i. p. 179.

[3] Then the residence of Lord Southampton; it had been built by Sir William Drury. The Olympic Theatre now occupies its site.

[4] Private Letter, dated 13th Jan., quoted by Lingard, vol. vi. p. 296.

summons to appear before the Council, but "the very same day, a little note was put into his hands (he knew not how) wherein he was warned to looke to himselfe and provide for his owne safetie. And the Earle fearing that somewhat had come to light, and so hee might perchance be committed againe, excused himselfe by reason of some distemper in his health, that he could not come to the Councell."[1]

On the next day, Sunday, the 8th of February, early in the morning, "comes to Essex House the Earles of Rutland and Southampton, the Lord Sands, &c., and almost 300 more of the best sort;" these he courteously entertained "and said there was waite laid for his life, that he was determined to get unto the Queen, and that the citie stood by him. All this while the gates were locked up and no man let in, but he that was well known, and no man let out that was once let in. At this very time the Queen commandes the Maior of London to see that all the citizens were ready at their doores at her command in an instant: and to the Earle of Essex she sent the Lord Keeper, the Earle of Worcester, Sir William Knolles, comptroller of the Queen's household and uncle to the Earle, and Popham, Lord Chiefe Justice of England, to know of him the reason of such a concourse. They were all let in at a wicket and their servants shut out, only except him that carried the seale before the Keeper."[2]

Essex told them his life was threatened and his letters counterfeited "both with hand and seale, and he contrived to get them into the middest of the house; in the mean time these harsh sounds fly about their eares, 'Kill them, kill them: away with the great seale: cast it out of the windows: shut them up fast enough,' so the Earle commanded the dores to be bolted, and left them there prisoners."[3]

He then went out into the streets with about two hundred men, and calling out "For the Queen! for the Queen! there is wait laid for my life," endeavoured to raise the citizens; "and so going through Cheapeside, he made all haste to

---

[1] Camden.   [2] Ibid.   [3] Ibid.

Smith's house, the Sheriffe, by Fenchurch Street." But the Londoners remained passive, and " Sheriffe Smith had withdrawn himself out at a postern gate and gone to the Lord Mayor's: in the meantime Lord Burghley,[1] and Dethicke,[2] Garter King at Armes, entering into the citie proclaimed Essex and all his complices traitors: so that when the Earl was about to return he findes his way chained up neerest the West gate of Pauls, and pikemen and muskets set against him, at the appointment of the Bishop of London, under the command of Sir J. Levison. Here first he drew his sword and commanded Blunt to assault them, which he did very manfully, having slaine one Wayte and he himselfe sore wounded, was taken. There was slaine also Henry Tracy a young man, and very dearely loved by the Earle, besides one or two citizens. The Earle's passage was stopped here, and his hat was shot through, so 'accompanied with a few that left him not yet (for most had), making haste downe to Queenehithe, he got boats, and came home to his house againe by water.'"[3]

His disappointment was great when he found that the Lord Keeper and the other lords, whom he thought to detain as hostages, had been allowed to depart; so he ordered his house to be fortified, and "he burnes many papers lest they should blabb too much," and "prepares for his defence." But the Lord Admiral[4] arrived almost immediately with troops, and invested the house, when a short parley took place. Essex's conditions were rejected, but a respite of two hours was granted, in order that the ladies with their female attendants might leave the house. At six o'clock the battering train arrived from the Tower, and then the Admiral repeated his summons: "about 6 of the cloke the Lord Admirall sent Sir Robert Sidney to somone the Earles and those that were with them, to yield themselves, and after the drume had somoned a parley, the Earl of

---

[1] Thomas Cecil, half-brother of Robert Cecil, afterwards Lord Salisbury, succeeded his father, Lord Burghley, in 1598; created Earl of Exeter in 1605; died 1622.

[2] Sir Gilbert Dethicke.
[3] Camden.
[4] Charles, Lord Howard of Effingham and Earl of Nottingham. Lord High Admiral from 1585 till 1619.

Southampton came upon the leads, and asked Sir Rob Sidney, calling him cossen Sidney, 'What would you have, would you have us yeeld to our enemies.'" Essex afterwards appeared on the leads, and also refused to surrender.

Ultimately, after a short assault, in which "there died only Owen Salisbury and one or two slaine within with the muskets," terms of capitulation were agreed upon, "whereupon they went down and opened the doors: and each of them upon his knee surrended his sword. So from thence they went to the places of their severall commitments."[1]

It was then ten o'clock at night, and Essex was "committed to the Archbishop of Canterburie's house at Lambeth and not taken straightway to the Tower, because it was so late, and the water not passable under London Bridge: but the next day by commission from the Queen, he and Lord Southampton were carried by boat unto the Tower."[2]

"The Queen," wrote Cecil[3] to Sir G. Carew, "when she heard of the proceedings of the Earl of Essex, was not more amazed than she would have been to have heard of a fray in Fleet Street;" and in a MS. in the Sloane collection, British Museum, called 'Observations on the Life and Raigne of Elizabeth, Queen of England,' it says that "when she heard the news (being then at dinner) she seemed nothing moved therewith, but only said, 'He that had placed her in that seat would preserve her in it,' and so continued her dinner, not showing any fear or distraction of mind."

On the 19th February, Essex, with the Earl of Southampton,[4] was brought to trial at Westminster Hall. "A plat-

---

[1] MS. account by Frances Bourchier, daughter of the Earl of Bath. See Lingard, vol. vi. p. 365.

[2] Camden. Essex was imprisoned in the Tower, which was called the Devilin, or Robyn the Devil's Tower; its title was changed to that of Devereux Tower after he had occupied it. It is now the official residence of the commanding officer of artillery.

[3] A list of the "prisoners and where they are prisoned" endorsed by Cecil, is preserved amongst the MSS. at Hatfield. See Lodge's 'Illustrations,' vol. ii. p. 545.

[3] Robert Cecil, born 1563; succeeded Walsingham as Secretary of State in 1590; created Earl of Salisbury in 1605; died 1612; and was buried at Hatfield. James I. called him "his little beagle."

[4] Henry Wriottesley, third Earl of Southampton; succeeded in 1581; attainted in 1598; restored by King James in 1603; died, 1624.

form 6 feet high and 36 feet square was erected at the upper end of the hall: the seat of the Lord Steward on the west side towards the King's Bench: on each side seats covered with green cloth for the Peers: in the middle a table covered with green cloth after the manner of the Exchequer, with seats round it for the Judges and counsel: on the north side a little square space was cut out for the Sergeant of the Mace: at the east end was the bar where the prisoners stood.[1]

Lord Buckhurst,[2] the Lord High Steward for the time being, preceded by the king of arms, bearing the white staff, and accompanied by seven sergeants with maces, having taken his seat, the Lieutenant[3] of the Tower produced the prisoners. On meeting at the bar the Earls kissed each other's hands, and embraced cheerfully. "The chief points," says Stow, "were (for holding of private counsels, conspiring to depryve the Queene of life and government, for attempting to surprise the person of the Queen at Whitehall; the imprysoning of the lordes which the Queen sent unto him as his good friends upon the day of his rysing, and his perswading them to stand for him; his warlike entrance to London, and to surprise the Tower; unto all which they pleaded Not guiltie: and very willingly submitted themselves to be tryed by their peeres. Their tryers were 24 in number, viz.: 8 earles, one viscount, and 15 barons; there were present divers others of right honorable rank and quallitie besides the reverend judges of the law."[4]

Camden was present, and gives his account of the trial: "Yelverton at large unfolds the matter, showing that it is to be reckoned as treason, even to thinke anything against the Majesty of a Prince. Then he compares Essex with Catiline; and then casts in his teeth the liberality and goodnesse of the Queene towards him, &c. Sir Edward Coke sollicitor too shows that the very inward thought of any

---

[1] Devereux's 'Earl of Essex,' vol. ii. p. 149.
[2] Thomas Sackville, Lord Buckhurst, was Lord High Treasurer from 1599 till 1603, when he was created Earl of Dorset; he died 19th April, 1609.
[3] Sir John Peyton. Lord Howard of Walden, the constable, was not present at the trial.
[4] Stow.

villany against the Prince was indeed treason. Then hee runnes thorow all the graces and favours of the Queene bestowed upon him, and having woven into his discourse an historicall narration of all the matter, about surprizing the Queene, and calling a parliament, hee concluded his speech with this bitter epiphonema, 'that it were to be wished, that this Robert should be the last of this name Earle of Essex, who affected to be Robert the first of that name King of England.' "[1]

The trial proceeded,[2] and witnesses appeared to give their evidence: when, amongst other witnesses, the name of Sir Walter Raleigh was called, Essex exclaimed, "What booteth it to swear this fox!"[3]

Having lasted until six at night, the trial then came to an end.

"By and by were both the Earles removed aside: and the peeres that past upon them, rising and separating themselves from the rest, conferred amongst themselves, and weighing the matter, within an houre returned againe to their seats; every one having found both the Earles guilty."[4]

Southampton was first sentenced[5]: and "then the Lord High Steward having made a very grave speech admonisheth the Earle of Essex to request the Queene's mercy and pardon, pronouncing upon him the doleful sentence of hanging, drawing, and quartering. And now the hatchet being turned towards them that before was turned from them,

---

[1] Camden, p. 312.

[2] A full and interesting account of the trial is given by Camden, and in Devereux's 'Earls of Essex,' vol. ii. p. 149, et seq. See also an interesting letter from the French ambassador in England to M. de Rohan, given in Winwood's 'Memorials,' vol. i. p. 296.

[3] "Words of a subject," wrote Raleigh afterwards, "do often take deeper root than the memory of ill deeds; the late Earl of Essex told Queen Elizabeth that her conditions were as crooked as her carcase; but it cost him his head, which his insurrection had not cost him, but for that speech."--Birch's 'Raleigh,' vol. i. p. 223.

[4] Camden.

[5] Southampton's life was spared, but he remained in prison until the accession of James I. A story is told that whilst in prison, he was visited by a favourite cat, which came from Southampton House, in Holborn, and found its way down a chimney into Lord Southampton's prison. There is a picture representing Lord Southampton seated with his cat in the possession of the Duke of Portland.

Essex said, 'This body might have done the Queene better service, if she had pleased; but I rejoyce that it is used any way for her:' requesting that before his death hee might receive the communion, and that Ashton,[1] a minister, might be still with him for his soule's health."[2]

Camden concludes his account of the trial with the words: "these things the author of the originall being there present, makes worth beleefe, who if he have omitted anything of note, wisheth it imputed to the fault of his memory, not of his will."[3]

Stow says, "there was a world of people pressing to see the event. The prisoners demeaned themselves very temperately and discreetly, and gave the Queene and the lordes most humble and heartie thankes for so speedie and honorable a tryall. "The newes of all this dayes businese was sodainely divulged throughout London; whereat many forsooke their suppers, and ran hastily into the streets to see the earle of Essex, as he returned to the Tower, who went a swift pace, bending his face towards the earth, and would not looke upon any of them, though some spake directly to him; concerning which with other passages, and the earles objections and answers I have written a more large discourse, according to the general expectation, whereunto by multitudes I have been infinitely urged, but for divers reasons it must be omitted at this time; therefore let this suffice without tarrying."[4]

On the next day, Friday, the 20th, Dr. Dove, Dean of Norwich, was sent by the Council to the Tower to urge Essex to confess and acknowledge his offences; Dr. Ashton, his chaplain, also visited him. After these visits, he asked Thomas, Lord Howard, Constable of the Tower, to move the Queen that he might "speake unto some of the Councell and particularly Cecill, who came to him (on the next day, 21st), with the admiral, treasurer, and Lord Keeper.[5] And first he asketh forgivenesse of the Lord Keeper for keeping

---

[1] Ashton was his chaplain.
[2] Camden.
[3] The records of the trial are preserved in the Baga de Secretis, Pouch lvi.
[4] Stow.
[5] Camden, pp. 322–3.

him in hold at his house: and then of Cecill, for traducing him in the case of the Infanta: so that on both sides there was made a charitable and christian reconciliation. And then he intimates unto them, that as long as he lived, the Queen could not be safe." He desired to die privately within the Tower,[1] fearing, it is alleged, that if he were executed on Tower Hill, his mind might be discomposed, and that the "acclamations of the citizens should have hoven him up."

Chamberlain writes to Sir Dudley Carleton:

"At his coming to the bar, his countenance was somewhat unsettled, but after that he was once in, I assure you I never saw any go through with such boldness and shew of resolution and contempt of death: but whether this courage were borrowed and put on for the time, or natural, it were hard to judge. I hear he now begins to relent, and among other faults, to acknowledge and be sorry for his arrogant, or rather, as the Secretary well termed it to his face, his impudent behaviour at his arraignment; and, what is more, to lay open the whole plot, and appeach divers others not yet called in question. His execution was expected on Saturday, then yesterday, now tomorrow or Thursday. Most of the council have been with him these three or four days together."[2]

Whether the oft-repeated story of Lady Nottingham and the Queen's ring is fact or fiction may be left to others to determine,[3] suffice it here to say that Essex did not himself make any direct appeal to the Queen for mercy; efforts were undoubtedly made to obtain a reprieve, and Lady Essex wrote an earnest appeal to Cecil,[4] to which there is reason to suppose he showed some inclination to listen, for Essex's old enemy Raleigh wrote also at about the same date to Cecil, urging him to execute Essex at once. The fact that he took no farewell of his wife or any of his friends has been considered as a strong proof that he expected a reprieve, if not a pardon.[5]

---

[1] Camden, pp. 322-3.
[2] 'Devereux, Earls of Essex,' vol. ii. pp. 170-1. His confession filled four sheets of paper, but its accuracy has been doubted. — Lingard, vol. vi. p. 302.
[3] See 'Devereux, Earls of Essex,' vol. ii. p. 177, et seq., where the question is discussed.
[4] Lansdowne MSS. Brit. Mus., No. 88, f. 14. Ellis's 'Original Letters,' 1st series, vol. iii. p. 55.
[5] 'Devereux, Earls of Essex,' vol. ii. p. 177.

Camden says, "The Queen, by reason of her good will alwaies to him, somewhat now moved in mind, commanded that he should not die, by Sir Edward Cary. But then on the other side, weighing his contumacy and stubbornesse, that scorned to aske her pardon; and that he had said, that as long as he lived the Queene could not live in safety; she altered her resolution, and by Darcy commanded the execution to proceed."

Notice of his approaching fate was communicated to him on Tuesday the 24th February, when "about eleven of the clocke at night, he opened the casement of his windowe and spake to the guard, 'My good friends pray for me, and tomorrow I shall leave an example behind me you shall all remember; you shall see in me a strong God in a weak man. I have nothing to give you, for I have nothing left, but that which I must pay to the Queen tomorrow in the morning."[1]

"Accordingly, on the 25th of February, being Ash Wednesday, about eight of the clocke in the morning, was the sentence of deathe executed upon Robert Devereux, earle of Essex,[2] within the Tower of London; a scaffold being set up in the court,[3] and a forme neere unto the place, whereon sat the earles of Cumberland and Hartford, the lord viscount Bindon, the lord Thomas Howard, the lord Darcy, and the lord Compton. The lieutenant, with some 16 partizans of the guard, was sent for the prysoner, who came in a gowne of wrought velvet, a blacke sattin sute, a felt hat blacke, a little ruffe about his necke, accompanied from his chamber with three divines, doctor Thomas Montford, doctor William Barlow and maister Ashton his chaplaine; them he had requested not to part from him, but observe him, and recall him if eyther his eye, countenance or speech should betray anything which might not beseeme him for that time."[4]

---

[1] See MS. account in 'European Magazine.'

[2] "On the 25th, early in the morning were sent unto him Thomas Mountford and William Barlowe, Doctors of Divinity, besides Ashton the minister, to confirme and strengthen his soule in her assurance of salvation."—Camden.

[3] "Erected in the courtyard in front of the chapel."—Camden.

[4] Stow.

"There were also present some of the Aldermen of London, and some Knights, and Sir Walter Rawleigh, to no other end (if we may beleeve him) than to answer him, if at his death he should chance to object anything to him; although many interpreted his being there to a worser sence, as though he had done it onely to feed his eyes with his torments, and to glut his hate with the Earles bloud: wherefore being admonished that he should not presse on him now he was dying, which was the property of base wilde beasts, he withdrew himself, and looked out upon him at the Armoury.[1]

"All the waye he desired the spectators to pray for him: and so arriving on the scaffolde, he vailed his hat, and with obeysance unto the lords, to this effect he spake, viz.:—

"My Lords, and you, my Christian brethren, who are to be witnesses of this my just punishment, I confesse, to the glory of God, that I am a most wretched sinner, and that my sinnes are more in number than the hayres of my head. I confesse that I have bestowed my youth in wantonnesse, lust, uncleannesse, that I have been puffed up with pride, vanitie, and love of this world's pleasures, and that, notwithstanding divers good motions inspired into mee by the spirit of God; the good which I would, I have not done, and the evill which I would not, that have I done. For all which I humblie beseech my Saviour Christ to be a mediatour to the eternall Majestie for my pardon: especially for this my last sinne, this great, this bloudie, this crying, this infectious sinne; whereby so many have for love to mee beene drawne to offend God, to offend their soveraigne, to offend the world: I beseech God to forgive it us, and to forgive it me, most wretched of all. I beseech her Majestie, and the state and ministers thereof, to forgive it us; and I beseech God to send her Majestie a prosperous raygne, and a long, if it be his will. O Lorde, graunte her a wise and understanding heart. O Lorde, blesse her, and the nobles, and the ministers of the Church and state! And I beseech you and the world to hold a charitable opinion of me for my intention towards her Majestie, whose

---

[1] Camden.
"Raleigh at his own execution, in his last speech said, 'it was said that I was a prosecutor at the death of the Earl of Essex, and stood in a window over against him, where he suffered, and puffed out tobacco in disdain of him. I take God to witness that my eyes shed tears for him when he died; and, as I hope to look God in the face, when he suffered, I was afar off, in the armoury, where I saw him, but he saw not me. And my soul hath been many times grieved that I was not near to him when he died, because I understood afterwards that he asked for me at his death, to be reconciled to me.'"—Edwards' 'Life of Raleigh,' vol. i. p. 704.

death I protest I never meant, nor violence towards her person. I never was, thanke God, Atheist, not believing the Word and Scriptures; neither papist, trusting in mine owne merits, but hope for salvation from God onely by the mercie and merites of my Saviour Christ Jesus. This faith was I brought up in, and herein I am now readie to die; beseeching you all to joyne your soules with me in prayer, that my soule may be lifted uppe by faith above all earthly things in my prayer; for nowe I will give myself to my private prayer: yet for that I beseech you to joyne with me. I will speake that you may heare me."

"And here he turned himself aside to put off his gowne, doctor Montford requested him to remember to pray to God to forgive all his enemies, if he had any. To whom he answered, 'I thanke you for it.' And so turning himself again to the lordes and the rest, he sayed, 'I desire all the world to forgive me, even as I doe freely and from my heart forgive all the world.' Then putting off his gown and ruffe, and presenting himselfe before the blocke, kneeling down, he was by doctor Barlow encouraged against the foare of death. To whom he answered, 'That having beene divers times in places of danger where death was neyther so present, nor yet so certaine, hee had felt the wekeness of the flesh, and therefore nowe in this great conflict desired God to assist and strengthen him;' and so with eyes fixed on heaven, after some passionate pauses and breathings, he beganne his prayer in effect following :

"O God, Creator of all things, Judge of all men, thou hast let mee know by warrant out of thy Word, that Sathan is then most busie when our end is neerest, and that Sathan being resisted will flee. I humbly beseech thee to assist me in this my last combat; and seeing thou acceptest even of our desires as of our actes; accept, I beseech thee, of my desires, to resist him, as of true resistance, and perfect by thy grace what thou seest in my flesh to bee frayle and weake; give mee patience to beare, as becometh me, this just punishment inflicted upon me by so honorable a tryall ; grant me the inward comfort of the spirit; let thy spirit seale unto my soule an assurance of thy manifolde mercies; lift my soule above all earthly cogitations; and when my life and bodie shall part, send thy blessed Angels which may receive my soule and convey it to thy joyes in heaven."

"He was wondrous patient and penitent.[1] Then concluding his prayer for all estates of the realme, he shut up all with the Lord's Prayer, reiterating this petition, 'Lord Jesus, forgive us our trespasses: Lord Jesus, receive my soule.' Then desiring to be informed what was fit for him to doe for disposing himselfe fitly for the blocke, the executioner, on his knees, presented himself, and asking him forgivenesse: to whom the earle sayd, 'I forgive thee: thou art welcome unto me, thou art the minister of justice.' At which time doctor Montford requested him to rehearse the Creed, which he did, repeating every article after the divines.[2] So opening and putting off his doublet, he was in a scarlet wastecoate, and then readie to lye downe, he said 'he would only stretch forth his armes and spread them abroad, for then he was readie:' so bowing towards the block, the doctors requested him to saye the two first verses of the 51st Psalme, which he did: and then, inclining his bodie, he sayd, 'In humilitie and obedience to thy commandement, in obedience to thy ordinance, to thy good pleasure, O God, I prostrate myself to my deserved punishment. Lord, be mercifull to thy prostrate servant.' So, lying flatte along on the boards, and laying downe his head and fitting it upon the blocke, he stretched out his arms, with these words, which he was requested to say, 'Lord, into thy hands I commend my spirit.'[3] But the collar of his doublet did hinder the executioner, because it did cover his necke. Then himself did say, 'My doublet dothe hinder thee, dothe it not?' and with that he rose upp againe and pulled it off, saying, 'What I must doe, I will doe,' and then givinge his bodie to the blocke again, and spreadinge his armes abroad, he bid the executioner strike home; and at three strokes he stroke off his head. And when his head was off and in the execu-

---

[1] Cecil, who was present, wrote: "The conflict between the flesh and the soul did thus far appear, that in his prayers he was fain to be helped; otherwise no man living could pray more christianly than he did."—Aikin's Eliz. vol. ii. p. 478.

[2] The doctor saying it softly before him.—MS. account in 'European Magazine.'

[3] Stow.

[4] Camden.

tioner's hand, his eyes did open and shut as in the time of his prayer; his bodie never stirred, neither anie part of him more than a stone, neither at the first nor the thirde stroke."[1]

"The hangman was beaten as he returned thence, so that the sheriffes of London were called to assist and rescue him from such as would have murdered him."

"His body and the head were removed into the Tower, put into a coffin ready prepared, and buried by the Earl of Arundel and Duke of Norfolk in the chancel of St. Peter's."[2]

The entry in the burial register is: "Robert Devereux, Earl of Essex, was beheaded in the Tower, and was buried in the Chappell the xvth of February."[3]

Sir Thomas Overbury.

Born 1581. Died, a prisoner in the Tower, 15th Sept., 1613.

Thomas Overbury was of a Gloucestershire family: he was an accomplished man and an elegant writer: he had been educated at Queen's College, Oxford, and after having travelled on the Continent, he returned to England "a finished gentleman, and soon found his way to King James's court." Here he became an intimate friend of Robert Carr, Earl of Rochester, the King's favourite,[4] and it was probably to his influence that Overbury owed the honour of knighthood, which was bestowed on him by the King, at Greenwich, on the 19th June, 1608.[5]

A quarrel arose between the two friends in 1611, and upon some trifling charge Overbury was sent to prison,

---

[1] MS. account in 'European Magazine.'
[2] Stow.
[3] See page 47.
[4] Robert Carr, third son of Thomas Ker or Car of Fennihurst, was page to King James in Scotland; was knighted and made gentleman of the bedchamber in 1607; the forfeited estates of Sir Walter Raleigh were granted to him in 1609; was created Viscount Rochester in 1611, and Earl of Somerset; was Lord Chamberlain from 1613 till 1615; he died in 1645.
[5] Nichols' 'Progresses of James I.' vol. ii. p. 200.

on 21st April: he was, however, soon released, as we find him again at court in the following year: but in the meantime he had made for himself a deadly enemy in the Countess of Essex,[1] because "he had oftentimes dissuaded his friend Carr to abstain from her company: yet now, having disclosed unto her his speech, she became much more revengeful, especially because he had taxed her with a bad name."[2]

It also happened that he had given offence to Queen Anne, and in the following manner: "She was looking out of her window, at Greenwich, into the gardens, where Somerset and Overbury were walking; and when the Queen saw them she said, 'there goes Somerset and his governor,' and a little while after, Overbury did laugh. The Queen conceiving that he had overheard her, thought they had laughed at her, whereupon she complained of him, and Overbury was committed. But when it did appear unto the Queen that they did not hear her, and that their laughter did proceed from a jest, which the King was pleased to use that day at dinner, then the Queen was well satisfied, and he was released."[3]

Yet the Queen did not forgive Overbury, for later, she writes to the Earl of Salisbury, who had interceded in his behalf.

MY LORD,—" The King hath told me that he will advise with you, and some other four or five of the council, *of that fellow*. I can say no more, either to make you understand the matter or my mind, than I said the other day. Only I recommend to your care how public the matter is now, both in court and city, and how far I have reason in that respect. I refer the rest to this bearer, and myself to your love. "ANNA R."

---

[1] Frances, daughter of Thomas Howard, Earl of Suffolk, married when young to the Earl of Essex, and afterwards divorced: she afterwards married Carr, and was tried with him for Overbury's murder and imprisoned in the Tower. She was released in 1622, and died in 1632.

[2] Saunderson's 'Aulicus Coquinariæ,' a book written in reply to Weldon's 'Court of James I.' The title is an allusion to Sir Anthony Weldon's origin, his father having been clerk in the royal kitchen, and he was clerk of the Board of Green Cloth.

[3] Goodman's 'James I.'

Overbury writes also about the same time to the Earl of Salisbury.

My honourable Lord,
As your Lordship was a judge of mine innocence before, so would I now crave that favour, that your Lordship would vouchsafe to be witness of the submission both of myself and cause to the Queen's mercy: which I desire you rather, because, as I understand, her Majesty is not fully satisfied of the integrity of my intent that way, and to that purpose if your Lordship will grant me access and audience I shall hold it as a great favour, and ever rest,
"Your Lordship's to be commanded,
"T. Overbury.
"London, 11ᵗʰ of September."

But soon his enemies began to plot against him and prepare his downfall and ultimate murder, and we find that this mysterious plot, one of the darkest blots of James's profligate reign, was thus commenced; Mr. Packer writes to Sir Ralph Winwood.

"London, 22 April, 1613, O.S.
" Right Honourable,
"Since I wrote to my lady, there is fallen out an accident whereof I thought fit to advertize your Lordship. Yesterday about six of the clock, my Lord Chancellor and my Lord of Pembroke were imployed by the King to speak with Sir Thomas Overbury, and to make him an offer of an Ambassage into the Low Countries, or France, which he would. Whereto he made answer, 'that he was not capable of such imployment, for want of language, nor able to undergoe it by reason of his weakness, being so exceedingly troubled with the spleen that if he had a long letter to write he was feign to give over: therefore he was not fit to attend any busyness, as in accepting this offer he must be forced to do. And whereas it was alleadged that his Majesty intended this for his good and preferment, he would not leave his country for any preferment in the world.' Some say he added some other speech which was very ill taken, but what it should be I cannot yet learn. But not to trouble your Lordship with length, this report being made to the King, he sent my Lord of Pembroke for the lords who were in councill (my Lord Chancellor staying still with his Majesty) to whom he declared when they were come, that he could not obtaine so much of a gentleman, and one of his servants, as to accept of an honourable imployment from him. In conclusion he gave them

order to send for him, and to send him to the Tower, where he is 'close prisoner.'"[1]

Another letter of interest is the following, written by Sir H. Wotton, to Sir Edmund Bacon.

"*From my chamber, this Thursday, St. George, his eve (i.e. 22 April)*, 1613.
"SIR,
"The last week, by reason of my being in Kent, was a week of silence: and this I think will appear unto you a week of wonder.

"Yesterday about six of the clock at evening, Sir Thomas Overbury was from the Council Chamber conveyed by a clerk of the council and two of the guard to the Tower; and there by warrant consigned to the Lieutenant as close prisoner: Which both by the suddenness, like a stroke of thunder, and more by the quality and relation of the person, breeding in the beholders (whereof by chance I was one) very much amazement: and being likely in some proportion to breed the like in the hearers, I will adventure for the satisfying of your thoughts about it, to set down the forerunning and leading causes of this accident, as far, as in so short a time I have been able to wade in so deep a water. It is conceived that the King hath a good while been much distasted with the said gentleman, even in his own nature, for too stiff a carriage of his fortune: besides that scandalous offence of the Queen at Greenwich,[2] which was never but a palliated cure. Upon which considerations, his Majesty resolving to sever him from my Lord of Rochester, and to do it not disgracefully or violently, but in some honourable fashion; he commanded not long since the Arch-Bishop by way of familiar discourse, to propound unto him the ambassage of France or of the archduke's court: whereof the one was shortly to be changed, and the other at the present vacant. In which proposition it seemeth, though shadowed under the Arch-Bishops good will, that the King was also contented some little light should be given him of his Majesties inclination unto it, grounded upon his merit. At this the Fish did not bite; whereupon the King took a rounder way, commanding my Lord Chancellor, and the Earl of Pembroke to propound joyntly the same unto him (which the Arch-Bishop had before moved) as immediately from the King, and to sweeten it the more, he had (as I hear) an offer made him of assurance before his going off the place, of Treasurer of the Chamber, which he expecteth after the death of the Lord Stanhope; whom belike the King would have drawn to some reasonable composition. Notwithstanding all which motives and impulses, Sir Thomas Overbury refused to be sent

[1] Winwood's 'Memorials,' vol. iii. p. 447; Nichols' 'Progresses of James I.' vol. ii. p. 628. [2] See *ante*, p. 232.

abroad, with such terms, as were by the council interpreted pregnant of contempt; in a Case where the King had opened his will; which refusal of his, I should for my part esteem, an eternal disgrace to our occupation, if withall I did not consider how hard it is to pull one from the bosome of a Favourite. Thus you see the point upon which one hath been committed standing in the second degree of power in the Court, and conceiving (as himself told me but two hours before) never better than at that present of his own fortunes and ends. Now in this whole matter there is one main and principal doubt, which doth travel all understandings, that is, Whether this were done without the participation of my Lord of Rochester. A point necessarily infolding two different consequences; for if it were done without his knowledge, we must expect of himself either a decadence or a ruine; if not, we must then expect a reparation by some other great publick satisfaction, whereof the world may take as much notice. These clouds a few dayes will clear: in the meanwhile I dare pronounce of Sir Thomas Overbury, that he shall return no more to this stage, unless Courts be governed every year by a new philosophy, for our old Principles will not bear it.

* * * * * *

"Your faithful poor friend and servant,

"H. WOOTTON."[1]

Again he writes to Sir E. Bacon,—

"London, this Thursday, the 29th April, 1613.

"Sir Thomas Overbury is still in the Tower, and the King hath, since his imprisonment, been twice here, and is twice departed, without any alteration in that matter or in other greater."[2]

The next information respecting Overbury is on the 6th May, when Mr. Chamberlain says, writing to Sir R. Winwood—

"Neither can you choose but be perfect in the true cause of Sir Thomas Overbury's committing to the Tower, which was a contemptuous answer, and refusing of foreign imployments, offered him in the King's name, and especially that he insisted that the King could not in law nor justice force him to forsake his country. But some say he was most urged to that of Muscovy, which drave him to that peremptory and unmannerly answer."[3]

[1] Sir H. Wotton's 'Reliquiæ,' p. 409.
[2] Ibid., p. 412.
[3] Nichols' 'Progresses of James I.' vol. ii. p. 641.

And there is no doubt that Overbury was a close prisoner, as Chamberlain continues:

"Sir Rob¹ Killigrew was yesterday committed to the Fleet from the counsayl table, for having some little speech with Sir Thomas Overbury, who called to him, as he passed by his window as he came from visiting Sir Walter Ralegh."[1]

His gaoler, Sir William Waad,[2] was considered to be too lenient to him, or else was regarded as too upright a man to lend himself to the dark deed contemplated by Carr and the Countess of Essex, so "Sir William Waade," writes Wootton, "was yesternight (*i.e.* 6th May, 1613) put "from the Lieutenancy of the Tower,"[3] and Sir Gervase Elwys[4] was appointed, as a more suitable gaoler, to guarantee that Overbury "should return no more to this stage."

Sir Symond D'Ewes says, "As soon as the Countess of Essex had gotten him cooped up there, she began to plot with Mrs. Anne Turner,[5] by what means she might make him away. Sir William Wade, Kn¹, an honest and upright man, was then Lieutenant of the Tower: during whose continuance in his place, which was but a few days after, he had fair and noble usage. But the Countess's revenge brooking no delay, and finding Sir William Wade's integrity to be corruption proof, so as remained no hope of making

---

[1] Winwood's 'Memorials,' vol. iii. p. 455.

[2] Sir William Waad was Clerk of the Council, employed on embassies to Germany, Spain, France, and other countries; was knighted in 1603, and appointed Privy Councillor: he was appointed Lieutenant of the Tower in Aug. 1605. He died in 1623. See Park's 'Hist. of Hampstead.'

[3] Sir H. Wotton's 'Reliquiæ,' p. 412.

[4] Sir Gervase Elwys or Elwes, a native of Lincolnshire, was knighted in 1603. He was hanged on Tower Hill 3 Nov. 1615, for his participation in Overbury's murder. For the spelling of his name see Amos, 'The Great Oyer of Poisoning,' p. 45. It is spelt "Ellowis" in the printed copy of his speech on the scaffold.

[5] Mrs. Ann Turner (Ann Norton), widow of an apothecary in Paternoster Row named Turner, was educated with the Countess of Somerset, and an accomplice in her many crimes. She was the inventor of "yellow starch" for ruffs, and was sentenced by Sir E. Coke to be hanged in a yellow ruff and cuffs at Tyburn for "procuring poison for Sir T. Overbury, and for witchcraft and magic." (Sir Simond D'Ewes, vol. i. p. 79.) She was executed 14th Nov. 1615. The hangman also "wearing his band and cuffs of the same colour." Yellow starch then went out of fashion.

him an instrument of murder, she used means at court to remove him out of his place, upon the 6th day of May next following, being about fifteen days after Sir Thomas Overbury's imprisonment."[1]

The gaoler who had the care of Overbury was next removed, and one Richard Weston, a creature of the Countess, received that appointment.[2]

On the 19th May, after he had only been two days in his new office, Weston poisoned Overbury's broth with some "water of a yellowish colour,"[3] and in the Harleian MSS., No. 7002, are some letters written by Overbury himself, in which he describes his symptoms. He says:

"I have now sent to the leiftenant to desire you (Mayerns[4] being absent) to send young Crag hither, and Nessmith: if Nessmith be away, send I pray Crag and Allen. This morning, notwithstanding my fasting till yesterday, I find a great heat continews in all my bodye: and the same desire of drinke and loathing of meat, etc. I was lett blood Wensday 10 o'clock; to this friday my heat slackens nott: the same loathing of meat, having eat not a bitt since thursday was sennight to this houre, and the same vomitting yesternight, about 8 o'clocke after Mr. Mayerns was gone I faynted."

On the 10th June, Mr. Chamberlain writes to Sir R. Winwood:

"Sir Thomas Overbury lyes still by it, and for ought I hear is like to do so."

And again on the 29th August, in a letter, Mr. Lorkin tells Sir Thomas Puckering;

"Sir Thomas Overbury is like to run a short course, being sick unto death. The Lieutenant of the Tower, together with the physicians that were there with him, have subscribed their hands that they hold him a man past all recovery."[5]

---

[1] Sir Symond D. Ewes, vol. i. p. 73.
[2] Rimbault's 'Life of Overbury,' p. l.
[3] In the indictment against the Earl and Countess of Somerset, it is called a "certain poison of a greenish and yellowish colour, called ' Rose acre.'"
[4] Sir Theodore de Mayerne Turquet, a French Protestant, born at Geneva in 1575. He was physician to Henry IV. of France, and then to James I. (who knighted him), to Charles I. and Charles II. successively. He died at Chelsea in 1655.
[5] Nichols' 'Progresses,' vol. ii. p. 675.

The poisoners had now nearly accomplished their end, and yet they became impatient that their victim still lingered. Weston was blamed for his dilatory conduct, and James Franklin and an apothecary named Paul de Lobell, were appointed to finish the dark deed more quickly : this, it is believed, they did, by administering a violent dose of corrosive sublimate, and Franklin afterwards stifled him with a pillow.[1]

In a letter written to Sir Dudley Carleton, on the 14th October, by Mr. Chamberlain, he says :

"Sir Thomas Overbury died on the 15th September, and is buried in the Tower. The manner of his death is not known ; for there was nobody with him, not so much as his keeper; but the foulness of the corpse gave much suspicion."[2]

His death took place at 5 o'clock in the morning of Wednesday, the 15th September,[3] and, writes a recent biographer, "it has been said that he was buried in the body of the choir of the church within the Tower, between three and four o'clock of the same day."[4]

In the entry in the Register[5] is the word "poysoned," which proves that, at any rate, the writer of that entry was at the time acquainted with the manner of his death.

In 1615, when the Earl of Somerset, whilst in the presence of the King, was arrested as a principal in the murder, it is recorded that James turned and said to him very coolly, as Somerset was removed from his presence; "now the de'il go with thee, for I will never see thy face any more."[6]

The following original letters will be found to be of considerable interest.

[1] Weldon's 'James I.' p. 76.
[2] Nichols' 'Progresses,' vol. ii. p. 678.
[3] See Elwys' 'Memorandum' at p. 8.
[4] Dr. Rimbault's 'Life of Overbury,' p. 53.
[5] See p. 47.
[6] Nichols' 'Progresses,' vol. i. p. 104.

Those who are desirous of examining further the question of Overbury's death will find the subject fully treated in the 'Great Oyer of Poisoning' (the Trial of the Earl and Countess of Somerset) by Andrew Amos, 1846. The trial is to be found in the Baga de Secretis, Pouch lxii., at great length.

The EARL OF NORTHAMPTON[1] *to* SIR GERVAISE HELWISE, *Lieutenant of the Tower.*

"WORTHY MR. LIEUTENANT,

"My Lord of Rochester,[2] desiring to do the last honour to his deceased friend, requires me to desire you to deliver the body of Sir Thomas Overbury to any friend of his that desires it, to do him honour at his funeral.

"Herein my Lord declares the constancy of his affection to the dead, and the meaning that he had in my knowledge to have given his strongest straine at this time of the King's being at Tiballes,[3] for his delivery. I fear no impediment to this honourable desire of my Lord's, but the unsweetness of the body.

"My fear is also that the body is already buried upon that cause whereof I write; which being so, it is too late to set out solemnity.

"Thus, with my kindest commendations I ende, and reste,

"Your affectionate and assured friend,

"H. NORTHAMPTON.

"P.S.—You see my Lord's earnest desire with my concurring care, that all respect be had to him that may be for the credit of his memory; but yet I wish withal that you do very discreetly enforme yourself whether this grace hath been afforded formerly to close prisoners, or whether you may grant my request in this case, who speak out of the sense of my Lord's affection, though I be a counsellor without offence or prejudice. For I would be loath to drawe either you or myself into censure, now I have well thought of the matter, though it be a work of charity."

On the back of this letter Sir Gervase Elwys has written a memorandum to the effect that Lord Northampton ordered him to summon a jury,[4] and to send for Sir John Lidcote,[5] and as soon as possible to bury the corpse "in the body of the Quire." That "Overbury died at 5 in the morning, and was buried at 4 in the afternoon," &c.; he then says:—

"The next day Sir John Lidcote came thither: I could not get him

---

[1] Henry Howard, first Earl of Northampton, born 1539, was Lord Privy Seal; he died July 1630. He was great uncle to the Countess of Somerset. He built Northumberland House at Charing Cross, recently pulled down. It was first called Northampton House.

[2] Carr. He was created Earl of Somerset on the 4th November following.

[3] Theobald's Park, in Hertfordshire.

[4] For Lord Northampton's letter, see Winwood, vol. iii. p. 481. For the evidence of the coroner, &c., see the 'Great Oyer of Poisoning,' by Amos.

[5] Sir John Lidcote, of Oxfordshire, knighted by King James at Hampton Court, 3rd October, 1609. He was Overbury's brother-in-law.

to bestow a coffin nor a winding-sheet upon him. The coffin I bestowed: but who did winde him I know not.

"GER: HELWYSSE."[1]

Wilson states that the people were forced to throw him in a loose sheet into a coffin, and bury him privately on Tower Hill,[2] but this is incorrect, as the register, as well as the foregoing letters, expressly records his burial in the church.

THOMAS GREY, LORD GREY OF WILTON.

Born, ——. Died a prisoner in the Tower, 16th July, 1614.

Sir Thomas Grey, fifteenth and last Lord Grey de Wilton, was summoned to Parliament from 24th October, 1597, to 27th October, 1601.

He was, though a violent Puritan, involved in those mysterious intrigues called "Ralegh's conspiracy," the ultimate objects of which are believed to have been, to re-establish the Roman Catholic religion and to place Arabella Stuart on the throne.

Although a young man of considerable promise, he appears to have been of a hasty and impetuous temper, which more than once brought him into trouble.

Cecil[3] writes to Sir Henry Neville:[4]

"From the court at Greenwich, 9th June, 1599.

"If you chance to heare any flying tale, that my Lord Grey should be committed in Ireland, the accident was only this; that he being only a colonell of horse, and my Lord of Southampton[5] Generall, he did charge without direction, and so, for order sake, was only committed to the Marshall one night."[6]

---

[1] Cotton. MSS. Titus, B. vii. f. 464. Winwood's 'Memorials,' vol. iii. pp. 481-2.

[2] Wilson's 'Life of James I.,' p. 73.

[3] Robert Cecil, second son of William Lord Burghley, created Earl of Salisbury in 1605.

[4] Sir Henry Neville was then Ambassador to France, having been appointed in April 1599. He was imprisoned in the Tower for complicity in Essex's conspiracy, but released on payment of 5000l. as a fine. He was not popular with James I., and died in 1615.

[5] Henry, third Earl of Southampton. See p. 222.

[6] Winwood's 'Memorials,' vol. i. p. 47.

This was a ground for future quarrels, for in the following year Sir Henry Neville writes to Winwood,[1]—

"London, 29th Jan: 1600.

" My Lord Grey, upon some new-conceived discontent, assaulted my Lord of Southampton on horseback in the street. For which contempt, against her Majesty's commandment, given before to them both, he was committed to the Fleet."[2]

He had also quarrelled with Robert Devereux, Earl of Essex, during the Irish campaign in 1598-9, and Sir Dudley Carleton writes from Windsor, 3rd July, 1603, to Sir Thomas Parry:[3]—

" The Lords of Southampton[4] and Grey, the first night the Queen (Anne of Denmark) came hither, renewed old quarrels, and fell flatly out in her presence.

" She was in discourse with the Lord Southampton, touching the Lord of Essex's action, and wondered, as she said, so many great men, did so little for themselves; to which Lord Southampton answered that the Queen being made a party against them, they were forced to yeald; but if that course had not been taken, there was none of theyr private enemys, with whom only their quarrel was, that durst have opposed themselves. This being overheard by the Lord Grey, he would maintain the contrary party durst have done more than they, upon which he had the lie erobled (levelled ?) at him.

" The Queen bad them remember where they were, and soon after sent them to their lodgings, to which they were committed with guard upon them.

" They next day were brought and heard before the council and condemned to be sent back to the tower.[5] But soon after the King sent for them, and taking the quarrel upon him, and the wrong and disgrace done to her Majesty, and not exchanged betwixt them, forgave it, to make them friends; which was accordingly effected, and they were presently set at liberty."[6]

---

[1] Sir Ralph Winwood, born 1565. His father was Lewis Winwood, secretary to Charles Brandon, Duke of Suffolk. He went to France with Sir H. Neville, and as ambassador to Holland in 1607. Was appointed Secretary of State in 1614; died in 1617.
[2] Winwood, vol. i. p. 292.
[3] Sir Thomas Parry, son of Sir Thomas Parry, who was Comptroller of the Household to Queen Elizabeth. He was minister resident in France from 1600 to 1607, when he was made Chancellor of the Exchequer.
[4] Lord Southampton had only been recently released from the Tower.
[5] *I.e.* in Windsor Castle, where they lodged.
[6] Nichols' 'Progresses of James I.,' vol. i. p. 198.

But on the 12th July, 1603, he was arrested and committed to the Tower, together with Sir Walter Raleigh, Sir Griffin Markham, Anthony Copley, and two Roman Catholic priests, named William Watson and William Clark.

These prisoners were frequently examined, and, after one of these examinations, Bishop Bancroft [1] reports that Lord Grey considers he "do rather deserve thanks and favour for diverting and breaking the plot, than to be imprisoned." [2]

He endeavoured to move Cecil on his behalf, and, in reply to an application from Lord Grey, Cecil writes to Sir G. Harvey, Lieutenant of the Tower:—

"20 Aug: 1603.

* * * * * *

"To my Lord Grey, I pray you, Sir, retourne this answer: that in anything wherein his case may be freended by me, without any prejudyce in duty or mislike in my Soverain,—I say it constantly, and never will be found untreu—that I will do as much for him as I wold ever have don for him in such a time when I held him dearest.

* * * * *

"For anything he will send me in writing of his case, lett him know I will receave nothing which I will not shew, at any time, to all my Lords Commissioners; and therefore lett him be resolved that my friendship must in such things have the precisest limitts.

"For any other privat letter of request, if you signe it I will at any time receave it. For his reader, I wish he had him, and will move my Lords. But if he come in he must not go out againe.

"Your loving and assured friend,
"Ro: CECYLL." [3]

Again Sir Thomas Edmonds [4] writes to the Earl of Shrewsbury: [5]

---

[1] Richard Bancroft, born in 1544; Prebendary of Westminster in 1591; Bishop of London and Dean of St. Paul's in 1597; Archbishop of Canterbury in 1604, in succession to Whitgift: he died Nov. 1610, and was buried at Lambeth.

[2] Edwards' 'Life of Ralegh,' vol. i. p. 369.

[3] Hatfield MSS. 'Cecil Papers,' vol. ci. p. 125. Edwards' 'Life of Ralegh,' vol. ii. p. 461.

[4] Sir Thomas Edmonds was actively employed abroad in diplomatic service, being sent to France in 1588: in 1596 he was appointed Secretary for the French tongue to Queen Elizabeth; sent to Flanders in 1599, and then to Paris until 1616. Sully alludes to him as "little Edmonds." He was knighted in 1603, and made Comptroller of the Household in 1616. He died in 1639.

[5] Gilbert, third Earl of Shrewsbury, died 1616.

"From the Court at Woodstock, the 17 Sept: 1609.

"Since the wryting of my last letters to your Lordship, there hath been order taken to proceade to the indictment of the prisoners in the Tower, which is appointed to be done at Staines, the 21st of this moneth, and it is intended that their arraignment shall followe shortlie after. There is order given that in the meane tyme they shall be kept close prisoners. I doe not understand that anie of them have confessed more of the scoape of the maynie practises than was discovered before your Lordship's departure hence, but some particular persons accused, whereof the most have been uppon examynation cleared and discharged. I learne that as yett there is a stronge purpose to proceade severely in the matter against the principall persons; but in the ende it is thought that Lord Grey will most move compassion."[1]

Lord Grey always persistently maintained that neither he nor Sir Griffin Markham had any part in the conspiracy of Raleigh; but it was nevertheless determined to bring them to trial, and the prisoners were therefore all removed to Winchester.[2] On "Monday, 7th November, 1603, Thomas, Lord Grey of Wilton, was conveyed in a coach from the Tower of London towards Winchester. He stayed at Bagshotte in Surrey, fower and twenty miles from London."

"On Wednesday the 9th, Thomas, Lord Grey, under the custody of Sir Richard Leveson, K\\\\t, was conducted by Sir Henry Wallop and Sir Hamden Powlet, Kts, the Sheriffs of the County of Southampton, well and strongly guarded with fiftie light horse-men of the same countie, from Bagshotte to the castle of Winchester, thirty miles from Bagshotte.[3]

Cecil writes to the Earl of Shrewsbury in reference to the approaching trial:

"From the Court at Wilton, at 12 o'clock at night 25 Oct: 1603.

"In the Commission all that were examiners with you are inserted: the Lord Chancellor is Lord Steward.[4] The first arraignment is the 15th, next the 17th of Sir Walter Ralegh alone; the 22nd the two Lords."

[1] Nichols' 'Progresses of James I.,' vol. i. p. 269.
[2] The trial was to take place at Winchester in consequence of the prevalence of the plague in London.
[3] Nichols' 'Progresses of James I.,' vol. i. p. 293.
[4] Thomas Egerton, Lord Ellesmere, natural son of Sir Richard Egerton. Lord Chancellor from 1596 to 1617, when he died.

"And thus, having at this time my hands full, I end, with a drowsy eye, which makes me scribble the best wishes, though in bad characters, to my Lady Justice, whose punishment I fear beyond Trent so much as I never mean to pass that water."[1]

"Your affectionate friend to command,

"Ro. Cecill."

The trial took place in Wolvesley Castle, the old palace of the bishops of Winchester; that of Lord Grey commenced on the 17th November, when the charges brought against him were—

"That on the 14th day of June he had held a meeting at Westminster with George Brooke and Sir Griffin Markham, when they declared their intention to seize the King's person, and that of Prince Henry, and to imprison them in the Tower, in order to extract three promises from them; viz. their own pardon for this imprisonment, a toleration of the Romish religion, and the exclusion of certain lords from the council: and that, on the 18th June, Lord Grey stipulated that after the King's imprisonment he should be made Earl Marshal and Master of the Horse.[2] Before his trial, and when in the Tower, Lord Grey admitted his complicity in the plot to seize the King in order to influence the Government; but he scouted the idea that he had anything to do with the Papists.[3]

Sir Dudley Carleton writes from Winchester on the 26th November that—

"After the abject defence of Cobham, Grey quite in another key began with great assurances and alacrity; telling the Lords, the judges and the King's counsel their duties in a long speech, and held them the whole day in subtle traverses and subterfuges; but the evidence that he was acquainted with the surprise of the King, was too conspicuous by Broke's and Markham's confessions. The Lords were long ere they could all agree, and loth to come out with so hard a censure against him; most of them strove with themselves, and would fain, as it seems, have dispensed with their consciences, to have shown him favour. After sentence he was asked what he would say against its

[1] 'Lodge's Illustrations,' vol. iii. p. 60.
[2] The original documents relating to the trial are in the Baga de Secretis, Pouch lviii.
[3] Edwards' 'Life of Ralegh,' vol. ii. p. 469.

being pronounced. He replied, 'I have nothing to say,' and there he paused long, 'and yet a word of Tacitus comes in my mouth, "Non eadem omnibus decora." The house of Wilton have spent many lives in their prince's service, and Grey cannot ask his.'

* * * * * *

"After he was sentenced he asked that one Travers, a divine,[1] might be sent for to come to him if he might live two days. If he were to die before that, then he might have one Field,[2] whom he thought to be near.

"There was great compassion had for this gallant young lord; for so clear and fiery a spirit had not been seen by any that had been present at the like trials. Yet the Lord Steward (Lord Ellesmere, the Chancellor) condemned his manner much, terming it Lucifer's pride, and preached much humiliation; and the judges liked him as little because he disputed with them against their laws. We cannot yet judge what will become of him or the rest."[3]

Mr. Michael Hicks[4] reports to the Earl of Shrewsbury:—

"From Ruckholts, 6 Dec: 1603.

"Touching my Lord Grey, I hard that he spent a day in his arraynment, and two houres at ye leaste in an oration, which I have hard was most eloquent, full of good wordes and sentences, and shewing good reading, and inveighing greatly against ye common lawe, touching many statutes. It is sayd he answered with such fervency or fury of spirit, that he was reproved and interrupted sometymes, but Mr. Atturney delt very mildly and respectably, both with my Lord Cobham and hym. Some thynk that neither Lord Cobham nor he shall dye, but be sent agayne to the Tower."[5]

On the 11th December, Sir Dudley Carleton, in a letter dated from Salisbury, relates how that Watson and Clarke had been executed, and—

"Grey in the meantime, with his minister, Field, having had the like summons for death, spent his time in great devotions; but with that careless regard of that which he was threatened with, that he was

---

[1] A Puritan divine whom Hooker, when engaged in controversy with him, mentioned as his "antagonist," but not his "enemy." Aikin's 'James I.', vol. i. p. 169.
[2] Dr. Richard Field.
[3] Nichols' 'Progresses,' vol. i. p. 299. Aikin's 'James I.' vol. i. pp. 168-9.

[4] Michael Hicks, son of a merchant in London. He was knighted in 1614, when the King visited him at Ruckholts, a manor near Leyton, in Essex. The house was pulled down in 1757.
[5] Lodge's 'Illustrations,' vol. iii. p. 77; Nichols' 'Progresses of James I.,' vol. i. p. 299.

observed neither to eat nor sleep the worse, or be anywise distracted from his accustomed fashions."[1]

The warrant for their execution was received by the Sheriff (Sir Benjamin Tichborne) "on Wednesday late at night," and on Friday, at ten of the clock, Markham and Grey were to be executed.

Markham was brought to the scaffold first, but the sheriff was then secretly "withdrawn by one John Gib, a Scotch groom of the bed-chamber, whereupon the execution was stayed, and Markham was sent for two hours respite into the Great Hall to walk with Prince Arthur. Lord Grey's turn was next, he was led to the scaffold by a troop of young courtiers, and was supported on both sides by two of his best friends; and, coming in this equipage, had such gaiety and cheer in his countenance, that he seemed a dapper young bridegroom. At his first coming on the scaffold[2] he fell on his knees, and his preacher made a long prayer to the present purpose, which he seconded himself with one of his own making, which, for the phrase, was somewhat affected and suited to his other speeches; but for the fashion, expressed the fervency and zeal of a religious spirit."

* * * * *

"After a long prayer for the King's good estate, which held us in the rain more than half-an-hour, he came to a full point, when the sheriff stayed him and said he had received orders from the King to change the order of the execution, and that the Lord Cobham was to go before him. Whereupon he was likewise led to Prince Arthur's Hall, and his going away seemed more strange unto him than his coming thither, for he had no more hope given him than of an hour's respite, neither could any man yet dive into the mystery of this strange proceeding."

"Lord Cobham was then brought on, and he was stayed by the sheriff, and Markham and Grey were then brought back, when the sheriff informed them that the King had spared

---

[1] Bayley, vol. ii. p. 533; Aikin's 'James I.' vol. i. p. 170.
[2] It is said that he first with his foot spurned away the straw on the scaffold, as if to see if there were any marks of blood there.

their lives. Cobham vowed openly, if ever he proved traitor again, not so much as to beg his life; and Grey, that since he had his life without begging, that he would deserve it. Markham returned with a merrier countenance than he came to the scaffold. Ralegh you must think (who had a window open that way) had hammers working in his head to beat out the meaning of this stratagem. His turn was to come on Monday next, but the King had pardoned him with the rest, and confined him with the two lords to the Tower of London, there to remain during pleasure."

Sir Dudley Carleton adds:—

"I send you a copy of the King's letter, which was privately written the Wednesday night, and the messenger despatched the Thursday about noon. But one thing had liked to have marred the play; for the letter was closed and delivered him unsigned, which the King remembered himself, and called for him back again. At Winchester there was another cross-adventure, for John Gib could not get so near the scaffold that he could speak to the sheriff, but was thrust out among the boys, and was forced to call out to Sir James Hayes,[1] or else Markham might have lost his neck. There were other bye-passages, if I could readily call them to mind, but here is enough already for 'un petit mot de lettre,' and therefore I bid you heartily farewell."[2]

On the 15th December Lord Grey was sent back to the Tower, but it is supposed before he left Winchester that he wrote the following letter to Cecil, offering to relate all he knew about the conspiracy.

"MY LORD,   "December 1603.

"I beseech you forget not to moov the King for my scoller,[3] whoe will yield me much comfort. If the King think my letter imperfect, or myself recluse in confession of what I knew concerning this business, shall your lordship, or any of whom the King shall command (but especially yourself) have occasion to cum this way, I will successively relate what passed by mee, eaven from my first entrance with George Brook,[4] whearin if I bee proved to have con-

---

[1] A Hampshire magistrate.
[2] Bayley, p. 536. See also Edwards' 'Life of Ralegh,' vol. i. p. 448 et seq.
[3] He had already asked leave to obtain the attendance upon him during his imprisonment of a youth who was to act as an amanuensis and reader. See p. 242.
[4] George Brook, brother of Lord Cobham, a prime mover in the plot, was executed at Winchester.

ccaled any man or passage which your lordship either had not in hand, or more against them than I could informe, which concerned the King or State, let mee dy without judgment; or if from my beginning with George Brook unto my breach with Markham I doe not demonstrate (soe farr as such a subject can permitt) a cleer heart of ill intention to the King and State of England. Think then, how unfortunate I am, and prejudg not my ends, for I much doubt you have to aunswear for your opinion of them. But with patience I will indure the King's pleasure, and doubt not to live to make the King and world see how I have been misjudged in this business, to him and my religion. And you will cleerly finde, however you have judged me, yet I never deserved but to be held your lovinge frend. And as I desire the King's favour, I know not the gentleman in his kingdom—out of this place—that I can say hath thought of innovasion.
"GREY."[1]

The capital part of his sentence had been remitted, but he remained a close prisoner in the Tower for the remainder of his days. The barony of Wilton expired with his attainder, and his estates became forfeited to the Crown.

The following letter refers to his imprisonment:—

"*From* SIR GEORGE HARVEY, *Lieutenant of the Tower, to the Right Honourable my very singular good lorde, the* LORDE CECILL, *His Majesties Princij all Secrtarie. At the Courte.*[2]

"Yesterday I receyved direction from your lordships for ease of my Lord Grey, to lodge him in the Brick Tower, which, belonging to the Master of the Ordinance, I have thought good to acquaint your lordship therwith, because he should not therebie take offence, notwithstanding that in my predecessors tyme, I have knowen divers of the prisoners there lodged. And so being readie therein to do anything that your lordships shall think fitt, do humbly take my leave.
"Your Lordship's ever most bounden,
"G. HARVEY."
"The Tower, 17th December, 1603."

Again, on the 23rd December, Cecil writes to the Earl of Shrewbury from Hampton Court:—

"You shall understand that since his Majesty's late mercy at Wynchester, the two late lords are in the Towre, and Sir W. Ralegh, where they remaine as condemned men."[3]

[1] Hatfield MSS. 'Cecil Papers,' vol. cii. p. 40; Edwards' 'Life of Ralegh,' vol. ii. p. 482.
[2] Endorsed by Lord Cecil, "17th Dec. 1603, Sir G. Harvey."
[3] Hatfield MSS., vol. cii. p. 77.

And under the same date Sir Thomas Edmonds also writes to the Earl of Shrewsbury from Hampton Court:—

"I know not whether your Lordship have already or no received the book which is published concerning the mercy shewed by the King's Majesty in respiting the execution of the prisoners at Winchester. I thought good to send your Lordship this, which was bestowed on me by my Lord Cecil.

"It is appoynted that Lord Grey shall be continued prisoner in the Tower."[1]

On the roll of the Barons of Parliament, dated 19th March, 1603-4, the word "attaynted" is affixed to Lord Grey's name.

And, again, his name appears on a list of prisoners in 1612 as a condemned person, together with that of Raleigh and Lord Cobham.

On the 6th May, 1613, Mr. Chamberlain writes to Sir Ralph Winwood:

"The Prince Palatine[2] before his going made a suit to the King for the enlargement of Lord Grey. The King told him he marvelled how he could become suitor for a man he neither knew nor ever saw. He answered that he was recommended to him by his uncle, Duke of Bouillon, the Prince Maurice, and the Count Henry, who had better knowledge of him. Then the King said, 'Son, when I come to Germany I will promise not to importune you for any of your prisoners.' Since that time Lord Grey hath been restrained and kept more straight for having had conference with one of the Lady Arbella's[3] women, who being strictly examined was faine to confess that it was only a matter of love and dalliance."[4]

Thus he remained a prisoner until death released him in 1614, when we find entered in the burial register: "1614, Lord Gray, a prisoner, buried the xvith of July in the chapel."

[1] Lodge's 'Illustrations,' vol. iii. p. 84; Nichols' 'Progresses of James I.,' vol. i. p. 302.

[2] Frederick, succeeded as Elector Palatine in 1610, married Elizabeth, daughter of James I. in 1618; was nominated King of Bohemia in 1619; was defeated at the battle of Prague, and fled in 1620. He died in Holland in 1631. The present Royal family are his direct descendants.

[3] Lady Arabella Stuart, born 1575, privately married to William Seymour in 1610, for which she was committed to the Tower: she finally lost her reason, and died there 27th Sept. 1615. She was buried in the Stuart vault at Westminster Abbey.

[4] Winwood's 'Memorials,' vol. iii. p. 454.

Sir John Eliot.

Born 20th April, 1590. Died in the Tower, 27th Nov. 1632.

The life of Sir John Eliot, and the critical period of our Parliamentary history in which he was one of the chief actors, have been most exhaustively treated by the late Mr. John Forster, and the following particulars are chiefly extracted from his volumes.[1]

Before the dissolution of Parliament in March, 1628-9, several members, including Sir John Eliot, Holles, Selden, &c., were summoned to appear before the Privy Council, and, on the 4th March, Eliot and the others, after their examination, were committed to the Tower. The warrant addressed to Sir Allan Apsley (the Lieutenant) directed him to keep each prisoner separate and in close custody "for notable contempts by him committed against ourself and our government, and for stirring up sedition against us." "Visitors desiring to see the prisoners were to be strictly reported upon and very sparingly admitted; and all books and papers, pens and ink, or any means of communicating with friends, were to be wholly denied to them."

This last provision appears to have been strictly carried out for a period of more than three months.

Soon after Sir John Eliot's imprisonment many of his friends desired to visit him, and Sir Allan Apsley reports on 20th March, that he had "sent to him a note in some haste of such as desired to have access to the prisoners."

Again later he writes:

"The Earl of Lincoln[2] and others would have induced Sir Allen's son to have taken them to Sir John Eliot's lodging, which hee refused, sayinge, 'hee could not justify yt.'" He also reports that Lord Rochford and Lord St. John's son, the Earl of Bolingbroke, had been caught "going obscurely by themselves directly to Sir John Elliotte's lodginge, and being

---

[1] 'Sir John Eliot: a Biography,' 2 vols. 1865.

[2] Theophilus, fourth Earl of Lincoln, born 1600; had fought under Count Mansfeldt in the Palatinate: he died in 1667.

stoppt by a warder I sett of purpose over his lodginge, then they desired to speake with Sir John's keeper, and would have had his keeper to have brought them to him, which he refused."

In another letter he reports, "On Monday last there was one Moreton, a minister, who came as neere Sir John Elliott's wyndowe as hee could, and called aloude to have spoken with him, but hee did not answer him."

Apsley denies that his son had carried any messages to the prisoners, and he writes to Lord Dorchester:—

"Tower, the xxth of Martch, 1628-9.

"The poore boy is soe afflicted as hee protestes to God hee had rather die instantly than live with his Majesties ill opinion. Hee is not xxiij. I doe not think that ever hee meddled with anything seryous, his witt lyinge a contrary waye."

Visitors continued to seek access to Eliot, and "at the close of April one Mr. Matthewes, of Dartmouth, came to enquire for his lodging, whereupon he was taken by a warder that stood watch of purpose and put out of the Tower."

In May, the Lieutenant was ordered to bring his prisoner before the Court of King's Bench, and he wrote, on the 14th May, to Lord Dorchester to know how he should convey Eliot to Westminster, "either by water or land publikly with a guard or silently without;" it was considered safest to bring him silently and by the river to Westminster. The enquiry was prolonged till June, when the Court closed without judgment having been pronounced.

One result of this enquiry however was that the rigour of his imprisonment was somewhat relaxed; the use of writing materials was allowed to him,[1] and permission was granted to Sir A. Apsley to let him have "liberty of the Tower, being kept safely but not as a 'close prisoner.'" His friend Richard Knightley, M.P. for Northamptonshire, was also allowed to visit him.

[1] Numerous letters written at that time are preserved among the MS. records at Port Eliot.

On 3rd October, Eliot and the other members were brought by writs to the Chief Justices' Chambers at Serjeants Inn at five o'clock in the afternoon, when arrangements were made for bailing them, but having declined to enter into the "good behaviour bond" which the Court proposed to them, they returned to the Tower.

On Thursday, the 29th October, Eliot and the others were taken by night from the Tower to the Chambers of the Chief Justice, and after being charged and required to answer, they were committed to the prison of the Marshalsea. Upon this Sir John Eliot playfully said "they left their palace in London, and betook themselves to their country house in Southwark."

On Monday, 25th January, 1629-30, the prisoners appeared again in the Court of King's Bench with their counsel, and their case was argued with little intermission until the morning of Friday the 12th of February, the last day of Hilary Term, when judgment was at length delivered.

Eliot writes that he was not able to be present "by reason of an indisposition of my healthe, contracted from cold and watching."

The sentence was, that each of the defendants should be imprisoned during the pleasure of the King. Sir John Eliot to be imprisoned in the Tower of London and the other defendants, Valentine and Holles, in other prisons. That Sir John Eliot, inasmuch as my Lord thought him the greatest offender and the ring-leader, should pay to the King a fine of 2000*l.*

Sir J. Eliot then sent a message to Sir Allan Apsley to express the "hope that a convenient lodging might be provided for him, and that he might be permitted to send his upholsterer to trim it up, for he had no prospect of quitting it speedily."

As to his fine, he said "he had two cloaks, two suits, two pairs of boots and gallashes, and a few books: that was his present substance, and if they could pick 2000*l.* out of that much good might it do them."

Owing to the absence of the judges on circuit some days

elapsed before his removal from the Marshalsea to the Tower took place.

After about a week, "the Marshal of the King's Bench, regarding him as a property or chattell, delivered him with an appropriate speech to Sir Allan Apsley at the Tower gate: 'Mr. Lieutenant, I have brought you this worthy knight whom I borrowed of you some months ago and now do repay him again.'"

"Thereupon," said Eliot, writing to Sir Oliver Luke on 3rd March, 1629,—

"The Marshall commanding my attendance, brought me to this place, and as a debt which formerly he had borrowed (to use his owne words) rendered me to the Lieutenant, whose prisoner I nowe am; soe taken and delivered in a compliment. This is all the newes which in our fortunes have occurred."

He never quitted the Tower again. He addressed letters to his friends during the two remaining years of his life, and in one letter, written to his friend Richard Knightley, July 1630, in reply to an announcement that there was a rumour of his release, he warned his friend—

"To have no confidence in such reports; sand was the best material on which they rested, and the many fancies of the multitude; unless they pointed at that kind of liberty, 'libertie of mynde.' But other libertie I knowe not, having soe little interest in her masters that I expect no service from her."

In December, 1631, a report became prevalent that Eliot had been allowed to leave the Tower; not only was this report baseless, but orders had been given by the Council forbidding the access of persons of several conditions to Sir John Eliot. His prison was also changed, and new restraints were put upon him, as he writes to John Hampden on 26th December:—

"My lodgings are removed. I am now where candle-light may be suffered, but scarce fire. None but my servant, hardly my sonnes may have admittance to me; my friends I must desire for their own sakes to forbear coming to the Tower."

His health appears soon to have broken down under the rigour of his imprisonment, and his prison was constantly changed—so often indeed that he said the many troubles of moving had awhile hindered his writing; he might say of "his lodging, as Jacob of his wages, now then ten times have they changed it."

The last letter written by him, which is preserved in the Port Eliot MSS., is dated 22nd March, 1631-2, and was addressed to John Hampden in reply to one received from him. He says:

"I thanke God lately my businesse has beene much with doctors and physitians, so that but by them I have had little trouble with myselfe. These three weekes I have had a full leisure to do nothing, and strictly tied unto it, either by their directions or my weakness. The cause originally was a cold, but the symptoms that did follow it spake more sickness, and a general indisposition it begot in all the faculties of the bodie. The learned said a consumption did attend it, but I thank God I do not feele or credit it. What they advise, as the ordinance that's appointed, I was content to use; and in the true show of patient, suffered whatever they imposed. Great is the authority of princes, but greater much is theirs who both command our persons and our wills. What the success of their government will be must be referred to Him that is master of their power."

Air and exercise were the prescriptions of his doctors, while for the one he had his "smoaky room," and for the other he was limited to his walk within the Tower.

The symptoms of his disease (consumption) increased, and his attorney, meeting a friend in St. Paul's Churchyard on the 12th November, said he had that morning been with Sir John in the Tower, and that he could not live a week longer.

His death was at last announced on the 27th November. "Not without suspicion of foul play," wrote Ludlow some years later. Some such impression must also have occurred to the minds of Hampden and Pym, who, at the meeting of Parliament in April, 1640, moved for a committee "to examine after what manner Sir John Eliot came to his death, his usage in the Tower, and to view the rooms and place where he was imprisoned and where he died, and to report the same to the House."

His son petitioned the King for permission to remove his father's remains to Cornwall and deposit them with his ancestors at Port Eliot. "Whereto was answered at the foot of the petition, 'Lett Sir John Eliot's body be buried in the Churche of the parish where he dyed,' and so he was buried in the Tower."

"No stone," adds his biographer, "marks the spot where he lies, but as long as freedom continues in England he will not be without a monument."

WILLIAM HOWARD, VISCOUNT STAFFORD.

Born 30th Nov., 1612. Beheaded on Tower Hill, 29th Dec., 1680.

Lord Stafford was a Roman Catholic, and in the autumn of 1678 was accused of being concerned in the so-called "Popish Plot."[1]

Parliament had met on the 21st October, and the King had, in his speech, alluded to a "design against his life by the Jesuits, which he should leave to the law," and assured the Houses that in the meantime he would take all due precautions against the introduction of Popery.

Immediately after the opening of Parliament, when the address to the speech was to be considered, there was a general cry of "the plot, the plot," raised in both Houses, and shortly afterwards, Titus Oates was summoned to the bar to give evidence before them. He then accused the five Catholic Lords, Powis, Stafford, Arundel, Petre, and Bellasis, of treason, and being accomplices in the plot.

---

[1] This plot was the absorbing topic of the day, the murder of Sir Edmondbury Godfrey having greatly excited the public mind. Subsequently a strong suspicion arose that the plot was entirely invented by Oates and his associates; but Dryden admitted, after he had become a Roman Catholic, that "some truth there was, but dashed and brewed with lies." Oates was, however, tried for perjury on the accession of James II., and sentenced to stand in the pillory five times a year during his life, and be whipped from Aldgate to Tyburn. He was released from Newgate by William III., who granted him a pension of 400*l.* a year. He died in 1705.

Lord Stafford, from his place in the House of Lords, declared his innocence, but a warrant for his committal to the Gate House was at once issued by the order of the House. On the 30th October, it was further resolved "that the Lords, with white staves, do attend His Majesty," humbly to desire that Ld Stafford might be removed from the prison of the King's Bench to remain a prisoner in the Tower; and accordingly, the King issued his warrant on 31st October, 1678, addressed to James, Earl of Northampton,[1] Constable, ordering the committal of Lord Stafford as a close prisoner to the Tower.[2]

Mr. Secretary Coventry writes on the following day to Sir John Robinson, who was then the Lieutenant, in reply to some enquiry, to say that Stafford and the other Lords are to remain prisoners, "as is expressed in the Order of the House of Lords."

On the 8th January, 1678-9, Robert, Earl of Lindsey, Lord Great Chamberlain; James, Earl of Salisbury; John, Earl of Bridgewater; Arthur, Earl of Essex; Sir Joseph Williamson, Secretary of State, and Edward Seymour, Speaker of the House of Commons, were sent to examine Lord Stafford, and the Archbishop of Canterbury[3] was also sent by the King, as the warrant states, "to confer with him upon certaine matters in which wee have given him our commands."

After the report of the Committee of Examination of their interview with Lord Stafford, the King issued an Order in Council on the 22nd January, 1678-9, permitting him for the benefit of his health to have "the liberty of the Tower, but so that he have neither meeting, nor conversation with any that are prisoners in that place:" permission was also

---

[1] James Compton, third Earl of Northampton, served at Edgehill, Newbury, &c., throughout the Civil War under Prince Rupert; was appointed Constable of the Tower in 1675, and died in 1681.

[2] Order and warrant in Tower Records.

[3] William Sancroft, born 1616; he had been Dean of York, and afterwards of St. Paul's. He was appointed archbishop in Jan. 1677-8: was committed with the other bishops to the Tower in 1688, having refused to take the oath of allegiance to William and Mary. He was ejected and deprived of his archbishopric in Feb. 1691. He died in 1693.

granted that several of his friends might visit him.[1] Again, on 29th January, special permission is granted to Francis Charleton to have access to Stafford, to discourse about his private affairs.

From time to time Stafford and the other Lords petitioned to be either put on their defence or admitted to bail, but without success. He remained a prisoner in the Tower, whence he addressed the following letter to his daughter Ursula, a nun in the convent of St. Augustine, at Louvain.

"From the Tower, 14th July, 1679.
"GOOD DAUGHTER,

"I know the misfortune that I am in is a greate griefe unto you, but I pray give yourselfe this assurance, that it is come upon me by my misfortune, and not by any faulte of myne, I being totally innocent of what I am so unjustly accused of, as I doute not but to make appeare by the grace of God; in the meantime, and allways I doe most willingly and cherefully submit to His holy will, beseeching him most humbly to grante me grace to make that good use that I ought to do.

"I am ever,
"Your most affectionate father,
"W. S.

"My most humble service to all your good company; this bearer Nicola can tell you particularly of our healths."[2]

It appears that in 1679 there was some intention of bringing him to trial, as he writes to Mr. Henry Vernon at Wolverhampton:

"From the Tower, 10th May, 1679.
"I desire you will doe mee the favor as to come to towne with all the haste that you can, to be heer at my tryall, I having an order from the House of Peers to that effect; and you will very much oblige me to come."[3]

On the 21st May, 1680, Lord Stafford was brought, by habeas corpus, before the Court of King's Bench, and there he demanded to be discharged on bail, as he had been eighteen

[1] Lady Stafford and his children, Earl of Bath, Lord Tretchville, Mr. William Blount, Mr. Ralph Lawson, Dr. Cox, and Mr. Hinton, his apothecary: also George Lee, Erasmus Jones, and Nicholas Fournier. See Tower Records.
[2] Tierney MSS. See Third Report of 'Histor. MSS. Commission,' p. 233, and Lingard, vol. ix. p. 258.
[3] MS. letter in possession of Lord Hatherton.

months in prison without being brought to trial. The Lord Chief Justice refused, on the ground that the Lords had declared that impeachments continued from Parliament to Parliament. In spite of Lord Stafford's arguments, the judges still declined to interfere, and advised him to petition the King. Several strict orders from the Council were given to the Lieutenant of the Tower, respecting Lord Stafford and his fellow-prisoners, and one was, that no Lords should visit them "without licence from the board, and that no commoners do visit them without leaving their names in a book for that purpose." Moreover, on the 24th October, 1680, the five Lords were ordered "to retrench their families to the number of six servants each, and that those be all Protestants."

In November, Stafford again petitioned either to be admitted to bail, or else that he should be put on his trial, and on the 18th November, the House of Lords ordered the Earl of Carlisle, and Lord Howard of Escrick, to go to the Tower and speak with Lord Stafford about the contents of his petition, and to give the House an account thereof. It was then resolved to bring Lord Stafford to trial, and the Lieutenant was summoned to produce his prisoner at the bar of the House in Westminster Hall, on Tuesday, the 30th November,[1] at nine o'clock in the morning.

"The trial," says Burnet, "was very august: the Earl of Nottingham[2] was the High Steward, and it continued for five days."[3]

Reresby, who was present, has left us his record of the proceedings:—

"But to turn our eyes upon what justly claimed the attention of all men, now came on the tryal of Lord Stafford by his peers. Westminster Hall was the place, and I think it was the deepest solemnity I ever saw. Great were the expectations of the issue of this event, it being doubtful

---

[1] This happened to be his birthday.
[2] Charles Heneage Finch, Lord Chancellor, created Earl of Nottingham 12th May, 1681. Born 1621; died 1682.
[3] The orders to the Lieutenant to bring Lord Stafford to Westminster on the 30th Nov., 1st, 2nd, 3rd, 4th, 6th and 7th Dec. are in the Tower records. It thus appears that the trial lasted seven days.

whether there were more who believed there was any plot by the Papists, in reality, against the King's life, than not.

"He was impeached by the Commons, and being deemed to be weaker than the other Lords in the Tower, for the same crime, and less able to labour his defence, was purposely marked out to be the first brought on: but he deceived them so far as to plead his cause to a miracle.

"The three chief evidences against him were Dr. Oates, Dugdale, and Tuberville: the first swore that his Lordship has brought him a commission signed by the Pope, to be paymaster of the army to be raised against the King: and the second, that he had offered him 500*l*. to kill the King: and the third, that he had offered him a reward for the dreadful deed, but at a different time. And so positive seemingly were they in this and other dangerous evidence, that I, who sat and heard most of the trial, had not known what to think, had the witnesses been but men of any the least credit, but indeed, such were the incoherences, and indeed contradictions, which seemed to me to arise towards the latter end, that considering them, and the very evil name of the people that swore against this Lord, I was fully satisfied that all was untruth they laid to his charge: but the poor gentleman was condemned by a majority of twenty-two. He heard his accusers, and defended himself with great steadiness and resolution, and received his sentence with great courage and composure: nor did he stoop beneath the weight of his doom, till he submitted his head to the block, with his last breath protesting his innocence and the cruel wrong he suffered. My Lord Halifax was one that gave his voice for him, and the King who heard all his trial, was extremely concerned at the rigour and abruptness of his fate."[1]

When the Lord High Steward announced the votes, and asked him "why sentence of death should not pass on him,"

---

[1] Reresby's 'Memoirs,' pp. 107-8. "King Charles secretly wished him well, and it is said had even solicited votes for his acquittal, though the Duchess of Portsmouth, probably bribed, had taken the contrary course."— Lodge.

he answered, " My Lord, I have little to say, I confess that I am surprised at it, for I did not expect it: but God's will be done. I will not murmur: God forgive them that have sworn falsely against me."

Judgment was then pronounced, when he for the last time thus addressed the Peers. " I thank you for all your favours to me. I do here, in the presence of God, declare that I have no malice in my heart against those who have condemned me. I know not who they are, nor desire to know; I forgive them all and beseech your Lordships all to pray for me. But I have one humble request to make, that for the short time I have to live, I may not be a close prisoner, as I have been of late, but may be allowed to see my wife and children, and friends."

Orders were given that this request should be granted,[1] and the Chancellor intimated also that the King would be petitioned to mitigate the ordinary sentence of treason to beheading:[2] upon this announcement he burst into tears, but suddenly collecting himself, he said, "My Lords, it is not your justice, but your kindness, that makes me weep."[3]

After his return to the Tower, he wrote again to his daughter in Belgium.

" GOOD DAUGHTER,

" I know you will beare what happens to me with patience and resignation. I thanke God that I knowe myself in every kind innocent, and that I have confydence in God's merceys, and doute not but through the mercy and passion of our Saviour to obtain everlasting happynoss. I pray God to blesse you.

" I am your affectionate father,

" For Ursula."[4] " WILLIAM.

On the 11th December, the Bishop of London,[5] and

---

[1] Dated "Tuesday, 7th Dec., all his relations and friends to have free access to him."—Tower Records.

[2] This the King granted, although some, and amongst others William Lord Russell, "stickled for the severer mode of executing the sentence."—Fox's 'Life of James II.'

[3] Lingard, vol. ix. p. 245; 'Trial of Lord Stafford,' p. 214.

[4] Ibid. p. 258.

[5] Henry Compton, born 1632, son of the Earl of Northampton, formerly in the army; appointed Bishop of London in 1675. Died in 1713.

Burnet,[1] went to him by his express desire. "We waited on him," writes Burnet, "when his design seemed to be only to possess us with an opinion of his innocence. He heard us speak of the points in difference between us and the Church of Rome with great temper and attention."

At parting he asked Burnet to return alone the next day: "when he again protested his innocence, and also to the Earl of Carlisle, who afterwards came in, and by the latter he sent a message to the House of Lords, that if sent for by them, he would disclose all he knew: upon that he was immediately sent for,[2] when he made a long statement about consultations for bringing in the Roman Catholic religion again, and said that Lord Bristol had advocated toleration of it: he then accused the Earl of Shaftesbury of a correspondence with Papists, when he was ordered to withdraw; the Lords would hear no more from him. He was sent back to the Tower, and then he composed himself in the best way he could to suffer: which he did with a constant and undisturbed mind. He supped and slept well the night before his execution, and died without any shew of fear or disorder."[3]

Wednesday, the 29th December, was fixed for Lord Stafford's execution:[4] a debate was raised on the 28th, in both Houses, on the question of the mitigation of his sentence by the King, but it was resolved, "this House is content the sheriffs should execute William, late Viscount Stafford, by severing his head from his body only." On the morning of the 29th December, he was brought out of the Tower, and he proceeded with a steady step and cheerful countenance to the place of execution. It was cold, and he asked for a cloak, lest if he should tremble through cold, and it might be taken for a symptom of fear. At his

---

[1] Gilbert Burnet was then preacher at the Rolls Chapel: made Bishop of Salisbury in 1689, died in 1715, and was buried at Clerkenwell.

[2] By warrants dated 18th Dec. See Tower Records.

[3] Burnet's 'Hist. of his Own Time,' vol. ii. p. 272.

[4] The warrant is dated 28th Dec., and endorsed by the sheriffs as receiving Lord Stafford on Wednesday 29th Dec. The King's signature and the seal have been removed from this document.—Tower Records.

appearance a few yells and groans were heard: and to his request that the sheriffs[1] would interfere, Cornish replied, "I am ordered to stop no one's mouth but your own." However, on the scaffold he delivered a long speech in a firm voice, and much animation.[2]

He repelled all the calumnies which had been uttered against his religion at the trial, and re-asserted his innocence. He declared Oates and Turberville to be perjured witnesses, and then, falling on his knees, he pronounced an extempore prayer, and again rising, protested his innocence.

Many of the spectators, with heads uncovered, exclaimed, "We believe you. God bless you, my Lord."[3]

Having embraced and taken leave of his friends, he knelt down and placed his head on the block: the executioner raised the axe high in the air, but then checking himself, suddenly lowered it.

Stafford raised his head and asked the reason of the delay: the executioner said he awaited the signal.[4] "I shall make no sign," he answered, "take your own time." The executioner asked his forgiveness. "I do forgive you," replied Stafford, and placing his head again in position, at one blow it was severed from his body.[5]

"He perished," says Sir J. Reresby, "in the firmest denial of what had been laid to his charge, and that in so cogent and persuasive a manner, that all the beholders believed his words, and grieved his destiny."[6]

The evidence of Oates was subsequently discredited, and in the year 1685 a bill was brought into the House of Lords to reverse the attainder of Lord Viscount Stafford, on the ground that no doubt could any longer exist of his innocence, or of the perjury of Titus Oates. It passed in

---

[1] John Cornish and Slingsby Bethel, the signature of the latter as endorsing the warrant is almost illegible.

[2] See 'Speech of William, late Lord Stafford,' printed by W. Bailey, 1680.

[3] Lingard, vol. ix. p. 248.

[4] It was customary to arrange that some signal should be given, so that it should be understood when the sufferer would remain quiet. The executioner asked Algernon Sidney when he laid his head on the block, whether he would rise again: "Not till the general resurrection, strike on," was the characteristic reply.

[5] 'Trial of Stafford,' p. 218; State Trials; Lingard, vol. ix. p. 248.

[6] Reresby's 'Memoirs,' p. 111.

a very full house, and may be considered as a vindication of his memory, by the same tribunal which had previously pronounced his condemnation.[1]

The burial of Lord Stafford in the chapel on the 29th December, 1680, is entered in the Register: but no record has been preserved in what part of the chapel he was interred.

ARTHUR CAPEL, EARL OF ESSEX.
Born 1635. Died in the Tower, 13th July, 1683.

Arthur Capel, Earl of Essex, born in 1635, was the eldest son of Arthur, Lord Capel, and was created Earl of Essex in 1661. In 1670 he went as ambassador to Denmark, and afterwards held the office of Lord Lieutenant of Ireland from 1672 till 1677. In June, 1683, he was implicated with Algernon Sidney, William Lord Russell, Lord Howard of Esrick, and others in the so-called "Rye House plot;" the object of which was to secure the succession of the Duke of Monmouth to the throne of England, and, as a means to that end, very probably to murder both Charles II. and his brother.

Lord Russell and several of the conspirators had already been arrested, when a party of horse was sent to Cashiobury to bring Lord Essex up to London, "who," says Burnet, "had staid all this while at his house in the country, and seemed so little apprehensive of danger that his own lady [2] did not imagine that he had any concern on his mind. He was offered to be conveyed away very safely, but he would not stir. His tenderness for Lord Russell was the cause of this, for he thought his going out of the way might incline the jury to believe the evidence the more for his absconding.[3] When the party came to bring him up, he was at first in some disorder, yet he recovered himself;

---

[1] Lingard, vol. x. p. 72.
[2] Elizabeth, Countess of Essex, daughter of Algernon, Earl of Northumberland.
[3] See also Lord Russell's 'Life of William, Lord Russell,' vol. ii. p. 25.

but when he came before the council he was in much confusion."[1]

He was committed to the Tower on Tuesday the 10th July, 1683, and placed for the night with Mr. Cheek in the Lieutenant's lodgings. Next day he was moved into the house of Major Hawley, the gentleman gaoler,[2] which adjoined it.

Burnet writes "that there he fell under a great depression of spirit; he could not sleep at all, he had fallen before that twice under great fits of the spleen, which returned now upon him with more violence. He sent by a servant, whom he had long trusted, and who was suffered to come to him, a very melancholy message to his wife, that what he was charged with was true; but he had sent for the Earl of Clarendon[3] to talk freely with him, who had married his sister."[4]

The permission for this visit was thus conveyed to Mr. Cheek by Sir Leoline Jenkins:—

"Whitehall, 12th July, 1683.

"Mr. Lieutenant,

"It is His Maties pleasure that you permit the Right Honble the Earl of Clarendon to speak with the Earl of Essex, without that you or any other be present.

"L. Jenkins."[5]

"Lord Clarendon," continues Burnet, "came to him upon his message, but he turned the matter so well with him, that Lord Clarendon went away in a great measure satisfied. His lady had another message that he was much calmer, and he ordered many things to be sent to him; and among other things he called at several times for a penknife, with which he used to pare his nails; when it did not come he called for a razor, and said that it would do as well."[4]

---

[1] Burnet, vol. ii. p. 373.

[2] The following is the "account of Thomas Cheeke for safe keeping Arthur Earle of Essex, from and for the 10th July, 1683, unto and for 14th July following, being 5 dayes at 10*l.* per week, ancient allowance, and 2*l.* 4*s.* 5*d.* per week, present demands according to retrenchment 7*l.* 11*s.* 8½*d.*"—Tower Records.

Cheek charges the 14th July in his account, yet Essex died on the morning of the 13th.

[3] Henry Hyde, second Earl of Clarendon, born 1638, died 1709.

[4] Burnet, vol. ii. p. 374.

[5] Tower Records.

On the morning of Friday the 13th July Lord Russell was brought out of his prison to be conveyed to the Old Bailey for trial; the King and the Duke of York had come early by water to the Tower, "as it was given out, to see some invention about the ordinance; but probably, with a curiosity unworthy of their rank, to see Russell pass out on his way."[1] "Essex was confined in the same apartments in the Tower[2] from which his father, Lord Capel, had been led to death, and in which his wife's grandfather, Lord Northumberland, had inflicted a voluntary death upon himself. When he saw his friend Lord Russell carried to what he reckoned certain fate, and their common enemies enjoying the spectacle, and reflected that it was he who had forced Lord Howard[3] upon the confidence of Russell, he retired, and by a Roman death put an end to his misery."[4]

As the King and his brother were returning to their barge "the cry came after them of what had happened to Lord Essex; for his servant, thinking he stayed longer than ordinary in his closet, looked through the key-hole and there saw him lying dead; upon which, the door being broken open, he was found with his throat cut, so that both the jugular and the gullet were cut a little above the aspera arteria."[5]

When the report of Essex's death reached Lord Russell in court he burst into tears; but Jeffreys in his speech to the jury turned the untimely fate of Essex into a "proof of his consciousness of the conspiracy."[6]

The circumstances of his death were suspicious, and as no definite decision resulted from the lengthened inquiry that was instituted in the matter, the question of suicide or murder must still remain unsolved.

---

[1] Dalrymple, vol. i. part i. book i. p. 44.
[2] "On the left hand, as you go up the mound, after passing the Bloody Gate:" the gaoler's house is between the Beauchamp Tower and the Lieutenant's House.
[3] Lord Howard of Esrick.
[4] Dalrymple, vol. i. part i. book i. p. 45. The condition of his friend seems to have pressed heavily on his mind. He had sent to the Earl of Bedford to say, that he was more concerned for his son's condition than even Lord Bedford himself.—'Life of William Lord Russell,' vol. ii. p. 30.
[5] Burnet, vol. ii. p. 375.
[6] Dalrymple, vol. i. part i. book i. p. 45.

Burnet says, "The coroner's jury found it 'self-murder;' and when his body was brought home to his own house, and the wound was examined by his own surgeon, he said to me that it was impossible the wound could be as it was, if given by any hand but his own; for except he had cast his head back, and stretched back his neck all he could, the aspera arteria must have been cut."[1]

In the following year Burnet writes: "I passed slightly over the suspicions raised upon Lord Essex's death when I mentioned this matter. This winter the business was brought to a trial. A boy and girl[2] did report that they heard a great crying in his lodgings, and that they saw a bloody razor flung out at window, which was taken up by a woman that came out of the house where he lodged. These children reported this confidently that very day, when they went to their homes. The boy went backward and forward in his story, sometimes affirming it and at other times denying it; but his father had an office in the Custom House, so it was thought he prevailed with him to deny it in open court; but the girl stood firmly to her story. The simplicity of the children, together with the ill opinion that was generally had of the court, inclined many to believe this."[3]

Lawrence Braddon, who had first reported this story of the children to the committee of enquiry, received permission, on the 24th January, 1684, from the House of the Lords "to see and view ye chamber in the Tower of London where the late Earle of Essex was found dead;"[4] but he was ultimately tried and convicted, "as a spreader of false reports; fined 2000*l*., and compelled to find sureties for good behaviour during his life, and committed until he had performed it."[5]

At a later period a committee of the House of Lords was appointed to enquire further into the circumstances of Lord Essex's death, and several persons were arrested in consequence. On 2nd February, 1688–9, "The close committee

---

[1] Burnet. "The Earle of Essex cutt his throat in the Tower, even whilst the Lord Russell was at Newgate upon his trial."—Sir J. Bramston's 'Autobiography,' p. 183.
[2] William Edward, aged 13, and Jane Lodeman, aged 13 years.
[3] Burnet, vol. ii. p. 403.
[4] Tower Records.
[5] Harris's 'Life of Charles II.' vol. ii. p. 353.

order that Mr. Merriton (Minister of Old Fish Street) be admitted, when and as often as the said Mr. Merriton pleases, to goe to and discourse alone with Thomas Russell,[1] now prisoner in the Tower, concerning the death of the said Earl. (Signed)

       BEDFORD. MORDAUNT.
       DEVONSHIRE. DELAMER."

And on the 21st of the same month they order that "Mr. Hawley[2] and Mr. Russell, now in custody concerning the said Earl's death, be brought before us on Saturday next at three of the clocke in the afternoone, at my Lord Devonshire's house at Gerrard Street in Soehoe."

Permission to liberate Hawley on bail was then granted, and Hawley was released on the 22nd February.

It is said that the committee examined nearly sixty witnesses, and much contradictory and unreliable evidence was produced. Paul Bomeney, the French valet, told his version,[3] and John Lloyd, the sentinel at Hawley's door, first said that he had allowed two men to enter, and then, after much prevarication, was sent to Newgate.[4]

The inquiry lingered on, but was never concluded, for after some time Lady Essex, considering it desirable to close the question, called a meeting of her relations, "at which the Lords Bedford and Devonshire and Bishop Burnet were present; she then declared that she believed Lord Essex had killed himself, and desired the business might be let fall."[5]

Hallam says, "Essex was a man of excellent qualities, but subject to constitutional melancholy, which overcame his fortitude; an event the more to be deplored as there seems to have been no possibility of his being convicted." He adds,

---

[1] Thomas Russell was the warder who had charge of Essex at the time of his death.

[2] The gentleman gaoler, or Tower Major, who had the custody of the Earl of Essex.

[3] He is said to have received a pension from the Treasury by order of King William till the day of his death.

[4] Robert Meek, another sentinel, who had made some remarks tending to prove that Essex had experienced foul play, was found murdered in the Tower ditch.

[5] 'Life of William Lord Russell,' vol. ii. p. 31.

"the suspicion of his murder is unsupported by any adequate evidence."[1]

In the burial register is the entry:

"Arthur, Earl of Essex, cutt his own throat within the Tower, July 13th, 1683. Buried in the chapel."

JAMES, DUKE OF MONMOUTH.

Born 1649. Beheaded on Tower Hill, 15th July, 1685.

When the Duke of Monmouth landed at Lyme Regis, the Mayor, Gregory Alford, wrote at once to the King to notify his arrival. This letter, dated "Honiton, 11th June, near twelve at night,"[2] was read in the House of Lords, and, says Sir J. Bramston, "The Kinge giving notice to the House of the landing of the Duke on the 11th of June, the House tooke the matter into consideration, and ordered the bringing a bill for the attaintinge him for treason, which the Sollicitor Finch,[3] by order withdrawinge, prepared immediately and presented it to the House, whoe read it the first and second tyme, ordered the ingrossinge, which was done against the afternoone, the House sitting purposely, when it had the third readinge, was passed, and sent up to the Lords. And an addresse was presented to the Kinge to sett a reward of 5000l. for any that should bringe him (Monmouth) in alive or dead; but the King deferred that until the bill was passed. Then by proclamation, taking notice that he was landed at Lyme, and in open rebellion, and attainted of treason by Act of Parliament,[4] and therefore, at the request of

---

[1] Hallam's 'Const. Hist.' vol. ii. p. 616. There is a satirical broadside in eight compartments, called a 'History of the New Plot, 1683.' No. 3 is 'cut his own throat,' and represents three figures murdering Lord Essex. The notched razor is lying on the ground.

[2] See Roberts, 'Life of Monmouth,' vol. i. p. 257.

[3] Heneage Finch, Solicitor-General from 1679 till 1686.

[4] The Act is 1 Jac. II. c. 2, and consists merely of these words: "Whereas James, Duke of Monmouth, has in an hostile manner invaded this kingdom, and is now in open rebellion, levying war against the King contrary to his allegiance, Be it enacted by the King's most excellent Majesty, by and with the advice and consent of the Lords spiritual and temporal and Commons in this parliament assembled, and by the

his Commons, he proposed 5000*l.* as a reward for any that brought him alive or dead." [1]

The King's troops under the Earl of Faversham advanced against Monmouth, the battle of Sedgmoor was fought, and between two and three o'clock on the morning of Monday, 6th July, the Duke of Monmouth, accompanied by Lord Grey, Dr. Oliver, and an officer named Busse, a native of Brandenburg, and William Williams, the Duke's servant, left the field. On the Monday night the Duke slept at Downside, 1½ mile from Shepton Mallet, in the house of Edward Strode, Esq. Next morning he started on his road towards the sea-coast, and on arriving at Cranbourne Chase, he got off his horse at Woodyates Inn, and there, having disguised himself as a shepherd, he wandered away on foot. Lord Lumley and Sir W. Portman with some dragoons, were searching the country in the neighbourhood, and learned from a cottager, named Amy Farrant, that she had seen two men getting over a hedge into a wood. The Duke and Busse remained concealed in that wood all night, but at five o'clock in the morning of Wednesday the 8th, Busse was discovered, and confessed that he had parted with the Duke at one o'clock that morning. 5000*l.* reward had been offered for the capture of the Duke, and the greatest diligence was now used in searching the wood.[2] At length a militiaman, named Henry Perkin,[3] found the Duke at the foot of an ash tree in a ditch, and covered with fern and brambles. In his pockets were merely a few peas, his watch, and the "George,"[4] together with "some papers in his own handwriting, containing charms and spells to open the doors of prisons, to obviate the danger of being wounded in battle; and some songs and prayers."[5]

---

authority of the same, That the said James Duke of Monmouth stand and be convicted and attainted of high treason, and that he suffer pains of death and incur all forfeitures as a traitor convicted and attainted of high treason."

[1] Sir J. Bramston's 'Autobiography,' pp. 202–3.

[2] It is now called "Monmouth's Close," at Woodlands, and belongs to the Earl of Shaftesbury.

[3] "The name of the trooper that tooke him was Perkin; he had twenty guineas and the other two troopers had ten guineas each."—Sir J. Bramston, p. 187.

[4] Dalrymple, vol. i. p. 184.

[5] Reresby, p. 213.

He was then taken to Holt Lodge, and brought before Anthony Etterick, Esq., a magistrate, who ordered him to be conveyed to London.

He first stopped at Ringwood, and it was from thence that he wrote the following letters to King James and to the Queen Dowager, Katharine of Braganza :—

"SIR, "8th July.

"Your Majesty may thinck it the misfortune I now lye under makes me make this application to you; but I doe assure your Majesty it is the remorse I now have in me of the wronge I have done you in severall things, and now in taking up armes against you. For my taking up arms, it was never in my thought since the Kinge died. The Prince and Princess of Orange will be witnes for me of the assurance I gave them, that I would never stirr against you. But my misfortune was such as to meete with some horrid people that made me believe things of your Majesty, and gave me soe manie false arguments, that I was fully led away to believe that it was a shame and a sin before God not to doe it. But, sir, I will not truble your Majesty at present with many things I could say of myselfe that I am sure would move your compassion, the chiefe end of this letter being only to begg of you that I may have that happiness as to speak to your Majesty, for I have that to say to you, sir, that I hope may give you a long and happy raign.

"I am sure, sir, when you heare me, you will be convinced of the zeale I have for your preservation, and how hartilie I repent of what I have done. I can say noe more to your Majesty now, seeinge this letter must be seene by those that keepe me. Therefore, sir, I shall make an end, in begginge of your Majesty to believe so well of me, that I would rather dye a thousand deaths than excuse anything I have done, if I did not really thinck myself the most in the wrong that ever a man was, and had not from the bottom of my hart an abhorrence for those that put me upon it, and for the action itselfe. I hope, sir, God Almighty will strike your hart with mercie and compassion for me, as He has done mine with the abhorrence of what I have done. Wherefore, sir, I hope I may live to show you how zealous I shall ever bee for your service; and could I but say one word in this letter you would be convinced of it; but it is of that consequence, I dare not do it. Therefore, sir, I doe begg of you once more to let me speake to you, for then you will be convinced how much I shall ever be,

"Your Majesty's most humble and dutifull,

"MONMOUTH."[1]

[1] Roberts, 'Life of Monmouth,' vol. ii. pp. 112–13.

"MADAM, "From Ringwood, the 9th.

"Being in this unfortunate condition, and having none left but your Majesty that I think may have compassion of me, and that for the last King's sake, makes me take this boldnes to beg of you to intersed for me.[1] I would not desire your Majesty to doe it, if I wear not from the botom of my hart convinced how I have bine disceaved in to it, and how angry God Almighty is with me for it; but I hope, Madam, your intersesion will give me life to repent of it, and to shew the King how really and truly I will serve him hereafter. And I hope, Madam, your Majesty will be convinced that the life you save shall ever be devoted to your service; for I have been, and ever shall be, your Majesty's most dutifull and obedient servant,

"MONMOUTH."[2]

He also wrote an abject letter to the Earl of Rochester,[3] the Secretary of State, imploring that his life should be spared.

On Saturday he was taken to Farnham Castle, on Sunday to Guildford, and on Monday the 13th he arrived at Vauxhall, where barges and troops were waiting to convey him and Lord Grey to Whitehall. They dined in Chiffinch's lodgings.[4] "It was after dinner, having his arms loosely tied behind him, that the King received Monmouth in the presence of Sunderland and Middleton, the two Secretaries of State. The interview lasted about forty minutes, the Duke declared he had been deceived by rogues, threw the "blame chiefly on the Duke of Argyll and Ferguson, who had stirred him to it, and disclaimed all title to the Crown, and said he was put upon assuming the style of King with a view that the quality would the sooner come into him. All this," says Sir J. Reresby, "I heard the King say." He concluded by asking for pardon, and begged his life of James.[5]

---

[1] Queen Katharine had already interceded successfully on his behalf after the discovery of the Rye House Plot.

[2] Lansdowne MSS. British Museum 1236, No. 130; 'Ellis's Orig. Letters,' 1st series, vol. iii. p. 343; Roberts, 'Life of Monmouth,' vol. ii. p. 119.

[3] Lawrence Hyde, Earl of Rochester, son of Edward, first Earl of Clarendon, died 1711; buried at Westminster Abbey.

[4] Son of Thomas Chiffinch, who was Keeper of the Jewels and the King's Closet to Charles II., &c., and died in 1666.

[5] Reresby's 'Memoirs,' pp. 212–13.

The King writes the following account of this interview to his son-in-law, William, Prince of Orange:

"Whitehall, July 14, 1685.

"I have had yours of the 17th, and now the Duke of Monmouth is brought up hither with Lord Grey and the Brandenburgher. The two first desired very earnestly to speak with me, as having things of importance to say to me; which they did, but did not answer my expectation in what they said to me. The Duke of Monmouth seemed more concerned and desirous to live, and did behave himself not so well as I expected, nor do as one ought to have expected from one who had taken upon him to be king. I have signed the warrant for his execution to-morrow."[1]

And again, on the 17th, he writes to his son-in-law:

"The Duke was beheaded on Wednesday on the Tower Hill. He died resolutely, and a downright enthusiast."[2]

At eight o'clock on the evening of the 13th Monmouth and Lord Grey[3] were carried to the Tower in the King's barges, guarded by several barges full of soldiers. The warrant for his committal is worded: "James, Duke of Monmouth, 13 July, for high treason in levying war against the King and assuming a title to the Crown."[4]

---

[1] "Monmouth having desired to see the Kinge, he was at Chiffins' lodgings, and the Kinge came down to him as I have heard, with the two Secretaries of State. He threw himself at the Kinge's feete, and begged his mercie. It is sayd he was soe disingenious in his answers to what the Kinge askt of him, that the Kinge turned from him, and bid him prepare for death. He stayd at Mr Chiffins' lodgeings untill the tyde served to carrie him to the Tower. Chiffins had prepared for him a short supper: Gray and the Brandenburgher eate with him."—Sir J. Bramston's 'Autobiography,' p. 186.

[2] Dalrymple's 'Memoirs,' vol. ii. App. part i. pp. 134—5.

[3] Forde, Lord Grey of Werke, the eldest son of the second Lord Grey: he is the "cold Caleb" in Dryden's 'Absalom and Achitophel.' He was in command of the cavalry at Sedgmoor, and has been accused of betraying Monmouth in revenge for the Duke's conduct to his wife.

"Next Monmouth came in with a party of fools,
Betrayed by his cuckold and other dull tools,
Who painted the turf of green Sedgmoor with gules."

Lord Grey was pardoned and released 12th Nov. 1685: he died in 1701.

[4] Tower MS. Records, and Bayley, p. 633.

His wife was admitted to see him that same evening,[1] and again she saw him on Wednesday, 15th, before his execution. These interviews are said to "have passed with decency, but without tokens of affection."[2]

On the 14th orders were received by the Lieutenant of the Tower that the Duke might have a servant, "but to be shut up with him;" that the Bishop of Ely[3] will acquaint the Duke that he may see his children if he desires it; that Lord Arundel of Wardour, and any other person to whom the Lord Privy Seal or the Bishop of Ely might grant permission, were to have access to the prisoner.[4]

The bill of attainder obviated the necessity of a trial, and the Duke's execution was to take place without delay. The King had determined that the execution should be public, so that no one could doubt Monmouth's death, as they had at first doubted his imprisonment.[5] On 14th July, the Duke wrote thus to the King:

"Tuesday.

"SIR,

"I have received your Majesty's order this day that I am to dye to-morrow. I was in hopes, Sir, by what your Majesty said to me yesterday, of taking care of my soul, that I should have had some little

---

[1] "Whitehall, 13th July, 1685.
"SIR,—His Majesty commands mee to signify his pleasure to you that you permitt and suffer the L⁴ Privy Seale, and the late Dutchesse of Monmouth, to have accesse to the late Duke of Monmouth,—I am, &c.,
"SUNDERLAND.
"To Mr. Cheek."

[2] His wife was Lady Anne Scott, daughter of the Duke of Buccleuch: she was married to him on 20th April, 1663, and on the day of his marriage they were created Duke and Duchess of Buccleuch. His English titles were forfeited by his attainder, but the Scotch titles, being conferred on him jointly with the Duchess, were inherited by her descendants.—Lodge.

[3] "Whitehall, 14th July, 1685.
"SIR,—I have acquainted the King with the contents of your letter, and he directs me to tell you that he allows the late Duke of Monmouth, and the late Lord Grey, should each of them have a servant, but to be shut up with them; that the Bishop of Ely will acquaint the late Duke of Monmouth he is to dy to-morrow, and that if he desires to see his children it may be allowed, they going with the Bishop of Ely, and coming away with him.—I am, &c.,
"SUNDERLAND.
"To the Lieutenant of the Tower."

[4] "Whitehall, July the 14th, 1685.
"SIR,—It is the King's pleasure that you allow any person or persons to see the late Duke of Monmouth, whom my Lord Privy Seale or the Bishop of Ely shall thinke fit.—I am, &c.
"SUNDERLAND.
"To Mr. Cheeke."

[5] A doubt nevertheless did prevail in the popular mind, whether the Duke of Monmouth really was executed.

more time; for truly, Sir, this is very short. I do beg of your Majesty, if it be possible, to let me have one day more, that I may go out of the world as a Christian ought.

"I had desired several times to speak with my Lord Arundel of Wardour, which I do desire still. I hope your Majesty will grant it me: and I do beg of your Majesty to let me know by him if there is nothing in this world that can recall your sentence, or at least reprieve me for some time. I was in hopes I should have lived to have served you, which I think I could have done to a great degree; but your Majesty does not think it fit. Therefore, Sir, I shall end my days with being satisfied that I had all the good intentions imaginable for it, and should have done it, being that I am your Majesty's most dutiful,

"MONMOUTH.

"I hope your Majesty will give Doctor Tennison[1] leave to come to me, or any other that you may be pleased to grant me.

"To the King."[2]

On the morning of Tuesday Dr. Turner, Bishop of Ely,[3] had been sent to him by the King, and Ken,[4] Bishop of Bath and Wells, came later in the day; they remained with him all night, and Dr. Hooper[5] and Dr. Tenison joined them on the morning of Wednesday.[6]

He took leave of his wife and children, but when Dr. Tenison asked him to be better reconciled to the Duchess, he excused himself, saying that "his heart was turned against her, because in his affliction she had gone to plays and into public companies; by which I know she did not love me."[7]

"He disowned his Duchess (says Reresby), who to him,

---

[1] Thomas Tenison, born 1636, Vicar of St. Martin's-in-the-Fields in 1685: he attended Monmouth on the scaffold, and in Nov. 1687 he preached "a notable funeral sermon" over Nell Gwyn; was Bishop of Lincoln in 1691, and Archbishop of Canterbury in 1694. Died 14th Dec. 1715.

[2] Harleian MSS. 7006-7198; Ellis's 'Orig. Letters,' 1st series, vol. iii. p. 346.

[3] Francis Turner, educated at Winchester with his friend Ken. Appointed Dean of Windsor in 1683 and Bishop of Rochester, and in 1684 was translated to Ely; was deprived and sent to the Tower as a non-juror in 1691. Died in 1700.

[4] Thomas Ken, born 1637, appointed Bishop of Bath and Wells in 1684. Deprived as a non-juror in 1691. Died in 1710.

[5] George Hooper was appointed Bishop of Bath and Wells in 1703, and died 1727.

[6] See letter of Dr. Lloyd, Bishop of St. Asaph, to Dr. Fell, Bishop of Oxford, dated 16th July, 1685, giving an account of Monmouth's last hours and execution. —Aubrey's Letters, No. xv.

[7] Reresby's 'Memoirs,' p. 213.

who had nothing of his own, had brought a fortune of ten thousand pounds; saying she was given to him as his wife in the days of his minority, but that the wife of his own choice was the Lady Henrietta Wentworth, the only daughter and heiress of the Earl of Cleveland, whom he had debauched, with whom he confessed he had lived according to the rules of his own convenience, though not according to the laws of the land, for two years past."

Monmouth begged the four divines to accompany him to the scaffold, and, at 10 A.M. on Wednesday the 15th July, the Lieutenant of the Tower conveyed him with the two bishops in a coach to the bars, a short distance outside the fortress, where he was delivered over to the sheriffs,[1] they conducted him on foot through a hedge of soldiers, preceded by three officers with pistols in their hands, who also ascended the scaffold and remained by him during the execution.

The following order had been received by the Sheriffs of London :—

"Whitehall, July 14, 1685.

"The King allows the scaffold for the execution of the late Duke of Monmouth to be covered with mourning, and that his body after execution shall be given to his friends to be disposed of as they shall think fit."

A murmur of sighs and groans greeted Monmouth's appearance on the scaffold, which was followed by a breathless silence, that all might hear what he had to utter.

On coming upon the scaffold he looked for the executioner and said, "Is this the man to do the business? Do your work well."

Monmouth made no set speech on the scaffold: what took place was of the nature more of question and answer between himself and the sheriffs, and of exhortations from the divines.[2]

---

[1] The warrant for the duke's execution is dated 13th July, and the writ for delivering him over to the sheriffs bears the same date. It is addressed to Sir William Gostling and Sir Peter Vanderputt, and is endorsed by them as receiving the Duke from the Lieutenant.—Tower Records.

[2] "The Duke made no speech on the scaffold (which was on Tower Hill), but gave a paper containing not above five or six lines for the King, in which he

His only speech was an endeavour to clear the character of Lady Harriet Wentworth.

The following paper he had delivered to the sheriffs on the scaffold:

"I declare that the title of King was forced upon me, and that it was very much contrary to my opinion when I was proclaimed. For the satisfaction of the world, I do declare, that the late King told me he was never married to my mother. Having declared this, I hope that the King, who is now, will not let my children suffer on this account. And to this I put my hand, this fifteenth day of July, 1685,

"MONMOUTH.

"This is a true account, witness our hands,
FRANCIS, ELY.   THOMAS TENISON.
THOMAS, BATH AND WELLS.   GEORGE HOOPER.
WILLIAM GOSTLIN, }
PETER VANDERPUTT, } Sheriffs."[1]

"After the devotionary and interrogatory part was over, he called his servant, Marshall, and gave him something like a toothpick-case, saying, 'Give this to the person to whom you are to deliver the other things.' He then went to that part of the scaffold where the block and axe lay,[2] the axe he took in his hand and tried it with his nail to see whether it was sharp enough, and, giving the executioner six guineas, said, 'Pray do your business well: do not serve me as you did my Lord Russell. I have heard you struck him three or four times; if you strike me twice I cannot promise you not to stir." He also told his servant to give the executioner six more guineas if he did his work well. He then took off his coat and threw off his peruke, and, having prayed, laid himself down and fitted his neck to the block with great composure of mind; but soon after he raised himself upon

---

disclaims all title to the Crown, acknowledges that the late King, his father, had indeed told him he was but his base son, and so desired his Majesty to be kind to his wife and children. This relation I had from Dr. Tenison, rector of St. Martin's, who, with the Bishops of Ely, and Bath and Wells, were sent to him by his Majesty, and were at the execution."— Evelyn's 'Diary,' July 1685.

[1] Roberts, 'Monmouth,' vol. ii. p. 149.

[2] Dalrymple writes: "The Duke examined the axe to satisfy himself, and expressed anxiety lest the executioner should not end his life at a blow, and said he was afraid to die, yet asked could any one perceive it by his countenance."—Dalrymple, vol. i. part i. book ii. p. 189.

his elbow and said to the executioner, 'Prithee, let me feel the axe,' and, feeling the edge, added, 'I fear it is not sharp enough.' 'It is sharp and heavy enough,' was the reply. Then the executioner proceeded to do his office. The Duke would have no cap, nor be bound, nor have anything on his face: and yet 'for all this,' writes an eye-witness, 'the botcherly dog did so barbarously act his pairt, that he could not at fyve stroaks of the ax sever the head from the body.' After the third stroke the executioner threw away the axe and offered forty guineas to any one who would finish the work. The bystanders threatened to kill him unless he took the axe again, and he completed his task; if there had been no guard he would have been torn to pieces by the crowd."[1]

James II. caused two commemorative medals, which have been called "savage medals," to be struck on this occasion.

On one is his own head, with the inscription, "Aras ad sceptra tuemur;" on the reverse, two headless trunks of Monmouth and Argyle, with "Ambitio malesuada ruit."

On the other medal is Monmouth's head, and on the reverse a young man falling in the attempt to climb a rock on which are three crowns, with the motto, "Superi risere, July 6, 1685."

"Thus, writes Evelyn," "ended this quondam Duke, darling of his father and the ladies, being extremely handsome and adroit; an excellent soldier and dancer, a favourite of the people, of an easy nature; seduced by knaves, who would have set him up only to make a property, and taken the opportunity of the King being of another religion, to gather a party of discontented men. He failed and perished. He was a lovely person, had a virtuous and excellent lady that brought him great riches and a second Dukedom in Scotland."[2]

---

[1] Contemporary Pamphlet. The executioner's name, "Jack Ketch," has since been the common name for all hangmen: he was deprived of his office after this wretched failure, and was succeeded by a man named Rose; but soon after Rose, for some crime, was executed at Tyburn, and Ketch was then reinstated. His frequent employment caused his name to be associated with that of Judge Jeffreys in popular verses of the day.

"While Jeffreys on the bench
Ketch on the gibbet sits."

[2] Evelyn's 'Diary,' July 1685.

"After his execution his body was put into a coffin covered with black velvet, and carried back in a herse into the Tower, where the head being sewed to the body, it was privately interred in St. Peter's Chapel there under the communion table."[1] The entry in the register is, "James, Duke of Monmouth, beheaded on Tower Hill y[e] 15th, and buryed y[e] 16th July."

He was buried "beneath the communion table," and there on the 11th November, 1876, his remains were seen.

GEORGE JEFFREYS, LORD JEFFREYS, OF WEM.

Born 1648. Died in the Tower, 18th April, 1689.

At three o'clock in the morning, of Tuesday the 11th December, 1688, King James II. fled from Whitehall, and Jeffreys, the ex-chancellor, who already on the 8th December had given up the seals to the King, considered it advisable to take precautions for his own safety. He dreaded the revenge of the mob, and so certain did he feel that punishment awaited him under the new government, that upon being asked if he knew what were the heads of the Prince of Orange's declaration, he replied, "I am sure that my head is one, whatever the rest may be."[2]

Between the hours of three and four o'clock, in the morning of Monday, 10th December, he withdrew privately from his house in Duke Street, Westminster, and retired to the obscure dwelling of one of his servants, in Westminster, near the river side, hoping to escape to France.[3] There he cut off his bushy eyebrows, and disguised himself "as a common sailor."[4]

---

[1] Sandford, pp. 643-4; Bayley, p. 121.
[2] Woolrych's 'Life of Jeffreys,' p. 361.
[3] Oldmixon, vol. ii. p. 185.
[4] "Jeffreys was prepared for sailing in a long tarpaulin gown;

Where is now his furious railing,
And his blood-congealing frown?
He took a collier's coat to sea to go:
Was ever chancellor arrayed so?"

There is a Dutch caricature portrait of him in this sailor's dress.

Arrangements had been made that he should be received on board a collier, which should clear out for Newcastle, but should first land him at Hamburg.

At dusk, next day, wearing an old tarry hat on his head, he took a boat, passed down through London Bridge, and went on board the collier: but he found she was not going to sail until the next day, so he took the precaution of going to pass the night on board another vessel that lay near.

Immediately he left the first vessel, the mate treacherously hurried on shore, and gave notice to some persons who were in search of Jeffreys, that the terrible ex-chancellor was on board the vessel: they at once went to one of the justices in the neighbourhood and applied for a warrant, but as no specific charge was sworn against Jeffreys, it was refused: the applicants then went to the Council Office, and obtained from the Lords, who were sitting, a warrant to arrest Jeffreys for high treason. They then returned to the collier, but Jeffreys was no longer there. He had escaped that danger, and slept quietly on board the second vessel.

His fatal habit of drinking, however, led to his arrest. On the morning of Wednesday, the 12th December, he went ashore to a public house bearing the sign of "The Red Cow," in Anchor and Hope Alley, King Edward's Stairs, Wapping, and having drunk a pot of ale he ventured to look out of the window, when a scrivener of Wapping, whom he had formerly grossly ill-treated when on the bench, passed, and saw the face looking out of the window.[1] He at once recognized the terrible look of the abusive judge, and went into the taproom to examine the countenance more closely. Jeffreys saw that he was eyed with suspicion, so he turned his face towards the wall and coughed, and held up the quart pot before his face.[2]

---

[1] Jeffreys had abused him and scowled at him to such a degree that the scrivener on leaving the court had remarked to a friend, "I shall never forget the terrors of that man's face while I live."

[2] Jeffreys had at one time said that his face was of brass: this was remembered in a street ballad of the day:

"George Jeffreys, who boasted his face was of brass,
Is now metamorphos'd into a Welsh ass."

The scrivener then gave the alarm, and Jeffreys was dragged out of the house, but "after a fair deliverance from the mob, that would have torn him to pieces,"[1] he was hurried into a coach and protected by some of the city train bands, armed with blunderbusses. He was then conveyed to the Lord Mayor: the mob yelling "Vengeance! Justice! Vengeance!"

Oldmixon, who was present in the crowd, tells us that "outside the Mansion House, the crowd was so great and the rabble so numerous, all crying out together, that the Lord Mayor[2] was forced to come out with his hat in his hand, and desired the people to go away and keep the peace, and did promise them that he had already sent to the Lords of the Council about the matter, and that they should have justice done them; and in the meantime their prisoner should be safely guarded. Whereupon the people withdrew, and soon after, my Lord, under a strong guard, was sent to the Tower."[3]

Jeffreys himself recommended that he should be taken without delay to the Tower, and this was accomplished under the protection of two regiments of train bands. Lord Lucas gave a receipt for the person of Jeffreys to Sir Harry Johnson, Sir John Friend, Champion Ashley, and Thomas Cooper, who had brought him safe into the Tower. The regular warrant, which is preserved in the Tower records, was subsequently sent to Lord Lucas.

"We the peers of this Realme being assembled with some of the Privy Councill, doe hereby will and require you to take into your custody the body of George Lord Jeffreys (herewith sent unto you)

---

[1] Kennet, vol. iii. p. 502.

[2] "Sir John Chapman, the Lord Mayor, either out of feare and amazement to find the great Lord Chancellor in that habit and in that condition, or else out of some indisposition, fell into a swooning fit, and a convulsion, which distorted his mouth very much" (Sir J. Bramston, p. 339): the excitement proved too great for him, for he died soon afterwards, and was succeeded in the mayoralty by Sir Thomas Pilkington. Sir R. Beach writes on 19th December, that when Jeffreys was brought to the Mansion House, he knelt to kiss the Lord Mayor's hand.—Orig. letter in possession of the Earl of Dartmouth.

[3] Oldmixon, vol. ii. p. 186; Burnet, vol. iii. p. 348, and Ellis's 'Orig. Letters,' 2nd series, vol. iv. p. 174.

and him to keep safe prisoner untill further order; for which this shall be your sufficient warrant.

"(Signed) HALIFAX.   CARLISLE.
          KENT.   BERKELEY.
          VAUGHAN & CARBERRY. SUSSEX.
          ANGLESEY.   NOTTINGHAM.
          NORTH & GREY.   CREWE.
          ROCHESTER.   P. WINCHESTER."[1]
          MULGRAVE.

"Council Chamber, Whitehall.
"The 12th of December, 1688.

"To the R^t Honble LORD LUCAS,
"Cheif Governor of the Tower of London."

This is a remarkable historical document, for it must be borne in mind that there was then no executive authority in the kingdom: no Sovereign, no Chancellor, and no Parliament sitting at the time, moreover the great seal was at the bottom of the Thames.

There had been considerable difficulty in conveying Jeffreys to the Tower, in consequence of the excitement of the people: two regiments of train bands escorted the coach in which he was seated, and the movements of the mob were so threatening that Jeffreys implored the soldiers "for the Lord's sake to keep them off," in the most imploring manner. "I saw him and heard him," says Oldmixon, "and I truly say without pity, though I never saw any malefactor in his distress without compassion or concern."[2] At length, a passage having been forced through the dense mob on Tower Hill, he was safely brought into the Tower.

On the following day, the Lords North, Grey, Chandos, and Ossulton, came to the Tower to examine Jeffreys, and especially to ask what he had done with the Great Seal: he replied that he had given it to the King on the previous Saturday, in Mr. Chiffinch's lodgings. In the report of their conversation with Jeffreys, which this deputation

---

[1] Peter Mew, Bishop of Winchester from 1684 till 1706.
[2] Oldmixon, vol. i. p. 762.

made to the other Lords, they said that "they were desired by the Lord Jeffreys to return his humble thanks for their care in preserving him from violence!" On the 22nd December the House of Lords "assembled in this extraordinary conjuncture," ordered that no one should speak to Jeffreys unless Lord Lucas were present, and that the names of all persons who should speak to him should be noted and "returned to their Lordships every morning when they meet."[1]

The public feeling was strongly displayed against Jeffreys, and his trial was clamorously demanded. Ballads, histories of his evil deeds, and such like literature, were hawked about the streets, and "the rabble congregated before his deserted mansion in Duke Street, read on the door with shouts of laughter, the bills that announced the sale of his property."[2]

He was known to be fond of oysters, and a barrel was sent to him, which appeared to contain Colchester natives: "Thank God," said he, "I have still some friends left." The barrel was opened, and out fell a heap of empty shells, and a halter.[3] He was visited by Dr. John Sharp, Dean of Norwich,[4] and Dr. John Scott, a prebendary of St. Paul's: to them he maintained that he had shown clemency in the administration of justice, and by so doing had incurred the displeasure of King James.

Richard Lapthorne writes to Richard Coffin:

"London, 29 Dec. 1688.

"The Lord Chancellor Jeffreys is close confined at one Mr. Bull's, a warder, but allowed pen, inke, and paper, which hee hath much used. The Tower church was very full on Sunday, in expectation to see him, but he came not out."[5]

On the 3rd day of January Lady Jeffreys was admitted to see her husband, and to "remain with him; and his health

---

[1] Tower Records.
[2] Macaulay, vol. iii. p. 339.
"The very boys, how they do grin and prate,
And giggle at the bills upon your gate."
                      Street ballad.
[3] Woolrych's 'Life of Jeffreys.'
[4] John Sharp, born 1644: appointed Dean of Norwich in 1681. In 1689 he was appointed Dean of Canterbury, and in 1691 Archbishop of York. He died in 1714.
[5] MS. letter in possession of J. Pine Coffin, Esq.

having so greatly failed, Dr. Richard Lower and Dr. Thomas Browne, doctors of phisick, were permitted to attend on him, and also Mr. Beaulieu, his chaplain." [1]

Robert Frampton, Bishop of Gloucester, also visited him, and he writes that he found Jeffreys "sitting in a low chair, with a long beard on, and a small pot of water by him, weeping with himself." [2]

His illness increased: decay of nature began to show itself; he was unable to take any food, and rejected all nourishment. He had formerly been corpulent, but now he shrank to a skeleton.

In a contemporary account we find "The manner of his death was this: he had been very much tormented with his old distemper (the stone), and rheumatism, almost ever since he has been in the Tower; and there has not been any help wanting that skill or art could invent for the continuation of his life: but it has been all as ineffectual and vain, as the supplications of the distressed were sometimes to him, in the time of his power. For about this month last past, he has been in a very languishing condition, still wasting away more and more, in which time he has hardly been in a capacity to take anything to sustain nature, unless a little sack to revive it.[3] About three weeks since, he had a mind to a bit of salmon, which he had, but could not digest it, nor scarce anything else, unless a poached egg. So he continued decaying till the 19th of this instant, April, 1689, when about half an hour after four in the morning [4] he died, in the forty first year of his age." [5]

He had been Chief Justice of the King's Bench at thirty-five, and Lord Chancellor at thirty-seven years of age.

One of the numerous ballads of the day gave his epitaph

---

[1] Tower Records. This order is signed "William D'Orange."

[2] Evans's 'Life of Frampton,' p. 195.

[3] Oldmixon says "he chose to save himself from a public death by large draughts of brandy, which soon despatched him."—Oldmixon, vol. i. p. 762.

[4] The record of his imprisonment is endorsed "Dyed 19th April, 1689, 35 minutes past four in the morning."

[5] 'A True and Full Account of the Death of George Lord Jeffreys: published by James Fraser, April, 1689.'

"at the request of the widows of the West, whose husbands were hanged without trial by this Lord Chancellor."

> "Here England's great Lord Chancellor is laid,
> Who King and Kingdom, Church and State betrayed:
> But may his crimes and bloodshed silent lie,
> And ne'er against the English nation cry."

On the 19th April, which according to the official record in the Tower, was the day of his death, an inquest was held on the body, and this warrant was then issued by the Earl of Shrewsbury under the sign manual of the King.

"William R.

"Whereas it hath been represented to us that George, Lord Jeffreys, a prisoner under your custody in our Tower of London, is deceased, and that (as it appears by an inquisition of a jury taken upon oath) of a naturall death, Our Will and Pleasure is, that you forthwith deliver the body of the said late Lord Jeffreys to his relations, in order to be buried in what place and in such manner as they shall think fitt, and for so doing this shall be your warrant.

"Given at our Court at Whitehall, the 19th day of Aprill, 1689, in the first year of our reign.

"By His Majesty's command,

"To Lord Lucas."   "SHREWSBURY.[1]

But Lady Jeffreys did not avail herself of this permission, and "the emaciated corpse was laid with all privacy, next to the corpse of Monmouth, in the chapel of the Tower."[2] The burial register records "George Lord Jeffreys, buried in the chapel, 20 April, 1689;"[3] but in 1692, during the absence of King William in Holland, an application was made to remove his body, and this warrant was issued by the Queen.

"Marie R.

"Our Will and pleasure is that you order the body of George, late Lord Jeffreys, to be delivered into the hands of his relations, and

---

[1] Charles Earl of Shrewsbury, K.G., born 1660. Secretary of State from Feb. 1688-9 till Dec. 1690, and again from March, 1693 till May, 1700: afterwards Lord Camberlain to Queen Anne, and Lord Lieutenant of Ireland. Died 1st Feb. 1718-9.

[2] Macaulay, vol. iv. p. 403.

[3] There was an impression current for some time that he had been buried at Enfield.

permit them to carry it in a private and decent manner out of the Tower, in order to the buriall of it in such place as they shall think fit, and for so doing this shall be your warrant.

"Given at our Court at Whitehall, the 30th day of September, 1692, in the fourth yeare of our Reigne.

"By Her Majesty's command,
"To Robert Lord Lucas."   "NOTTINGHAM.[1]

It was not, however, until the 2nd November, 1693, that the body was disinterred and deposited in a vault under the Communion Table in the church of St. Mary, Aldermanbury, "near the body of his rakish son, Lord Wem."[2]

In the year 1810, when the church was undergoing some repairs, his coffin was seen, with the name "Lord Chancellor Jeffreys" on it.[3]

JOHN ROETTIER, OR ROTIER.

Born ——. Died in the Tower, 17th June, 1703.

John Roettier was the head of a family of medallists. He was the son of a goldsmith and banker at Antwerp, who had assisted Charles II. with money during his exile.

He came over to England in 1661, shortly after the Restoration, and received employment in the Mint under Simon the medallist, upon the recommendation of the King. Simon resigned his appointment soon afterwards, and in 1662 Roettier and his brothers, James and Philip, were appointed medallists, with a salary and a residence in the Tower; they also were allowed 200*l.* for each broad seal, and they probably earned 300*l.* a year in addition by selling medals at home and abroad.

On 9th March, 1662-3, Pepys records that—

"About noon, Sir J. Robinson, Lord Mayor, desiring way through the garden from the Tower, called in at the office, and there invited me and Sir W. Pen, who happened to be in the way, to dinner, and we

---

[1] Daniel Finch, second Earl of Nottingham, born 1647, son of the chancellor. Was Secretary of State to William and Mary, and afterwards to Queen Anne. then President of the Council. He died in 1730.

[2] Pennant, p. 414.

[3] 'Gentleman's Magazine,' vol. lxxx. part ii. p. 584.

did go: and there had a great Lent dinner of fish, and little flesh. There dined with us Mr. Slingsby, master of the Mint, who showed us all the new pieces (both gold and silver), examp'es of them all that were made for the King by Blondeau's way, and compared them with those made for Oliver. The pictures of the latter were made by Symons (Simon) and of the King by one Rotyr, a German I think, that dined with us also. He (Slingsby) extols those of Rotyr above the others, and indeed I think they are the better, because the sweeter of the two."[1]

Pepys also visited him in the Tower on 26th March, 1666, and writes:

"My Lord Brouncker and I to the Tower, to see the famous engraver Roetier, to get him to grave a seal for the office (Admiralty). And did see some of the finest pieces of work, in embossed work, that ever I did see in my life for fineness and smallness of the images thereon, and I will carry my wife thither to show them to her. Here I also did see bars of gold melting, which was a fine sight."

In the next year, on 25th February, 1666-7, Pepys again writes:

"At my goldsmith's did observe the King's new medall, where in little there is Mrs. Stewart's face, as well done as ever I saw anything in my whole life, I think; and a pretty thing it is, that he should choose her face to represent Britannia by."

It is said that John Roettier was in love with the fair Mrs. Stewart, Duchess of Richmond, and represented her likeness under the form of Britannia, on the reverse of a large medal with the King's head."[2] This figure, with some variations, is still preserved, and handed down to us on the reverse of the copper coinage of the present day.[3]

---

[1] They were evidently comparing the coins of Roettier with those of Simon. The head of the King on Simon's "petition crown" is certainly somewhat hard and harsh.

[2] Walpole's 'Anecdotes.' This medal, which is called "the Great Britannia," has the King's head on the obverse, and on the reverse is a figure of Britannia seated on the sea-shore, holding a shield and a sloping spear. Ships are in the distance, and above is the sun in the meridian: below is the word "Britannia," and the legend is "Favente Deo"; around the rim is the inscription "Carolus secundus pacis et imperii restitutor augustus;" this medal having been struck in commemoration of the peace of Breda. Walpole had in his description of the "Britannia" confused together two totally different medals.

[3] There is also a one-sided medal with a bust of the Duchess on a much larger scale, which was evidently the first study for her portrait. The die of this medal was purchased by the Mint authorities from Roettier's representatives after his death. A fine specimen is in the British Museum.

A warrant was issued on 6th March, 1666-7, directing Roettier to make a new great seal, which was to cost 246*l*. 3*s*. 2*d*., and was to replace the great seal which Simon had made for the King in 1662.

In 1669 the three brothers Roettier were collectively appointed engravers to the Mint, with a yearly allowance of 450*l*.,[1] and under the guidance of John Roettier, who was the eldest, they continued to conduct the coinage of the country for some years; but John had two sons, Norbert and James,[2] who were much employed by their father; their uncles therefore became jealous of them and left England, James going over to Paris, and Philip Roettier settling in Flanders in the service of Spain.

We find John Evelyn visiting the Mint on 20th July, 1678:

"I went to the Tower to try a metal at the Assay Master's, which only proved sulphur; then saw Monsieur Roticre, that excellent graver belonging to the Mint, who emulates even the ancients, in both metal and stone; he is now moulding a horse for the King's statue, to be cast in silver of a yard high. I dined with Mr. Slingsby, Master of the Mint."

In spite of his great reputation, Roettier, however, appears not to have received very liberal treatment at the hands of the Government, and already, in 1684, he petitioned the Treasury to pay him 400*l*. for engraving "two broad seales;" 200*l*. was issued to him on account, but he then prayed for the payment of the remaining 200*l*., "being in great want and necessity to maintain his family, and put to hard difficulties and shiftes for procuring money, being a stranger here in England."

His appeal appears to have been unsuccessful if we may judge by the following letter, which he addressed to the Earl of Rochester:[3]

"MY LORD,

"Necessity forceth me againe to trouble your Lordship, begging your Lordship's order and directions for the £200 in full, of the £400

---

[1] Of which they could seldom obtain regular payment.
[2] James died soon after.
[3] Lawrence Hyde, Earl of Rochester, Lord High Treasurer from 1679 till 1684, and again from 1685 to 1687. He died in 1711.

for making the two great seales, before your Lordship's adjournment, which I heare will be speedily, otherwise we shall be ruined, being put to great straightes for monyes for maintaining my family, and paying the workemen att the Mint. This favour and good worke I hop your Lordship will doe, and me and mine shall be ever bound to pray for your Lordship.

"I am, your Lordship's most humble servant,

"27 Aug. 1684."[1]   "Jo: ROETTIER.

"On the accession of James II. Roettier was confirmed in his appointment, and in April, 1685, he engraved the King's Coronation Medal. In 1687, Henry Slingsby, master and worker of the Mint, was for "non-fulfilment of his duty" compelled to resign his appointment, and being in difficulties, he offered his collection of twenty five of "Monsieur Roettier's medals with cases" for sale to Pepys.[2]

"SIR,   "11 Oct. 1687.

"You being my ancient friend and good acquaintance, I cannot doe less than offer to put into your hands a general collection of all the medals made by Roettiers, of which I had an opportunity to chuse the best struck off, and I am sure so full a collection no man in England has beside myself, which you shall have at the same rate I paid. When Roettier happens to die, they may be worth five or ten pounds more, and yet are not to be had, many of the stamps being broke and spoiled. I have sent you the list to peruse, which if you approve of, I shall much rejoice at; if not, pray return the list, for I have several friends will be glad to have them of,

"Sir, your very affectionate friend and humble servant,

"H. SLINGSBY.

"If you desire any off the King and Queen's coronation medals I have six of them I can spare, at six shillings each."[3]

Roettier remained undisturbed in his house within the Tower after the accession of King William, and until January, 1696-7, when suspicions arose that he was carrying on a treasonable correspondence with the Jacobite party abroad, and a report was spread that even King James was in England and concealed in Roettier's house. Some dies were

---

[1] 'Numismatic Chronicle,' vol. ii. p. 198, and vol. iii. p. 173.
[2] A list of them with the prices affixed is given by Walpole.
[3] 'Numismatic Chronicle,' 1840-1, p. 175.

stated to be missing from the Mint, and it was alleged that he had struck coins with the stamp and for the service of King James. A committee of the House of Commons was therefore appointed to enquire into the conduct of Roettier, and they reported that "it is too great a trust and may be of dangerous consequence for the said Roettier to have the custody of the dies, he being a Roman Catholic and keeping an Irish Papist in his house, and having the custody of the said dies, it lies in his power to let them out when he pleases, or to coin false money in the Tower. That the Lord Lucas has complained that the Tower is not safe while so many Papists are entertained in Roettier's house."

"And that it appears that the said Roettier is a very dangerous person; and that the Master of the Mint, the Warden of the Mint, and the Engraver, all declared the coinage might be carried on without the assistance of Roettier. And that the Committee had directed the House should be moved, that they would give directions for securing the dies and punchions in the Tower. Ordered: that all the punchions, dies, presses, and other things belonging to His Majesty's Mint, in the hands of Mr. Roettier in the Tower, be immediately seized by the officers of the Mint," &c.

"The Committee do observe that old Roettier is still continued in the graver's house in the Tower, though he will not, nor did ever, own the King, or do any one thing as a graver since the Revolution;[1] and that the Governor of the Tower hath declared to some members of this Committee that he is a dangerous person to be in the Tower, and that he would remove him if he could: Resolved that it is the opinion of this Committee that no officer of the Mint ought to have or enjoy any place in the same for life."[2]

In consequence of the report of this Committee, and the unfavourable opinion of Roettier which the Constable of the

---

[1] His son James executed a large medal with a portrait of William III., which was to be worn with a collar, which collar and medal, valued then at 1000*l.*, were presented by the King to the Mayor of Dublin to replace that which had been lost in the war between James II. and William III.

[2] 'Numismatic Chronicle,' 1841-2, pp. 183-4.

Tower entertained, the following letter was addressed to Lord Lucas by the Secretary of State:—

"MY LORD, "Whitehall, 28 March, 1696.

"There being an information that one of the Rotiers, engravers in the Tower, was acquainted with some of the persons accused of having conspired the murther and assassination of the King, and it being suspected that some of them may be concealed in their lodgings in the Tower, his Majesty commands me to signify his pleasure to y^r Lordship that you forthwith cause a search to bee made in the lodgings of the said Rotier for any suspected persons, and if such bee found that they bee secured.

"I am, my Lord, your L^{d}ships most humble servant,

"Ld Lucas. "SHREWSBURY."[1]

Roettier was regarded with suspicion, as this letter, written by Sir Isaac Newton, then Master of the Mint, will show.

"SIR, "Mint Office, Oct. 22, 1698.

"Pray let Mr. James Roettiers have the use of the great Crown Press in the long Press room for coyning of Medalls, and let some person whom you can confide in, attend to see that Mr. Roettiers make no other use of the said press or press room there for coyning of Medalls.

"To Mr. John Braint, "Is: NEWTON.
"Provost of the Moniers."

No actual coercive measures appear to have been enforced against him, but it is said that Lord Lucas by placing a guard about his house, rendered Roettier so uneasy that he left the Tower, and went to reside in Red Lion Square: this removal is believed to have been but of short duration, as he was again residing in the Tower in 1703, when Sir Godfrey Kneller visited him there by desire of Queen Anne, and gave him a commission to engrave a medal of the Queen. He however died before it was finished.

The burial register records his death, and his burial in the chapel on the 17th June, 1703. Several members of his family were also buried in the chapel.

[1] Tower Records.

EDWARD, LORD GRIFFIN.

Born ——. Died a prisoner in the Tower, 15th Nov., 1710.

On the 3rd December, 1688, Edward Griffin of Braybrooke Castle, Northamptonshire, was created Baron Griffin by King James II.: and soon after the accession of William III. he was suspected of intriguing against the new government, and favouring the cause of the exiled King.

He had never taken his seat in the House of Lords, or subscribed the roll of Peers, and a summons desiring him to attend for that purpose had more than once been sent to him. Moreover, there appeared to be such undoubted proofs of his disaffection, that in 1689, the House of Lords forwarded an address to the King, requesting "His Majesty to summon Lord Griffin, by his royal proclamation, at such a day as His Majesty should appoint, either to their house (if then actually sitting), or to one of the Secretaries of State," and Lord Griffin being accordingly summoned, surrendered himself to the Lord Nottingham. On the 19th October, he made his appearance before the House of Lords, when the Speaker told him, "that he knew what to do before his sitting in that house." Whereupon his Lordship "desired time to consider of taking the oaths, he not being prepared for it: which was readily granted."

"But immediately after this, a pacquet was intercepted, which plainly discovered how little he was inclined to own the present government. This discovery happened in the following manner. His Lordship having caused a large pewter bottle to be made, with a double bottom, ordered his cook, at an unseasonable hour of the night, to get the false bottom solder'd. The pewterer finding a pacquet between the two bottoms of the bottle, began to suspect something; and the cook not giving a satisfactory answer about its contents, the pewterer made bold to open it. The superscription of several letters directed to King James, the Duke of Berwick, and others, justified the pewterer's suspicion, who immediately seized the Lord Griffin's cook, and carried him to one of the

Secretaries of State, but he being gone to bed, and his servants refusing to admit the pewterer to their master's presence, the Lord Griffin, who by this time began to apprehend what had befallen his messenger, took this opportunity to make his escape.[1] Besides the letters, there was found an account of some private resolutions of the Council, and an exact list of all the land and sea forces of England. Whereupon Lord Griffin's house and papers were searched, his Lady committed to the Tower, several suspected persons arrested, and the customs house officers ordered to stop all unknown persons, that offered to cross the seas without passes. Lord Griffin having already absconded himself some few days, and finding it difficult to go out of the kingdom, surrendered himself to the Earl of Shrewsbury (Secretary of State), who having examined him, committed him to the custody of a messenger, from whence he was sent to the Tower."[2]

The warrant for his committal, dated 2nd November, 1689, and addressed to Lord Lucas, the "Chief Governor of the Tower," states that Edward, Lord Griffin "is sent unto you for holding correspondencyes with their Majesty's enemyes, and contriving and carrying on treasonable and seditious practices against their Majestys and ye government."[3]

As soon as his committal to the Tower was announced, the House of Commons appointed a committee " to enquire how the Lord Griffin came to know a resolution which the King had communicated to four persons only:" and the Lords addressed His Majesty to let him understand that the said Lord being one of their number, they were consequently his proper judges. The King having left the cognizance of this affair to the Peers, they began to examine the papers intercepted in the pewter bottle, which were the only evidence against the Lord Griffin: and because, some days before, it had been resolved that "Colonel Algernon Sidney was unjustly condemned, nothing but writings

[1] Burnet, vol. iv. p. 67.
[2] Kennet's 'Hist. of England,' vol. ii. p. 545. Oldmixon, p. 32.
[3] Tower Records.

found in his closet having been produced against him," the Earl of Rochester argued from a parity of reason, in favour of the Lord Griffin.[1] He was also brought to be examined at the bar of the House of Lords on the following Monday, and again on the 12th November, and on the latter day was recommitted to the Tower for "contriving and carrying on treasonable practices."

On the 5th December the following order was made by the House of Lords.

"Dies Jovis, 5 Decemb: 1689.

"Upon reading the peticion of Edward Lord Griffin, now prisoner in the Tower, showing that he is truely sensible and sorry for the misfortune of living under the displeasure of this house, and that his confinement is very prejudiciall to his health, and praying that he may be bayled: It is thereupon ordered by the Lords spirituall and temporall in Parliament assembled, that the Chiefe Governour of their Maties Tower of London, or his Deputy, doe bring the said Edward Lord Griffin to the barr of this house to-morrow, at ten of the clocke in the forenoone, in order to his being bayled. And that the Lord Griffin doe bring two persons with him to be bound in five thousand pounds each, and himselfe in ten thousand pounds, for his appearance at such time as the house shall think fitt to appoint.

"Jo: Browne,
"Cler: Parliamtar:
" To the
" R^t Honble Lord Lucas."

He was then released, but in the following year he was again arrested upon suspicion of treasonable conduct, and by warrant of the Privy Council, dated 24th June, 1690, committed to the Tower, upon a charge of high treason.

He had, however, several influential friends, and they had already by their efforts interceded on his behalf, so that "he should be gently dealt with."[2] Accordingly, on the 15th August, 1690, when King William was absent in Holland, a resolution was passed by the Privy Council, the Queen presiding, that Lord Griffin, with several other prisoners, should be admitted to bail. In the Tower records is the order of Sir John Holt, Chief Justice,[3] desiring the Constable

---

[1] Kennett, vol. iii. p. 545.
[2] Burnet, vol. iv. p. 67.
[3] Sir J. Holt was Lord Chief Justice of the King's Bench from April 1689 until 1709.

of the Tower to bring Lord Griffin to "my chamber at Sergeants' Inn, in Chancery Lane, in order to be bayled." Soon afterwards Lord Griffin was set at liberty.

We hear nothing more of him until May, 1692, when Jacobite intrigues becoming too prevalent, a special proclamation was issued ordering all Papists to depart from London and Westminster, and that both Houses of Parliament should meet on the 24th May. "Warrants were expedited for apprehending divers disaffected persons: and they withdrawing themselves from their respective places of abode, another proclamation was published for discovering them and bringing them to justice. Lord Griffin, and several others, however, found means to elude the search, and escaped to France."[1] There he remained at the Jacobite Court until 1708, when a French expedition for Scotland was fitted out at Dunkirk, consisting of five ships of the line, and twenty frigates, under the command of Admiral Forbin. The old chevalier James Francis Edward, was on board one ship, and Lord Griffin on board another. This expedition set sail on the 13th March, but having experienced much bad weather, and being pursued by the British squadron, under Sir George Byng, the vessels put back to Dunkirk. Sir George Byng writes, "the enemy worked their ships in a handsome manner to cut some of our ships off from the rest of the fleet; but in the darkness of the night they all got out of sight, except the *Salisbury*, which falling in amongst our headmost ships, the *Leopard* entered men on board her."[2] One ship (the *Salisbury*) was, therefore, captured, and Lord Griffin being found on board of it, he was taken prisoner, and again in his old age lodged in the Tower on the 19th April, by warrant from the Earl of Sunderland,[3] addressed to Major General William Cadogan, the Lieutenant of the Tower.[4]

"Shortly afterwards, on the 15th May, he was brought to

---

[1] Smollett, vol. i. p. 155.
[2] Oldmixon, p. 404.
[3] Charles, third Earl of Sunderland, born 1674, appointed Secretary of State in 1707, Lord Lieutenant of Ireland and subsequently Lord Privy Seal in 1714. In 1718 he became Prime Minister. He died in 1722.
[4] Tower Records.

the King's Bench, and the whole record of the indictment and outlawry was read to him, and he was demanded if he had aught to say why execution should not be done; and he not making any material objection, the Court ordered execution to be done, but Sir James Montague, Solicitor-General (there being then no Attorney-General), prayed that judgment, as in case of high treason, might be pronounced, or at least entered on the roll in the award of execution; but Powell and the Court held that the award of execution should be general, for the judgment in the outlawry implieth all the particulars, and no second judgment ought to be given."[1]

Judgment was therefore recorded, and on the 12th June, 1708, Queen Anne signed the warrant ordering his execution on Wednesday the 16th; but on the 15th the sheriffs received an order respiting him until the 30th, "certaine causes and considerations us especially thereunto moving," and further respite of his sentence was again granted, probably in great measure on account of his infirm health. On the 2nd May, in the following year, Colonel Farewell, the Lieutenant, is desired, in consequence of Lord Griffin's representation, to let him have any other apartment " that he should think more for his conveniency, and to allow him to walk abroad within the Tower, for the benefit of the air, at convenient hours, and in the company of the gentleman porter or gentleman gaoler."

Again, on the 10th May, "further indulgence is granted that he might walk out with one or two of the warders if the gentleman gaoler was engaged, provided this enlarging of the liberty given him is consistent with the care that ought to be taken of his being safely kept."[2]

His health, however, gradually failed, and he died on the 10th November, 1710, when the following letter was addressed by the Secretary of State to the Lieutenant of the Tower.

"SIR, "Whitehall, 10 Nov: 1710.

"The Lord Griffin being dead, you are to give notice to the Coroner of the Tower, that he do forthwith impannell a jury to inquire on view

[1] Howell's 'State Trials.'   [2] Tower Records.

of the body, whether my Lord died a natural death, or by any violence, and such inquisition being taken, the body may be delivered to his relations if they desire it, otherwise it is to be buried in the Tower Church.

"I am,

(Signed) "QUEENSBERRY.[1]

"Major D'Oyly."

His body was not claimed by his relatives, but was buried in the chapel, as appears by the entry in the register, "buried on 15 Nov^r."

WILLIAM, MARQUIS OF TULLIBARDINE.

Born 1689. Died a prisoner in the Tower, 9th July, 1746.

William, Marquis of Tullibardine, was the second son of John, second Marquis and first Duke of Athol, and his elder brother, John, having been killed at the battle of Malplaquet (31st August, 1709), he then became Marquis of Tullibardine.

He was one of the first that joined the Earl of Mar in the rebellion of August 1715, and was therefore by the Act 1 George I. st. 11, ch. 32, attainted of high treason. His father then went up to Court, and obtained from George I. an order that a bill should be brought into Parliament for vesting the honours, titles, and estates in Lord James Murray, the Duke's second surviving son; this Act (1 Geo. I. cap. 34, Private Acts) was duly passed, and in virtue of it, Lord James succeeded his father as Duke in 1724.

In the meantime William, Marquis of Tullibardine, who had fled to France upon his attainder, returned again to Scotland in 1719, with a handful of Spanish troops sent over by Cardinal Alberoni, and joined the insurgents in Kintail. After their defeat by General Wightman, at Glenshiel, on the 18th June, 1719, a proclamation was issued, dated 20th July, for the apprehension of William Murray, Marquis of

[1] William, first Earl of Queensberry, died 1711.

Tullibardine, the Earl Marischal,[1] and the Earl of Seaforth,[2] and a reward of 2000*l*. was offered for the capture of any one of them.[3]

The Marquis retreated in safety to the Isle of Lewis, and shortly after escaped to France, where he lived in exile for twenty-six years.[4]

He resided chiefly at Puteaux, near Paris, and before the year 1745 his health had begun to fail: writing to the old Chevalier he says, "These seven or eight years have sufficiently shown me how unfit I am for meddling with the deep concerns of state."[5]

He was the chief in rank of the seven attendants who sailed from Belleisle on the 2nd July, 1745, with Prince Charles Edward on board the *Doutelle*, and he landed with the Prince at Borodale on the 25th July.

He unfurled the standard (a banner of red silk with a white space in the middle), at Glenfinnan on the 19th August, and being supported by a man on each side, in consequence of the infirm condition of his health, he held the staff, whilst the manifesto, dated 23rd December, 1743, and the commission of Regency, dated Paris, 16th May, 1745, were read.[6]

"The Marquis now took possession of the family estates, raised the followers of his house, and assumed the title of Duke of Atholl, by virtue of a patent[7] which he had received some years before from the old Chevalier."[8]

---

[1] George Keith, last of the Earls Marischal, born 1693. He was attainted for his share in the insurrection in 1715, but escaped to Spain: he returned to Scotland in 1719, and after the defeat at Glenshiel again fled to Spain. He then, with his brother, James Keith, entered the Prussian service, and was sent on missions to France, Spain, &c. He was subsequently appointed Governor of Neuchatel, and there he became the friend of Rousseau. He died at Potsdam in 1778.

[2] Kenneth, fifth Earl of Seaforth: he escaped to Spain, and died in 1740.

[3] Oldmixon, p. 685.

[4] Douglas's 'Peerage,' vol. ii. pp. 196–7.

[5] 'Athol Correspondence,' printed for the Abbotsford Club, Appendix, p. 229.

[6] Chambers's 'History of Rebellion of 1745–6,' p. 42.

[7] It is doubtful whether there was any such patent; the Jacobites denied the validity of his attainder, and considered that upon the death of his father he had succeeded to the title. This patent may refer to the grant to him by the old Chevalier of the title of Duke of Rannoch. On only two papers does the signature of "Atholl" occur in the series of his papers, printed for the Abbotsford Club. See Hist. MSS. Commission, 4th Report, p. 528.

[8] Collins's 'Peerage,' vol. vii. p. 104.

He was appointed Commander-in-Chief of the Jacobite forces in Scotland when Prince Charles Edward advanced into England in September, 1745, after the battle of Preston Pans, and the following is a copy of his commission:

"CHARLES, *Prince of Wales, and Regent of Scotland, England, France and Ireland, and the dominions thereunto belonging, to our right trusty and well beloved* WILLIAM, *Duke of Atholl.*

"WE reposeing especial trust and confidence in your loyalty, courage, and good conduct, do hereby constitute and appoint you, in terms of your former commission from his Majesty, to act as Commander-in-chief of the King's forces, (we finding it necessary to remain in the southern portion of the kingdom,) benorth Forth, so long as we shall continue on this side, and hereby authorise you to do whatever you shall think most condusive to his Majesty's interest, and requiring all his Majesty's officers to obey you.

"Given in our camp att Pinkey, this 22^d of Septr 1745."[1]

After the decisive battle of Culloden on 16th April, 1746, where he held the rank of Lieutenant-General, Lord Tullibardine fled to the westward, intending to reach the Isle of Mull, but he became too ill to travel far on horseback, although a saddle was arranged for him in which he could sit sideways, as in a chair; and at length, on the 27th of April, he was compelled to surrender himself to Mr. Buchanan of Drumakill, who was a connection of his family. But Buchanan was a devoted loyalist, and having at once sent word to Dumbarton,[2] some soldiers arrived on the following day, and Tullibardine was committed to Dumbarton Castle; from thence he was conveyed to Edinburgh, where he remained until the 13th May, when he was sent to Leith and put on board the *Eltham* man of war, but he did not reach London until the third week in June,[3] the ship

---

[1] 'Athol Correspondence.'

[2] Years afterwards it was remembered in the district how the marquis's French servants were seen sitting "greeting (Anglicè, crying) and roaring like women" at the gate of Drumakill after their master had been carried off as a prisoner. In consequence of this betrayal Buchanan was shunned by his neighbours, his family gradually sunk, and is said to have become extinct.

[3] "Saturday, 20th June, 1746. Several ships with rebel prisoners on board came up the river: the Marquis of Tullibardine, Mr. Murray, and another person were committed to the Tower." 'Gentleman's Magazine,' 1746, p. 326. Walpole writes to Sir H. Mann 20th June, 1746, "Old Marquis Tullibardine with another set of rebels is come."

having gone elsewhere to fetch other prisoners. On his arrival he was committed to the Tower, by warrant dated 17th June, 1746, and signed by the Duke of Newcastle.[1]

He was in a very indifferent condition of health when he arrived, and on the 24th June permission is given to Lord Cornwallis, the Constable of the Tower, "to allow Dr. Willmott to attend the person formerly called Marquess of Tullibardine, a prisoner in your custody, from time to time as he shall desire during his indisposition; provided the same to be in the presence of you or the Lieutenant."[2]

The following letters, copied from the originals in the possession of the Duke of Athol, have been kindly furnished me by his Grace; they will be read with much interest:—

"My Lord,   "Tower of London, June the 26, 1746.

"I think it my Duty to acquaint your Grace, that the Marquis of Tullibarden, who came very sick to us last Friday, continues so ill that it is thought he is in great danger of sinking under it; he has been visited by the King's Physician, Doctor Willmot, and by Doctor Harvey, to whom I refer your Grace for the further account of his distemper, and beg leave to assure you that we do all here that is in our power, for his support and recovery, and that I am with the greatest respect,

"Your Grace's most obedient and most humble servant,
"A. WILLIAMSON.

"P.S.—I had heard your Grace was not in town, or you should have heard sooner from me.
"To His Grace of Athol."

"My Lord,   "July y⁰ 7th, 1746.

"General Williamson sends me word that L⁴ Tullibardine is extremely ill in y⁰ Tower, and y⁰ Phisicians think him in great danger, unless his Distemper should soon take a more favourable turn. The General tells me no proper care is wanting, which I have recommended him to be assiduous in.

"I am, with great respect, my Lord,
"Your Grace's most obedient and most humble servant,
"CORNWALLIS."

---

[1] Tower Records.   [2] Ibid.

"Tower of London, July the 9th, 1746.
"Ten a'clock in the morning.

"MY LORD DUKE,

"Just now your Brother, the Marquis of Tullibarden expired. I assure your Grace, no care, pains, or trouble was wanting for his recovery. I wait your Grace's orders, how further to act for him.

"I am, your Grace's most respectful and obedient serv',

"A. WILLIAMSON.

"To His Grace the Duke of Athol,
"In Savel Row."

The Duke replied as follows to General Williamson's letter:

"SIR,

"I am very much obliged to you for the civilities which you have shewed upon this occasion, of which I shall ever retain a very grateful sense.

"As to what now remains to be done, I shall give you as little further trouble as I can; and as I find that it is thought that the Chappel in the Tower will be the properest place for the burial, to which my Lord Cornwallis consents, I have sent the Bearer, who will follow your directions, to give the necessary orders for that purpose."

* * * * * *

The Duke inquired whether he might be permitted to wear mourning for his brother, and he received the King's permission in a letter dated "Kensington, 10 July, 1746."

The Marquis of Tullibardine died in the 58th year of his age, and was privately buried in the chapel of the Tower.

"In his last moments he declared, that although he had been as much as any man attached to the Pretender, if he might now advise his countrymen, it should be never more to enter into rebellious measures, for after having failed in their late attempt they might be sure never to succeed in any other." [1]

In the burial register his interment is thus recorded: "William Murray, Esq., alias Marquis of Tullibardine, Prisoner in ye Tower, on 11th July." No record or means of identifying the spot where he was buried has been preserved.

[1] Douglas's 'Peerage,' vol. i. p. 150. See also 'Athol Correspondence,' printed for the Abbotsford Club: introductory notice.

WILLIAM, EARL OF KILMARNOCK.

Born 1704. Beheaded on Tower Hill, 18th Aug. 1746.

ARTHUR, LORD BALMERINO.

Born 1688. Beheaded on Tower Hill, 18th Aug. 1746.

William, the fourth Earl of Kilmarnock, succeeded to his father's title in 1717.

On the 14th and 15th September, 1745, he entertained Prince Charles Edward at Callender House, and, saluting him as his sovereign, assured him of his earnest devotion to the Jacobite cause. At the battle of Culloden he was taken prisoner whilst fighting at the head of his regiment.[1] Arthur, Lord Balmerino, who had also been present at the battle, had afterwards with 800 of his followers, surrendered to the Grants, they then delivered him up as a prisoner to the Duke of Cumberland, and these two Lords, together with Lord Cromarty, were then sent by sea to London.[2] On their arrival they were committed to the Tower "for high treason and levying war against His Majesty," by warrant dated the 27th May, 1746, signed by Thomas Holles, Duke of Newcastle, and addressed to Lord Cornwallis, the Constable of the Tower.

Permission is given on the 13th of June to Andrew Stone, secretary to the Duke of Newcastle, to visit Lord Kilmarnock and "to be alone with him," and, on the 30th June, Mr. John Sharpe, Solicitor to the Treasury, and Mr. Richard Wright, his clerk, are authorized to have "free access to the three prisoners."

Arrangements were then made for their trial. Monday, 23rd June, the grand jury found a true bill against them, and on the 27th June the Committee of the House of Lords, which had been appointed to search for precedents for the trial of criminal peers, made their report, when it was

---

[1] It is said that, being half blinded with the smoke, in the confusion of the fight, he mistook a party of English dragoons for Fitzjames' horse, and was thus made prisoner.

[2] In the 'London Gazette' for 17th May, 1746, it is announced that the Earls of Cromartie and Kilmarnock, and Lord Balmerino, were to set out on the 9th from Inverness for London.

ordered that an address be presented to His Majesty, desiring him to appoint a Lord High Steward for the trials; that Westminster Hall be prepared for the ceremony, and that the Lord Chancellor should summon all the Peers to attend in their robes.

On the 4th July permission is given that George Rose and John Maule may visit the Lords Kilmarnock and Balmerino "for one time only, and to have the use of ink and paper for drawing up petitions, but not for writing letters."[1]

The Constable of the Tower was ordered on the 23rd July by the House of Lords to produce his prisoners at Westminster Hall on the following Monday, when it was arranged that the trial should commence.

"On the 28th July at eight in the morning, the judges in their robes, with Garter King-of-Arms, the Usher of the Black Rod, and the Sergeant-at-Arms, waited on the Lord High Steward[2] at his house in Ormond Street;[3] Garter in his coat of the King's arms, Black Rod having the white staff, and the Sergeant-at-Arms his mace: the three last waited in an apartment while the judges went to the Lord High Steward to pay their compliments to his Grace. After a short stay, his Grace came to his coach in the following order:—

"His Grace's twenty gentlemen, two and two, uncovered. His Serjeant-at-Arms and Seal-bearer, both uncovered; one with his mace, and the other with the purse. The Black Rod, with the Lord High Steward's staff, and Garter King-of-Arms on his right hand, in his coat of arms, both uncovered.

"His Grace, the Lord High Steward, in his rich gown, his train bore, followed by the chief justices and judges.

"His Grace seated himself on the hinder seat of the coach singly, Garter and the Seal-bearer on the other seat over against his Grace, uncovered, the Black Rod in the right

---

[1] Tower Records.
[2] Philip Yorke, Lord Hardwicke, born 1690. Was appointed Lord Chancellor in 1766, which office he held from February 1737 to November 1756.
[3] Powis House, on the north side of the street, where Powis Place now stands. It was taken down in 1777. There is a good engraving of it by T. Bowles, 1714.

hand side boot with his Grace's white staff, and his Grace's Serjeant-at-Arms in the left boot with his mace; his Grace's gentlemen in the five leading coaches, and the judges followed his Grace in their own coaches.

"His Grace thus attended passed through Red Lion Square, across Holborn, down Little and Great Queen Street, Long Acre, St. Martin's Lane, and King Street, to the Old Palace Yard, the soldiers resting their muskets and the drums beating as to the Royal family, and so they went up the stairs to the House of Peers, through the Painted Chamber.

"The Peers in their robes, and the mace deposited upon the uppermost woolsack, his Grace passed on to the Lord Chancellor's room; the staff was not brought within the House of Peers.

"His Grace having stayed there a while, came into the House again, and prayers began. Then the Peers were called over, Garter or his deputy being allowed to come to the Clerks' table, to make a list at the same time of the Peers present; which done, and the Black Rod being sent to see that the Court in Westminster Hall, and the passages to it, were clear, and giving an account to the House that they were so, they proceeded towards Westminster Hall thus: His Grace the Lord High Steward's Gentlemen attendants two and two; four Clerks of the House two and two. The two Clerks of the Crown bearing the commission of the Lord High Steward. Masters in Chancery two and two; Attorney-General; judges: peers' eldest sons: peers minors. Four Sergeants-at-Arms, with their maces, two and two. The Yeoman Usher of the House of Peers. The Peers according to their degrees and precedency, two and two, the youngest barons first, all covered. Four Serjeants-at-Arms more, with their maces, two and two. His Grace's Seal-bearer and Serjeant-at-Arms. The Black Rod and Garter. The Lord High Steward alone, covered, his train borne.

"The Lords being seated on their benches, and the judges and masters in Chancery below on their seats, the Lord High Steward, making a reverence to the State, and saluting the Peers, seated himself on the woolsacks as Speaker of the House of Lords.

"The two clerks of the Crown being ready at the clerks' table, and the Clerk of the Crown in Chancery, having the King's commission to his Grace in his hand, both made three reverences to him, and at the third, coming before the woolsack, kneeled down, and the Clerk of the Crown in Chancery, on his knee, presents the commission to his Grace, who delivers it to the Clerk of the Crown in the King's Bench, and they, making three reverences, returned to the clerks' table; the Clerk of the Crown in the King's Bench opened the commission and read it, having first directed his Grace's Serjeant-at-Arms to make proclamation for silence, which he did with his mace upon his shoulder.

"While the commission was reading his Grace and the Lords stood up, all uncovered; after which his Grace, making obeysance, reseated himself, and then Garter and the Black Rod, with three reverences, jointly presented the white staff on their knees to his Grace; and, being fully invested in his office, he, with the white staff in his hand, removed from the woolsack to the chair placed for him, on an ascent before the throne, and sat down."[1]

In the meantime, "at about 8 o'clock in the morning, the three rebel Lords, prisoners in the Tower, were carried from thence in three coaches, the Earl of Kilmarnock, with Governor Williamson and another gentleman captain of the guard, in the first: the Earl of Cromartie attended by Captain Marshall, in the second; and Lord Balmerino, attended by Mr. Fowler, gentleman gaoler, who had the axe covered by him, in the third, under a strong guard of foot soldiers to Westminster Hall, where the Lord High Steward and the Peers, having taken their seats, proclamation was made for the Lieutenant of the Tower of London to return the precept to him directed, with the bodies of the prisoners: which done, the gentleman gaoler of the Tower brought his prisoners to the bar: and the proclamation being made for the King's evidence to come forth, the King's Counsel, by his Grace's direction, opened the indictment; then his Grace moved the House, that he might advance forwards for the better hearing of the evidence, which was done."[2]

[1] 'Gentleman's Magazine,' 1746, pp. 338-9. [2] Ibid. p. 382.

EARL OF KILMARNOCK AND LORD BALMERINO. 305

An interesting account of the scene of the trial is to be found in the following letter addressed by Horace Walpole to Sir H. Mann.

"Arlington Street, 1 Aug. 1746.

"I am this moment come from the conclusion of the greatest and most melancholy scene I ever yet saw! You will easily guess it was the trials of the rebel Lords. As it was the most interesting sight, it was the most solemn and fine; a coronation is a puppet show, and all the splendour of it idle: but this sight at once feasted one's eyes and engaged all one's passions. It began last Monday: three parts of Westminster Hall were enclosed with galleries and hung with scarlet; and the whole ceremony was conducted with the most awful solemnity and decency, except in the one point of leaving the prisoners at the bar, amidst the idle curiosity of some crowd, and even with the witnesses who had sworn against them, while the Lords adjourned to their own house to consult.

"No part of the Royal Family was there, which was a proper regard to the unhappy men, who were become their victims. One hundred and thirty-nine Lords were present, and made a noble sight on their benches, frequent and full! The Chancellor was Lord High Steward; but, though a most comely personage with a fine voice, his behaviour was mean, curiously searching for occasion to bow to the Minister,[1] that is no Peer, and consequently applying to the other ministers in a manner for their orders: and not even ready at the ceremonial. To the prisoners he was peevish: and, instead of keeping up to the humane dignity of the law of England, whose character it is to point out favour to the criminal, he crossed them, and almost scolded at any offer they made towards defence.

"Lord Kilmarnock is past forty, but looks younger. He is tall and slender, with an extreme fine person: his behaviour a most just mixture between dignity and submission: if in anything to be reprehended, a little affected, and his hair too exactly dressed for a man in his situation: but when I say this, it is not to find fault with him, but to show how little fault there was to be found.

"For Lord Balmerino, he is the most natural brave old fellow I ever saw; the highest intrepidity, even to indifference. At the bar he behaved like a soldier and a man: in the intervals of form, with carelessness and humour. He pressed extremely to have his wife, his pretty Peggy,[2] with him in the Tower."[3]

---

[1] Henry Pelham.
[2] Margaret, daughter of Captain Chalmers.
[3] Permission is granted to Lady Balmerino to see her husband on 4th July, and again on 18th July, and on subsequent occasions.—Tower Records.

x

"When they were to be brought from the Tower in separate coaches, there was some dispute in which the axe must go, old Balmerino cried, 'Come, come, put it with me.' At the bar he plays with his fingers upon the axe, while he talks to the gentleman gaoler; and one day somebody coming up to listen, he took the blade and held it like a fan between their faces.[1]

"During the trial a little boy was near him, but not tall enough to see; he made room for the child and placed him near himself.

"When the trial began, the two Earls (Kilmarnock and Cromartie) pleaded guilty: Balmerino not guilty,[2] saying he could prove his not being at the taking of the castle of Carlisle, as was laid in the indictment. Then the King's Counsel opened, and Sergeant Skinner pronounced the most absurd speech imaginable.

"Then some witnesses were examined; whom afterwards the old hero shook cordially by the hand. The Lords withdrew to their house, and returning, demanded of the judges whether, one point not being proved, though all the rest were, the indictment was false? to which they unanimously answered in the negative. Then the Lord Steward asked the Peers severally whether Lord Balmerino was guilty, all said, 'Guilty upon honour,'[3] and then adjourned, the prisoner having begged pardon for giving them so much trouble."

* * * *

"On Wednesday the prisoners were again brought to Westminster Hall, at about 11 o'clock, to receive sentence: and being asked what they had to say, Lord Kilmarnock, with a fine voice, read a very fine speech, confessing the extent of his crime, but offering his principles as some alleviation."[4]

They were remanded back to the Tower, until Friday, when sentence was pronounced by the Lord High Steward in "a speech, which," says

Processional Axe.

---

[1] "On getting into the coach, he said to the gaoler, 'Take care or you will break my shins with this damned axe.'"—Walpole to G. Montagu, p. 31. This axe is kept in the Tower in charge of the Resident Governor.

[2] Balmerino said, that one of his reasons for pleading "not guilty," was that so many ladies might not be disappointed of their show.

[3] When Lady Townshend heard her husband vote, she said, "I always knew my Lord was guilty, but I never thought he would own it *upon his honour*." Ethelreda Harrison, wife of Charles, 3rd Viscount Townshend, mother of the Rt. Hon. Charles Townshend, the celebrated wit.

[4] 'Walpole to Mann,' vol. ii. pp. 147-152.

Walpole, "was very long and very poor, with only one or two good passages."[1]

The execution of the two Lords was fixed to take place at noon on the 18th August. Rev. James Foster, a friend of Kilmarnock, announced the fact to him, and General Williamson informed Lord Balmerino of his approaching death.

It was whilst Lady Balmerino was seated at dinner with her husband in the Tower that Williamson stated that the warrant for his execution on the following Monday had been received. "Lady Balmerino being very much surprised, he desired her not to be concerned at it: 'If the King had given me mercy,' said he, 'I should have been glad of it, but since it is otherwise, I am very easy, for it is what I have expected, and therefore it does not at all surprise me.'

"His Lady seemed very disconsolate, and rose immediately from table, on which he started from his chair, and said, 'Pray, my Lady, sit down, for it shall not spoil my dinner,'[2] upon which her Ladyship sat down again, but could eat nothing."[3]

Walpole again writes to Sir H. Mann:

"Windsor, 21st Aug. 1746.

"On the 18th August the execution took place.

"Just before they came out of the Tower, Lord Balmerino drank a bumper to King James's health. As the clock struck ten they came forth on foot, Lord Kilmarnock all in black, his hair unpowdered in a bag, supported by Forster, the great Presbyterian, and by Mr. Home, a young clergyman, his friend. Lord Balmerino followed, alone, in a

---

[1] The Earl of Cromartie received a pardon on the 9th August, his countess having petitioned every lord of the council on his behalf. She had also waylaid the King at Kensington Palace on his way to chapel, and, presenting a petition to him, fainted away at his feet.
The Earl of Kilmarnock petitioned the King, the Prince of Wales, and the Duke of Cumberland; but it is believed that the unfavourable opinion which the latter had received of Lord Kilmarnock's character rendered his appeal for mercy nugatory. The warrant for his execution was signed on the 11th August. He wrote a long letter of instructions to his factor, Robert Paterson, on the 16th, and also to his son, Lord Boyd, on the 17th August.

[2] "Lieutenant," he said, turning to General Williamson, "with your damned warrant you have spoiled my Lady's dinner."—'Memoirs of the Jacobites,' vol. iii. p. 452.

[3] 'Life of Lord Balmerino' (contemporary pamphlet).

blue coat turned up with red, his rebellious regimentals:[1] a flannel waistcoat and his shroud beneath: their hearses following.

"At the outer gate they were received by the sheriffs,[2] and conducted through deep lines of military,[3] to a house near the scaffold, where their friends were admitted to see them.[4]

"The room forwards had benches for spectators; in the second, Lord Kilmarnock was put, and in the third, backwards, Lord Balmerino.[5] All three chambers were hung with black.

"Here they parted: Balmerino embraced the other, and said, 'My Lord, I am heartily sorry to have your company in this expedition, I wish I could suffer for both.'

"He had scarce left him, before he desired again to see him, and then asked him, 'My Lord Kilmarnock, do you know anything of the resolution taken in our army the day before the battle of Culloden to put the English prisoners to death?' He replied, 'My Lord, I was not present; but since I came hither, I have had all the reason in the world to believe that there was such order taken, and I hear the Duke has the pocket-book with the order.' Balmerino answered, 'It was a lie, raised to excuse their barbarity to us.' Take notice that the Duke's charging this on Lord Kilmarnock (certainly on misinformation) decided this unhappy man's fate. The most now pretended is, that it would have come to Lord Kilmarnock's turn to have given the word for the slaughter, as lieutenant-general, with the patent for which he was immediately drawn into the rebellion, after having been staggered by his wife, her mother, his own poverty, and the defeat of Cope.

"He remained an hour and a half in the house, and shed tears.[6] At

---

[1] "He said he would go to the scaffold in the regimentals which he wore when first taken, and that he would have a woollen shirt next his skin, which would serve him instead of a shroud to be buried in. Being then asked why he would not have a new suit of black, he replied, "It would be thought very imprudent in a man to repair an old house when the lease of it was so near expiring, for the lease of mine will expire next Monday.""—Contemporary pamphlet.

[2] "The Lieutenant of the Tower then informed Mr. Sheriff Blatchford that he must not have the stage pulled down, for that he had received orders it must be kept standing."—Contemporary pamphlet.

[3] "A troop of Lifeguards, another of Horse Grenadiers, and 1000 foot soldiers."

[4] The accompanying illustration is taken from the engraving by Canot of the picture by G. Budd. "A true representation of Tower Hill as it appeared from a raised point of view on the north side, 18th August, 1746, when the Lords were beheaded."

[5] Balmerino was attended by the Rev. Cornelius Humphreys, Chaplain of the Tower, and another clergyman of the Church of England.

[6] Whilst in the house, he, and all those in the room with him, knelt down and joined in prayer delivered by Mr. Foster, after which, and taking a bit of bread and a glass of wine, he expressed a desire that Lord Balmerino might precede him to the scaffold; but on being told that this could not be, as he was named first in the warrant, he seemed satisfied, and saluting his friend, said, "he would make no speech, but desired the ministers to assist in his last moments."—Bayley, p. 647.

To face p. 308.

last he came to the scaffold, certainly much terrified, but with a resolution that prevented his behaving in the least meanly or unlike a gentleman.[1] He took no notice of the crowd, only to desire that the baize might be lifted up from the rails that the mob might see the spectacle. He stood and prayed some time with Foster, who wept over him, exhorted and encouraged him. He delivered a long speech to the sheriff, and with a noble manliness stuck to the recantation he made at his trial; declaring he wished that all who embarked in the same cause might meet the same fate. He then took off his bag, coat, and waistcoat with great composure, and after some trouble put on a napkin-cap, and then several times tried the block, the executioner, who was in white with a white apron, out of tenderness concealing the axe behind himself. At last the Earl knelt down with a visible unwillingness to depart, and after five minutes dropped his handkerchief, the signal, and his head was cut off at once and received in a scarlet cloth by four of the undertaker's men kneeling, who wrapped it up and put it into the coffin with the body, orders having been given not to expose the heads as used to be the custom."[2]

Whilst Lord Kilmarnock was on the scaffold, Balmerino remained in the house conversing with his friends, he twice refreshed himself with a bit of bread and a glass of wine, and desired the company to drink to him, "ain degrae ta haiven," but above all, he called frequently on God, and appeared both prepared and willing to die.

Upon the sheriffs coming into the apartment, his Lordship said, "I suppose Lord Kilmarnock is no more:" and having asked how the executioner performed his duty, upon receiving the account, added, "then it was well done, and now, gentlemen, I will detain you no longer, for I desire not to protract my life." He then saluted the company in a manner so cheerful as to draw tears from every eye, and hastened to the scaffold, which he mounted with so undaunted a step as surprised every spectator, walked round it, bowed to the people, and read the inscription upon his

---

[1] He was struck with the appalling objects around him, and the immense concourse of people, and turning to Mr. Home, he said, "Home, this is terrible:" but he said it without a change of voice or countenance.—See 'Tracts relating to the Pretender.'

[2] Walpole to Mann, vol. ii. pp. 160-2. A sum of 100*l.* had been placed in the hands of Mr. Fowler, the gentleman gaoler, for the use of Lord Kilmarnock whilst in the Tower. He signed a receipt for 25*l.* on the 11th July, and for 60*l.* on the 27th July. On the 17th August (which happened to be Sunday) William Boyd signs for 15*l.* "the remainder part of the 100*l.* above mentioned."—Tower Records.

coffin, said it was right, and then looking on the block with apparent pleasure, styled it his pillow of rest. He then took out a paper, and putting on his spectacles, read it to the few who were near him.[1] It contained a declaration of his unshaken adherence to the House of Stuart, and of his regret for ever having served in the armies of their enemies, Queen Anne and George I., which he considered the only faults of his life, tending to justify his present fate.[2]

His Lordship then called for the executioner, who, being introduced, was about to ask forgiveness, but he stopped him, and said, "Friend, you need not ask me forgiveness. The execution of your duty is commendable." Then presenting him with three guineas, he said, "Friend, I never have had much money, this is all I have, I wish it was more for your sake; I am sorry I can add nothing else but my coat and waistcoat," which he instantly took off and laid upon his coffin.

He then prepared himself for the block, and took his last farewell of his friends; and, having once more taken a view of the great number of spectators, said, "I am afraid there are some who may think my behaviour bold;" and turning to a gentleman near him added, "Remember, sir, what I tell you, it arises from a confidence in God, and a clear conscience."

Then taking the axe from the executioner, he felt its edge, and returned it to him again, at the same time shewing him where to strike the blow, and animating him to do it with resolution, "For in that, friend," said he, "will consist your mercy."[3]

Walpole writes:

"After the execution of Kilmarnock the scaffold was immediately new strewed with saw-dust, the block new covered, the executioner new dressed, and a new axe brought. Then came old Balmerino, treading with the air of a general. As soon as he mounted the scaffold he read the inscription on his coffin, as he did again afterwards: he then

---

[1] It has been said that when he had finished reading his speech, he breathed on his spectacles, and then wiping them put them carefully in their case again. To such an extent are we the creatures of habit.

[2] Chambers's 'Hist. of the Rebellion of 1745-6,' p. 387.

[3] Douglas's 'Peerage,' vol. i. p. 189.

surveyed the spectators, who were in amazing numbers, even upon masts of ships in the river; and, pulling out his spectacles, read a treasonable speech,[1] which he delivered to the sheriff, and said the young Pretender was so sweet a Prince that flesh and blood could not resist following him;[2] and, lying down to try the block, he said, 'If I had a thousand lives I would lay them all down here in the same cause.' He said, if he had not taken the sacrament the day before, he would have knocked down Williamson, the Lieutenant of the Tower, for his ill-usage of him. He took the axe and felt it, and asked the headsman how many blows he had given Lord Kilmarnock, and gave him three guineas. Two clergymen who attended him coming up, he said, 'No, gentlemen, I believe you have already done me all the service you can.' Then he went to the corner of the scaffold, and called very loud for the warder and gave him his periwig, which he took off and put on a night cap of Scotch plaid, and then pulled off his coat and waistcoat and lay down; but, being told he was on the wrong side, vaulted round immediately and gave the sign by tossing up his arm, as if he were giving the signal for battle.[3] He received three blows, but the first certainly took away all sensation. He was not a quarter of an hour on the scaffold, Lord Kilmarnock above half a one. Balmerino certainly died with the intrepidity of a hero, but with the insensibility of one too. As he walked from his prison to execution, seeing every window and top of house filled with spectators, he cried out, 'Look, look, how they are piled up like rotten oranges!'"[4]

The bodies of the two Lords were conveyed into the Tower, and "at their interment Mr. Humphreys,[5] curate of the Chapel, read the service, and on pronouncing that part of it where it says, 'Ashes to ashes, dust to dust,' two gentlemen, friends of the deceased, took up the spade, and performed that part of the office instead of the grave-diggers."[6]

---

[1] For the speech see 'Memoirs of the Jacobites,' vol. iii. p. 460. It is said, being too treasonable a publication, a garbled version was circulated, and afterwards printed in the State Trials.

[2] The Lieutenant of the Tower, on delivering the two prisoners to the sheriffs, had concluded his address with "God bless King George": to this Kilmarnock bowed respectfully. But Balmerino, with a stern voice, and yet a sterner look, replied, "God bless King James."—Bayley, p. 648.

[3] He laid his head on the block, and said, "O Lord! reward my friends, forgive mine enemies, bless and restore the King, preserve the prince and the Duke of York, and receive my soul."—'Tracts relating to the Pretender.' Bayley, p. 649.

[4] "My Lady Townshend, who fell in love with Lord Kilmarnock at his trial, will go nowhere to dinner for fear of meeting with a rebel-pie, she says every body is so bloody-minded, that they eat rebels."—Horace Walpole's 'Letters to Mann,' vol. ii. pp. 160-3.

[5] Rev. Cornelius Humphreys.

[6] Contemporary pamphlet, 'Life, of Lord Balmerino.'

312   ST. PETER AD VINCULA.

"Under the gallery, at the western end of the Chapel, were deposited the headless bodies of the penitent Earl of Kilmarnock, the undaunted Balmerino, and the infamous Simon Lord Lovat, leaders in the memorable rebellion of 1745. As they were associates in crime, they are companions in sepulchre, being all buried in the same grave."[1] Some years ago, on opening the adjoining ground, their coffin plates were discovered. Those of Kilmarnock and Balmerino are of pewter, that of Lord Lovat is of lead, and much corroded; they are now placed on the west wall of the Chapel.

Coffin-Plates of the three Scotch Lords.

A flat stone, in which are cut three marks, two circular and one lozenge shape, with a line drawn through them, denotes the spot of their interment.[2]

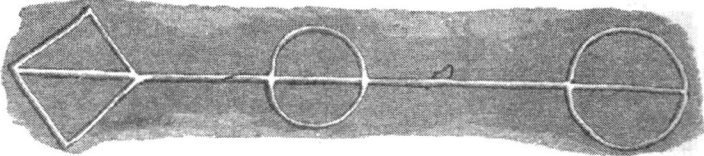

Gravestone of Scotch Lords.

---

[1] Bayley, pp. 121–2.
[2] Wilkinson, 'Londina Illustrata.' It was not precisely known where they had been buried, nor what this peculiarly marked stone denoted, until the coffin plates were found beneath it.

SIMON, LORD FRASER OF LOVAT.

Born 1667. Beheaded on Tower Hill, 9th April, 1747.

Simon Lord Lovat had led a wild and eventful life: born in 1667, he had first served in the army, then soon quitting it, he went over to France, where he became a Roman Catholic. In 1702 he was sent by Prince James Francis Edward to Scotland, to endeavour to raise the country, but he betrayed the plot to the English Government, for which act of treachery he was, on his return to France, imprisoned in the Bastile.

In 1715 he fought against Prince Charles Edward, but subsequently joined the Jacobite cause, and took part with the Prince in the rebellion of 1745.

After the defeat at Culloden, at which, however, he was not present, he fled to Castle Cawdor, and from thence to a refuge on the Lake of Muilly, his object being to get on board some ship and escape to France.

After hiding in caverns, hollow trees, &c., Lord Lovat was finally apprehended in the district of Morar, on the western coast, by a party from the *Furnace* sloop, which had been sent to search the isles and the coast. From his retreat in Loch Muilly, he must have travelled seventy miles over the wildest country of Scotland to reach this spot, and for all this exertion he must have been indebted to the labours of his faithful clansmen, for he could not walk a step unsupported.

In the Lake of Morar he had hidden himself in an island, which, as he had the command of the only boat on the lake, he considered impregnable. As, however, the western extremity of the lake was very close to the sea, a boat was towed by some man-of-war's men, under the command of Captain Mellon, over the peninsula, and launched on the lake. He was then discovered within a hollow tree, in which he was able to stand upright, after having entered by an orifice below, through which opening the sailors were astonished to see two human legs muffled up in flannel like those of a gouty alderman.[1]

After his capture he wrote this letter to His Royal Highness the Duke of Cumberland:—

"SIR, "Fort William, June 12, 1746.

"This letter is most humbly addressed to your royal highness by the very unfortunate Simon Lord Frazier of Lovat. I durst not presume to solicit or petition your royal highness for any favour, if it was not very well known to the best people in this country attach'd to the Government, such as the Lord President, and by those that frequented the Court at that time, that I did more essential service to your royal family in the great rebellion in the year 1715, with the hazard of my life, and the loss of my only brother, than any of my rank in Scotland; for which I had three letters of thanks from my royal master, by the hands of Earl Stanhope, then Secretary of State; in which his Majesty strongly promised to give me such marks of his favour as should oblige all the country to be faithful to him; therefore the gracious King was as good as his word to me, for as soon as I arrived at Court, and was introduced to the King by the late Duke of Argyll, I became, by degrees, to be as great a favourite as any Scotchman about the Court; and I often carried your royal highness in my arms in the parks of Kensington and Hampton Court, to hold you up to your royal grandfather, that he might embrace you, for he was very fond of you and the young princesses. Now, sir, all that I have to say in my present circumstances is, that your royal highness will be pleased to extend your goodness towards me, in a generous and compassionate manner, in my deplorable situation; and, if I have the honour to kiss your royal highness's hand, I would easily demonstrate to you, that I can do more service to the King and Government, than the destroying an hundred such old, and very infirm men like me pass'd 70 (without the least use of my hands, legs, or knees) can be of advantage in any shape to the government.

"Your royal father, our present sovereign, was very kind to me in the year 1715. I presented on my knees to his Majesty a petition in favour of the laird of M'Intosh, to obtain a protection for him, which he granted me, and gave it to Charles Cathcart, then groom of his bed-chamber, and ordered him to deliver it into my hands, that I might give it to the laird of M'Intosh. This was but one testimony of several marks of goodness his Majesty was pleased to bestow on me while the King was at Hanover; so I hope I shall feel that the same compassionate blood runs in your royal highness's veins.

[1] Fraser's 'Life of Lord Lovat,' p. 249.

"Major-General Campbell told me that he had the honour to acquaint your royal highness, that he was sending me to Fort William, and that he begged of your Royal Highness to order a litter to be made for me to carry me to Fort Augustus; as I am in such a condition, that I am not able to stand, walk, or ride.

"I am, with the utmost submission and most profound respect,
"Sir,
"Your Royal Highness's obedient
and most faithful humble servant,
"LOVAT."

His request for a litter was complied with, and the following is an extract from a letter quoted in the 'Gentleman's Magazine':—

"Fort Augustus, 17 June.

"Yesterday I had the pleasure of seeing that old rebel Lord Lovat, with his two aide de camps, and about sixty of his clan brought in here prisoners: he is 78 years of age, has a fine comely head to grace Temple Bar, and his body is so large, that I imagine the doors of the Tower must be altered to get him in. He can neither walk nor ride, and was brought in here in a horse litter, or rather a cage, as hardened as ever."[1]

He was conveyed in a litter by easy stages[2] through Stirling to Edinburgh, and thence by Berwick to London, and ultimately lodged in the Tower.[3]

It was at the "White Hart Inn," at St. Albans, that Hogarth saw him, and drew the well-known portrait. Hogarth had been invited to St. Albans by Dr. Webster to be introduced to Lovat, and he was, through the Doctor's introduction, received with much cordiality, "even to the kiss fraternal," which was, perhaps, not very pleasant, as at that moment, he was under the barber's hands. Lovat rested for

[1] 'Gentleman's Magazine,' vol. xvi. p. 350.
[2] His journey was divided into twenty stages: the escort of sixty dragoons was commanded by Major Gardiner.
[3] A story is told, that on the journey a young officer was desirous of seeing the actual features of Lovat, who had been described as such a monster. Lovat heard of this, and pretended to be asleep, snoring loudly. The young man gently drew the curtains and looked in, when Lovat, starting up, seized him by the nose, and gave it a twinge not easily to be forgotten.— 'Life of Lord Lovat,' p. 251.

two or three days at St. Albans. Hogarth said that the portrait was taken when he was relating on his fingers the numbers of the rebel forces, 'Such a General had so many men,' &c. When the engraving was finished, a printseller offered its weight in gold for it. It was published 25th August, 1746, and the impressions could not be taken off as fast as they were wanted, though the press was at work all night for a week together; for several weeks Hogarth received for them at the rate of twelve pounds a day."[1]

On the 11th November, 1746, he was brought from the Tower, at nine o'clock at night, to the Cockpit, Whitehall, and, after examination before the Secretaries of State, was remanded back to prison.

Formal arrangements were then made for his impeachment, and on the 18th December he was taken to the House of Lords, where the articles of his impeachment were read to him; to which he replied in a speech of considerable length, much in the sense of his letter to the Duke of Cumberland, and he concluded by saying that his extreme deafness had prevented him from hearing one word of the charge against him. He was therefore remanded, in order that he might deliver a written reply to the impeachment, which he accordingly did.

After several postponements the trial commenced on Monday, 9th March, and at "about ten o'clock he was brought from the Tower, attended by Mr. Fowler, the gentleman gaoler, under a strong guard to Westminster Hall.[2]

"Soon after, the Lord High Steward, in his state coach drawn by six horses, with five led coaches, and followed in a grand procession by the Lord Chief Justice Willes, the Lord Chief Baron Parker, and the rest of the judges, and the Masters in Chancery, went to the House of Peers. After which they adjourned into Westminster Hall, and being

---

[1] Nichols' 'Hogarth,' vol. i. pp. 131-2.
[2] A plan of the seats and arrangements for the trial in Westminster Hall is given in the 'Gentleman's Magazine,' 1747, p. 149.

there seated in their robes, the commission for appointing a Lord High Steward was presented to his Lordship by the Clerk of the Crown, and by him read, and all present stood uncovered according to proclamation.

"Then the articles of impeachment,[1] which had been exhibited against Lord Lovat, with his Lordship's answer, and the replication of the Commons, were read."[2]

The trial proceeded on the next day and on Wednesday, but Lovat then signified that he was very infirm, and had had two fainting fits the day before, and was obliged to get up at three or four o'clock in the morning, so he begged a day's respite, which was granted.

The court met again on Friday, on the following Monday and Wednesday, when the Lords pronounced him guilty.

He was then remanded back to the Tower, the warrant stating that he was to be brought the next day at eleven o'clock to Westminster Hall, " to proceed further, in order to the giving of judgment upon the said Lord."[3]

On Thursday, the 19th, " the Speaker, with his mace, went to the bar of the House of Lords, and, in the name of all the Commons of England, demanded judgment against Simon, Lord Lovat, for high treason. Then the Lords adjourned to Westminster Hall, and the prisoner, being brought to the bar, was asked if he had anything to offer why judgment of death should not be pronounced against him, to which he answered he had not. The Lord High Steward then passed sentence, and, standing up, broke his staff and declared his commission to be void.

" Then Lord Lovat desired the Lords to recommend him to His Majesty's mercy, and said to the managers of the Commons, 'I hope as ye are stout, ye will be merciful;' and going from the bar he said, "God bless you all, I wish you an everlasting farewell, for we shall never meet again in this place.' "[4]

[1] The articles of impeachment, and Lord Lovat's reply to them, will be found in the 'Gentleman's Magazine' for 1747, p. 151 et seq.
[2] Ibid. p. 111.
[3] Tower Records.
[4] 'Gentleman's Magazine,' 1747, p. 116.

Walpole writes to Mann:—

"Arlington Street, 20th March, 1747.

"I have been living at old Lovat's trial, and was willing to have it over before I talked to you of it.

"It lasted seven days; the evidence was as strong as possible; and, after all he had denounced, he made no defence. The Solicitor-General,[1] who was one of the managers for the House of Commons, shone extremely; the Attorney-General,[2] who is a much greater lawyer, is cold and tedious. The old creature's behaviour has been foolish, and at last indecent.

* * * * *

"When he came to the Tower, he told them that if he were not so old and infirm; they would find it difficult to keep him there. They told him they had kept much younger. 'Yes,' said he, 'but they were inexperienced ; they had not broke so many gaols as I have.' At his own house he used to say, that for thirty years of his life he never saw a gallows but it made his neck ache. His last act was to shift his treason upon his eldest son, whom he forced into the rebellion. He told Williamson, the Lieutenant of the Tower, 'We will hang my eldest son, and then my second shall marry your niece.' He has a sort of ready humour at repartee, not very well adapted to his situation. One day that Williamson complained that he could not sleep, he was so haunted with rats; he replied, 'What do you say, that you are so haunted with Ratcliffes?'[3] The first day, as he was brought to his trial, a woman looked into the coach, and said, 'You ugly old dog, don't you think you will have that frightful head cut off?' He replied, 'You ugly old ——, I believe I shall.'

"At his trial he affected great weakness and infirmities, but often broke out into passions ; particularly at the first witness, who was his vassal, he asked him how he dared to come thither; the man replied, to satisfy his conscience.

* * * * *

"The two last days he behaved ridiculously, joking and making everybody laugh, even at the sentence. He said to Lord Ilchester, who sat near the bar, ' Je meurs pour ma patrie, et ne m'en soucie guère.' When he withdrew, he said, ' Adieu, my Lords, we shall never meet again in the same place.' He says he will be hanged, for that

---

[1] Sir William Murray, then Solicitor-General; appointed Lord Chief Justice of the King's Bench in 1756 ; and created Earl of Mansfield in 1776 ; he died in 1793, aged 89.

[2] Sir Dudley Ryder, then Attorney-General, which office he held for seventeen years; appointed Lord Chief Justice of the King's Bench in 1754; he died in 1756.

[3] Charles Ratcliffe, younger brother of the Earl of Derwentwater, committed to the Tower in 1746, and beheaded on 8th Dec. 1746.

his neck is so short and bended that he should be struck in the shoulders.'[1] I did not think it possible to feel so little as I did at so melancholy a spectacle, but tyranny and villany wound up by buffoonery took off all edge of concern."[2]

On the 24th March and 6th April permission is granted that any of his friends and relations should be admitted to see him, but "that no more than two of the said persons be at one time admitted to him."[3]

Thursday, April 9, was fixed for his execution. "On that day he waked about three in the morning, and was heard to pray with great devotion; at five he rose, called for a glass of wine and water as usual, appeared cheerful, sat and read till seven, and then drank another glass of wine and water. At eight he desired his wig might be sent, that the barber might have time to comb it out genteely, and provided himself with a purse to hold the money, which he intended for the executioner.

"At about half an hour after nine his Lordship eat very heartily of minced veal, ordering coffee and chocolate for his friends, whose healths he drank in wine and water.

"About eleven the Sheriffs sent to demand his body, upon which he desired the gentlemen would retire for a few moments, while he said a prayer; and this being immediately complied with, he presently called for them again, saying, 'I am ready.'

"At the bottom of the first pair of stairs, General Williamson invited him into his rooms to rest himself, which he accepted, and on his entrance paid his respects to the company politely, and talked freely. He desired of the General in French that he might take leave of his lady, and thank her for her civilities. But the General told his Lordship in the same language, that she was too much affected with

---

[1] Hogarth, when drawing his portrait at St. Albans, remarked, "that the muscles of Lord Lovat's neck appeared of unusual strength, more so than he had ever seen."—Nichols' 'Hogarth,' vol. i. p. 131.

[2] 'Walpole to Mann,' vol. ii. pp. 189–191.

[3] Tower Records.

his Lordship's misfortunes to bear the shock of seeing him, and, therefore, hoped his Lordship would excuse her.

"He then took his leave and proceeded; at the door he bowed to the spectators, and was conveyed from thence to the outward gate in the Governor's coach, where he was delivered to the Sheriffs, who conducted him in another coach to the house (hired for the two former Lords) near the scaffold, in which was a room lined with black cloth, and hung with sconces, for his reception.[1]

"His friends were at first denied entrance, but upon application made by his Lordship to the Sheriffs for their admittance, it was granted. Soon after his Lordship, addressing himself to the Sheriffs, thanked them for the favour, and taking a paper out of his pocket delivered it to one of them, saying he should make no speech, and that they might give the word of command when they pleased.

"A gentleman present beginning to read a prayer to his Lordship, while he was sitting, he called one of the warders to help him up that he might kneel. He then prayed silently for a short time, and was afterwards set again in his chair; being asked by one of the Sheriffs if he would refresh himself with a glass of wine, he declined it because no warm water could be had to mix with it, and took a little burnt brandy and bitters in its stead.

"He desired that his clothes might be delivered to his friends with his corps, and said that for that reason he should give the executioner ten guineas. He also desired of the Sheriffs that his head might be received in a cloth, and put into the coffin, which the Sheriffs, after conferring with some gentlemen present, promised should be done, and that the holding up the head at the corners of the scaffold should be dispensed with, as it had been of late years at the execution of Lords, though they had no written order to the contrary in the warrant, and without it, might be liable to censure.

---

[1] This house is on Tower Hill, at the north corner of Catherine Court; a raised platform was arranged from the window of the first floor to the scaffold. It had formerly been the Transport Office.

"When his Lordship was going up the steps to the scaffold, assisted by two warders, he looked round, and seeing so great a concourse of people, 'God save us,' says he, 'why should there be such a bustle about taking off an old grey head, that cannot get up three steps without three bodies to support it?'[1]

"Turning about, and observing one of his friends much dejected, he clapped him on the shoulder, saying, 'Cheer up thy heart, man, I am not afraid, why should you be?'

"As soon as he came upon the scaffold, he asked for the executioner, and presented him with ten guineas in a purse; then desiring to see the axe, he felt the edge, and said he believed it would do.

"Soon after he rose from the chair, which was placed for him, and looked at his coffin, on which was written—

SIMON DOMINUS FRASER DE LOVAT,
Decollat. April 9, 1747.
Ætat. suae 80.

He then sat down again, and repeated from Horace:—

"Dulce et decorum pro patriâ mori."

And afterwards from Ovid:—

"Nam genus et proavos, et quæ non fecimus ipsi,
Vix ea nostra voco."[2]

"He then desired all the people to stand off except his two warders, who supported his Lordship while he said a prayer; after which he called his solicitor and agent in Scotland, Mr. William Frazer, and, presenting his gold-headed cane, said, 'I deliver you this cane in token of my sense of your

---

[1] See also Fraser's 'Life of Lord Lovat.'
[2] These ejaculations being told to a gentleman, he replied instantly, to the first:

"With justice may Lovat this adage apply,
For the good of their country all criminals die."

To the second:

"Thine alone is the honour of all thou hast done,
Such father no honour transmits to his son."

faithful services, and of my committing to you all the power I have upon earth,' and then embraced him. He also called for Mr. James Frazer, and said, 'My dear James, I am going to Heaven, but you must continue to crawl a little longer in this evil world.'[1] Then taking leave of both, he delivered his hat, wig, and clothes to Mr. William Frazer, and desired him to see that the executioner did not touch them. He ordered his cap to be put on, and, unloosing his neck-cloth and collar of his shirt, he kneeled down at the block,[2] and pulled the cloth, which was to receive his head, close to him.

"But being placed too near the block, the executioner desired him to remove a little further back, which, with the warder's assistance, was immediately done, and his neck being properly placed, he told the executioner he would say a short prayer, and then give the signal by dropping his handkerchief. In this posture he remained about half a minute, and then throwing his handkerchief on the floor, the executioner at one blow severed his head from his body, which was received in the cloth, and, together with his body, put into the coffin, and carried in a hearse back to the Tower, where it remained till four o'clock, and was then taken away by an undertaker, in order to be sent to Scotland and deposited in his own tomb in the church of Kirkill, but leave not being given, as was expected, it was again brought back to the Tower, and interred near the bodies of the other Lords."[3]

The following is the account of the execution which was written by Walpole to his friend Mann :—

"Arlington Street, 10th April, 1747.

"I deferred writing to you as long as they deferred the execution of old Lovat, because I had a mind to send you some account of his death, as I had of his trial. He was beheaded yesterday, and died extremely well, without passion, affectation, buffoonery, or timidity;

---

[1] See also 'Life of Lord Lovat,' p. 265.
[2] A new block had been made for the occasion : it is still shown in the Tower armoury.
[3] The 'Gentleman's Magazine,' vol. xvii. pp. 160-2.

his behaviour was natural and intrepid. He professed himself a Jansenist; made no speech, but sat down a little while in a chair on the scaffold, and talked to the people round him.

"He said he was glad to suffer for his country, 'Dulce est pro patriâ mori:' that he did not know how, but he had always loved it, 'nescio quâ natale solum,' &c.; that he had never swerved from his principles; that this was the character of his family, who had been gentlemen for five hundred years. He lay down quietly, gave the sign soon, and was despatched at a blow. I believe it will strike some terror into the Highlands, when they hear there is any power great enough to bring so potent a tyrant to the block. A scaffold fell down and killed several persons, one a man that had rid post from Salisbury the day before to see the ceremony, and a woman was taken up dead with a live child in her arms."[1]

It was intended that Lord Lovat's body should be removed to Scotland, but this was countermanded, as will be seen by the following letter:—

"Whitehall, 16th April, 1747.

"SIR,—Mr. Stevenson, the undertaker, in whose custody the body of Lord Lovat now remains, being directed to convey the same to the Tower of London, and there to deliver it into your hands, in order to its being interred, I am commanded to signify to you His Majesty's pleasure, that you do accordingly receive the said body from Mr. Stevenson, and that you take care that it be interred within the Tower in a private manner.

"I am, Sir, yours,
(Signed) "HOLLES, NEWCASTLE.

"To the Commanding Officer
    in the Tower."

His body was laid by the side of the Lords Kilmarnock and Balmerino, at the western end of the chapel, and a stone on which three marks are cut, indicates the spot of their burial.[2] The remains of the three Lords, had however, been so much disturbed that it was impossible to identify them, when the spot was recently uncovered. A small fragment

---

[1] Walpole's 'Letters,' vol. ii. pp. 192-3.
[2] See page 312. The lozenge-shaped mark is believed to have been added when Lord Lovat was buried.

of a coffin plate, on which is the Lovat arms, was, however, found on the spot.

Lord Lovat is the last person who has suffered death by beheading in this country.

Axe, Block, and Executioner's Mask.

APPENDIX A.

PEDIGREE OF THE HOUSE OF NORFOLK AND ARUNDEL.

JOHN HOWARD, First Duke of Norfolk.
("Jockey of Norfolk.")
Created Duke of Norfolk and Earl Marshal by Richard III. in 1483.
Killed at Bosworth, 22nd Aug. 1485, and buried at Thetford.
His son was

THOMAS HOWARD, Second Duke of Norfolk, K.G.
Created Earl of Surrey in 1483; Was Lord High Treasurer in 1501: Created Earl Marshal in 1510;
Served as General-in-Chief at Flodden, 9th Sept. 1513: Restored as Duke of Norfolk, 1st Feb. 1514.
Died 21st May, 1524, and was buried at Thetford.
His children were

- **EDWARD HOWARD, K.G.**
  Lord High Admiral.
  Killed off Brest, 25th April, 1513.

- **EDMUND HOWARD.**
  Served at Flodden.
  One of his daughters was
  KATHARINE HOWARD, wife of
  HENRY VIII.

- **ELIZABETH HOWARD,**
  who married THOMAS BOLEYN,
  EARL OF WILTSHIRE.
  Their daughter was
  ANNE BOLEYN, wife of HENRY VIII,
  and mother of
  QUEEN ELIZABETH.

THOMAS HOWARD, Third Duke of Norfolk, K.G.
Lord Admiral in 1513: Lord Lieutenant of Ireland in 1520:
Lord Treasurer in 1522:
Succeeded his father in 1524. Died 25th Aug. 1554,
and was buried at Framlingham.
He married, first, ANNE, daughter of EDWARD IV.; and,
secondly, ELIZABETH, daughter of the DUKE OF BUCKINGHAM.
Their son was

HENRY HOWARD, Earl of Surrey, K.G.
Who was arraigned for high treason, and executed on
Tower Hill, 1st Jan. 1547.
Buried in the church of All Hallows, Barking, but removed
by his son to Framlingham.
His son was

THOMAS HOWARD, Fourth Duke of Norfolk, K.G.
Succeeded his grandfather in 1554;
Was arraigned for high treason, and executed on Tower Hill,
2nd June, 1572.
Buried in St. Peter's Chapel in the Tower.
He married MARY FITZALAN, daughter and heiress of
HENRY EARL OF ARUNDEL.
Their son was

PHILIP HOWARD. Twenty-third Earl of Arundel.
Arraigned for high treason in 1689, and died in the
Tower, 19th Oct. 1595.
He was buried in St. Peter's Chapel in the Tower, but
removed to Arundel in 1624.

APPENDIX B.

Baga de Secretis.

IN 1836 the legal records of the Court of King's Bench were transferred to the custody of the Master of the Rolls, and in 1841 the Deputy Keeper of the Public Records published in his Third Report an account of the "Baga de Secretis," in which had been preserved the official papers connected with many important state trials. This "Baga de Secretis" had been formerly kept under three keys; one in the custody of the Lord Chief Justice, another by the Attorney-General, and the third by the Master of the Crown Office.

The great "Baga" had long since disappeared, but was represented by a closet, of which the keys were kept as above mentioned, and in which the records were deposited upon the shelves; the principal part however of the ancient proceedings were in small bags or pouches, and generally speaking were found in good condition as to soundness, though crushed and crumpled in consequence of the mode in which they had been stowed. These records consist of indictments and attainders for high treason and other state offences, as well as other proceedings on the Crown side of the Court.

The greater part are of very considerable value, both in a legal and historical point of view. With the exception of extracts in the State Trials, and other works of the like description, they have hitherto been nearly unknown; and one of the most important, the conviction of Queen Anne Boleyn and her brother Lord Rochford, was supposed to have been suppressed and destroyed.[1]

The earliest trials amongst these documents bear the dates of 1477, Edward IV.'s reign, and the series terminates in the year 1813, in the reign of George III.

These state papers are contained in ninety-one pouches, and they have been fully calendared in the Third, Fourth, and Fifth Reports of the Deputy Keeper of the Public Records.

[1] Third Report of the Deputy Keeper of Public Records, 1842, pp. 16, 211.

APPENDIX B.

The following are the most interesting among the trials that are preserved:—

Pouch II. Trial of EDWARD PLANTAGENET, EARL OF WARWICK, in 1499.

Pouch IV. Trials of EDMUND DUDLEY and SIR RICHARD EMPSON in 1509, and of EDWARD STAFFORD, DUKE OF BUCKINGHAM, in 1521.

Pouch VII. Trials of BISHOP FISHER and SIR THOMAS MORE in 1535.

Pouch VIII. Trials of SMEATON, NORREYS, BRYERTON, and WESTON, in 1536.

Pouch IX. Trial of QUEEN ANNE BOLEYN and the LORD ROCHFORD in 1536.

Pouch XI. Trials of HENRY POLE, LORD MOUNTACUTE, and HENRY, MARQUIS OF EXETER, in 1538, for "treasonable adherence to Cardinal Pole and treasonable discourses."

Pouch XIII. Trials relating to the charges against QUEEN KATHARINE HOWARD, in 1541.

Pouch XIV. Trial of HENRY, EARL OF SURREY, in 1547, for "high treason in assuming the arms of Edward the Confessor."

Pouch XIX. Trial of EDWARD SEYMOUR, DUKE OF SOMERSET, in 1551, for "felony and high treason, exciting the citizens of London to rebellion, and compassing the King's death."

Pouch XX. Trial of SIR RALPH FANE, SIR THOMAS ARUNDEL, SIR MILES PARTRICHE, and SIR MICHAEL STANHOPE, in 1551-2, for "felony, and instigating the Duke of Somerset to insurrection."

Pouches XXI. and XXII. Trials of JOHN DUDLEY, DUKE OF NORTHUMBERLAND, and others, in 1553, for "high treason, levying war against the Queen, and proclaiming Lady Jane Grey."

Pouch XXIII. Trials of LADY JANE GREY, ARCHBISHOP CRANMER, GUILDFORD DUDLEY, SIR AMBROSE DUDLEY, and HENRY DUDLEY, in 1553, for "high treason," &c.

Pouch XXV. Trial of SIR ROBERT DUDLEY, in 1553-4, for "high treason and proclaiming Lady Jane Grey."

Pouches XXVI. and XXVII. Trials of SIR THOMAS WYATT and his accomplices, in 1553-4.

Pouch XXVIII. Trial of HENRY GREY, DUKE OF SUFFOLK, in 1553-4, for "high treason and levying war against the Queen."

Pouches XXXVIII. and XXXIX. Trials connected with the SURRENDER OF CALAIS in 1559.

Pouch XL. Trial of ARTHUR POOLE, or POLE, "pretending to the title of Duke of Clarence," EDMUND POOLE, and others, in

1562-3, for "high treason, conspiring to depose the Queen and proclaim Mary Queen of Scots."

Pouch XLII. Trial of THOMAS HOWARD, DUKE OF NORFOLK, 16th January, 1571-2, for "high treason, conspiring to dethrone the Queen, and seeking a marriage with Mary Queen of Scots."

Pouch XLVIII. Trial of ANTHONY BABYNGTON and others, in 1586.

Pouch XLIX. Trial of PHILIP HOWARD, EARL OF ARUNDEL, 14th April, 1589.

Pouch L. Trial of SIR JOHN PERROTT, 27th April, and 16th June, 1592, for "high treason and correspondence with the King of Spain."

Pouch LVI. Trial of the EARLS OF ESSEX AND SOUTHAMPTON, 19th February, 1600-1, for "high treason and conspiracy to seize the Queen's person."

Pouch LVII. Trials of G. BROOKE, SIR WALTER RALEIGH, HENRY LORD COBHAM, and THOMAS, LORD GREY DE WILTON, in 1603, for "high treason, conspiring to seize and imprison the King and Prince Henry, and to raise one Arbella Stuart to the Crown of England."

Pouches LIX., LX., and LXI. The GUNPOWDER PLOT Trials.

Pouch LXII. Trial of the EARL AND COUNTESS OF SOMERSET, in 1616, for the murder of Sir Thomas Overbury.

&c. &c. &c.

INDEX.

Alberoni, Cardinal, 296.
Alford, Gregory, mayor of Lyme, 268.
Allen, Cardinal William, 205, 211.
Anne, Queen of James I., her letter to Cecil, 232, 241.
Apsley, Sir Allan, his burial, 25, 48; his monument, 35, 48, 250, 251, 252, 253.
——— House built, 36.
Arundel, Henry, Earl of, 154, 157, 180, 186.
——— House, 205.
———, Humphrey, 150.
———, Sir John, 150.
———, Philip, Earl of, buried, 47, 50, 53; letter from his father, 195; his birth, 205; confined to his house, 205; examined by Council, 205, 209; embarks for France, 206; arrested and committed to the Tower, 206; his trial, 210; sentence, 212; his letter to Sir C. Hatton, 212; his life in prison, 213; poisoned, 215; his interview with Sir M Blount, 215; his death and burial, 216; removal of his remains, 217; inscription on his coffin, 217, 231.
———, Sir Thomas, buried, 43, 50, 149; committed to the Tower, 150; brought to trial, 151; sentenced to death, 152; executed and buried, 153.

Ashley, Champion, 280.
Ashton, Dr., attends Earl of Essex, 225, 227.
Athol, Duke of, 296, 297, 298, 299, 300.
Audley, Thomas, Lord Chancellor, 69, 80, 95, 101, 105, 122, 186.

Baga de Secretis, trials in, 103, 326.
Baker, Sir John, 128, 130.
Baldwin, Sir John, 80.
Balfour, Sir W., 7.
Balmerino, Lady, 305, 307.
———, Arthur, Lord, 15; buried, 49, 51; committed to the Tower, 301; trial of, 302; his execution, 309; buried in chapel, 311.
Bancroft, Richard, Archbishop of Canterbury, 242.
Barham, Nicholas, 193.
Barlowe, Dr. William, attends Earl of Essex, 227, 229.
Barnes, Thomas, 202.
Baskerville, —, 160.
Baynton, Lady, 123.
Beauchamp Tower, inscriptions in, 157, 208; Earl of Arundel imprisoned in, 206, 208.
Bell, Doyne C., 17, 19, 20, 22, 23, 26, 30, 31.
——— Tower, account of, 63, 64, 208.
Bellasis, Lord, 255.
Benson, or Boston, William, Abbot of Westminster, 77.

Bennet, William, 209, 211.
Beresford, Hannah, 22.
Berwick, Duke of, 291.
Bill, Dr. William, 152.
Bindon, Thomas, third Viscount, 227.
Blatchford, Mr. Sheriff, 308.
Bloody Tower, prison of Duke of Norfolk, 194.
Blount, Lyster, buried, 34.
———, Lady Mary, buried, 47.
———, Sir Michael, his monument, 33; list of prisoners, 46, 213, 202; interview with Earl of Arundel, 214, 215.
———, Sir Richard, his monument, 33.
Boleyn, Queen Anne, 17, 20; discovery of her remains, 21, 22, 26, 27, 50, 51; sent to the Tower, 95; her letter to Henry VIII., 99; trial of, 101; execution of, 105; burial of, 107, 150, 163.
———, Lady, 101, 103.
Bolingbroke, Earl of, 250.
Bomeney, Paul, 267.
Bonall's Court, 202.
Bounds of parish, 4.
Boyd, William, 309.
Braddon, Lawrence, 266.
Bray, William, 206.
Brereton, William, buried, 42; arrested, 91; tried, 92; executed, 93.
Brick Tower, prison of Lord Grey, 248.
Bridges, William, his monument, 39.
Bridgewater, John, Earl of, 256.
Britannia, figure of, on coins, 286.
Brooke, George, 244, 247.
Browne, Sir Anthony, 145, 173.
———, Dr. Thomas, 283.
Brydges, Sir John, 159, 174 (*see also* Chandos).

Brydges, Thomas, 175.
Buchanan of Drumakill, 298.
Buckhurst, Thomas Sackville, Lord, 201; presides at trial of Lord Essex, 223.
Burbace, W., 206.
Burghley, Thomas, Lord, 221.
———, William, Lord, 112, 190, 196, 209.
Burgoyne, Sir John, 17, 20, 21, 23; his memorial tablet, 41, 148.
Burnet, Gilbert, Bishop of Salisbury, 261.
Busse, —, 269.
Byng, Sir George, captures the *Salisbury*, 294.

Cadogan, Major-General William, 294.
Camden, William, Duke of Norfolk's trial, 191.
Carew, Sir George, 222.
———, Sir Peter, 35, 192.
Carey, Sir E., 227.
———, Sir George, 206.
———, Lady Maria, 36.
Carleton, Sir Dudley, 241, 244, 245, 247.
Carr, Robert (*see* Somerset, Earl of).
Cecil, Robert, Earl of Salisbury, 138, 143.
Chamberlain, John, his letters, 235, 236, 237, 238, 249.
Chancel, decoration of, 1; restoration of, 17.
Chandos, Lord, 95, 174 (*see also* Brydges).
Chapel, foundation of, 1, 2; dedication of, 3; is a benefice donative, 6.
Chaplains, allowances to, 3, 4.
Chapman, Sir John, 280.
Charles I., tradition of his burial at Naseby, 108.
——— II. visits the Tower, 265.
——— Edward, Prince, 297, 301.

INDEX.   331

Charter House, residence of Duke of Norfolk, 189.
Cheeke, Thomas, 264.
Cheney, Sir Thomas, 130.
Chiffinch, Thomas, 271.
Cholmondeley, Lady, her funeral, 43.
———, Sir Richard, his monument, 32, 33, 43.
———, Sir Roger, his monument, 33, 43.
Christ Church, Salisbury chapel at, 121.
Clarence, George, Duke of, 116.
Clarendon, Henry, second Earl of, 264.
Clark, William, 242.
Clement, Margaret, 84, 87.
Cleves, Anne of, 109.
Cobham, Henry Brooke, Lord, 244, 245, 246, 249.
Coffin, Richard, 282.
Coke, Sir Edward, 223.
Collegiate establishment proposed, 3, 4.
Collie, Dorothy, 83, 87.
Compton, Henry, Bishop of London, 260.
———, Lord, 227.
Cooper, Thomas, 280.
Copley, Anthony, 242.
Cornish, John, 262.
Cornwallis, Lord, Constable of the Tower, 299.
Cosyns, Mrs., 101.
Courtney, Edward, 180.
Cowdray Castle, 117.
Cox, Richard, Bishop of Ely, 146, 147.
Cranmer, Archbishop, intercedes on behalf of Bishop of Fisher, 63; writes on behalf of Queen Anne Boleyn, 96; she confesses to him, 103; his letter on behalf of Cromwell, 110; interview with Katharine Howard, 122; tried at Guildhall, 169.

Cromartie, Earl of, his trial, 304; he is pardoned, 307.
Cromwell, Sir Richard, 77.
———, Thomas, Earl of Essex, 50, 95, 105; his origin, 109; committed to the Tower, 109; Cranmer intercedes for him, 110; examined in Tower, 111; his attainder, 111; his letters to Henry VIII., 112, 113; execution of, 113; speech on scaffold, 114, 115; burial of, 115; his character, 115, 119.
Crypt, position of, 16.
Culloden, battle of, 298, 308.
Cumberland, George Clifford, 3rd Earl of, 227.
———, William, Duke of, 314.

Dalby, William, letters of, 160, 163.
Darcy, Sir Arthur, 139, 152.
———, Lord, 227.
Daubeney, Robert, 215.
Delaroche, Paul, picture by, 176.
Delawarr, Lord, 193.
Denny, Sir Anthony, 130.
Derby, Henry, fourth Earl of, 210.
De Ros, Lord, vii., 10, 37, 41.
Dethicke, Sir Gilbert, 221.
Devereux Tower, 174, 222; Earl of Essex, confined in, 222.
Devil's Tower, 174.
Dove, Dr., Dean of Norwich, 225.
D'Oyly, Major, 296.
Drury House, 219.
Dublin, Lord Mayor's chain and medal, 289.
Dudley, Lord Ambrose, 159, 169.
———, Lord Guildford, 50, 53; imprisoned, 164, 168, 169; his trial, 169; his letter to his father, 171; execution of, 173-177.
———, Lord Harry, 168.

332   INDEX.

Edmonds, Sir Thomas, 242.
Edward VI., his account of Duke of Somerset's trial, 140.
——, William, 266.
Edwards, Talbot, 37, 48, 49.
Effingham, Charles, Lord Howard of, 201, 221.
Egerton, Thomas, Lord Chancellor, 243.
Eliot, Sir John, 50; committed to the Tower, 250; brought before Court of King's Bench, 251; transferred to the Marshalsea, 252; committed to the Tower, 252; his letters, 253, 254; his death, 254; buried in the Tower, 255.
Elizabeth, Queen, at the Tower, 95; delays execution of Duke of Norfolk, 196, 218, 219, 220, 222, 227.
Elrington, J. H., his tablet and vault, 40, 41.
Ely, Thomas Goodrich, Bishop of, 116, 117, 132.
Essex, Earl of (see Cromwell).
——, Arthur, Earl of, 48, 50, 256; arrested, 263; committed to the Tower, 264; found with his throat cut, 265; enquiry respecting his death, 266; burial of, 268.
——, Elizabeth, Countess of, 263, 267.
——, Robert Devereux, Earl of, 47, 50, 53, 217; confined in York House, 218; his letters to Queen Elizabeth, 219; besieged in Essex House, 221; his trial, 222; sentenced, 224; Lady Nottingham and the ring, 226; his execution, 227, 229, 230; his speech on scaffold, 228; his burial, 231, 241.
Etterick, Anthony, 270.
Evelyn, John, visits the Mint, 287.
Exeter, Gertrude, Marchioness of, 118, 120.
——, Henry, first Marquis of, 92.

Fane, Hon. S. Ponsonby, 17, 19, 22, 30, 31.
——, Sir Ralph (see Vane).
Farewell, Colonel, 295.
Farnham Castle, 186.
Faversham, Earl of, 269.
Feckenham, John Howman, 171, 172, 174, 175.
Fell, Dr., Bishop of Oxford, 274.
Field, Dr. Richard, 245.
Finch, Heneage, 268.
Fisher, John, Bishop of Rochester, 50; summoned to Parliament, 61; appears before Commissioners, 62; imprisoned in Bell Tower, 63; his letters to Cromwell, 61, 65; inscription of, in White Tower, 65; made a cardinal, 67; his trial, 68; his execution, 70; his burial, &c., 75; his tomb, 76.
Fitzalan, Lady Mary, 155, 186, 205.
Fitzgerald, Lady Elizabeth, 60.
——, Lieutenant, 189.
——, Lord Thomas, inscription by him, 59.
Fitzherbert, Sir Anthony, 80.
——, Sir Thomas, 46.
Fitzjames, Sir John, 80.
Fleetwood, William, Recorder of London, 190.
Font, fragments of, 6.
Fortescue, Sir John, 201.
Foster, Rev. James, 307, 308, 309.
Fowler, Mr., the gentleman gaoler, 304, 307, 316.
Foxley, William, buried, 45.
Frampton, Robert, Bishop of Gloucester, 283.
Franklin, James, 238.
Frazer, William, 321.
Frederick, King of Bohemia, 249.
Frewin, Henry, 214.
Friend, Sir John, 280.

INDEX. 333

Gage, John, imprisoned, 46, 47.
———, Sir John, Constable, 95, 159, 161.
Galleries, erected, 7; removed, 17.
Gaoler's house, 167, 265.
Gardiner, Major, 315.
———, Stephen, Bishop of Winchester, 113, 157, 161.
Gates, Sir John, 159, 161, 162, 163.
Geraldine, the Fair, 60.
Gerrard, Sir Thomas, 209, 211.
Gibb, John, 246, 247.
Giggs, Margaret, 83.
Glenshiel, battle of, 296.
Godfrey, Sir Edmondbury, 255.
Gold, George, 67.
Gore, John, his tablet, 39.
Gostling, Sir William, 275, 276.
Gresham, Sir John, 136.
———, Sir Thomas, 191.
Grey, Forde, Lord Grey of Werke, 269, 271, 272.
———, Lady Jane, 50, 58; tradition of burial at Bradgate, 108, 153, 160, 163; enters the Tower as Queen, 164; at dinner at Parttridge's house, 167; her trial, 169; her letters to the Duke of Suffolk, 170, 171; exhortation to her sister, 172; her speech on scaffold, 175; her execution, 176; her letter to Sir John Brydges, 176.
———, Lord John, 178, 179.
———, Lord Thomas, 179, 180.
———, Lord Grey de Wilton, 47, 50; his quarrels with Lord Southampton, 240, 241; committed to the Tower, 242; sent to Winchester, 243; his trial, 244; preparation for his execution, 246; respited, 247; his letters to Cecil, 247; dies, and is buried in the Tower, 249.
Griffin, Edward, Lord, 49, 51; summoned to Parliament, 291; committed to the Tower, 292; released, but re-arrested, 293; escapes to France, 294; captured and recommitted to the Tower, 294; his illness and death, 295.
Griffiths, Henry F., his tablet, 40.
Gurwood, Colonel John, his tablet, 40.

Hagioscope discovered, 5, 17.
Hampden, John, 253, 254.
Hardwicke, Philip Yorke, Lord, 302.
Harrington, Sir John, interview with Queen Elizabeth, 218, 219.
Hartop, Mr., 160.
Harvey, Sir George, 242, 248.
Hatton, Sir Christopher, 201, 209, 212.
Hawley, Major, 264, 267.
Hayes, Mr., 6.
———, Sir James, 247.
Heath, Nicholas, Bishop of Rochester, 123, 161.
Helwys, Sir Gervas, 53, 231, 239.
Heneage, Sir Thomas, 209.
Hertford, Edward, Earl of, 227.
Hicks, Michael, 245.
Higford, or Hickford, secretary to the Duke of Norfolk, 189.
Hoby, Sir Philip, 136, 139.
Hogarth, William, his portrait of Lord Lovat, 315, 319.
Holt, Sir J., 293.
Home, Rev. Mr., 307, 309.
Hooper, George, Bishop of Bath and Wells, 274, 276.
Hopton, Sir Owen, 6, 192, 194, 203, 213.
———, Sir Ralph, 139.
———, Ralph, burial of, 60.
Hornden on the Hill, 108.
Howard, Charles, Lord Howard of Effingham, 201.
——— of Esrick, Lord, 263, 264.

334 INDEX.

Howard, Queen Katharine, 17, 22, 23, 24, 25, 27, 50, 51, 53; accusations against, 122; removed to Sion House, 123; bill of attainder against, 124; sent to the Tower, 125; execution of, 126; burial of, 127.
——— de Walden, Lord, 223, 225.
Howman, John (*see* Feckenham).
Hubbock, Rev. Mr., 6.
Humphreys, Rev. Cornelius, 308, 311.
Hungerford, Walter, Lord, 113.
Hunsdon, Lord, 201, 203, 205, 206, 209.
Huntingdon, Francis, Earl of, 136, 155, 179, 180.
Hutchinson, Lucy, 35.

James Francis Edward, Prince, 294, 313.
Jeffreys, George, Lord, 24, 25, 48, 51, 277; flees in disguise, 278; arrested in Wapping, 279; committed to the Tower, 280; warrant for committal, 281; examination by Privy Council, 281; his illness and death in Tower, 283; burial of, 284; removed to St. Mary, Aldermanbury, 285.
Jenkins, Sir Leoline, 264.
Johnson, Otwell, his letter, 126.
———, Sir Harry, 280.

Katharine of Braganza, Queen, 270, 271.
———, Saint, altar of, 2.
Kelloway, Captain, 206.
Ken, Thomas, Bishop of Bath and Wells, 274, 276.
Kenninghall in Norfolk, 186.
Kerry, Thomas, 201.
Ketch, Jack, 277.
Kildare, Gerald, Earl of, 50; committed to the Tower, 59; burial of, 59.
Killigrew, Sir R., 236.
Kilmarnock, William, Earl of, 15, 49, 51; taken prisoner and committed to the Tower, 301; trial of, 302; his execution, 307; buried in Chapel, 311.
Kingston, Lady, 103, 104.
———, Sir William, 81; his letters to Cromwell, 91, 92, 93, 95, 96, 99, 100, 104; attends Anne Boleyn at trial, 101, 103.
Kintail, battle of, 296.
Kneller, Sir Godfrey, 290.
Knightly, Richard, 251.
Knollys, Sir Francis, 207.
———, Sir William, 220.

Lapthorne, Richard, 282.
Lassells, Bryan, 207.
Latimer, Hugh, Bishop of Gloucester, 132, 134.
Laud, Archbishop, burial of, 51.
Leads, liberty of the, 169.
Lee, Sir Henry, 199.
———, Rowland, Bishop of Lichfield, 64.
Leicester, Robert Dudley, Earl of, 186, 205.
Lennox, Margaret, Countess of, 64.
Leveson, Sir Richard, 243.
Levison, Sir J., 221.
Lewknor, or Lecknolle, Mr., 44.
Leybourne, Margaret, 186.
———, Sir Thomas, 186.
Lidcote, Sir John, 239, 240.
Lincoln, Theophilus, Earl of, 250.
Lindsey, Robert, Earl of, 256.
Lloyd, Dr., Bishop of St. Asaph, 274.
Lobell, Paul de, 238.
Locke, Thomas, 160.
———, Sir William, 136.
Lodeman, Jane, 266.

INDEX.   335

London, Bishop of, his jurisdiction, 5, 6.
Lorkin, Mr., 237.
Lovat, Simon, Lord, 15, 49, 51; arrested, 313; his letter to Duke of Cumberland, 314; conveyed to London, 315; committed to the Tower, 316; his trial, 317; his execution, 319; buried in the Chapel, 322, 323.
Lower, Dr. Richard, 283.
Lucas, Robert, Lord, 280, 284, 285, 289, 290, 293.
Luke, Sir Oliver, 253.
——, Sir Walter, 80.
Lumley, Lord, 269.
Lyster, Sir Richard, 80.

Macaulay, Lord, his impressions of state of Chapel, 8.
Mackellar, Archibald, 7.
Maclean, Colonel, 26.
McCleish, Mr., 18.
Maitland, Major-General C. L., 16, 17, 30, 31.
Mansfield, William Murray, Earl of, 318.
Marischal, George Keith, Earl, 296.
Markham, Sir Griffin, arrested, 242, 243, 244; preparations for his execution, 246, 248.
————, Sir John, 152.
Mary, Queen, daughter of Henry VIII., 104, 116, 154.
—— Queen of Scots, proposed marriage, 186; her letter to Duke of Norfolk, 189, 191, 205.
Marshall, Captain, 304.
Mathew, Rev. Mr., his sermon, 6
Maule, John, 302.
Mayerne, Sir Theodore, 237.
Meek, Robert, 267.
Mellon, Captain, 313.
Merriton, Mr., 267.

Mildmay, Sir W., 112.
Milman, Colonel G. Bryan, 16, 17, 19, 22, 23, 26, 30, 31.
Mitford, A. B., 19, 20, 22, 23, 26, 30, 31, 184.
Mitton, Richard, 179.
Monmouth, James, Duke of, 17, 21, 25, 48, 50, 53; tradition respecting his execution, 108, 273; lands at Lyme, 268; attainted, 268; arrested, 269; his letters to James II., Queen Katharine, and Lord Rochester, 270, 271, 273; interview with James II., 271; committed to the Tower, 272; interview with his wife, the Bishop of Ely, &c., 273; his execution, 275; commemorative medals, 277; burial of, 278.
Montague, Sir James, 295.
Moore, Sir George, 35.
More, Cecilia, 83.
——, Cresacre, 84.
——, Elizabeth, 83.
——, John, 82, 84.
——, Sir Jonas, 38, 48.
——, Sir Thomas, 50; correspondence with Bishop Fisher, 67; summoned to Lambeth, 76; committed to the Tower, 77; letters to Margaret Roper, 78, 83; visited by his wife, 79; examined by Privy Council, 80; his trial, 80; list of jury, 81; his return to the Tower, 82; his execution, 86; his burial, 87; his head buried at Canterbury, 88; tomb at Chelsea, 89; his appearance, 90.
Mouat, Dr. F. J., 19, 20, 22, 23, 26, 29, 184.
Mountford, Thomas, 227, 229.
Murray, Earl of, 189.

Needham, Francis, 201.
Neville, Sir Henry, 189, 240, 241.

Newcastle, Thomas Holles, Duke of, 301, 323.
Newse, Clement, 160.
Newton, Sir Isaac, Master of the Mint, 290.
Nicholas, altar of Saint, 2.
Noel, Rt. Hon. G. J., 19, 22, 23, 26.
Norfolk, Dukes of, 101, 325.
———, Thomas Howard, third Duke, 50, 92, 155; his letter to Henry VIII., 101, 102, 112, 113, 122.
———, Thomas Howard, fourth Duke, 185; arrested, 189; his correspondence seized, 189; summoned before Privy Council, 190; trial of, 191; sentenced, 193; letters to his children and others, 194, 195; his execution delayed, 196; his speech on scaffold, 197; his execution, 197; burial of, 200, 231.
Norris, Henry, 42, 91, 92, 93.
Northampton, Henry Howard, Earl of, 239.
————, James, Earl of, 256.
————, William, Marquis of, 154, 159, 174.
Northumberland House, 239.
————————, Henry, Earl of, 92, 102.
————————, John Dudley, Duke of, 17, 22, 23, 24, 27, 50, 51, 53, 128, 148, 149, 150, 153; arrested, 154; committed to the Tower, 155; his trial, 156; sentenced, 157; preparations for execution, 158; attends mass, 159; his execution, 161; his speech on scaffold, 162; his burial, 163, 164, 177.
Nottingham, Charles Heneage Finch, Earl of, 258.
————, Daniel Finch, Earl of, 285.
————, Henry, Earl of, 201.

Nottingham, Lady, 226.
Nowell, Alexander, Dean of St. Paul's, 197, 200.

Oates, Titus, 255, 259, 262.
Offley, Sir Thomas, 174.
Oliver, Dr., 269.
Overbury, Sir Thomas, 47, 50, 53; knighted, 231; quarrels with Carr, 232; his letter to Cecil, 233; sent to the Tower, 234; attempts to poison him, 237; his death and burial, 238, 239, 240.

Palmer, Mr., 80, 81.
————, Sir Thomas, 159, 162, 163.
Parker, Chief Baron, 316.
————, Dr. Matthew, 152.
Parr, Queen Katharine, 127, 154.
Parry, Sir Thomas, 241.
Partridge, Sir Miles, executed, 153.
————, Nathaniel, 45, 167, 168, 174.
Paterson, Robert, 307.
Pavement, removed, 15; in chancel, 18, 20.
Pawlett, Sir Hampden, 243.
Payler, George, his monument, 36.
Peckham, Sir Edmond, 161.
Pelham, Henry, 305.
Pen, Sir W., 285.
Pepys, Samuel, visits the Chapel, 7; his opinion of coins, 285; his visit to the Mint, 286.
Perkin, Henry, 269.
Perlin, Stephen, 163.
Perne, William, 152.
Peryn, William, 152.
Petre, Lord, 255.
Perrott, Sir John, 45, 46, 47, 50, 200; committed to the Tower, 201; appeals to Council, 202; his oath, 203; his trial, 203; his supposed parentage, 204; his death, 204; burial of, 205.

INDEX. 337

Pewter bottle, Lord Griffin's, 291.
Peyton, Sir John, 223.
Philip II., King of Spain, 205.
Phillips, Thomas, 202.
Piers, John, 149.
Pietro in Vincoli, Church of, 3.
Piscina discovered, 5, 17.
Pole, Cardinal, 74, 114, 116, 118, 120.
——, Reginald, 116.
——, Sir Richard, 116.
Ponet, Bishop, 150.
Poole, Arthur, buried, 44; inscription by, 45.
——, Edmund, buried, 44; inscriptions by, 44.
——, Geoffrey, inscription by, 45.
Pope, Sir Thomas, 84.
Popham, Sir John, 203, 211, 220.
Porch removed, 10.
Port, Sir John, 80.
Portman, Sir William, 269.
Portuguese letter, 93, 105.
Powis House, 302.
——, Lord, 255.
Puckering, Sir Thomas, 237.
Pyne, Valentine, 37.

Queensberry, William, Earl of, 296.

Raimberd, Nicholas, 215.
Raleigh, Sir Walter, burial of, 51; witness at Earl of Essex's trial, 224, 226; at Earl of Essex's execution, 228, 236: committed to the Tower, 242; trial at Winchester, 248.
Randolf, Friar, 4.
Rannoch, Duke of, 297.
Ratcliffe, Charles, 318.
Register of burials, 42.
Reresby, Sir John, 258.
Rich, Sir Richard, Lord Chancellor, 68, 80, 130, 133, 135.
Richmond, Frances Stewart, Duchess of, 286.

Richmond, Henry Fitzroy, Duke of, 105.
Ridolfi, ——, agent of the Papal Court, 198.
Robinson, Sir J., 7, 256, 285.
Rochester, Bishop of (*see* Fisher).
————, Lawrence Hyde, Earl of, 271, 287.
————, Nicholas Heath, Bishop of, 123, 161.
Rochford, George Viscount, 21, 22, 50, 53; his arrest, 91; trial of, 92; his execution, 93; his speech, 93; his burial, 94.
————, Henry Carey, Lord, 250.
————, Jane, Viscountess, 23, 24, 25, 27, 50, 53; arrested and sent to Sion House, 123; attainted, 124; sent to the Tower, 125; execution of, 126; burial of, 127.
Roettier, James, 285, 287.
————, or Rotier, John, 48, 61; comes to England and is appointed Medallist, 285; engraves coronation medal, 288; suspected as a Jacobite, 288, 289, 290; his death and burial, 290.
————, Norbert, 287.
————, Philip, 285, 287.
Rogers, Rev. E. Jordan, 30, 31.
Rookwood, Thomas, 216.
Roper, Margaret, 82, 87, 88.
Rose, George, 302.
Rougham, Dennis, 46, 202, 203.
Russell, Thomas, 267.
————, William, Lord, 260; arrested, 263; his trial, 265.
Rutland, Roger, Earl of, 220.
Ryder, Sir Dudley, 318.

Sackville, Lady Margaret, 206.
Sadler, Sir Ralph, 112, 190.
Salisbury, James, Earl of, 256.
————, Margaret, Countess of, 23, 24, 25, 27, 29, 50, 53; com-

mitted to the Tower, 116, 118; arrested at Warblingon, 117; accusations against her, 118, 119; execution of, 120; burial of, 120; clothes sent to her, 121; her chapel, 121, 155.
Salisbury, Owen, 222.
———, Robert Cecil, Earl of, 222, 230, 232, 240, 243 (*see also* Cecil).
Salisbury, man-of-war, captured, 294.
Salle Church, 107.
Salmonby, John, 4.
Salt Tower, 208.
Salvin, Mr. A., 15, 18.
Sancroft, William, Archbishop of Canterbury, 256.
Sands, Lord, 220.
Sandwich, Ralph de, Constable, 2.
Scaffold on Tower Green, site of, 108.
Scharf, George, 184, 185.
Scotch Lords, burial-place of, 15, 312.
Scott, Sir Gilbert, 184.
———, Dr. John, 282.
Seaforth, Kenneth, Earl of, 297.
Sedgmoor, Battle of, 269.
Seymour, Lady Anne, 138.
———, Edward, 256.
———, Thomas Lord, of Sudeley, 50, 127; committed to the Tower, 128; examination of, 129, 130; desires an interview with his brother, 131; warrant for his execution, 132; execution of, 133, 134; letters found in his shoe, 133.
Sharp, Dr. John, 282.
Sharpe, John, 301.
Shelley, Mr., 209.
Shipsen, Dr., 7.
Shrewsbury, Charles, Earl of, 284.
———, George, Earl of, 190.

Shrewsbury, Gilbert, Earl of, 242, 243.
Sidney, Algernon, 262, 292.
———, Sir Robert, 221, 222.
Simon, Thomas, 285, 286.
Sion House, 123.
Sleg, Roger, 154.
Slingsby, Henry, Master of the Mint, 286, 287, 288.
Smeaton, Mark, 42, 91, 92, 93.
Smith, Sir Thomas, 132.
Somerset, Edward, Duke of, 17, 22, 50, 51, 53; letter to his brother, 127; committed to the Tower, 134, 136; arrest of, 135; released, 137; recommitted to the Tower, 138; trial of, 139; sentenced, 142; execution of, 143, 147; speech on scaffold, 144, 146; burial of, 148, 150, 163.
———, Frances, Countess of, 232.
———, Robert Carr, Earl of, 231, 236, 238.
Southampton, Henry, Earl of, 219, 220, 222, 224, 240, 241.
———, Thomas, Earl of, 136.
———, William, Earl of, 116, 117, 125.
Southwell, Sir Richard, 77, 80, 81.
Spellman, Sir John, 80.
Stafford, William, Viscount, 48, 50; accused by Titus Oates, 255; committed to Tower, 256; letters to his daughter, 257, 260; his trial, 259; sentenced, 260; execution of, 261, 262; burial of, 263.
Stanhope, Sir Michael, 152.
Stewart, Frances, Duchess of Richmond, 286.
Stone, Andrew, 301.
Strafford, Wentworth, Earl of, 51.
Strode, Edward, 269.
Stuart, Lady Arabella, 51, 249.
Stutt, John, 121.

INDEX.

Suffolk, Charles Brandon, Duke of, 92, 101, 102, 105, 125.
———, Henry Grey, Duke of, 50, 53, 169; letters to, 170, 171; arrested, 177, 178; escapes to Leicester, 178; committed to the Tower, 179; his trial, 179, 180; his execution, 181, 182; burial of, 183; supposed head of, 184; portraits of, 185.
Sunderland, Charles, Earl of, 273, 294.
Surrey, Henry, Earl of, 51, 101.

Taylor, John, 15, 18.
Tenison, Thomas, Archbishop of Canterbury, 274, 276.
Thirlby, Thomas, Bishop of Westminster, 125.
Throckmorton, Lady, 164.
Throgmorton, John, 173, 189.
Tichborne, Sir Benjamin, 246.
Tobacco-pipe found, 25.
Townshend, Lady, 306, 311.
Tracy, Henry, 221.
Travers, Dr., 245.
Trinity Church in the Minories, 184.
Tudor, John, 49.
Tullibardine, John, Marquis of, 296.
——————, William, Marquis of, 49, 51; joins rebels in 1715, 296; escapes to France, 297; appointed to command in 1745, 298; surrender, 298; committed to the Tower, 299; his illness, 299; his death and burial, 300.
Turner, Anne, 236.
———, Francis, Bishop of Ely, 274, 276.
Tylney, Elizabeth, 175.

Vanderputt, Sir Peter, 275, 276.
Vane, Sir Ralph, 43, 50; committed to the Tower, 149; his trial, 150; sentenced, 151; executed and buried, 153.
Vernon, Henry, 257.
Vestry, new, built in 1877, 17.

Waade, Sir William, 6, 236.
Wales, Petty, 3.
Wallop, Sir Henry, 243.
———, Sir John, 69.
Walpole, Horace, his letters, 305, 306, 307, 310, 311, 318, 322.
Walsingham, Sir Edward, 67, 81, 102, 121.
Warblington Castle, 117.
Warren, Sir Ralph, 136.
Warwick, Earl of (see Northumberland).
——————, Edward, Earl of, 116.
Watson, William, 242.
Weldon, Sir A., 124, 232.
Wem, Lord, 285.
Wentworth, Lady Henrietta, 275, 276.
West Horsley, 217.
Westminster Abbey, door at, 184.
——————, Bishop of, 125.
Weston, Sir Francis, 42, 91, 92, 39.
———, Dr. Hugh, 181.
———, Richard, 236, 238.
Whistler, Lawrence, 215.
White, Thomas, Lord Mayor, 169.
Wightman, General, 296.
Willes, Chief Justice, 316.
William III., 272, 284.
Williams, Sir Thomas, 45, 46.
Williamson, General Adam, 299, 304, 307, 311, 318, 319.
——————, Sir Joseph, 256.
Willmott, Dr., 299.
Wilson, Dr., Vicar of Croydon, 77.
Wiltshire, Thomas, Earl of, 92.
Winchester, trials at, 244.
——————, William Paulet, Marquis of, 139, 143.

Wingfield, Sir Anthony, 136.
——, Sir Richard, 77.
Winwood, Sir Ralph, his letters, 233, 235, 237, 241.
Wood, John A., 78.
Worcester, Edward, Earl of, 220.
Wotton, Sir Henry, 218, 234, 235.
Wright, Richard, 301.
Wrottesley, Col. Hon. G., 17.

Wyatt, Sir Thomas, 115, 169, 177, 181.

Yarmouth, sailors mutiny at, 153.
Yelverton, Christopher, 223.
York House, 218.
—— Place, 91.
Yorke, Sir Charles, 10, 16, 30, 31.
——, Sir John, 135, 137.

50A, ALBEMARLE STREET, LONDON,
January, 1876.

MR. MURRAY'S

GENERAL LIST OF WORKS.

ALBERT (THE) MEMORIAL. A Descriptive and Illustrated Account of the National Monument erected to the PRINCE CONSORT at Kensington. Illustrated by Engravings of its Architecture, Decorations, Sculptured Groups, Statues, Mosaics, Metalwork, &c. With Descriptive Text. By DOYNE C. BELL. With 24 Plates. Folio. 12*l*. 12*s*.
——— (PRINCE) SPEECHES AND ADDRESSES with an Introduction, giving some outline of his Character. With Portrait. 8vo. 10*s*. 6*d*.; or *Popular Edition*, fcap. 8vo. 1*s*.
ALBERT DÜRER; his Life and Works. By DR. THAUSING, Keeper of Archduke Albert's Art Collection at Vienna. Translated from the German. With Portrait Illustrations. Medium 8vo.
[*In the Press.*
ABBOTT'S (REV. J.) Memoirs of a Church of England Missionary in the North American Colonies. Post 8vo. 2*s*.
ABERCROMBIE'S (JOHN) Enquiries concerning the Intellectual Powers and the Investigation of Truth. Fcap. 8vo. 3*s*. 6*d*.
——— Philosophy of the Moral Feelings. Fcap. 8vo. 2*s*. 6*d*.
ACLAND'S (REV. CHARLES) Popular Account of the Manners and Customs of India. Post 8vo. 2*s*.
ÆSOP'S FABLES. A New Version. With Historical Preface. By Rev. THOMAS JAMES. With 100 Woodcuts, by TENNIEL and WOLF. Post 8vo. 2*s*. 6*d*.
AGRICULTURAL (ROYAL) JOURNAL. (*Published half yearly.*)
AIDS TO FAITH: a Series of Theological Essays. 8vo. 9*s*.

CONTENTS.

Miracles	DEAN MANSEL.
Evidences of Christianity	BISHOP FITZGERALD.
Prophecy & Mosaic Record of Creation	Dr. MCCAUL.
Ideology and Subscription	Canon COOK.
The Pentateuch	Canon RAWLINSON.
Inspiration	BISHOP HAROLD BROWNE.
Death of Christ	ARCHBISHOP THOMSON.
Scripture and its Interpretation	BISHOP ELLICOTT.

AMBER-WITCH (THE). A most interesting Trial for Witchcraft. Translated by LADY DUFF GORDON. Post 8vo. 2*s*.
ARMY LIST (THE). *Published Monthly by Authority.*
ARTHUR'S (LITTLE) History of England. By LADY CALLCOTT. *New Edition, continued to* 1872. With 36 Woodcuts. Fcap. 8vo. 1*s*. 6*d*.
AUSTIN'S (JOHN) LECTURES ON GENERAL JURISPRUDENCE; or, the Philosophy of Positive Law. Edited by ROBERT CAMPBELL. 2 Vols. 8vo. 32*s*.
——— STUDENT'S EDITION, compiled from the above work. Post 8vo. 12*s*.
ARNOLD'S (THOS.) Ecclesiastical and Secular Architecture of Scotland: The Abbeys, Churches, Castles, and Mansions. With Illustrations. Medium 8vo. [*In Preparation.*

B

LIST OF WORKS

ADMIRALTY PUBLICATIONS; Issued by direction of the Lords Commissioners of the Admiralty:—
A MANUAL OF SCIENTIFIC ENQUIRY, for the Use of Travellers. *Fourth Edition.* Edited by ROBERT MAIN, M.A. Woodcuts. Post 8vo. 8s. 6d.
GREENWICH ASTRONOMICAL OBSERVATIONS 1841 to 1846, and 1847 to 1871. Royal 4to. 20s. each.
MAGNETICAL AND METEOROLOGICAL OBSERVATIONS. 1840 to 1847. Royal 4to. 20s. each.
APPENDICES TO OBSERVATIONS.
  1837. Logarithms of Sines and Cosines in Time. 8s.
  1842. Catalogue of 1439 Stars, from Observations made in 1836 to 1841. 4s.
  1845. Longitude of Valentia (Chronometrical). 3s.
  1847. Description of Altazimuth. 3s.
        Twelve Years' Catalogue of Stars, from Observations made in 1836 to 1847. 4s.
        Description of Photographic Apparatus. 2s.
  1851. Maskelyne's Ledger of Stars. 3s.
  1852. I. Description of the Transit Circle. 3s.
  1853. Refraction Tables. 3s.
  1854. Description of the Zenith Tube. 3s.
        Six Years' Catalogue of Stars, from Observations. 1848 to 1853. 4s.
  1862. Seven Years' Catalogue of Stars, from Observations. 1854 to 1860. 10s.
        Plan of Ground Buildings. 3s.
        Longitude of Valentia (Galvanic). 2s.
  1864. Moon's Semid. from Occultations. 2s.
        Planetary Observations, 1831 to 1835. 2s.
  1868. Corrections of Elements of Jupiter and Saturn. 2s.
        Second Seven Years' Catalogue of 2760 Stars for 1861 to 1867. 4s.
        Description of the Great Equatorial. 3s.
  1856. Descriptive Chronograph. 3s.
  1860. Reduction of Deep Thermometer Observations. 2s.
  1871. History and Description of Water Telescope. 3s.
  Cape of Good Hope Observations (Star Ledgers). 1856 to 1863. 2s.
  —————————— 1856. 5s.
  —————————— Astronomical Results. 1857 to 1858. 5s.
  Report on Teneriffe Astronomical Experiment. 1856. 5s.
  Paramatta Catalogue of 7385 Stars. 1822 to 1826. 4s.
ASTRONOMICAL RESULTS. 1847 to 1871. 4to. 3s. each.
MAGNETICAL AND METEOROLOGICAL RESULTS. 1847 to 1871. 4to. 3s. each.
REDUCTION OF THE OBSERVATIONS OF PLANETS. 1750 to 1830. Royal 4to. 20s. each.
—————————— LUNAR OBSERVATIONS. 1750 to 1830. 2 Vols. Royal 4to. 20s. each.
—————————— 1831 to 1851. 4to. 10s. each.
BERNOULLI'S SEXCENTENARY TABLE. 1779. 4to. 5s.
BESSEL'S AUXILIARY TABLES FOR HIS METHOD OF CLEARING LUNAR DISTANCES. 8vo. 2s.
ENCKE'S BERLINER JAHRBUCH, for 1830. *Berlin,* 1828. 8vo. 9s.
HANSEN'S TABLES DE LA LUNE. 4to. 20s.
LAX'S TABLES FOR FINDING THE LATITUDE AND LONGITUDE. 1821. 8vo. 10s.

ADMIRALTY PUBLICATIONS—*continued.*
 LUNAR OBSERVATIONS at GREENWICH. 1783 to 1819. Compared with the Tables, 1821. 4to. 7s. 6d.
 MACLEAR ON LACAILLE'S ARC OF MERIDIAN. 2 Vols. 20s. each.
 MAYER'S DISTANCES of the MOON'S CENTRE from the PLANETS. 1822, 3s.; 1823, 4s. 6d. 1824 to 1835. 8vo. 4s. each.
 ———— TABULÆ MOTUUM SOLIS ET LUNÆ. 1770. 5s.
 ———— ASTRONOMICAL OBSERVATIONS MADE AT GOTTINGEN, from 1756 to 1761. 1826. Folio. 7s. 6d.
 NAUTICAL ALMANACS, from 1767 to 1877. 2s. 6d. each.
 ———————————— SELECTIONS FROM, up to 1812. 8vo. 5s. 1834-54. 5s.
 ———————————— SUPPLEMENTS, 1828 to 1833, 1837 and 1838. 2s. each.
 ———————————— TABLE requisite to be used with the N.A. 1781. 8vo. 5s.
 SABINE'S PENDULUM EXPERIMENTS to DETERMINE THE FIGURE OF THE EARTH. 1825. 4to. 40s.
 SHEPHERD'S TABLES for CORRECTING LUNAR DISTANCES. 1772. Royal 4to. 21s.
 ———————— TABLES, GENERAL, of the MOON'S DISTANCE from the SUN, and 10 STARS. 1787. Folio. 5s. 6d.
 TAYLOR'S SEXAGESIMAL TABLE. 1780. 4to. 15s.
 ———— TABLES OF LOGARITHMS. 4to. 60s.
 TIARK'S ASTRONOMICAL OBSERVATIONS for the LONGITUDE of MADEIRA. 1822. 4to. 5s.
 ———— CHRONOMETRICAL OBSERVATIONS for DIFFERENCES of LONGITUDE between DOVER, PORTSMOUTH, and FALMOUTH. 1823. 4to. 5s.
 VENUS and JUPITER: OBSERVATIONS of, compared with the TABLES. London, 1822. 4to. 2s.
 WALES' AND BAYLY'S ASTRONOMICAL OBSERVATIONS. 1777. 4to. 21s.
 ———— REDUCTION OF ASTRONOMICAL OBSERVATIONS MADE IN THE SOUTHERN HEMISPHERE. 1764—1771. 1788. 4to. 10s. 6d.

BARBAULD'S (MRS.) Hymns in Prose for Children. With Illustrations. Crown 8vo. 5s.
BARROW'S (SIR JOHN) Autobiographical Memoir, from Early Life to Advanced Age. Portrait. 8vo. 16s.
———— (JOHN) Life, Exploits, and Voyages of Sir Francis Drake. Post 8vo. 2s.
BARRY'S (SIR CHARLES) Life and Works. By CANON BARRY. With Portrait and Illustrations. Medium 8vo. 15s.
BATES' (H. W.) Records of a Naturalist on the River Amazon during eleven years of Adventure and Travel. Illustrations. Post 8vo. 7s. 6d.
BAX'S (CAPTAIN) Russian Tartary, Eastern Siberia, China, Japan, and Formosa. A Narrative of a Cruise in the Eastern Seas. With Map and Illustrations. Crown 8vo. 12s.
BEAUCLERK'S (LADY DIANA) Summer and Winter in Norway. With Illustrations. Small 8vo. 6s.
BELCHER'S (LADY) Account of the Mutineers of the 'Bounty,' and their Descendants; with their Settlements in Pitcairn and Norfolk Islands. With Illustrations. Post 8vo. 12s.
BELL'S (SIR CHAS.) Familiar Letters. Portrait. Post 8vo. 12s.

LIST OF WORKS

BELT'S (THOS.) Naturalist in Nicaragua, including a Residence at the Gold Mines of Chontales; with Journeys in the Savannahs and Forests; and Observations on Animals and Plants. Illustrations. Post 8vo. 12s.

BERTRAM'S (JAS. G.) Harvest of the Sea: an Account of British Food Fishes, including sketches of Fisheries and Fisher Folk. With 50 Illustrations. 8vo. 9s.

BIBLE COMMENTARY. EXPLANATORY and CRITICAL. With a REVISION of the TRANSLATION. By BISHOPS and CLERGY of the ANGLICAN CHURCH. Edited by F. C. COOK, M.A., Canon of Exeter. Medium 8vo. VOL. I., 30s. VOLS. II. and III., 36s. VOL. IV., 24s. Vol. V., 20s. Vol. VI., 20s.

Vol. I. { GENESIS. EXODUS. LEVITICUS. NUMBERS. DEUTERONOMY. }

Vols. II. and III. { JOSHUA. JUDGES, RUTH, SAMUEL. KINGS, CHRONICLES, EZRA, NEHEMIAH, ESTHER. }

VOL. IV. { JOB. PSALMS. PROVERBS. ECCLESIASTES. SONG OF SOLOMON. }

Vol. V. { ISAIAH. JEREMIAH. }

Vol. VI. { EZEKIEL. DANIEL. MINOR PROPHETS. }

BIRCH'S (SAMUEL) History of Ancient Pottery and Porcelain: Egyptian, Assyrian, Greek, Roman, and Etruscan. With Coloured Plates and 200 Illustrations. Medium 8vo. 42s.

BIRD'S (ISABELLA) Hawaiian Archipelago; or Six Months Among the Palm Groves, Coral Reefs, and Volcanoes of the Sandwich Islands. With Illustrations. Crown 8vo. 12s.

BISSET'S (ANDREW) History of the Commonwealth of England, from the Death of Charles I. to the Expulsion of the Long Parliament by Cromwell. Chiefly from the MSS. in the State Paper Office. 2 vols. 8vo. 30s.

———— (GENERAL) Sport and War in South Africa from 1834 to 1867, with a Narrative of the Duke of Edinburgh's Visit. With Map and Illustrations. Crown 8vo. 14s.

BLACKSTONE'S COMMENTARIES; adapted to the Present State of the Law. By R. MALCOLM KERR. LL.D. *Revised Edition*, incorporating all the Recent Changes in the Law. 4 vols. 8vo.

BLUNT'S (REV. J. J.) Undesigned Coincidences in the Writings of the Old and New Testaments, an Argument of their Veracity: containing the Books of Moses, Historical and Prophetical Scriptures, and the Gospels and Acts. Post 8vo. 6s.

———— History of the Church in the First Three Centuries. Post 8vo. 6s.

———— Parish Priest; His Duties, Acquirements and Obligations. Post 8vo. 6s.

———— Lectures on the Right Use of the Early Fathers. 8vo. 9s.

———— University Sermons. Post 8vo. 6s.

———— Plain Sermons. 2 vols. Post 8vo. 12s.

BLOMFIELD'S (BISHOP) Memoir, with Selections from his Correspondence. By his Son. Portrait, post 8vo. 12s.

BOSWELL'S (JAMES) Life of Samuel Johnson, LL.D. Including the Tour to the Hebrides. By Mr. CROKER. *New Edition*. Portraits. 4 vols. 8vo. [*In Preparation.*

BRACE'S (C. L.) Manual of Ethnology; or the Races of the Old World. Post 8vo. 6s.

BOOK OF COMMON PRAYER. Illustrated with Coloured Borders, Initial Letters, and Woodcuts. 8vo. 18s.

BORROW'S (GEORGE) Bible in Spain; or the Journeys, Adventures, and Imprisonments of an Englishman in an Attempt to circulate the Scriptures in the Peninsula. Post 8vo. 5s.
―――― Gypsies of Spain; their Manners, Customs, Religion, and Language. With Portrait. Post 8vo. 5s.
―――― Lavengro; The Scholar—The Gypsy—and the Priest. Post 8vo. 5s.
―――― Romany Rye—a Sequel to "Lavengro." Post 8vo. 5s.
―――― WILD WALES: its People, Language, and Scenery. Post 8vo. 5s.
―――― Romano Lavo-Lil; Word-Book of the Romany, or English Gypsy Language; with Specimens of their Poetry, and an account of certain Gypsyries. Post 8vo. 10s. 6d.
BRAY'S (MRS.) Life of Thomas Stothard, R.A. With Portrait and 60 Woodcuts. 4to. 21s.
―――― Revolt of the Protestants in the Cevennes. With some Account of the Huguenots in the Seventeenth Century. Post 8vo. 10s.6d.

BRITISH ASSOCIATION REPORTS. 8vo.

York and Oxford, 1831-32, 13s. 6d.
Cambridge, 1833, 12s.
Edinburgh, 1834, 15s.
Dublin, 1835, 13s. 6d.
Bristol, 1836, 12s.
Liverpool, 1837, 16s. 6d.
Newcastle, 1838, 15s.
Birmingham, 1839, 13s. 6d.
Glasgow, 1840, 15s.
Plymouth, 1841, 13s. 6d.
Manchester, 1842, 10s. 6d.
Cork, 1843, 12s.
York, 1844, 20s.
Cambridge, 1845, 12s.
Southampton, 1846, 15s.
Oxford, 1847, 18s.
Swansea, 1848, 9s.
Birmingham, 1849, 10s.
Edinburgh, 1850, 15s.
Ipswich, 1851, 16s. 6d.
Belfast, 1852, 15s.
Hull, 1853, 10s. 6d.
Liverpool, 1854, 18s.
Glasgow, 1855, 15s.
Cheltenham, 1856, 18s.
Dublin, 1857, 15s.
Leeds, 1858, 20s.
Aberdeen, 1859, 15s.
Oxford, 1860, 25s.
Manchester, 1861, 15s.
Cambridge, 1862, 20s.
Newcastle, 1863, 25s.
Bath, 1864, 18s.
Birmingham, 1865, 25s
Nottingham, 1866, 24s.
Dundee, 1867, 26s.
Norwich, 1868, 25s.
Exeter, 1869, 22s.
Liverpool, 1870, 18s.
Edinburgh, 1871, 16s.
Brighton, 1872, 24s.
Bradford, 1873, 25s.
Belfast, 1874.

BROUGHTON'S (LORD) Journey through Albania, Turkey in Europe and Asia, to Constantinople. Illustrations. 2 Vols. 8vo. 30s.
―――― Visits to Italy. 2 Vols. Post 8vo. 18s.
BROWNLOW'S (LADY) Reminiscences of a Septuagenarian. From the year 1802 to 1815. Post 8vo. 7s. 6d.
BRUGSCH'S (PROFESSOR) History of Ancient Egypt. Derived from Monuments and Inscriptions. *New Edition.* Translated by H. DANBY SEYMOUR. 8vo. [*In Preparation.*
BUCKLEY'S (ARABELLA B.) Short History of Natural Science, and the Progress of Discovery from the time of the Greeks to the present day, for Schools and young Persons. Illustrations. Post 8vo. 9s.
BURGON'S (REV. J. W.) Christian Gentleman; or, Memoir of Patrick Fraser Tytler. Post 8vo. 9s.
―――― Letters from Rome. Post 8vo. 12s.
BURN'S (COL.) Dictionary of Naval and Military Technical Terms, English and French—French and English. Crown 8vo. 15s.
BURROW'S (MONTAGU) Constitutional Progress. A Series of Lectures delivered before the University of Oxford. Post 8vo. 6s.

BUXTON'S (CHARLES) Memoirs of Sir Thomas Fowell Buxton, Bart. With Selections from his Correspondence. Portrait. 8vo. 16s.
Popular Edition. Fcap. 8vo. 5s.

——————— Notes of Thought. With Biographical Sketch. By Rev. LLEWELLYN DAVIES. With Portrait. Crown 8vo. 10s. 6d.

BURCKHARDT'S (DR. JACOB) Cicerone; or Art Guide to Painting in Italy. Edited by REV. DR. A. VON ZAHN, and Translated from the German by MRS. A. CLOUGH. Post 8vo. 6s.

BYLES' (SIR JOHN) Foundations of Religion in the Mind and Heart of Man. Post 8vo. 6s.

BYRON'S (LORD) Life, Letters, and Journals. By THOMAS MOORE. *Cabinet Edition.* Plates. 6 Vols. Fcap. 8vo. 18s.; or One Volume, Portraits. Royal 8vo, 7s. 6d.

——————— and Poetical Works. *Popular Edition.* Portraits. 2 vols. Royal 8vo. 15s.

—— Poetical Works. *Library Edition.* Portrait. 6 Vols. 8vo. 45s.
    Cabinet Edition. Plates. 10 Vols. 12mo. 30s.
——————— *Pocket Edition.* 8 Vols. 24mo. 21s. *In a case.*
——————— *Popular Edition.* Plates. Royal 8vo. 7s. 6d.
    Pearl Edition. Crown 8vo. 2s. 6d.

——————— Childe Harold. With 80 Engravings. Crown 8vo. 12s.
——————— ——————— 16mo. 2s. 6d.
——————— ——————— Vignettes. 16mo. 1s.
——————— ——————— Portrait. 16mo. 6d.
——————— Tales and Poems. 24mo. 2s. 6d.
——————— Miscellaneous. 2 Vols. 24mo. 5s.
——————— Dramas and Plays. 2 Vols. 24mo. 5s.
——————— Don Juan and Beppo. 2 Vols. 24mo. 5s.
——————— Beauties. Poetry and Prose. Portrait. Fcap. 8vo. 3s. 6d.

BUTTMAN'S Lexilogus; a Critical Examination of the Meaning of numerous Greek Words, chiefly in Homer and Hesiod. By Rev. J. R. FISHLAKE. 8vo. 12s.

——————— Irregular Greek Verbs. With all the Tenses extant—their Formation, Meaning, and Usage, with Notes, by Rev. J. R. FISHLAKE. Post 8vo. 6s.

CALLCOTT'S (LADY) Little Arthur's History of England. *New Edition, brought down to 1872.* With Woodcuts. Fcap. 8vo. 1s. 6d.

CARNARVON'S (LORD) Portugal, Gallicia, and the Basque Provinces. Post 8vo. 3s. 6d.

——————— Reminiscences of Athens and the Morea. With Map. Crown 8vo. 7s. 6d.

——————— Recollections of the Druses of Lebanon. With Notes on their Religion. Post 8vo. 5s. 6d.

CASTLEREAGH (THE) DESPATCHES, from the commencement of the official career of Viscount Castlereagh to the close of his life. 12 Vols. 8vo. 14s. each.

CAMPBELL'S (LORD) Lord Chancellors and Keepers of the Great Seal of England. From the Earliest Times to the Death of Lord Eldon in 1838. 10 Vols. Crown 8vo. 6s. each.
———— Chief Justices of England. From the Norman Conquest to the Death of Lord Tenterden. 4 Vols. Crown 8vo. 6s. each.
———— Lords Lyndhurst and Brougham. 8vo. 16s.
———— Shakspeare's Legal Acquirements. 8vo. 5s. 6d.
———— Lord Bacon. Fcap. 8vo. 2s. 6d.
———— (SIR NEIL) Account of Napoleon at Fontainebleau and Elba. Being a Journal of Occurrences and Notes of his Conversations, &c. Portrait. 8vo. 15s.
———— (SIR GEORGE) India as it may be: an Outline of a proposed Government and Policy. 8vo.
———— (THOS.) Essay on English Poetry. With Short Lives of the British Poets. Post 8vo. 3s. 6d.
CATHCART'S (SIR GEORGE) Commentaries on the War in Russia and Germany, 1812-13. Plans. 8vo. 14s.
CAVALCASELLE AND CROWE'S History of Painting in NORTH ITALY, from the 14th to the 16th Century. With Illustrations. 2 Vols. 8vo. 42s.
———— Early Flemish Painters, their Lives and Works. Illustrations. Post 8vo. 10s. 6d.; or Large Paper, 8vo. 15s.
CHILD'S (G. CHAPLIN, M.D.) Benedicite; or, Song of the Three Children; being Illustrations of the Power, Beneficence, and Design manifested by the Creator in his works. Post 8vo. 6s.
CHISHOLM'S (Mrs.) Perils of the Polar Seas; True Stories of Arctic Discovery and Adventure. Illustrations. Post 8vo. 6s.
CHURTON'S (ARCHDEACON) Gongora. An Historical Essay on the Age of Philip III. and IV. of Spain. With Translations. Portrait. 2 Vols. Small 8vo. 12s.
———— Poetical Remains, Translations and Imitations. Portrait. Post 8vo. 7s. 6d.
———— New Testament. Edited with a Plain Practical Commentary for Families and General Readers. With 100 Panoramic and other Views, from Sketches made on the Spot. 2 vols. 8vo. 2s.
CICERO'S LIFE AND TIMES. His Character as a Statesman, Orator, and Friend, with a Selection from his Correspondence and Orations. By WILLIAM FORSYTH, M.P. With Illustrations. 8vo. 10s. 6d.
CLARK'S (SIR JAMES) Memoir of Dr. John Conolly. Comprising a Sketch of the Treatment of the Insane in Europe and America. With Portrait. Post 8vo. 10s. 6d.
CLIVE'S (LORD) Life. By REV. G. R. GLEIG. Post 8vo. 3s. 6d.
CLODE'S (C. M.) Military Forces of the Crown; their Administration and Government. 2 Vols. 8vo. 21s. each.
———— Administration of Justice under Military and Martial Law, as applicable to the Army, Navy, Marine, and Auxiliary Forces. 8vo. 12s.
COLCHESTER (THE) Papers. The Diary and Correspondence of Charles Abbott, Lord Colchester, Speaker of the House of Commons, 1802-1817. Portrait. 3 Vols. 8vo. 42s.

LIST OF WORKS

CHURCH (THE) & THE AGE. Essays on the Principles and Present Position of the Anglican Church. 2 vols. 8vo. 26s. Contents:—

VOL. I.
Anglican Principles.—Dean Hook.
Modern Religious Thought.—Bishop Ellicott.
State, Church, and Synods.—Rev. Dr. Irons.
Religious Use of Taste.—Rev. R. St. John Tyrwhitt.
Place of the Laity.—Professor Burrows.
Parish Priest.—Rev. Walsham How.
Divines of 16th and 17th Centuries.—Rev. A. W. Haddan.
Liturgies and Ritual, Rev. M. F. Sadler.
Church & Education.—Canon Barry.
Indian Missions.—Sir Bartle Frere.
Church and the People.—Rev. W. D. Maclagan.
Conciliation and Comprehension.—Rev. Dr. Weir.

VOL. II.
Church and Pauperism.—Earl Nelson.
American Church.—Bishop of Western New York.
Church and Science. — Prebendary Clark.
Ecclesiastical Law.—Isambard Brunel.
Church & National Education.—Canon Norris.
Church and Universities.—John G. Talbot.
Toleration.—Dean Cowie.
Eastern Church and Anglican Communion.—Rev. Geo. Williams.
A Disestablished Church.—Dean of Cashel.
Christian Tradition.—Rev. Dr. Irons.
Dogma.—Rev. Dr. Weir.
Parochial Councils. — Archdeacon Chapman.

COLERIDGE'S (SAMUEL TAYLOR) Table-Talk. Portrait. 12mo. 3s. 6d.

COLLINGWOOD'S (CUTHBERT) Rambles of a Naturalist on the Shores and Waters of the China Sea. With Illustrations. 8vo. 16s.

COLONIAL LIBRARY. [See Home and Colonial Library.]

COOK'S (Canon) Sermons Preached at Lincoln's Inn. 8vo. 9s.

COOKE'S (E. W.) Artist's Portfolio. Being Sketches made during Tours in Holland, Germany, Italy, Egypt, &c. 50 Plates. Royal 4to. [In Preparation.

COOKERY (MODERN DOMESTIC). Founded on Principles of Economy and Practical Knowledge. By a Lady. Woodcuts. Fcap. 8vo. 5s.

COOPER'S (T. T.) Travels of a Pioneer of Commerce on an Overland Journey from China towards India. Illustrations. 8vo. 16s.

CORNWALLIS (THE) Papers and Correspondence during the American War,—Administrations in India,—Union with Ireland, and Peace of Amiens. 3 Vols. 8vo. 63s.

COWPER'S (COUNTESS) Diary while Lady of the Bedchamber to Caroline, Princess of Wales, 1714–20. Portrait. 8vo. 10s. 6d.

CRABBE'S (REV. GEORGE) Life and Poetical Works. With Illustrations. Royal 8vo. 7s.

CRAWFORD & BALCARRE'S (Earl of) Etruscan Inscriptions. Analyzed, Translated, and Commented upon. 8vo. 12s.

——— Argo ; or the Quest of the Golden Fleece. In Ten Books. 8vo.

CROKER'S (J. W.) Progressive Geography for Children. 18mo. 1s. 6d.

——— Stories for Children, Selected from the History of England. Woodcuts. 16mo. 2s. 6d.

——— Boswell's Life of Johnson. Including the Tour to the Hebrides. New Edition. Portraits. 4 vols. 8vo. [In Preparation.

——— Early Period of the French Revolution. 8vo. 15s.

——— Historical Essay on the Guillotine. Fcap. 8vo. 1s.

CUMMING'S (R. GORDON) Five Years of a Hunter's Life in the Far Interior of South Africa. Woodcuts. Post 8vo. 6s.

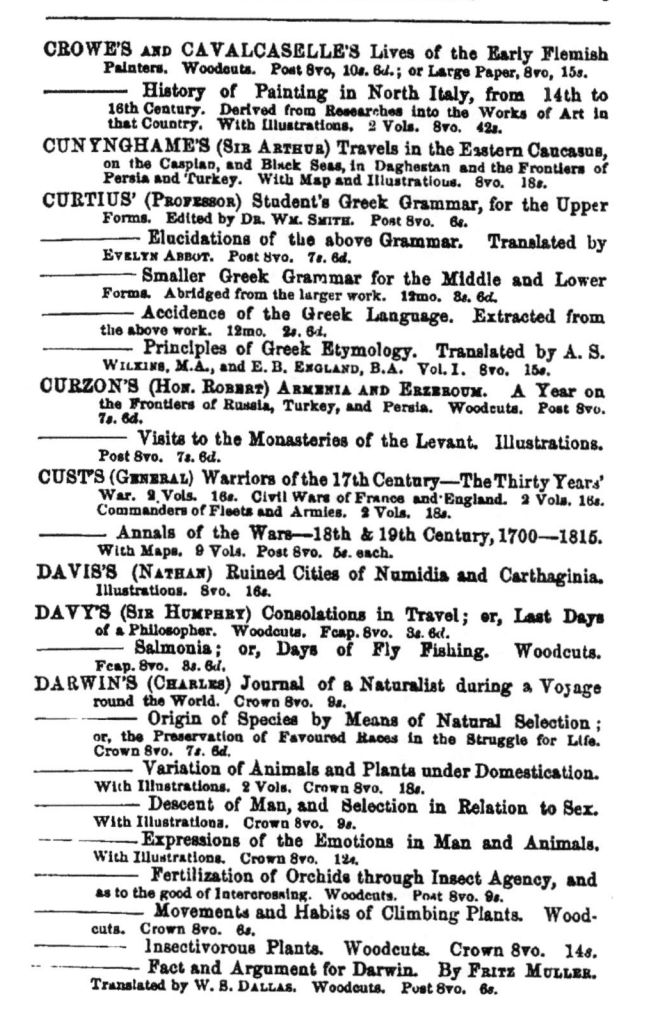

CROWE'S AND CAVALCASELLE'S Lives of the Early Flemish Painters. Woodcuts. Post 8vo, 10s. 6d.; or Large Paper, 8vo, 15s.
———— History of Painting in North Italy, from 14th to 16th Century. Derived from Researches into the Works of Art in that Country. With Illustrations. 2 Vols. 8vo. 42s.
CUNYNGHAME'S (SIR ARTHUR) Travels in the Eastern Caucasus, on the Caspian, and Black Seas, in Daghestan and the Frontiers of Persia and Turkey. With Map and Illustrations. 8vo. 18s.
CURTIUS' (PROFESSOR) Student's Greek Grammar, for the Upper Forms. Edited by DR. WM. SMITH. Post 8vo. 6s.
———— Elucidations of the above Grammar. Translated by EVELYN ABBOT. Post 8vo. 7s. 6d.
———— Smaller Greek Grammar for the Middle and Lower Forms. Abridged from the larger work. 12mo. 3s. 6d.
———— Accidence of the Greek Language. Extracted from the above work. 12mo. 2s. 6d.
———— Principles of Greek Etymology. Translated by A. S. WILKINS, M.A., and E. B. ENGLAND, B.A. Vol. I. 8vo. 15s.
CURZON'S (HON. ROBERT) ARMENIA AND ERZEROUM. A Year on the Frontiers of Russia, Turkey, and Persia. Woodcuts. Post 8vo. 7s. 6d.
———— Visits to the Monasteries of the Levant. Illustrations. Post 8vo. 7s. 6d.
CUST'S (GENERAL) Warriors of the 17th Century—The Thirty Years' War. 2 Vols. 16s. Civil Wars of France and England. 2 Vols. 16s. Commanders of Fleets and Armies. 2 Vols. 18s.
———— Annals of the Wars—18th & 19th Century, 1700—1815. With Maps. 9 Vols. Post 8vo. 5s. each.
DAVIS'S (NATHAN) Ruined Cities of Numidia and Carthaginia. Illustrations. 8vo. 16s.
DAVY'S (SIR HUMPHRY) Consolations in Travel; or, Last Days of a Philosopher. Woodcuts. Fcap. 8vo. 3s. 6d.
———— Salmonia; or, Days of Fly Fishing. Woodcuts. Fcap. 8vo. 3s. 6d.
DARWIN'S (CHARLES) Journal of a Naturalist during a Voyage round the World. Crown 8vo. 9s.
———— Origin of Species by Means of Natural Selection; or, the Preservation of Favoured Races in the Struggle for Life. Crown 8vo. 7s. 6d.
———— Variation of Animals and Plants under Domestication. With Illustrations. 2 Vols. Crown 8vo. 18s.
———— Descent of Man, and Selection in Relation to Sex. With Illustrations. Crown 8vo. 9s.
———— Expressions of the Emotions in Man and Animals. With Illustrations. Crown 8vo. 12s.
———— Fertilization of Orchids through Insect Agency, and as to the good of Intercrossing. Woodcuts. Post 8vo. 9s.
———— Movements and Habits of Climbing Plants. Woodcuts. Crown 8vo. 6s.
———— Insectivorous Plants. Woodcuts. Crown 8vo. 14s.
———— Fact and Argument for Darwin. By FRITZ MULLER. Translated by W. S. DALLAS. Woodcuts. Post 8vo. 6s.

LIST OF WORKS

DELEPIERRE'S (OCTAVE) History of Flemish Literature. 8vo. 9s.
——————— Historic Difficulties & Contested Events. Post 8vo. 6s.
DENISON'S (E. B.) Life of Bishop Lonsdale. With Selections from his Writings. With Portrait. Crown 8vo. 10s. 6d.
DERBY'S (EARL OF) Iliad of Homer rendered into English Blank Verse. 2 Vols. Post 8vo. 10s.
DE ROS'S (LORD) Young Officer's Companion; or, Essays on Military Duties and Qualities: with Examples and Illustrations from History. Post 8vo. 9s.
DEUTSCH'S (EMANUEL) Talmud, Islam, The Targums and other Literary Remains. 8vo. 12s.
DILKE'S (SIR C. W.) Papers of a Critic. Selected from the Writings of the late CHAS. WENTWORTH DILKE. With a Biographical Sketch. 2 Vols. 8vo. 24s.
DOG-BREAKING; the Most Expeditious, Certain, and Easy Method, whether great excellence or only mediocrity be required. With a Few Hints for those who Love the Dog and the Gun. By LIEUT.-GEN. HUTCHINSON. With 40 Woodcuts. Crown 8vo. 9s.
DOMESTIC MODERN COOKERY. Founded on Principles of Economy and Practical Knowledge, and adapted for Private Families. Woodcuts. Fcap. 8vo. 5s.
DOUGLAS'S (SIR HOWARD) Life and Adventures. Portrait. 8vo. 15s.
——————— Theory and Practice of Gunnery. Plates. 8vo. 21s.
——————— Construction of Bridges and the Passage of Rivers, in Military Operations. Plates. 8vo. 21s.
——————— (WM.) Horse-Shoeing; As it Is, and As it Should be. Illustrations. Post 8vo. 7s. 6d.
DRAKE'S (SIR FRANCIS) Life, Voyages, and Exploits, by Sea and Land. By JOHN BARROW. Post 8vo. 2s.
DRINKWATER'S (JOHN) History of the Siege of Gibraltar, 1779-1783. With a Description and Account of that Garrison from the Earliest Periods. Post 8vo. 2s.
DUCANGE'S MEDIÆVAL LATIN-ENGLISH DICTIONARY. Translated by Rev. E. A. DAYMAN, M.A. Small 4to. [In preparation.
DU CHAILLU'S (PAUL B.) EQUATORIAL AFRICA, with Accounts of the Gorilla, the Nest-building Ape, Chimpanzee, Crocodile, &c. Illustrations. 8vo. 21s.
——————— Journey to Ashango Land; and Further Penetration into Equatorial Africa. Illustrations. 8vo. 21s.
DUFFERIN'S (LORD) Letters from High Latitudes; a Yacht Voyage to Iceland, Jan Mayen, and Spitzbergen. Woodcuts. Post 8vo. 7s. 6d.
DUNCAN'S (MAJOR) History of the Royal Artillery. Compiled from the Original Records. With Portraits. 2 Vols. 8vo. 30s.
DYER'S (THOS. H.) History of Modern Europe, from the taking of Constantinople by the Turks to the close of the War in the Crimea. With Index. 4 Vols. 8vo. 42s.
EASTLAKE'S (SIR CHARLES) Contributions to the Literature of the Fine Arts. With Memoir of the Author, and Selections from his Correspondence. By LADY EASTLAKE. 2 Vols. 8vo. 24s.

EDWARDS' (W. H.) Voyage up the River Amazons, including a Visit to Para. Post 8vo. 2s.

EIGHT MONTHS AT ROME, during the Vatican Council, with a Daily Account of the Proceedings. By POMPONIO LETO. Translated from the Original. 8vo. [*Nearly ready*.

ELDON'S (LORD) Public and Private Life, with Selections from his Correspondence and Diaries. By HORACE TWISS. Portrait. 2 Vols. Post 8vo. 21s.

ELGIN'S (LORD) Letters and Journals. Edited by THEODORE WALROND. With Preface by Dean Stanley. 8vo. 14s.

ELLESMERE'S (LORD) Two Sieges of Vienna by the Turks. Translated from the German. Post 8vo. 2s.

ELLIS'S (W.) Madagascar, including a Journey to the Capital, with notices of Natural History and the People. Woodcuts. 8vo. 16s.

—————— Madagascar Revisited. Setting forth the Persecutions and Heroic Sufferings of the Native Christians. Illustrations. 8vo. 16s.

—————— Memoir. By HIS SON. With his Character and Work. By REV. HENRY ALLON, D.D. Portrait. 8vo. 10s. 6d.

—————— (ROBINSON) Poems and Fragments of Catullus. 16mo. 5s.

ELPHINSTONE'S (HON. MOUNTSTUART) History of India—the Hindoo and Mahomedan Periods. Edited by PROFESSOR COWELL. Map. 8vo. 18s.

—————— (H. W.) Patterns for Turning; Comprising Elliptical and other Figures cut on the Lathe without the use of any Ornamental Chuck. With 70 Illustrations. Small 4to. 15s.

ENGLAND. See CALLCOTT, CROKER, HUME, MARKHAM, SMITH, and STANHOPE.

ESSAYS ON CATHEDRALS. With an Introduction. By DEAN HOWSON. 8vo. 12s.

CONTENTS.

Recollections of a Dean.—Bishop of Carlisle.
Cathedral Canons and their Work.—Canon Norris.
Cathedrals in Ireland, Past and Future.—Dean of Cashel.
Cathedrals in their Missionary Aspect.—A. J. B. Beresford Hope.
Cathedral Foundations in Relation to Religious Thought.—Canon Westcott.
Cathedral Churches of the Old Foundation.—Edward A. Freeman.
Welsh Cathedrals.—Canon Perowne.
Education of Choristers.—Sir F. Gore Ouseley.
Cathedral Schools.—Canon Durham.
Cathedral Reform.—Chancellor Massingberd.
Relation of the Chapter to the Bishop. Chancellor Benson.
Architecture of the Cathedral Churches.—Canon Venables.

ELZE'S (KARL) Life of Lord Byron. With a Critical Essay on his Place in Literature. Translated from the German. With Portrait. 8vo. 16s.

FARRAR'S (A. S.) Critical History of Free Thought in reference to the Christian Religion. 8vo. 16s.

FERGUSSON'S (JAMES) History of Architecture in all Countries from the Earliest Times. With 1,600 Illustrations. 4 Vols. Medium 8vo. 31s. 6d. each.

Vol. I. & II. Ancient and Mediæval.
Vol. III. Indian and Eastern. Vol. IV. Modern.

—————— Rude Stone Monuments in all Countries; their Age and Uses. With 230 Illustrations. Medium 8vo. 24s.

—————— Holy Sepulchre and the Temple at Jerusalem. Woodcuts. 8vo. 7s. 6d.

FLEMING'S (Professor) Student's Manual of Moral Philosophy. With Quotations and References. Post 8vo. 7s. 6d.

FLOWER GARDEN. By Rev. Thos. James. Fcap. 8vo. 1s.

FORD'S (Richard) Gatherings from Spain. Post 8vo. 3s. 6d.

FORSYTH'S (William) Life and Times of Cicero. With Selections from his Correspondence and Orations. Illustrations. 8vo. 10s. 6d.

―――― ―――― Hortensius; an Historical Essay on the Office and Duties of an Advocate. Illustrations. 8vo. 12s.

―――― ―――― History of Ancient Manuscripts. Post 8vo. 2s. 6d.

―――― ―――― Novels and Novelists of the 18th Century, in Illustration of the Manners and Morals of the Age. Post 8vo. 10s. 6d.

FORTUNE'S (Robert) Narrative of Two Visits to the Tea Countries of China, 1843-52. Woodcuts. 2 Vols. Post 8vo. 18s.

FORSTER'S (John) Life of Jonathan Swift. Vol. I. 1667-1711. With Portrait. 8vo. 15s.

FOSS' (Edward) Biographia Juridica, or Biographical Dictionary of the Judges of England, from the Conquest to the Present Time, 1066-1870. Medium 8vo. 21s.

―――――――― Tabulæ Curiales; or, Tables of the Superior Courts of Westminster Hall. Showing the Judges who sat in them from 1066 to 1864. 8vo. 10s. 6d.

FRANCE. *⁎* See Markham—Smith—Student's.

FRENCH (The) in Algiers; The Soldier of the Foreign Legion— and the Prisoners of Abd-el-Kadir. Translated by Lady Duff Gordon. Post 8vo. 2s.

FRERE'S (Sir Bartle) Indian Missions. Small 8vo. 2s. 6d.

―――― ―――― Eastern Africa as a field for Missionary Labour. With Map. Crown 8vo. 5s.

―――――――― Bengal Famine. How it will be Met and How to Prevent Future Famines in India. With Maps. Crown 8vo. 5s.

GALTON'S (Francis) Art of Travel; or, Hints on the Shifts and Contrivances available in Wild Countries. Woodcuts. Post 8vo. 7s. 6d.

GEOGRAPHICAL SOCIETY'S JOURNAL. (*Published Yearly.*)

GEORGE'S (Ernest) Mosel; a Series of Twenty Etchings, with Descriptive Letterpress. Imperial 4to. 42s.

―――――― Loire and South of France; a Series of Twenty Etchings, with Descriptive Text. Folio. 42s.

GERMANY (History of). See Markham.

GIBBON'S (Edward) History of the Decline and Fall of the Roman Empire. Edited by Milman and Guizot. Edited, with Notes, by Dr. Wm. Smith. Maps. 8 Vols. 8vo. 60s.

―――――― (The Student's Gibbon); Being an Epitome of the above work, incorporating the Researches of Recent Commentators. By Dr. Wm. Smith. Woodcuts. Post 8vo. 7s. 6d.

GIFFARD'S (EDWARD) Deeds of Naval Daring; or, Anecdotes of the British Navy. Fcap. 8vo. 3s. 6d.
GLADSTONE'S (W. E.) Financial Statements of 1853, 1860, 63–65. 8vo. 12s.
———— Rome and the Newest Fashions in Religion. Three Tracts. *Collected Edition.* With a new Preface. 8vo. 7s. 6d.
GLEIG'S (G. R.) Campaigns of the British Army at Washington and New Orleans. Post 8vo. 2s.
———— Story of the Battle of Waterloo. Post 8vo. 3s. 6d.
———— Narrative of Sale's Brigade in Affghanistan. Post 8vo. 2s.
———— Life of Lord Clive. Post 8vo. 3s. 6d.
———— Sir Thomas Munro. Post 8vo. 3s. 6d.
GOLDSMITH'S (OLIVER) Works. Edited with Notes by PETER CUNNINGHAM. Vignettes. 4 Vols. 8vo. 30s.
GORDON'S (SIR ALEX.) Sketches of German Life, and Scenes from the War of Liberation. Post 8vo. 3s. 6d.
———— (LADY DUFF) Amber-Witch: A Trial for Witchcraft. Post 8vo. 2s.
———— French in Algiers. 1. The Soldier of the Foreign Legion. 2. The Prisoners of Abd-el-Kadir. Post 8vo. 2s.
GRAMMARS. See CURTIUS; HALL; HUTTON; KING EDWARD; MATTHIÆ; MAETZNER; SMITH.
GREECE. *See* GROTE—SMITH—Student.
GREY'S (EARL) Correspondence with King William IVth and Sir Herbert Taylor, from 1830 to 1832. 2 Vols. 8vo. 30s.
———— Parliamentary Government and Reform; with Suggestions for the Improvement of our Representative System. *Second Edition.* 8vo. 9s.
GUIZOT'S (M.) Meditations on Christianity, and on the Religious Questions of the Day. 3 Vols. Post 8vo. 30s.
GROTE'S (GEORGE) History of Greece. From the Earliest Times to the close of the generation contemporary with the death of Alexander the Great. *Library Edition.* Portrait, Maps, and Plans. 10 Vols. 8vo. 120s. *Cabinet Edition.* Portrait and Plans. 12 Vols. Post 8vo. 6s. each.
———— PLATO, and other Companions of Socrates. 3 Vols. 8vo. 45s.
———— ARISTOTLE. 2 Vols. 8vo. 32s.
———— Minor Works. With Critical Remarks on his Intellectual Character, Writings, and Speeches. By ALEX.BAIN, LL.D. Portrait. 8vo. 14s.
———— Fragments on Ethical Subjects. Being a Selection from his Posthumous Papers. With an Introduction. By ALEXANDER BAIN, M.A. 8vo.
———— Personal Life. Compiled from Family Documents, Private Memoranda, and Original Letters to and from Various Friends. By Mrs. Grote. Portrait. 8vo. 12s.
———— (MRS.) Memoir of Ary Scheffer. Portrait. 8vo. 8s. 6d.
HALL'S (T. D.) School Manual of English Grammar. With Copious Exercises. 12mo. 3s. 6d.
———— Primary English Grammar for Elementary Schools. 16mo. 1s.
———— Child's First Latin Book, including a Systematic Treatment of the New Pronunciation, and a full Praxis of Nouns, Adjectives, and Pronouns. 16mo. 1s. 6d.

HALLAM'S (HENRY) Constitutional History of England, from the Accession of Henry the Seventh to the Death of George the Second. *Library Edition.* 3 Vols 8vo. 30s. *Cabinet Edition.* 3 Vols. Post 8vo. 12s.
————— Student's Edition of the above work. Edited by WM. SMITH, D.C.L. Post 8vo. 7s. 6d.
————— History of Europe during the Middle Ages. *Library Edition.* 3 Vols. 8vo. 30s. *Cabinet Edition,* 3 Vols. Post 8vo. 12s.
————— Student's Edition of the above work. Edited by WM. SMITH, D.C.L. Post 8vo. 7s. 6d.
————— Literary History of Europe, during the 15th, 16th and 17th Centuries. *Library Edition.* 3 Vols. 8vo. 36s. *Cabinet Edition.* 4 Vols. Post 8vo. 16s.
————— (ARTHUR) Literary Remains; in Verse and Prose. Portrait. Fcap. 8vo. 3s. 6d.
HAMILTON'S (GEN. SIR F. W.) History of the Grenadier Guards. From Original Documents in the Rolls' Records, War Office, Regimental Records, &c. With Illustrations. 3 Vols. 8vo. 63s.
HART'S ARMY LIST. (*Published Quarterly and Annually.*)
HAY'S (SIR J. H. DRUMMOND) Western Barbary, its Wild Tribes and Savage Animals. Post 8vo. 2s.
HEAD'S (SIR FRANCIS) Royal Engineer. Illustrations. 8vo. 12s.
————— Life of Sir John Burgoyne. Post 8vo. 1s.
————— Rapid Journeys across the Pampas. Post 8vo. 2s.
————— Bubbles from the Brunnen of Nassau. Illustrations. Post 8vo. 7s. 6d.
————— Emigrant. Fcap. 8vo. 2s. 6d.
————— Stokers and Pokers; or, the London and North Western Railway. Post 8vo. 2s.
————— (SIR EDMUND) Shall and Will; or, Future Auxiliary Verbs. Fcap. 8vo. 4s.
HEBER'S (BISHOP) Journals in India. 2 Vols. Post 8vo. 7s.
————— Poetical Works. Portrait. Fcap. 8vo. 3s. 6d.
————— Hymns adapted to the Church Service. 16mo. 1s. 6d.
HERODOTUS. A New English Version. Edited, with Notes and Essays, historical, ethnographical, and geographical, by CANON RAWLINSON, assisted by SIR HENRY RAWLINSON and SIR J. G. WILKINSON. Maps and Woodcuts. 4 Vols. 8vo. 48s.
HERSCHEL'S (CAROLINE) Memoir and Correspondence. By MRS. JOHN HERSCHEL. With Portraits. Crown 8vo.
HATHERLEY'S (LORD) Continuity of Scripture, as Declared by the Testimony of our Lord and of the Evangelists and Apostles. 8vo. 6s. *Popular Edition.* Post 8vo. 2s. 6d.
HOLLWAY'S (J. G.) Month in Norway. Fcap. 8vo. 2s.
HONEY BEE. By REV. THOMAS JAMES. Fcap. 8vo. 1s.
HOOK'S (DEAN) Church Dictionary. 8vo. 16s.
————— (THEODORE) Life. By J. G. LOCKHART. Fcap. 8vo. 1s.
HOPE'S (T. C.) ARCHITECTURE OF AHMEDABAD, with Historical Sketch and Architectural Notes. With Maps, Photographs, and Woodcuts. 4to. 5l. 5s.
————— (A. J. BERESFORD) Worship in the Church of England. 8vo. 9s., or, *Popular Selections from.* 8vo. 2s. 6d.

FOREIGN HANDBOOKS.

HAND-BOOK—TRAVEL-TALK. English, French, German, and Italian. 18mo. 3s. 6d.

———— HOLLAND,—BELGIUM, RHENISH PRUSSIA, and the Rhine from Holland to Mayence. Map and Plans. Post 8vo. 6s.

———— NORTH GERMANY,—From the Baltic to the Black Forest, the Hartz, Thüringerwald, Saxon Switzerland, Rügen, the Giant Mountains, Taunus, Odenwald, and the Rhine Countries, from Frankfort to Basle. Map and Plans. Post 8vo. 6s.

———— SOUTH GERMANY,— Wurtemburg, Bavaria, Austria, Styria, Salzburg, the Austrian and Bavarian Alps, Tyrol, Hungary, and the Danube, from Ulm to the Black Sea. Map. Post 8vo. 10s.

———— PAINTING. German, Flemish, and Dutch Schools. Illustrations. 2 Vols. Post 8vo. 24s.

———— LIVES OF EARLY FLEMISH PAINTERS. By CROWE and CAVALCASELLE. Illustrations. Post 8vo. 10s. 6d.

———— SWITZERLAND, Alps of Savoy, and Piedmont. Maps. Post 8vo. 9s.

———— FRANCE, Part I. Normandy, Brittany, the French Alps, the Loire, the Seine, the Garonne, and the Pyrenees. Post 8vo. 7s. 6d.

———— Part II. Central France, Auvergne, the Cevennes, Burgundy, the Rhone and Saone, Provence, Nimes, Arles, Marseilles, the French Alps, Alsace, Lorraine, Champagne, &c. Maps. Post 8vo. 7s. 6d.

———— MEDITERRANEAN ISLANDS—Malta, Corsica, Sardinia, and Sicily. Maps Post 8vo. [In the Press.

———— ALGERIA. Algiers, Constantine, Oran, the Atlas Range. Map. Post 8vo. 9s.

———— PARIS, and its Environs. Map. 16mo. 3s. 6d.
*** MURRAY'S PLAN OF PARIS, mounted on canvas. 3s. 6d.

———— SPAIN, Madrid, The Castiles, The Basque Provinces, Leon, The Asturias, Galicia, Estremadura, Andalusia, Ronda, Granada, Murcia, Valencia, Catalonia, Aragon, Navarre, The Balearic Islands, &c. &c. Maps. 2 Vols. Post 8vo. 24s.

———— PORTUGAL, LISBON, Porto, Cintra, Mafra, &c. Map. Post 8vo. 9s.

———— NORTH ITALY, Turin, Milan, Cremona, the Italian Lakes, Bergamo, Brescia, Verona, Mantua, Vicenza, Padua, Ferrara, Bologna, Ravenna, Rimini, Piacenza, Genoa, the Riviera, Venice, Parma, Modena, and Romagna. Map. Post 8vo. 10s

———— CENTRAL ITALY, Florence, Lucca, Tuscany, The Marches, Umbria, and the late Patrimony of St. Peter's. Map. Post 8vo. 10s.

———— ROME AND ITS ENVIRONS. Map. Post 8vo. 10s.

———— SOUTH ITALY, Two Sicilies, Naples, Pompeii, Herculaneum, and Vesuvius. Map. Post 8vo. 10s.

———— KNAPSACK GUIDE TO ITALY. 16mo.

———— PAINTING. The Italian Schools. Illustrations. 2 Vols. Post 8vo. 30s.

———— LIVES OF ITALIAN PAINTERS, FROM CIMABUE to BASSANO. By Mrs. JAMESON. Portraits. Post 8vo. 12s.

———— NORWAY, Christiania, Bergen, Trondhjem. The Fjelds and Fjords. Map. Post 8vo. 9s.

———— SWEDEN, Stockholm, Upsala, Gothenburg, the Shores of the Baltic, &c. Post 8vo. 6s.

———— DENMARK, Sleswig, Holstein, Copenhagen, Jutland, Iceland. Map. Post 8vo. 6s.

HAND-BOOK—RUSSIA, St. Petersburg, Moscow, Poland, and Finland. Maps. Post 8vo. 15s.
——— GREECE, the Ionian Islands, Continental Greece, Athens, the Peloponnesus, the Islands of the Ægean Sea, Albania, Thessaly, and Macedonia. Maps. Post 8vo. 15s.
——— TURKEY IN ASIA—Constantinople, the Bosphorus, Dardanelles, Broussa, Plain of Troy, Crete, Cyprus, Smyrna, Ephesus, the Seven Churches, Coasts of the Black Sea, Armenia, Mesopotamia, &c. Maps. Post 8vo. 15s.
——— EGYPT, including Descriptions of the Course of the Nile through Egypt and Nubia, Alexandria, Cairo, and Thebes, the Suez Canal, the Pyramids, the Peninsula of Sinai, the Oases, the Fyoom, &c. Map. Post 8vo. 15s
——— HOLY LAND—Syria, Palestine, Peninsula of Sinai, Edom, Syrian Deserts, Petra, Damascus, and Palmyra. Maps. Post 8vo.
*** Travelling Map of Palestine. In a case. 12s.
——— INDIA — Bombay and Madras. Map. 2 Vols. Post 8vo. 12s. each.

ENGLISH HANDBOOKS.

HAND-BOOK—MODERN LONDON. Map. 16mo. 3s. 6d.
——— EASTERN COUNTIES, Chelmsford, Harwich, Colchester, Maldon, Cambridge, Ely, Newmarket, Bury St. Edmunds, Ipswich, Woodbridge, Felixstowe, Lowestoft, Norwich, Yarmouth, Cromer, &c. Map and Plans. Post 8vo. 12s.
——— CATHEDRALS of Oxford, Peterborough, Norwich, Ely, and Lincoln. With 90 Illustrations. Crown 8vo. 18s.
——— KENT AND SUSSEX, Canterbury, Dover, Ramsgate, Sheerness, Rochester, Chatham, Woolwich, Brighton, Chichester, Worthing, Hastings, Lewes, Arundel, &c. Map. Post 8vo. 10s.
——— SURREY AND HANTS, Kingston, Croydon, Reigate, Guildford, Dorking, Boxhill, Winchester, Southampton, New Forest, Portsmouth, and Isle of Wight. Maps. Post 8vo. 10s.
——— BERKS, BUCKS, AND OXON, Windsor, Eton, Reading, Aylesbury. Uxbridge, Wycombe, Henley, the City and University of Oxford, Blenheim, and the Descent of the Thames. Map. Post 8vo. 7s. 6d.
——— WILTS, DORSET, AND SOMERSET, Salisbury, Chippenham, Weymouth, Sherborne, Wells, Bath, Bristol, Taunton, &c. Map. Post 8vo. 10s.
——— DEVON AND CORNWALL, Exeter, Ilfracombe, Linton, Sidmouth, Dawlish, Teignmouth, Plymouth, Devonport, Torquay, Launceston, Truro, Penzance, Falmouth, the Lizard, Land's End, &c. Maps. Post 8vo. 12s.
——— CATHEDRALS of Winchester, Salisbury, Exeter, Wells, Chichester, Rochester, Canterbury. With 110 Illustrations. 2 Vols. Crown 8vo. 24s.
——— GLOUCESTER, HEREFORD, and WORCESTER, Cirencester, Cheltenham, Stroud, Tewkesbury, Leominster, Ross, Malvern, Kidderminster, Dudley, Bromsgrove, Evesham. Map. Post 8vo. 9s.
——— CATHEDRALS of Bristol, Gloucester, Hereford, Worcester, and Lichfield. With 50 Illustrations. Crown 8vo. 16s.
——— NORTH WALES, Bangor, Carnarvon, Beaumaris, Snowdon, Llanberis, Dolgelly, Cader Idris, Conway, &c. Map. Post 8vo. 7s.
——— SOUTH WALES, Monmouth, Llandaff, Merthyr, Vale of Neath, Pembroke, Carmarthen, Tenby, Swansea, and The Wye, &c. Map. Post 8vo. 7s.

HAND-BOOK—CATHEDRALS OF BANGOR, ST. ASAPH, Llandaff, and St. David's. With Illustrations. Post 8vo. 15s.

——— DERBY, NOTTS, LEICESTER, STAFFORD, Matlock, Bakewell, Chatsworth, The Peak, Buxton, Hardwick, Dove Dale, Ashborne, Southwell, Mansfield, Retford, Burton, Belvoir, Melton Mowbray, Wolverhampton, Lichfield, Walsall, Tamworth. Map. Post 8vo. 9s.

——— SHROPSHIRE, CHESHIRE AND LANCASHIRE —Shrewsbury, Ludlow, Bridgnorth, Oswestry, Chester, Crewe, Alderley, Stockport, Birkenhead, Warrington, Bury, Manchester, Liverpool, Burnley, Clitheroe, Bolton, Blackburn, Wigan, Preston, Rochdale, Lancaster, Southport, Blackpool, &c. Map. Post 8vo. 10s.

——— YORKSHIRE, Doncaster, Hull, Selby, Beverley, Scarborough, Whitby, Harrogate, Ripon, Leeds, Wakefield, Bradford, Halifax, Huddersfield, Sheffield. Map and Plans. Post 8vo. 12s.

——— CATHEDRALS of York, Ripon, Durham, Carlisle, Chester, and Manchester. With 60 Illustrations. 2 Vols. Crown 8vo. 21s.

——— DURHAM AND NORTHUMBERLAND, Newcastle, Darlington, Gateshead, Bishop Auckland, Stockton, Hartlepool, Sunderland, Shields, Berwick-on-Tweed, Morpeth, Tynemouth, Coldstream, Alnwick, &c. Map. Post 8vo. 9s.

——— WESTMORLAND AND CUMBERLAND—Lancaster, Furness Abbey, Ambleside, Kendal, Windermere, Coniston, Keswick, Grasmere, Ulswater, Carlisle, Cockermouth, Penrith, Appleby. Map. Post 8vo. 6s.

⁎ MURRAY'S MAP OF THE LAKE DISTRICT, on canvas. 3s. 6d.

——— SCOTLAND, Edinburgh, Melrose, Kelso, Glasgow, Dumfries, Ayr, Stirling, Arran, The Clyde, Oban, Inverary, Loch Lomond, Loch Katrine and Trossachs, Caledonian Canal, Inverness, Perth, Dundee, Aberdeen, Braemar, Skye, Caithness, Ross, Sutherland, &c. Maps and Plans. Post 8vo. 9s.

——— IRELAND, Dublin, Belfast, Donegal, Galway, Wexford, Cork, Limerick, Waterford, Killarney, Munster, &c. Maps. Post 8vo. 12s.

HORACE; a New Edition of the Text. Edited by DEAN MILMAN. With 100 Woodcuts. Crown 8vo. 7s. 6d.

——— Life of. By DEAN MILMAN. Illustrations. 8vo. 9s.

HOUGHTON'S (LORD) Monographs, Vol. I., Personal and Social. With Portraits. Crown 8vo. 10s. 6d.

——— POETICAL WORKS. Collected Edition. With Portrait. 2 Vols Fcap. 8vo. 12s.

HUME'S (The Student's) History of England, from the Invasion of Julius Cæsar to the Revolution of 1688. Corrected and continued to 1868. Woodcuts. Post 8vo. 7s. 6d.

HUTCHINSON (GEN.), on the most expeditious, certain, and easy Method of Dog-Breaking. With 40 Illustrations. Crown 8vo. 9s.

HUTTON'S (H. E.) Principia Græca; an Introduction to the Study of Greek. Comprehending Grammar, Delectus, and Exercise-book, with Vocabularies. *Sixth Edition.* 12mo. 3s. 6d.

IRBY AND MANGLES' Travels in Egypt, Nubia, Syria, and the Holy Land. Post 8vo. 2s.

JACOBSON'S (BISHOP) Fragmentary Illustrations of the History of the Book of Common Prayer; from Manuscript Sources (Bishop SANDERSON and Bishop WREN). 8vo. 5s.

JAMES' (REV. THOMAS) Fables of Æsop. A New Translation, with Historical Preface. With 100 Woodcuts by TENNIEL and WOLF. Post 8vo. 2s. 6d.

c

HOME AND COLONIAL LIBRARY. A Series of Works adapted for all circles and classes of Readers, having been selected for their acknowledged interest, and ability of the Authors. Post 8vo. Published at 2s. and 3s. 6d. each, and arranged under two distinctive heads as follows:—

CLASS A.
HISTORY, BIOGRAPHY, AND HISTORIC TALES.

1. SIEGE OF GIBRALTAR. By JOHN DRINKWATER. 2s.
2. THE AMBER-WITCH. By LADY DUFF GORDON. 2s.
3. CROMWELL AND BUNYAN. By ROBERT SOUTHEY. 2s.
4. LIFE OF SIR FRANCIS DRAKE. By JOHN BARROW. 2s.
5. CAMPAIGNS AT WASHINGTON. By REV. G. R. GLEIG. 2s.
6. THE FRENCH IN ALGIERS. By LADY DUFF GORDON. 2s.
7. THE FALL OF THE JESUITS. 2s.
8. LIVONIAN TALES. 2s.
9. LIFE OF CONDÉ. By LORD MAHON. 3s. 6d.
10. SALE'S BRIGADE. By REV. G. R. GLEIG. 2s.
11. THE SIEGES OF VIENNA. By LORD ELLESMERE. 2s.
12. THE WAYSIDE CROSS. By CAPT. MILMAN. 2s.
13. SKETCHES OF GERMAN LIFE. By SIR A. GORDON. 3s. 6d.
14. THE BATTLE OF WATERLOO. By REV. G. R. GLEIG. 3s. 6d.
15. AUTOBIOGRAPHY OF STEFFENS. 2s.
16. THE BRITISH POETS. By THOMAS CAMPBELL. 3s. 6d.
17. HISTORICAL ESSAYS. By LORD MAHON. 3s. 6d.
18. LIFE OF LORD CLIVE. By REV. G. R. GLEIG. 3s. 6d.
19. NORTH-WESTERN RAILWAY. By SIR F. B. HEAD. 2s.
20. LIFE OF MUNRO. By REV. G. R. GLEIG. 3s. 6d.

CLASS B.
VOYAGES, TRAVELS, AND ADVENTURES.

1. BIBLE IN SPAIN. By GEORGE BORROW. 3s. 6d.
2. GYPSIES OF SPAIN. By GEORGE BORROW. 3s. 6d.
3 & 4. JOURNALS IN INDIA. By BISHOP HEBER. 2 Vols. 7s.
5. TRAVELS IN THE HOLY LAND. By IRBY and MANGLES. 2s.
6. MOROCCO AND THE MOORS. By J. DRUMMOND HAY. 2s.
7. LETTERS FROM THE BALTIC. By a LADY. 2s.
8. NEW SOUTH WALES. By MRS. MEREDITH. 2s.
9. THE WEST INDIES. By M. G. LEWIS. 2s.
10. SKETCHES OF PERSIA. By SIR JOHN MALCOLM. 3s. 6d.
11. MEMOIRS OF FATHER RIPA. 2s.
12 & 13. TYPEE AND OMOO. By HERMANN MELVILLE. 2 Vols. 7s.
14. MISSIONARY LIFE IN CANADA. By REV. J. ABBOTT. 2s.
15. LETTERS FROM MADRAS. By a LADY. 2s.
16. HIGHLAND SPORTS. By CHARLES ST. JOHN. 3s. 6d.
17. PAMPAS JOURNEYS. By SIR F. B. HEAD. 2s.
18. GATHERINGS FROM SPAIN. By RICHARD FORD. 3s. 6d.
19. THE RIVER AMAZON. By W. H. EDWARDS. 2s.
20. MANNERS & CUSTOMS OF INDIA. By REV. C. ACLAND. 2s.
21. ADVENTURES IN MEXICO. By G. F. RUXTON. 3s. 6d.
22. PORTUGAL AND GALLICIA. By LORD CARNARVON. 3s. 6d.
23. BUSH LIFE IN AUSTRALIA. By REV. H. W. HAYGARTH. 2s.
24. THE LIBYAN DESERT. By BAYLE ST. JOHN. 2s.
25. SIERRA LEONE. By A LADY. 3s. 6d.

* Each work may be had separately.

JAMESON'S (Mrs.) Lives of the Early Italian Painters—and the Progress of Painting in Italy—Cimabue to Bassano. With 50 Portraits. Post 8vo. 12s.

JENNINGS' (L. J.) Eighty Years of Republican Government in the United States. Post 8vo. 10s. 6d.

JERVIS'S (Rev. W. H.) Gallican Church, from the Concordat of Bologna, 1516, to the Revolution. With an Introduction. Portraits. 2 Vols. 8vo. 28s.

JESSE'S (Edward) Gleanings in Natural History. Fcp. 8vo. 3s. 6d.

JEX-BLAKE'S (Rev. T. W.) Life in Faith: Sermons Preached at Cheltenham and Rugby. Fcap. 8vo.

JOHNS' (Rev. B. G.) Blind People; their Works and Ways. With Sketches of the Lives of some famous Blind Men. With Illustrations. Post 8vo. 7s. 6d.

JOHNSON'S (Dr. Samuel) Life. By James Boswell. Including the Tour to the Hebrides. Edited by Mr. Croker. *New Edition.* Portraits. 4 Vols. 8vo. [*In Preparation.*]

———— Lives of the most eminent English Poets, with Critical Observations on their Works. Edited with Notes, Corrective and Explanatory, by Peter Cunningham. 3 vols. 8vo. 22s. 6d.

JUNIUS' Handwriting Professionally investigated. By Mr. Chabot, Expert. With Preface and Collateral Evidence, by the Hon. Edward Twisleton. With Facsimiles, Woodcuts, &c. 4to. £3 3s.

KEN'S (Bishop) Life. By a Layman. Portrait. 2 Vols. 8vo. 18s.

———— Exposition of the Apostles' Creed. 16mo. 1s. 6d.

KERR'S (Robert) Gentleman's House; or, How to Plan English Residences from the Parsonage to the Palace. With Views and Plans. 8vo. 24s.

———— Small Country House. A Brief Practical Discourse on the Planning of a Residence from 2000l. to 5000l. With Supplementary Estimates to 7000l. Post 8vo. 3s.

———— Ancient Lights; a Book for Architects, Surveyors, Lawyers, and Landlords. 8vo. 5s. 6d.

———— (R. Malcolm) Student's Blackstone. A Systematic Abridgment of the entire Commentaries, adapted to the present state of the law. Post 8vo. 7s. 6d.

KING EDWARD VIth's Latin Grammar. 12mo. 3s. 6d.

———— ———— First Latin Book. 12mo. 2s 6d.

KING GEORGE IIIrd's Correspondence with Lord North, 1769-82. Edited, with Notes and Introduction, by W. Bodham Donne. 2 vols. 8vo. 32s.

KING'S (R. J.) Archæology, Travel and Art; being Sketches and Studies, Historical and Descriptive. 8vo. 12s.

KIRK'S (J. Foster) History of Charles the Bold, Duke of Burgundy. Portrait. 3 Vols. 8vo. 45s.

KIRKES' Handbook of Physiology. Edited by W. Morrant Baker, F.R.C.S. With 240 Illustrations. Post 8vo. 12s. 6d.

KUGLER'S Handbook of Painting.—The Italian Schools. Revised and Remodelled from the most recent Researches. By Lady Eastlake. With 140 Illustrations. 2 Vols. Crown 8vo. 30s.

———— Handbook of Painting.—The German, Flemish, and Dutch Schools. Revised and in part re-written. By J. A. Crowe. With 60 Illustrations. 2 Vols. Crown 8vo. 24s.

LANE'S (E. W.) Account of the Manners and Customs of Modern Egyptians. With Illustrations. 2 Vols. Post 8vo. 12s

c 2

LAWRENCE'S (SIR GEO.) Reminiscences of Forty-three Years' Service in India; including Captivities in Cabul among the Affghans and among the Sikhs, and a Narrative of the Mutiny in Rajputana. Crown 8vo. 10s. 6d.

LAYARD'S (A. H.) Nineveh and its Remains. Being a Narrative of Researches and Discoveries amidst the Ruins of Assyria. With an Account of the Chaldean Christians of Kurdistan; the Yezedis, or Devil-worshippers; and an Enquiry into the Manners and Arts of the Ancient Assyrians. Plates and Woodcuts. 2 Vols. 8vo. 36s.
*** A POPULAR EDITION of the above work. With Illustrations. Post 8vo. 7s. 6d.

────── Nineveh and Babylon; being the Narrative of Discoveries in the Ruins, with Travels in Armenia, Kurdistan and the Desert, during a Second Expedition to Assyria. With Map and Plates. 8vo. 21s.
*** A POPULAR EDITION of the above work. With Illustrations. Post 8vo. 7s. 6d.

LEATHES' (STANLEY) Practical Hebrew Grammar. With the Hebrew Text of Genesis i.—vi., and Psalms i.—vi. Grammatical Analysis and Vocabulary. Post 8vo. 7s. 6d.

LENNEP'S (REV. H. J. VAN) Missionary Travels in Asia Minor. With Illustrations of Biblical History and Archæology. With Map and Woodcuts. 2 Vols. Post 8vo. 24s.

────── Modern Customs and Manners of Bible Lands in Illustration of Scripture. With Coloured Maps and 300 Illustrations. 2 Vols. 8vo. 21s.

LESLIE'S (C. R.) Handbook for Young Painters. With Illustrations. Post 8vo. 7s. 6d.

────── Life and Works of Sir Joshua Reynolds. Portraits and Illustrations. 2 Vols. 8vo. 42s.

LETTERS FROM THE BALTIC. By a LADY. Post 8vo. 2s.

────── MADRAS. By a LADY. Post 8vo. 2s.

────── SIERRA LEONE. By a LADY. Post 8vo. 3s. 6d.

LEVI'S (LEONE) History of British Commerce; and of the Economic Progress of the Nation, from 1763 to 1870. 8vo. 16s.

LIDDELL'S (DEAN) Student's History of Rome, from the earliest Times to the establishment of the Empire. With Woodcuts. Post 8vo. 7s. 6d.

LLOYD'S (W. WATKISS) History of Sicily to the Athenian War; with Elucidations of the Sicilian Odes of Pindar. With Map. 8vo. 14s.

LISPINGS from LOW LATITUDES; or, the Journal of the Hon. Impulsia Gushington. Edited by LORD DUFFERIN. With 24 Plates. 4to. 21s.

LITTLE ARTHUR'S HISTORY OF ENGLAND. By LADY CALLCOTT. New Edition, continued to 1872. With Woodcuts. Fcap. 8vo. 1s. 6d.

LIVINGSTONE'S (DR.) Popular Account of his First Expedition to Africa, 1840-56. Illustrations. Post 8vo. 7s 6d.

────── Popular Account of his Second Expedition to Africa, 1858-64. Map and Illustrations. Post 8vo. 7s. 6d.

────── Last Journals in Central Africa, from 1865 to his Death. Continued by a Narrative of his last moments and sufferings. By Rev. HORACE WALLER. Maps and Illustrations. 2 Vols 8vo. 28s.

LIVONIAN TALES. By the Author of "Letters from the Baltic." Post 8vo. 2s.

LOCH'S (H. B.) Personal Narrative of Events during Lord Elgin's Second Embassy to China. With Illustrations. Post 8vo. 9s.

LOCKHART'S (J. G.) Ancient Spanish Ballads. Historical and Romantic. Translated, with Notes. With Portrait and Illustrations. Crown 8vo. 5s.

—————— Life of Theodore Hook. Fcap. 8vo. 1s.

LONSDALE'S (Bishop) Life. With Selections from his Writings. By E. B. Denison. With Portrait. Crown 8vo. 10s. 6d.

LOUDON'S (Mrs.) Gardening for Ladies. With Directions and Calendar of Operations for Every Month. Woodcuts. Fcap. 8vo. 3s. 6d.

LUCKNOW: A Lady's Diary of the Siege. Fcap. 8vo. 4s. 6d.

LYELL'S (Sir Charles) Principles of Geology; or, the Modern Changes of the Earth and its Inhabitants considered as illustrative of Geology. With Illustrations. 2 Vols. 8vo. 32s.

—————— Student's Elements of Geology. With Table of British Fossils and 600 Illustrations. Post 8vo. 9s.

—————— Geological Evidences of the Antiquity of Man, including an Outline of Glacial Post-Tertiary Geology, and Remarks on the Origin of Species. Illustrations. 8vo. 14s.

—————— (K. M.) Geographical Handbook of Ferns. With Tables to show their Distribution. Post 8vo. 7s. 6d.

LYTTELTON'S (Lord) Ephemera. 2 Vols. Post 8vo. 19s. 6d.

LYTTON'S (Lord) Memoir of Julian Fane. With Portrait. Post 8vo. 5s.

McCLINTOCK'S (Sir L.) Narrative of the Discovery of the Fate of Sir John Franklin and his Companions in the Arctic Seas. With Illustrations. Post 8vo. 7s. 6d.

MACDOUGALL'S (Col.) Modern Warfare as Influenced by Modern Artillery. With Plans. Post 8vo. 12s.

MACGREGOR'S (J.) Rob Roy on the Jordan, Nile, Red Sea, Gennesareth, &c. A Canoe Cruise in Palestine and Egypt and the Waters of Damascus. With Map and 70 Illustrations. Crown 8vo. 7s. 6d.

MACPHERSON'S (Major) Services in India, while Political Agent at Gwalior during the Mutiny. Illustrations. 8vo. 12s.

MAETZNER'S English Grammar. A Methodical, Analytical, and Historical Treatise on the Orthography, Prosody, Inflections, and Syntax of the English Tongue. Translated from the German. By Clair J. Grece, LL.D. 3 Vols. 8vo. 36s.

MAHON (Lord), see Stanhope.

MAINE'S (Sir H. Sumner) Ancient Law: its Connection with the Early History of Society, and its Relation to Modern Ideas. 8vo. 12s.

—————— Village Communities in the East and West. 8vo. 9s.

—————— Early History of Institutions. 8vo. 12s.

MALCOLM'S (Sir John) Sketches of Persia. Post 8vo. 3s. 6d.

MANSEL'S (Dean) Limits of Religious Thought Examined. Post 8vo. 8s. 6d.

—————— Letters, Lectures, and Papers, including the Phrontisterion, or Oxford in the XIXth Century. Edited by H. W. Chandler, M.A. 8vo. 12s.

—————— Gnostic Heresies of the First and Second Centuries. With a sketch of his life and character. By Lord Carnarvon. Edited by Canon Lightfoot. 8vo. 10s. 6d.

MANUAL OF SCIENTIFIC ENQUIRY. For the Use of Travellers. Edited by Rev. R. Main. Post 8vo. 3s. 6d. (*Published by order of the Lords of the Admiralty.*)

MARCO POLO. The Book of Ser Marco Polo, the Venetian. Concerning the Kingdoms and Marvels of the East. A new English Version. Illustrated by the light of Oriental Writers and Modern Travels. By Col. Henry Yule. Maps and Illustrations. 2 Vols. Medium 8vo. 63s.

MARKHAM'S (Mrs.) History of England. From the First Invasion by the Romans to 1867. Woodcuts. 12mo. 3s. 6d.
—————— History of France. From the Conquest by the Gauls to 1861. Woodcuts. 12mo. 3s. 6d.
—————— History of Germany. From the Invasion by Marius to 1867. Woodcuts. 12mo. 3s. 6d.
MARLBOROUGH'S (Sarah, Duchess of) Letters. Now first published from the Original MSS. at Madresfield Court. With an Introduction. 8vo. 10s. 6d.
MARRYAT'S (Joseph) History of Modern and Mediæval Pottery and Porcelain. With a Description of the Manufacture. Plates and Woodcuts. 8vo. 42s.
MARSH'S (G. P.) Student's Manual of the English Language. Post 8vo. 7s. 6d.
MATTHIÆ'S Greek Grammar. Abridged by Blomfield. Revised by E. S. Crooke. 12mo. 4s.
MAUREL'S Character, Actions, and Writings of Wellington. Fcap. 8vo. 1s. 6d.
MAYNE'S (Capt.) Four Years in British Columbia and Vancouver Island. Illustrations. 8vo. 16s.
MEADE'S (Hon. Herbert) Ride through the Disturbed Districts of New Zealand, with a Cruise among the South Sea Islands. With Illustrations. Medium 8vo. 12s.
MELVILLE'S (Hermann) Marquesas and South Sea Islands. 2 Vols. Post 8vo. 7s.
MEREDITH'S (Mrs. Charles) Notes and Sketches of New South Wales. Post 8vo. 2s.
MESSIAH (THE) The Life, Travels, Death, Resurrection, and Ascension of our Blessed Lord. By A Layman. Map. 8vo. 18s.
MILLINGTON'S (Rev. T. S.) Signs and Wonders in the Land of Ham, or the Ten Plagues of Egypt, with Ancient and Modern Illustrations. Woodcuts. Post 8vo. 7s. 6d.
MILMAN'S (Dean) History of the Jews, from the earliest Period down to Modern Times. 3 Vols. Post 8vo. 18s.
—————— Early Christianity, from the Birth of Christ to the Abolition of Paganism in the Roman Empire. 3 Vols. Post 8vo. 18s.
—————— Latin Christianity, including that of the Popes to the Pontificate of Nicholas V. 9 Vols. Post 8vo. 54s.
—————— Annals of St. Paul's Cathedral, from the Romans to the funeral of Wellington. Portrait and Illustrations. 8vo. 18s.
—————— Character and Conduct of the Apostles considered as an Evidence of Christianity. 8vo. 10s. 6d.
—————— Quinti Horatii Flacci Opera. With 100 Woodcuts. Small 8vo. 7s. 6d.
—————— Life of Quintus Horatius Flaccus. With Illustrations. 8vo. 9s.
—————— Poetical Works. The Fall of Jerusalem—Martyr of Antioch—Balshazzar—Tamor—Anne Boleyn—Fazio, &c. With Portrait and Illustrations. 3 Vols. Fcap. 8vo. 18s.
—————— Fall of Jerusalem. Fcap. 8vo. 1s.
—————— (Capt. E. A.) Wayside Cross. Post 8vo. 2s.
MIVART'S (St. George) Lessons from Nature; as manifested in Mind and Matter. 8vo.
MODERN DOMESTIC COOKERY. Founded on Principles of Economy and Practical Knowledge. *New Edition.* Woodcuts. Fcap. 8vo. 5s.

MONGREDIEN'S (AUGUSTUS) Trees and Shrubs for English Plantation. A Selection and Description of the most Ornamental which will flourish in the open air in our climate. With Classified Lists. With 30 Illustrations. 8vo. 16s.

MOORE & JACKMAN on the Clematis as a Garden Flower. Descriptions of the Hardy Species and Varieties, with Directions for their Cultivation. 8vo. 10s. 6d.

MOORE'S (THOMAS) Life and Letters of Lord Byron. *Cabinet Edition.* With Plates. 6 Vols. Fcap. 8vo. 18s.; *Popular Edition*, with Portraits. Royal 8vo. 7s. 6d.

MOSSMAN'S (SAMUEL) New Japan; the Land of the Rising Sun; its Annals and Progress during the past Twenty Years, recording the remarkable Progress of the Japanese in Western Civilisation. With Map. 8vo. 15s.

MOTLEY'S (J. L.) History of the United Netherlands: from the Death of William the Silent to the Twelve Years' Truce, 1609. *Library Edition.* Portraits. 4 Vols. 8vo. 60s. *Cabinet Edition.* 4 Vols. Post 8vo. 6s. each.

——— Life and Death of John of Barneveld, Advocate of Holland. With a View of the Primary Causes and Movements of the Thirty Years' War. *Library Edition.* Illustrations. 2 Vols. 8vo. 28s. *Cabinet Edition.* 2 vols. Post 8vo. 12s.

MOUHOT'S (HENRI) Siam, Cambojia, and Lao; a Narrative of Travels and Discoveries. Illustrations. 2 Vols. 8vo.

MOZLEY'S (CANON) Treatise on Predestination. 8vo. 14s.

——— Primitive Doctrine of Baptismal Regeneration. 8vo. 7s. 6d.

MUIRHEAD'S (JAS.) Vaux-de-Vire of Maistre Jean Le Houx, Advocate of Vire. Translated and Edited. With Portrait and Illustrations. 8vo.

MUNRO'S (GENERAL) Life and Letters. By REV. G. R. GLEIG. Post 8vo. 3s. 6d.

MURCHISON'S (SIR RODERICK) Siluria; or, a History of the Oldest rocks containing Organic Remains. Map and Plates. 8vo. 18s.

——— Memoirs. With Notices of his Contemporaries, and Rise and Progress of Palæozoic Geology. By ARCHIBALD GEIKIE. Portraits. 2 Vols. 8vo. 30s.

MURRAY'S RAILWAY READING. Containing:—
WELLINGTON. By LORD ELLESMERE. 6d.
NIMROD ON THE CHASE. 1s.
MUSIC AND DRESS. 1s.
MILMAN'S FALL OF JERUSALEM. 1s.
MAHON'S "FORTY-FIVE." 3s.
LIFE OF THEODORE HOOK. 1s.
DEEDS OF NAVAL DARING. 3s. 6d.
THE HONEY BEE. 1s.
ÆSOP'S FABLES. 2s. 6d.
NIMROD ON THE TURF. 1s. 6d.
ART OF DINING. 1s. 6d.
MAHON'S JOAN OF ARC. 1s.
HEAD'S EMIGRANT. 2s. 6d.
NIMROD ON THE ROAD. 1s.
CROKER ON THE GUILLOTINE. 1s.
HOLLWAY'S NORWAY. 2s.
MAUREL'S WELLINGTON. 1s. 6d.
CAMPBELL'S LIFE OF BACON. 2s. 6d.
THE FLOWER GARDEN. 1s.
TAYLOR'S NOTES FROM LIFE. 2s.
REJECTED ADDRESSES. 1s.
PENN'S HINTS ON ANGLING. 1s.

MUSTERS' (CAPT.) Patagonians; a Year's Wanderings over Untrodden Ground from the Straits of Magellan to the Rio Negro. Illustrations. Post 8vo. 7s. 6d.

NAPIER'S (SIR CHAS.) Life, Journals, and Letters. Portraits. 4 Vols. Crown 8vo. 48s.

——— (SIR WM.) Life and Letters. Portraits. 2 Vols. Crown 8vo. 28s.

——— English Battles and Sieges of the Peninsular War. Portrait. Post 8vo. 9s.

NAPOLEON AT FONTAINEBLEAU AND ELBA. A Journal of Occurrences and Notes of Conversations. By SIR NEIL CAMPBELL, C.B. With a Memoir. By REV. A. N. C. MACLACHLAN, M.A. Portrait. 8vo. 15s.

NASMYTH AND CARPENTER. The Moon. Considered as a Planet, a World, and a Satellite. With Illustrations from Drawings made with the aid of Powerful Telescopes, Woodcuts, &c. 4to. 30s.

NAUTICAL ALMANAC (THE). (*By Authority.*) 2s. 6d.
NAVY LIST. (Monthly and Quarterly.) Post 8vo.
NEW TESTAMENT. With Short Explanatory Commentary. By ARCHDEACON CHURTON, M.A., and ARCHDEACON BASIL JONES, M.A. With 110 authentic Views, &c. 2 Vols. Crown 8vo 21s. *bound.*
NEWTH'S (SAMUEL) First Book of Natural Philosophy; an Introduction to the Study of Statics, Dynamics, Hydrostatics, Optics, and Acoustics, with numerous Examples. Small 8vo. 3s. 6d.
——————— Elements of Mechanics, including Hydrostatics, with numerous Examples. Small 8vo. 8s. 6d.
——————— Mathematical Examinations. A Graduated Series of Elementary Examples in Arithmetic, Algebra, Logarithms, Trigonometry, and Mechanics. Small 8vo. 8s. 6d.
NICHOLS' (J. G.) Pilgrimages to Walsingham and Canterbury. By ERASMUS. Translated, with Notes. With Illustrations. Post 8vo. 6s.
——————— (SIR GEORGE) History of the English, Irish and Scotch Poor Laws. 4 Vols. 8vo.
NICOLAS' (SIR HARRIS) Historic Peerage of England. Exhibiting the Origin, Descent, and Present State of every Title of Peerage which has existed in this Country since the Conquest. By WILLIAM COURTHOPE. 8vo. 30s.
NIMROD, On the Chace—Turf—and Road. With Portrait and Plates. Crown 8vo. 5s. Or with Coloured Plates. 7s. 6d.
NORDHOFF'S (CHAS.) Communistic Societies of the United States; including Detailed Accounts of the Shakers, The Amana, Oneida, Bethell, Aurora, Icarian and other existing Societies; with Particulars of their Religious Creeds, Industries, and Present Condition. With 40 Illustrations. 8vo. 15s.
OLD LONDON; Papers read at the Archæological Institute. By various Authors. 8vo. 12s.
ORMATHWAITE'S (LORD) Astronomy and Geology—Darwin and Buckle—Progress and Civilisation. Crown 8vo. 6s.
OWEN'S (LIEUT.-COL.) Principles and Practice of Modern Artillery, including Artillery Material, Gunnery, and Organisation and Use of Artillery in Warfare. With Illustrations. 8vo. 15s.
OXENHAM'S (REV. W.) English Notes for Latin Elegiacs; designed for early Proficients in the Art of Latin Versification, with Prefatory Rules of Composition in Elegiac Metre. 12mo. 3s. 6d.
PALGRAVE'S (R. H. I.) Local Taxation of Great Britain and Ireland. 8vo. 5s.
——————— NOTES ON BANKING IN GREAT BRITAIN AND IRELAND, SWEDEN, DENMARK, AND HAMBURG, with some Remarks on the amount of Bills in circulation, both Inland and Foreign. 8vo. 6s.
PALLISER'S (MRS.) Brittany and its Byeways, its Inhabitants, and Antiquities. With Illustrations. Post 8vo. 12s.
——————— Mottoes for Monuments, or Epitaphs selected for General Use and Study. With Illustrations. Crown 8vo. 7s. 6d.
PARIS' (DR.) Philosophy in Sport made Science in Earnest; or, the First Principles of Natural Philosophy inculcated by aid of the Toys and Sports of Youth. Woodcuts. Post 8vo. 7s. 6d.
PARKMAN'S (FRANCIS) Discovery of the Great West; or, The Valleys of the Mississippi and the Lakes of North America. An Historical Narrative. Map. 8vo. 10s. 6d.
PARKYNS' (MANSFIELD) Three Years' Residence in Abyssinia: with Travels in that Country. With Illustrations. Post 8vo. 7s. 6d.
PEEK PRIZE ESSAYS. The Maintenance of the Church of England as an Established Church. By REV. CHARLES HOLE—REV. R. WATSON DIXON—and REV. JULIUS LLOYD. 8vo. 10s. 6d.
PEEL'S (SIR ROBERT) Memoirs. 2 Vols. Post 8vo. 15s.

PENN'S (RICHARD) Maxims and Hints for an Angler and Chess-player. Woodcuts. Fcap. 8vo. 1s.

PERCY'S (JOHN, M.D.) Metallurgy. Vol. I., Part 1. FUEL, Wood, Peat, Coal, Charcoal, Coke, Refractory Materials, Fire-Clays, &c. With Illustrations. 8vo. 30s.

——— Vol. I., Part 2. Copper, Zinc, Brass. With Illustrations. 8vo. *[In the Press.*

——— Vol. II. Iron and Steel. With Illustrations. 8vo. *[In Preparation.*

——— Vol. III. Lead, including part of SILVER. With Illustrations. 8vo. 30s.

——— Vols. IV. and V. Gold, Silver, and Mercury, Platinum, Tin, Nickel, Cobalt, Antimony, Bismuth, Arsenic, and other Metals. With Illustrations. 8vo. *[In Preparation.*

PERSIA'S (SHAH OF) Diary during his Tour through Europe in 1873. Translated from the Original. By J. W. REDHOUSE. With Portrait and Coloured Title. Crown 8vo. 12s.

PHILLIPS' (JOHN) Memoirs of William Smith. 8vo. 7s. 6d.

——— Geology of Yorkshire, The Coast, and Limestone District. Plates. 2 Vols. 4to.

——— Rivers, Mountains, and Sea Coast of Yorkshire. With Essays on the Climate, Scenery, and Ancient Inhabitants. Plates. 8vo. 15s.

——— (SAMUEL) Literary Essays from "The Times." With Portrait. 2 Vols. Fcap. 8vo. 7s.

POPE'S (ALEXANDER) Works. With Introductions and Notes, by REV. WHITWELL ELWIN. Vols. I., II., VI., VII., VIII. With Portraits. 8vo. 10s. 6d. each.

PORTER'S (REV. J. L.) Damascus, Palmyra, and Lebanon. With Travels among the Giant Cities of Bashan and the Hauran. Map and Woodcuts. Post 8vo. 7s. 6d.

PRAYER-BOOK (ILLUSTRATED), with Borders, Initials, Vignettes, &c. Edited, with Notes, by REV. THOS. JAMES. Medium 8vo. 18s. cloth ; 31s. 6d. calf ; 36s. morocco.

PRINCESS CHARLOTTE OF WALES. A Brief Memoir. With Selections from her Correspondence and other unpublished Papers. By LADY ROSE WEIGALL. With Portrait. 8vo. 8s. 6d.

PUSS IN BOOTS. With 12 Illustrations. By OTTO SPECKTER. 16mo. 1s. 6d. Or coloured, 2s. 6d.

PRINCIPLES AT STAKE. Essays on Church Questions of the Day. 8vo. 12s. Contents :—

Ritualism and Uniformity.—Benjamin Shaw.
The Episcopate.—Bishop of Bath and Wells.
The Priesthood.—Dean of Canterbury.
National Education.—Rev. Alexander R. Grant.
Doctrine of the Eucharist.—Rev. G. H. Sumner.
Scripture and Ritual.—Canon Bernard.
Church in South Africa. — Arthur Mills.
Schismatical Tendency of Ritualism. —Rev. Dr. Salmon.
Revisions of the Liturgy.—Rev. W. G. Humphry.
Parties and Party Spirit.—Dean of Chester.

PRIVY COUNCIL JUDGMENTS in Ecclesiastical Cases relating to Doctrine and Discipline. With Historical Introduction, by G. C. BRODRICK and W. H. FREMANTLE. 8vo. 10s. 6d.

QUARTERLY REVIEW (THE). 8vo. 6s.

RAE'S (EDWARD) Land of the North Wind; or Travels among the Laplanders and Samoyedes, and along the Shores of the White Sea. With Map and Woodcuts. Post 8vo. 10s. 6d.

RAMBLES in the Syrian Deserts. Post 8vo. 10s. 6d.

LIST OF WORKS

RANKE'S (LEOPOLD) History of the Popes of Rome during the 16th and 17th Centuries. Translated from the German by SARAH AUSTIN. 3 Vols. 8vo. 30s.

RASSAM'S (HORMUZD) Narrative of the British Mission to Abyssinia. With Notices of the Countries Traversed from Massowah to Magdala. Illustrations. 2 Vols. 8vo. 28s.

RAWLINSON'S (CANON) Herodotus. A New English Version. Edited with Notes and Essays. Maps and Woodcut. 4 Vols. 8vo. 48s.

———— Five Great Monarchies of Chaldæa, Assyria, Media, Babylonia, and Persia. With Maps and Illustrations. 3 Vols. 8vo. 42s.

———— (SIR HENRY) England and Russia in the East: a Series of Papers on the Political and Geographical Condition of Central Asia. Map. 8vo. 12s.

REED'S (E. J.) Shipbuilding in Iron and Steel; a Practical Treatise, giving full details of Construction, Processes of Manufacture, and Building Arrangements. With 5 Plans and 250 Woodcuts. 8vo.

———— Iron-Clad Ships; their Qualities, Performances, and Cost. With Chapters on Turret Ships, Iron-Clad Rams, &c. With Illustrations. 8vo. 12s.

REJECTED ADDRESSES (THE). By JAMES AND HORACE SMITH. Woodcuts. Post 8vo. 3s. 6d.; or Popular Edition, Fcap. 8vo. 1s.

RESIDENCE IN BULGARIA; or, Notes on the Resources and Administration of Turkey, &c. By S. G. B. ST.CLAIR and CHARLES A. BROPHY. 8vo. 12s.

REYNOLDS' (SIR JOSHUA) Life and Times. By C. R. LESLIE, R.A. and TOM TAYLOR. Portraits. 2 Vols. 8vo.

RICARDO'S (DAVID) Political Works. With a Notice of his Life and Writings. By J. R. M'CULLOCH. 8vo. 16s.

RIPA'S (FATHER) Thirteen Years' Residence at the Court of Peking. Post 8vo. 2s.

ROBERTSON'S (CANON) History of the Christian Church, from the Apostolic Age to the Reformation, 1517. *Library Edition*. 4 Vols. 8vo. *Cabinet Edition*. 8 Vols. Post 8vo. 6s. each.

———— How shall we Conform to the Liturgy. 12mo. 9s.

ROME. *See* LIDDELL and SMITH.

ROWLAND'S (DAVID) Manual of the English Constitution. Its Rise, Growth, and Present State. Post 8vo. 10s. 6d.

———— Laws of Nature the Foundation of Morals. Post 8vo. 6s.

ROBSON'S (E. R.) SCHOOL ARCHITECTURE. Being Practical Remarks on the Planning, Designing, Building, and Furnishing of School-houses. With 300 Illustrations. Medium 8vo. 31s. 6d.

RUNDELL'S (MRS.) Modern Domestic Cookery. Fcap. 8vo. 5s.

RUXTON'S (GEORGE F.) Travels in Mexico; with Adventures among the Wild Tribes and Animals of the Prairies and Rocky Mountains. Post 8vo. 3s. 6d.

ROBINSON'S (REV. DR.) Biblical Researches in Palestine and the Adjacent Regions, 1838—52. Maps. 3 Vols. 8vo. 42s.

———— Physical Geography of the Holy Land. Post 8vo. 10s. 6d.

———— (WM.) Alpine Flowers for English Gardens. With 70 Illustrations. Crown 8vo. 12s.

———— Wild Gardens; or, our Groves and Shrubberies made beautiful by the Naturalization of Hardy Exotic Plants. With Frontispiece. Small 8vo. 6s.

———— Sub-Tropical Gardens; or, Beauty of Form in the Flower Garden. With Illustrations. Small 8vo. 7s. 6d.

SALE'S (SIR ROBERT) Brigade in Affghanistan. With an Account of the Defence of Jellalabad. By REV. G. R. GLEIG. Post 8vo. 2s.

SCHLIEMANN'S (DR. HENRY) Troy and Its Remains. A Narrative of Researches and Discoveries made on the Site of Ilium, and in the Trojan Plain. Edited by PHILIP SMITH, B.A. With Maps, Views, and 500 Illustrations. Medium 8vo. 42s.

SCOTT'S (SIR G. G.) Secular and Domestic Architecture, Present and Future. 8vo. 9s.

—— (DEAN) University Sermons. Post 8vo. 8s. 6d.

SHADOWS OF A SICK ROOM. With a Preface by Canon LIDDON. 16mo. 2s 6d.

SCROPE'S (G. P.) Geology and Extinct Volcanoes of Central France. Illustrations. Medium 8vo. 30s.

SHAW'S (T. B.) Manual of English Literature. Post 8vo. 7s. 6d.

—— Specimens of English Literature. Selected from the Chief Writers. Post 8vo. 7s. 6d.

—— (ROBERT) Visit to High Tartary, Yarkand, and Kashgar (formerly Chinese Tartary), and Return Journey over the Karakorum Pass. With Map and Illustrations. 8vo. 16s.

SHIRLEY'S (EVELYN P.) Deer and Deer Parks; or some Account of English Parks, with Notes on the Management of Deer. Illustrations. 4to. 21s.

SIERRA LEONE; Described in Letters to Friends at Home. By A LADY. Post 8vo. 3s. 6d.

SINCLAIR'S (ARCHDEACON) Old Times and Distant Places. A Series of Sketches. Crown 8vo. 9s.

SMILES' (SAMUEL) British Engineers; from the Earliest Period to the death of the Stephensons. With Illustrations. 5 Vols. Crown 8vo. 7s. 6d. each.

—— George and Robert Stephenson. Illustrations. Medium 8vo. 21s.

—— Boulton and Watt. Illustrations. Medium 8vo. 21s.

—— Self-Help. With Illustrations of Conduct and Perseverance. Post 8vo. 6s. Or in French, 5s.

—— Character. A Sequel to "SELF-HELP." Post 8vo. 6s.

—— THRIFT. A Companion Volume to "Self-Help" and "Character." Post 8vo. 6s.

—— Boy's Voyage round the World. With Illustrations. Post 8vo. 6s.

STANLEY'S (DEAN) Sinai and Palestine, in connexion with their History. 20th Thousand. Map. 8vo. 14s.

—— Bible in the Holy Land; Extracted from the above Work. Second Edition. Woodcuts. Fcap. 8vo. 2s. 6d.

—— Eastern Church. Fourth Edition. Plans. 8vo. 12s.

—— Jewish Church. 1st & 2nd Series. From the Earliest Times to the Captivity 8vo. 24s.

—— Third Series. From the Captivity to the Destruction of Jerusalem. 8vo.

—— Church of Scotland. 8vo. 7s. 6d.

—— Memorials of Canterbury Cathedral. Woodcuts. Post 8vo. 7s. 6d.

—— Westminster Abbey. With Illustrations. 8vo. 21s.

—— Sermons during a Tour in the East. 8vo. 9s.

—— ADDRESSES AND CHARGES OF THE LATE BISHOP STANLEY. With Memoir. 8vo. 10s. 6d.

—— Epistles of St. Paul to the Corinthians. 8vo. 18s.

SMITH'S (Dr. Wm.) Dictionary of the Bible; its Antiquities, Biography, Geography, and Natural History. Illustrations. 3 Vols. 8vo. 105s.

———— Concise Bible Dictionary. With 300 Illustrations. Medium 8vo. 21s.

———— Smaller Bible Dictionary. With Illustrations. Post 8vo. 7s. 6d.

———— Christian Antiquities. Comprising the History, Institutions, and Antiquities of the Christian Church. With Illustrations. Vol. I. 8vo. 31s. 6d.

———— ———— Biography and Doctrines; from the Times of the Apostles to the Age of Charlemagne. 8vo. [*In Preparation.*]

———— Atlas of Ancient Geography—Biblical and Classical. Folio. 6l. 6s.

———— Greek and Roman Antiquities. With 500 Illustrations. Medium 8vo. 28s.

———— ———— Biography and Mythology. With 600 Illustrations. 3 Vols. Medium 8vo. 4l. 4s.

———— ———— Geography. 2 Vols. With 500 Illustrations. Medium 8vo. 56s.

———— Classical Dictionary of Mythology, Biography, and Geography. 1 Vol. With 750 Woodcuts. 8vo. 18s.

———— Smaller Classical Dictionary. With 200 Woodcuts. Crown 8vo. 7s. 6d.

———— ———— Greek and Roman Antiquities. With 200 Woodcuts. Crown 8vo. 7s. 6d.

———— Latin-English Dictionary. With Tables of the Roman Calendar, Measures, Weights, and Money. Medium 8vo. 21s.

———— Smaller Latin-English Dictionary. 12mo. 7s. 6d.

———— English-Latin Dictionary. Medium 8vo. 21s.

———— Smaller English-Latin Dictionary. 12mo. 7s. 6d.

———— School Manual of English Grammar, with Copious Exercises. Post 8vo. 3s. 6d.

———— ———— Modern Geography. 12mo. [*Nearly ready.*]

———— Primary English Grammar. 16mo. 1s.

———— ———— History of Britain. 12mo. 2s. 6d.

———— French Principia. Part I. A First Course, containing a Grammar, Delectus, Exercises, and Vocabularies. 12mo. 3s. 6d.

———— ———— Part II. A Reading Book, containing Fables, Stories, and Anecdotes, Natural History, and Scenes from the History of France. With Grammatical Questions, Notes and copious Etymological Dictionary. 12mo. 4s. 6d.

———— ———— Part III. Prose Composition, containing a Systematic Course of Exercises on the Syntax, with the Principal Rules of Syntax. 12mo. [*In the Press.*]

———— German Principia, Part I. A First German Course, containing a Grammar, Delectus, Exercise Book, and Vocabularies. 12mo. 3s. 6d.

———— ———— Part II. A Reading Book; containing Fables, Stories, and Anecdotes, Natural History, and Scenes from the History of Germany. With Grammatical Questions, Notes, and Dictionary. 12mo. 3s. 6d.

———— ———— Part III. An Introduction to German Prose Composition; containing a Systematic Course of Exercises on the Syntax, with the Principal Rules of Syntax. 12mo. [*In the Press.*]

SMITH'S (Dr. Wm.) Principia Latina—Part I. First Latin Course, containing a Grammar, Delectus, and Exercise Book, with Vocabularies. 12mo. 3s. 6d.

In this Edition the Cases of the Nouns, Adjectives, and Pronouns are arranged both as in the ORDINARY GRAMMARS and as in the PUBLIC SCHOOL PRIMER, together with the corresponding Exercises.

—————— Part II. A Reading-book of Mythology, Geography, Roman Antiquities, and History. With Notes and Dictionary. 12mo. 3s. 6d.

—————— Part III. A Poetry Book. Hexameters and Pentameters; Eclog. Ovidianæ; Latin Prosody. 12mo. 3s. 6d.

—————— Part IV. Prose Composition. Rules of Syntax with Examples, Explanations of Synonyms, and Exercises on the Syntax. 12mo. 3s. 6d.

—————— Part V. Short Tales and Anecdotes for Translation into Latin. 12mo. 3s.

—————— Latin-English Vocabulary and First Latin-English Dictionary for Phædrus, Cornelius Nepos, and Cæsar. 12mo. 3s. 6d.

—————— Student's Latin Grammar. Post 8vo. 6s.

—————— Smaller Latin Grammar. 12mo. 3s. 6d.

—————— Tacitus, Germania, Agricola, &c. With English Notes. 12mo. 3s. 6d.

—————— Initia Græca, Part I. A First Greek Course, containing a Grammar, Delectus, and Exercise-book. With Vocabularies. 12mo. 3s. 6d.

—————— Part II. A Reading Book. Containing Short Tales, Anecdotes, Fables, Mythology, and Grecian History. 12mo. 3s. 6d.

—————— Part III. Prose Composition. Containing the Rules of Syntax, with copious Examples and Exercises. 12mo. 3s. 6d.

—————— Student's Greek Grammar. By PROFESSOR CURTIUS. Post 8vo. 6s.

—————— Smaller Greek Grammar. 12mo. 3s. 6d.

—————— Greek Accidence. Extracted from the above work. 12mo. 2s. 6d.

—————— Plato. The Apology of Socrates, the Crito, and Part of the Phædo; with Notes in English from Stallbaum and Schleiermacher's Introductions. 12mo. 3s. 6d.

—————— Smaller Scripture History. Woodcuts. 16mo. 3s. 6d

—————— Ancient History. Woodcuts. 16mo. 3s. 6d.

—————— Geography. Woodcuts. 16mo. 3s. 6d.

—————— Rome. Woodcuts. 16mo. 3s. 6d.

—————— Greece. Woodcuts. 16mo. 3s. 6d.

—————— Classical Mythology. Woodcuts. 16mo. 3s. 6d.

—————— History of England. Woodcuts. 16mo. 3s. 6d.

—————— English Literature. 16mo. 3s. 6d.

—————— Specimens of English Literature. 16mo. 3s. 6d

—————— (PHILIP) History of the Ancient World, from the Creation to the Fall of the Roman Empire, A.D. 455. *Fourth Edition.* 3 Vols. 8vo. 31s. 6d.

—————— (REV. A. C.) Nile and its Banks. Woodcuts. 2 Vols. Post 8vo. 18s.

SIMMONS' (CAPT.) Constitution and Practice of Courts-Martial. *Seventh Edition.* 8vo. 15s.

LIST OF WORKS

——— STUDENT'S OLD TESTAMENT HISTORY; from the Creation to the Return of the Jews from Captivity. Maps and Woodcuts. Post 8vo. 7s. 6d.

——— NEW TESTAMENT HISTORY. With an Introduction connecting the History of the Old and New Testaments. Maps and Woodcuts. Post 8vo. 7s. 6d.

——— ECCLESIASTICAL HISTORY. A History of the Christian Church from its Foundation to the Eve of the Protestant Reformation. Post 8vo. 7s 6d.

——— ANCIENT HISTORY OF THE EAST; Egypt, Assyria, Babylonia, Media, Persia, Asia Minor, and Phœnicia. Woodcuts. Post 8vo. 7s. 6d.

——— GEOGRAPHY. By Rev. W. L. Bevan. Woodcuts. Post 8vo. 7s. 6d.

——— HISTORY OF GREECE; from the Earliest Times to the Roman Conquest. By Wm. Smith, D.C.L. Woodcuts. Crown 8vo. 7s. 6d.
*** Questions on the above Work, 12mo. 2s.

——— HISTORY OF ROME; from the Earliest Times to the Establishment of the Empire. By Dean Liddell. Woodcuts. Crown 8vo. 7s. 6d.

——— GIBBON'S Decline and Fall of the Roman Empire. Woodcuts. Post 8vo. 7s. 6d.

——— HALLAM'S HISTORY OF EUROPE during the Middle Ages. Post 8vo. 7s 6d.

——— HALLAM'S HISTORY OF ENGLAND; from the Accession of Henry VII. to the Death of George II. Post 8vo. 7s. 6d.

——— HUME'S History of England from the Invasion of Julius Cæsar to the Revolution in 1688. Continued down to 1863. Woodcuts. Post 8vo. 7s. 6d.
*** Questions on the above Work, 12mo. 2s.

——— HISTORY OF FRANCE; from the Earliest Times to the Establishment of the Second Empire, 1852. By Rev. H. W. Jervis. Woodcuts. Post 8vo. 7s. 6d.

——— ENGLISH LANGUAGE. By Geo. P. Marsh. Post 8vo. 7s. 6d.

——— LITERATURE. By T. B. Shaw, M.A. Post 8vo. 7s. 6d.

——— SPECIMENS of English Literature from the Chief Writers. By T. B. Shaw. Post 8vo. 7s. 6d.

——— MODERN GEOGRAPHY; Mathematical, Physical, and Descriptive. By Rev. W. L. Bevan. Woodcuts. Post 8vo. 7s. 6d.

——— MORAL PHILOSOPHY. By William Fleming, D.D. Post 8vo. 7s. 6d.

——— BLACKSTONE'S Commentaries on the Laws of England. By R. Malcolm Kerr, Ll.D. Post 8vo. 7s. 6d.

SPALDING'S (Captain) Tale of Frithiof. Translated from the Swedish of Esias Tegner. Post 8vo. 7s. 6d.

STEPHEN'S (Rev. W. R.) Life and Times of St. Chrysostom. With Portrait. 8vo. 15s.

ST. JAMES (The) LECTURES. Companions for the Devout Life. By the following authors. 8vo. 7s. 6d.
Imitation of Christ. Rev Dr. Farrar.
Pascal's Pensees. Dean Church.
S. François de Sales. Dean Goulbourn.
Baxter's Saints' Rest. Archbishop Trench.
S. Augustine's Confessions. Bishop Alexander.
Jeremy Taylor's Holy Living and Dying. Rev. Dr Humphry

ST. JOHN'S (CHARLES) Wild Sports and Natural History of the Highlands. Post 8vo. 3s. 6d.
——————— (BAYLE) Adventures in the Libyan Desert. Post 8vo. 2s.
STORIES FOR DARLINGS. With Illustrations. 16mo. 5s.
STREET'S (G. E.) Gothic Architecture in Spain. From Personal Observations made during several Journeys. With Illustrations. Royal 8vo. 30s.
——————— in Italy, chiefly in Brick and Marble. With Notes of Tours in the North of Italy. With 60 Illustrations. Royal 8vo. 26s.
STANHOPE'S (EARL) England during the Reign of Queen Anne, 1701—13. *Library Edition.* 8vo. 16s. *Cabinet Edition.* Portrait. 2 Vols. Post 8vo. 10s.
——————— from the Peace of Utrecht to the Peace of Versailles, 1713-83. *Library Edition.* 7 vols. 8vo. 93s. *Cabinet Edition,* 7 vols. Post 8vo. 5s. each.
——————— British India, from its Origin to 1783. 8vo. 3s. 6d.
——————— History of "Forty-Five." Post 8vo. 3s.
——————— Historical and Critical Essays. Post 8vo. 3s. 6d.
——————— Life of Belisarius. Post 8vo. 10s. 6d.
——————— Condé. Post 8vo. 3s. 6d.
——————— William Pitt. Portraits. 4 Vols. 8vo. 24s.
——————— Miscellanies. 2 Vols. Post 8vo. 13s.
——————— Story of Joan of Arc. Fcap. 8vo. 1s.
——————— Addresses Delivered on Various Occasions. 16mo. 1s.
STYFFE'S (KNUTT) Strength of Iron and Steel. Plates. 8vo. 12s.
SOMERVILLE'S (MARY) Personal Recollections from Early Life to Old Age. With Selections from her Correspondence. Portrait. Crown 8vo. 12s.
——————— Physical Geography. Portrait. Post 8vo.
——————— Connexion of the Physical Sciences. Portrait. Post 8vo.
——————— Molecular and Microscopic Science. Illustrations. 2 Vols. Post 8vo. 21s.
SOUTHEY'S (ROBERT) Book of the Church. Post 8vo. 7s. 6d.
——————— Lives of Bunyan and Cromwell. Post 8vo. 2s.
SWAINSON'S (CANON) Nicene and Apostles' Creeds; Their Literary History; together with some Account of "The Creed of St. Athanasius." 8vo.
SYBEL'S (VON) History of Europe during the French Revolution, 1789—1795. 4 Vols. 8vo. 48s.
SYMONDS' (REV. W.) Records of the Rocks; or Notes on the Geology, Natural History, and Antiquities of North and South Wales, Siluria, Devon, and Cornwall. With Illustrations. Crown 8vo. 12s.
TAYLOR'S (SIR HENRY) Notes from Life. Fcap. 8vo. 2s.
THIELMAN'S (BARON) Journey through the Caucasus to Tabreez, Kurdistan, down the Tigris and Euphrates to Nineveh and Babylon, and across the Desert to Palmyra. Translated by CHAS. HENEAGE. Illustrations. 2 Vols. Post 8vo. 18s.
THOMS' (W. J.) Longevity of Man; its Facts and its Fiction. Including Observations on the more Remarkable Instances. Post 8vo. 10s. 6d.
THOMSON'S (ARCHBISHOP) Lincoln's Inn Sermons. 8vo. 10s. 6d.
——————— Life in the Light of God's Word. Post 8vo. 5s.

LIST OF WORKS PUBLISHED BY MR. MURRAY.

TOCQUEVILLE'S State of Society in France before the Revolution, 1789, and on the Causes which led to that Event. Translated by HENRY REEVE. 8vo. 12s.

TOMLINSON (CHARLES); The Sonnet; Its Origin, Structure, and Place in Poetry. With translations from Dante, Petrarch, &c. Post 8vo. 9s.

TOZER'S (REV. H. F.) Highlands of Turkey, with Visits to Mounts Ida, Athos, Olympus, and Pelion. 2 Vols. Crown 8vo. 24s.

—————— Lectures on the Geography of Greece. Map. Post 8vo. 9s.

TRISTRAM'S (CANON) Great Sahara. Illustrations. Crown 8vo. 15s.

—————— Land of Moab; Travels and Discoveries on the East Side of the Dead Sea and the Jordan. Illustrations. Crown 8vo. 15s.

TWISLETON (EDWARD). The Tongue not Essential to Speech, with Illustrations of the Power of Speech in the case of the African Confessors. Post 8vo. 6s.

TWISS' (HORACE) Life of Lord Eldon. 2 Vols. Post 8vo. 21s.

TYLOR'S (E. B.) Early History of Mankind, and Development of Civilization. 8vo. 12s.

—————— Primitive Culture; the Development of Mythology, Philosophy, Religion, Art, and Custom. 2 Vols. 8vo. 24s.

VAMBERY'S (ARMINIUS) Travels from Teheran across the Turkoman Desert on the Eastern Shore of the Caspian. Illustrations. 8vo. 21s.

VAN LENNEP'S (HENRY J.) Travels in Asia Minor. With Illustrations of Biblical Literature, and Archæology. With Woodcuts. 2 Vols. Post 8vo. 24s.

—————— Modern Customs and Manners of Bible Lands, in illustration of Scripture. With Maps and 300 Illustrations. 2 Vols. 8vo. 21s.

WELLINGTON'S Despatches during his Campaigns in India. Denmark, Portugal, Spain, the Low Countries, and France. Edited by COLONEL GURWOOD. 8 Vols. 8vo. 20s. each.

—————— Supplementary Despatches, relating to India, Ireland, Denmark, Spanish America, Spain, Portugal, France, Congress of Vienna, Waterloo and Paris. Edited by his SON. 14 Vols. 8vo. 20s. each. *,* An Index. 8vo. 20s.

—————— Civil and Political Correspondence. Edited by his SON. Vols. I. to V. 8vo. 20s. each.

—————— Despatches (Selections from). 8vo. 18s.

—————— Speeches in Parliament. 2 Vols. 8vo. 42s.

WHEELER'S (G.) Choice of a Dwelling; a Practical Handbook of Useful Information on Building a House. Plans. Post 8vo. 7s. 6d.

WHYMPER'S (FREDERICK) Travels and Adventures in Alaska. Illustrations. 8vo. 16s.

WILBERFORCE'S (BISHOP) Essays on Various Subjects. 2 vols. 8vo. 21s.

—————— Life of William Wilberforce. Portrait. Crown 8vo. 6s.

WILKINSON'S (SIR J. G.) Popular Account of the Ancient Egyptians. With 500 Woodcuts. 2 Vols. Post 8vo. 12s.

WOOD'S (CAPTAIN) Source of the Oxus. With the Geography of the Valley of the Oxus. By COL. YULE. Map. 8vo. 12s.

WORDS OF HUMAN WISDOM. Collected and Arranged by E. S. With a Preface by CANON LIDDON. Fcap. 8vo. 3s. 6d.

WORDSWORTH'S (BISHOP) Athens and Attica. Plates. 8vo. 5s.

—————— Greece. With 600 Woodcuts. Royal 8vo.

YULE'S (COLONEL) Book of Marco Polo. Illustrated by the Light of Oriental Writers and Modern Travels. With Maps and 80 Plates 2 Vols. Medium 8vo. 63s.

89098638729

b89098638729a